1968 in Europe

PALGRAVE MACMILLAN TRANSNATIONAL HISTORY SERIES

Series Editors: Akira Iriye (Harvard University) and Rana Mitter (University of Oxford)

This distinguished series seeks to: develop scholarship on the transnational connections of societies and peoples in the nineteenth and twentieth centuries; provide a forum in which work on transnational history from different periods, subjects, and regions of the world can be brought together in fruitful connection; and explore the theoretical and methodological links between transnational and other related approaches such as comparative history and world history.

Editorial Board: Thomas Bender, University Professor of the Humanities, Professor of History, and Director of the International Center for Advanced Studies, New York University; Jane Carruthers, Professor of History, University of South Africa; Mariano Plotkin, Professor, Universidad Nacional de Tres de Febrero, Buenos Aires, and member of the National Council of Scientific and Technological Research, Argentina; Pierre-Yves Saunier, Researcher at the Centre National de la Recherche Scientifique, France; Ian Tyrrell, Professor of History, University of New South Wales

Titles include:

Glenda Sluga
THE NATION, PSYCHOLOGY AND INTERNATIONAL POLITICS, 1870–1919

Sebastian Conrad and Dominic Sachsenmaier (*editors*)
COMPETING VISIONS OF WORLD ORDER: GLOBAL MOMENT AND MOVEMENTS, 1880s–1930s

Eri Hotta
PAN-ASIANISM AND JAPAN'S WAR 1931–1945

Erika Kuhlman
WOMEN, GENDER, AND POSTWAR RECONCILIATION BETWEEN NATIONS

Martin Klimke and Joachim Scharloth (*editors*)
1968 IN EUROPE: A HISTORY OF PROTEST AND ACTIVISM, 1956–1977

Forthcoming:

Matthias Middell, Michael Geyer, and Michel Espagne
EUROPEAN HISTORY IN AN INTERCONNECTED WORLD

Gregor Benton and Terence Gomez
THE CHINESE IN BRITAIN, 1800-PRESENT: ECONOMY, TRANSNATIONALISM, IDENTITY

D. K. Lahiri-Choudhury
TELEGRAPHIC IMPERIALISM: CRISIS AND PANIC IN THE INDIAN EMPIRE, c. 1850–1920

Kris Manjapra and Sugata Bose (*editors*)
COSMOPOLITAN THOUGHT ZONES: INTELLECTUAL EXCHANGE BETWEEN SOUTH ASIA AND EUROPE, 1870–1945

Jonathan Gantt
IRISH TERRORISM IN THE ATLANTIC COMMUNITY, 1865–1922

1968 in Europe
A History of Protest and Activism, 1956–1977

Edited by Martin Klimke and Joachim Scharloth

palgrave
macmillan

1968 IN EUROPE
Copyright © Martin Klimke and Joachim Scharloth, 2008.
All rights reserved. No part of this book may be used or reproduced in
any manner whatsoever without written permission except in the
case of brief quotations embodied in critical articles or reviews.

First published in 2008 by
PALGRAVE MACMILLAN™
175 Fifth Avenue, New York, N.Y. 10010 and
Houndmills, Basingstoke, Hampshire, England RG21 6XS.
Companies and representatives throughout the world.

PALGRAVE MACMILLAN is the global academic imprint of the
Palgrave Macmillan division of St. Martin's Press, LLC and of Palgrave
Macmillan Ltd. Macmillan® is a registered trademark in the United
States, United Kingdom and other countries. Palgrave is a registered
trademark in the European Union and other countries.

ISBN-13: 978-0-230-60620-3 (paperback)
ISBN-10: 0-230-60620-2 (paperback)

Library of Congress Cataloging-in-Publication Data

1968 in Europe : a history of protest and activism, 1956–77 /
edited by Martin Klimke and Joachim Scharloth.
    p. cm.
Includes bibliographical references and index.
ISBN 0–230–60619–9 — ISBN 0–230–60620–2
    1. Protest movements—Europe. 2. Protest movements—Europe—
Case studies. I. Klimke, Martin. II. Scharloth, Joachim.

HN377.A15 2008
303.48'409409045—dc22   2007041541

A catalogue record of the book is available from the British Library.

Design by Scribe Inc.

First edition: April 2008

10 9 8 7 6 5 4 3 2 1

Printed in the United States of America.

Transferred to Digital Printing in 2008

Contents

Foreword   vii

1968 in Europe: An Introduction   1
    Martin Klimke and Joachim Scharloth

Part 1: Transnational Roots of the 1968 Protest Movements

Chapter 1	**Subcultural Movements: The Provos**	13
	Niek Pas	
Chapter 2	**Situationism**	23
	Thomas Hecken and Agata Grzenia	
Chapter 3	**The International Peace Movement**	33
	Michael Frey	
Chapter 4	**The Origins of the British New Left**	45
	Madeleine Davis	
Chapter 5	**Music and Protest in 1960s Europe**	57
	Detlef Siegfried	
Chapter 6	**Motions and Emotions**	71
	Jakob Tanner	

Part 2: Protest Histories in Different European Countries

Chapter 7	**Italy**	83
	Jan Kurz and Marica Tolomelli	
Chapter 8	**West Germany**	97
	Martin Klimke	
Chapter 9	**France**	111
	Ingrid Gilcher-Holtey	
Chapter 10	**Great Britain**	125
	Holger Nehring	
Chapter 11	**Northern Ireland**	137
	Niall ó Dochartaigh	
Chapter 12	**Belgium**	153
	Louis Vos	

Chapter 13   **Czechoslovakia**   163
                  Jan Pauer

Chapter 14   **Poland**   179
                  Stefan Garsztecki

Chapter 15   **East Germany**   189
                  Timothy S. Brown

Chapter 16   **Romania**   199
                  Corina Petrescu and Serban Pavelescu

Chapter 17   **Hungary**   209
                  Máté Szabó

Chapter 18   **Yugoslavia**   219
                  Boris Kanzleiter

Chapter 19   **Switzerland**   229
                  Nicole Peter

Chapter 20   **Scandinavia**   239
                  Thomas Ekman Jørgensen

Chapter 21   **Spain and Greece**   253
                  Kostis Kornetis

Part 3: Transnational Networks and Narratives after 1968

Chapter 22   **Terrorism**   269
                  Dorothea Hauser

Chapter 23   **The Women's Movement**   281
                  Kristina Schulz

Chapter 24   **The Environmental Movement**   295
                  Christopher Rootes

Chapter 25   **Narratives of Democratization:**
                  1968 in Postwar Europe   307
                  Philipp Gassert

Afterword   **The Future of 1968's "Restless Youth"**   325
                  Tom Hayden

About the Authors   333

Index   339

Foreword

Like other volumes in the Palgrave Series in Transnational History, this book makes a valuable contribution to the study of modern history in a transnational framework. It focuses on "1968," the year that symbolizes protest movements in many parts of Europe and marked a point separating two worlds, one defined primarily by sovereign nations, in particular the great powers, and the other that came to be shaped as much by smaller countries and by nonnational, global, and transnational forces, as by geopolitical and national agendas.

As the essays in this volume demonstrate, "1968" was a transnational phenomenon across Europe, both Western and Eastern. Although the "revolution" took many shapes and exhibited varying degrees of intensity in different countries, what happened in one part of Europe had an almost immediate impact elsewhere. The "revolutionaries" were aware that they were players not just within their national boundaries but also on the world stage. Although the book focuses on Europe, various chapters refer to developments in the United States, China, and other countries. Those involved in the movement spoke similar, often identical, languages, and the way they looked at their societies and at themselves made the "the long 1960s" (from around 1956 to around 1977) a major landmark in contemporary history—the age of protest on a global scale.

The history of the world after the Second World War is usually understood in the framework of such large themes as the Cold War and decolonization. Undoubtedly, these were among the overarching themes in the history of the world in the second half of the twentieth century, but it should be noted that the Cold War was an international geopolitical phenomenon, whereas decolonization was something that led to nation-building. In other words, the nation was the key to both developments. One important aspect of "1968" was the questioning of the presumed omnipotence of the nation and the state, as various essays in the book show. The New Left, as distinct from the Old Left, challenged the privileging of the national community and the authority of the state as the fundamental definers and regulators of human beings. To the radicals espousing the new movement, the national or state framework as the key source of identity was too restrictive of individual rights and social movement. There was, to be sure, nothing new about the ideas of individual liberty or social reform. But in "the long 1960s," these became such a transnational aspiration precisely because during the preceding several decades, human beings throughout the world had tended to be conceptualized in terms of nationality and citizenship. That is why "1968" came to be seen both as an occasion for profound political transformation and a "cultural revolution," for it was a cultural aspiration to pit the individual against the all powerful state, a political entity, and to organize social groupings outside of national affiliations.

But can individuals and social groups, liberated from restrictive state and national identities, construct an alternative order, whether within national boundaries or worldwide? That question was bequeathed to the following decades, which may have answered the question by developing a world of globalization, a transnational world order that is interconnected by technology, goods, and capital. Is this the world the generation of "1968" dreamed of? Hardly, so the inevitable question would be how to connect the cultural revolution of the 1960s to the global economic order forty years later. The contributors to this book help us get started in that exploration.

Akira Iriye
Rana Mitter

1968 in Europe
An Introduction

Martin Klimke and Joachim Scharloth

On June 13, 1968, the popular British broadcaster Robert McKenzie brought together student activists from across Europe, the United States, and Japan in a BBC television show entitled "Students in Revolt" to discuss their aims and objectives in the aftermath of the events in Paris the previous month.[1] McKenzie compared the emergence of a "student class" to the emergence of the working class in the nineteenth century, arguing that in both Western and Eastern Europe, student activists were carrying their protest into the larger society, thereby "clearly influencing the political course of history." The discussion featured such prominent student leaders as Daniel Cohn-Bendit and Alan Geismar from France, Tariq Ali from Great Britain, Karl-Dietrich Wolff from West Germany, and Jan Kavan from Czechoslovakia, among others, who also insisted that they were not leaders but, rather, "megaphones" of a far larger movement that included both members of the young generation and workers.

Decrying the alienation and the lack of democratic participation in their societies, students from Western Europe largely blamed capitalism for the rise of technocratic and authoritarian structures. As Tariq Ali pointed out, "what unites us, those of us from capitalist societies, is our feeling that capitalism is inhumane and unjust and that we are all in favor of its overthrow." In this process, the universities could serve as "centers of revolutionary protest" to prevent domestic repression, connect to the working class, and transform the underlying roots of society to stop further imperialist wars such as the Vietnam War from taking place. Student representatives from Eastern Europe similarly criticized the bureaucracy, party oligarchy, and lack of freedom in Socialist societies, emphasizing the need for a greater opening and a turn to true socialism. As Jan Kavan explained, "the current situation in Czechoslovakia gives us the hope this may be the first country where a system of socialist democracy could be created." All participants agreed that the protest movement had transcended national borders in its attempt to realize an alternative society and world order and, in a remarkable display of this mutual transnational solidarity, rose up and jointly intoned the Communist Internationale in their native tongue at the end of the program.

The BBC meeting was extraordinary because it highlighted not only the transnational but, most important, the truly European experience of "1968." Although research on the transnational and global nature of the events of "1968" has been blossoming for several years, the specific European dimension of protest movements and their subcultures during the Cold War has only been analyzed marginally and within closed national contexts.[2] This extensive gap in historical research is all the more regrettable because Europe at the time of the Cold War can be considered a microcosm for global political events. It was here that the geopolitical fault line between East and West was most visible, with the Berlin Wall as its symbolic embodiment. As a consequence, not only this unique geopolitical environment but also the variety of national experience ranging from the Communist East European states of the Warsaw Pact to the democratic nations of Western Europe, as well as the dictatorships of Spain, Portugal, and Greece, practically offer themselves for a more thorough examination of border transcending cultures of domestic dissent. The goal of this volume is to therefore present a concise reference for students and researchers of the protest movements of the 1960s and 1970s in Europe. It aims at presenting information on the history of the various national protest movements to facilitate comparative studies, on the multifaceted transnational aspects of the protest movements to gain a deeper understanding of the similarities between the various national movements, and on the common narratives and cultures of memory to further the discussion on the consequences and relevance of domestic protest in the various countries as well as for Europe as a whole.

One of the outstanding historical characteristics of "1968" was that it transgressed the ideological fronts of the Cold War. This "magical year" can be viewed as the climax of various developments that had been set in motion by the immense speed of the social and economic transformations after the Second World War: demographic changes and dramatic increase in university enrollment, a globalization of communication channels, an unprecedented economic prosperity that brought the arrival of consumer society, and a generational gap expressed in differing expectations and hopes for the future.[3] Whether we regard "1968" as a transition point to a postindustrial modernity, a revolution in the world system, a global revolutionary movement, or a conglomerate of national movements with similar characteristics, the transnational dimension of 1960s protest perceived by contemporaries was one of its crucial motors. This aspect is particularly distinguished in the following four areas: roots and cognitive orientation, personal and institutional networks, action repertoires, and alternative lifestyles and emotional dispositions.[4]

Roots and Cognitive Orientation

The roots of many of these movements reach back to the beginning of the 1960s and the previous decade, making a strong case for extending the general periodization to the "long 1960s," dating roughly from 1956 to 1977. In this book, "1968" thus stands as a metaphor used to capture the broad history of European protest and activism, encapsulated by events such as the Polish riots and Hungarian revolt of 1956 and the climax of political violence and terrorism in Germany and Italy in 1977 and afterwards, to name but a few examples. The late 1950s already saw the emergence of a transnational New Left that was significantly influenced by the international peace movement.[5] Developed in British Leftist circles, the New Left was a distinctively European product that found its way across the Atlantic through, among others, the American sociologist C. Wright Mills, who popularized the concept with his "Letter to the New Left" in the fall of 1960.[6] At the same time, several Socialist youth organizations from West Germany, France, Great Britain, Belgium, and the Netherlands, among others, formed an international New Left nucleus at International Union of Socialist Youth meetings and began loose cooperation. With the programmatic Port Huron Statement of 1962 by the American Students for a Democratic Society, the New Left also acquired its specific characteristics in the United States and continued to establish itself in a transatlantic framework. What united activists on both sides of the Atlantic was a departure from orthodox Marxism and its focus on the working class; a fundamental discontent with Cold War, its anti-Communism, the deterrence policy, and the threat of nuclear extinction; and a deep-seated frustration with the apathy, materialism, and capitalist competitiveness of their societies.

In Eastern Europe, in contrast, the worker's uprising in East Germany in 1953, as well as the riots in Poland in the summer and the Hungarian revolt in the fall of 1956, had already highlighted the potential magnitude of dissatisfaction in the Warsaw Pact states. Although the de-Stalinization policies of Krushchev had promised limited liberalization, the Kremlin's grip on its satellite states in Eastern Europe remained firm and only allowed very narrow niches for any forms of dissent throughout the 1960s. Dissenters either articulated their demands on the basis of the official ideology of their countries' Communist parties or opposed Soviet ideologies with the classical works of Marx and Lenin—references to their harsh living conditions or their lack of democratic participation. The opportunities for these expressions, however, depended heavily on the lenience the individual governments were willing to grant and differed substantially from country to country. Whereas in Czechoslovakia the reform movement of the Prague

Spring brought a liberalization from above, party officials in East Germany were unyielding toward any modifications of the party line. In nonaligned Yugoslavia, in contrast, protesters enjoyed relative freedom to express their criticism of society and the shortcomings of both Eastern and Western regimes.

Across Europe, the stumbling blocks for the conflicts between young activists and state institutions were thus strikingly different. Even though anti-imperialism, anti-capitalism, and international solidarity were diffuse but common elements of the cognitive orientation of these movements, specific national issues generally determined the characteristics of protesters. In Belgium, the dominance of the French language in the Flemish university of Leuven triggered major protests among Flemish students, which had a strong nationalist current. In Italy, and even more in Germany, activists turned their anger on their parents' Fascist past. In Greece and Spain, the dictatorships of the colonels and of General Franco were the main targets of criticism.

Personal and Institutional Networks

Transnational networks between activists from different countries were nonetheless an essential factor in the European dimension of 1960s/1970s protests. Mediated exchange between student organizations from all over Europe led to a permanent diffusion of ideas, with networks such as the Underground Press Syndicate intensifying the spread of new concepts and symbolic forms. Events such as the International Vietnam Congress in Berlin in 1968 gave activists from all over Europe and other parts of the world the opportunity to meet and share their experiences while at the same time discussing their views on forms and tactics of protest. As platforms for international solidarity between the various youth movements, these events also gave activists the opportunity not only to present transnational solutions for what they perceived as global problems, such as capitalism and imperialism, but also to help prepare a global revolutionary strategy that would result in a revolutionary transformation of the Cold War system.

Despite similar political concerns and countercultural inspirations, however, national and regional idiosyncrasies were still pervasive. Whereas activists in Western Europe frequently attacked the United States for its imperialist interventions, most notably in Vietnam, dissenters in Eastern Europe often used American cultural items such as music or clothing to voice their grievances. Although the young generation in Eastern Europe, for example, welcomed efforts such as the Prague Spring, it was partially denounced as reformist by their Western counterparts. International encounters, often tightly controlled or manipulated by Eastern European authorities, occasionally illustrated these differences in ideological concepts and political realities. Events like the

World Youth Festival in Sofia in 1968 displayed the deep trenches between the leftist ideologies among the European movements: the Czech and the West German delegations were fiercely offended by representatives of more dogmatic Communist and Socialist delegations from Bulgaria, the Soviet Union, and Eastern Germany. The many international contacts and meetings between European activists therefore did not always lead to tight and permanent networks transcending national borders but could equally showcase the dissent among activists triggered by the antagonisms of the Cold War.[7]

Action Repertoires

A major effect of these personal and institutional networks, however, was the rapid spread and mixture of new forms and tactics of protest that clearly distinguished the protest movements of "1968" from their historical predecessors. Students held teach-ins to generate a critical public in egalitarian discussions, go-in activists put forward their claims to ensure their participation in the debates and decision-making processes of the authorities, and anti-ritualism aimed at disturbing the order of everyday life and suspending the social cohesion constructed in conventional ritual performances. Whereas the roots of direct action strategies lay in the African American civil rights movement and the Free Speech Movement at Berkeley, other features such as *détournement*, happening, and subversive anti-ritualism were inspired by aesthetic avantgardist and neoavantgardist movements from Europe such as surrealism, Situationism, and Provo.

Moreover, these forms of direct action were not just appellative and symbolic expressions of dissent addressed to the public. In fact, their goal was to change the activists themselves. By exposing the often hostile response of society and the authorities, direct actions were designed to raise protesters' awareness of society's "repressive" character. In addition, these protest techniques served as anticipations of the new society: Activists acted as if the norms of the actual society had been temporarily suspended, and by autonomously following their own rules, they were prefiguring the alternative society they envisioned.

Even though these protest techniques were only selectively adopted by the various national protest movements according to the different opportunity structures of their countries, they formed a widespread resource for mobilization and thereby markedly amplified the action repertoire of 1968's activists in Eastern and Western Europe.

Alternative Lifestyles and Emotional Dispositions

The rise of alternative lifestyles and countercultures as additional forms of dissent was another truly transnational aspect of the protest movements in the late 1960s and 1970s. A global popular culture, inspired by new aesthetics emerging in art, music, film, architecture, graphic design, and fashion, joined with hippie ideologies and lifestyles and melted into a set of symbolic forms, which became an infinite resource of mobilization in both the East and the West. Long hair, beards, colorful and exotic clothes, casual behavior, and a hedonistic search for pleasure and ostentatious informality became distinctive marks of a rebelling youth. The youths' belief that they were more sentient than their parents' generation, and the hope of building a new society founded on tenderness met with the search for the "new man" in psychedelic music and drug experiences, in "free" sexuality, and in new forms of living and communication. The synaesthetic nature of rock music served as the colorful display and global transmitter of these new symbolic forms of living and communication. Portraits of musicians like Jimi Hendrix promised the same freedom as the images of Che Guevara or Ho Chi Minh, the only difference being that their freedom could be gained in the here and now.

Meanwhile, these new symbolic forms of living and communication often provoked conflicts with both conservative elements in societies and state authorities and thus acquired a political dimension. Concerts by the Rolling Stones or Jimi Hendrix often ended in outbreaks of violence. In Zurich, the riots succeeding the "Monster Concerts" in the late spring of 1968 triggered political protest against the brutal intervention of the police and hardened the antagonism between youths and the local authorities. Given the limited room for dissent in the dictatorial regimes of Eastern Europe, young people often used these aspects of Western popular culture to voice their grievances. Communist authorities, however, met long hair, unconventional clothing, and beat music with suppression and interpreted it as a dangerous deviance from state ideology and as symbols of Western decadence.

Drawing on a variety of these transnational orientations, even the U.S. Department of State concluded in 1969 that student protest in Europe was not a "national phenomenon" anymore but had become "European in character."[8] A profound identity crisis and fundamental disaffection with the existing political system would continue to spur youthful activism and was beginning to occupy a firm place in all European societies: "Armed with a sophisticated knowledge of society's ills at an earlier age than ever before, more and more European young people are becoming actively hostile towards the prevailing values of their elders and towards the official government ideology in both East and West Europe. Evidence in several countries—notably

France, Germany and Eastern Europe—indicates that radicalism has taken root in secondary schools where it was never known before. This is an important indication of what can be expected from future student generations."[9]

Feeling that most of the current student dissident leaders would occupy influential political positions in the future, a transformation in the domestic political landscape and social fabric of European countries seemed to be the natural consequence.

Nobody today seriously doubts that European societies were fundamentally transformed as a result of the events of "1968." As many eyewitnesses of this "miraculous" year start to reflect on their own lives, the turbulent events of the 1960s and 1970s are slowly passing into the continent's cultural memory. When closely examining the politics of memory involved in this process, it is remarkable to see that in almost all European countries, the actual historical events have been transformed by subsequent narratives illustrating a vast array of nostalgia, condemnation, and myth-making. On the one hand, "1968" is blamed for the disintegration of traditional family structures—an atomization of society or even terrorism; on the other hand, it is used as a foundational date for a greater liberalization and democratization of society and for the enlargement of individual freedoms and as a forerunner for the fall of Communism in 1989.[10] As Kristin Ross has rightly pointed out with respect to the French May, the "afterlives" of "1968" have developed a life of their own.[11]

This book and the online and teaching guide that accompanies it provide a starting point for the historical events and the legacy they formed and for an analysis of their afterlives on both a national level and European level.[12] The goal is to inspire further examinations of the significance of "1968" for Europe as a whole, both in terms of memory culture but also as "a transnational moment of crisis and opportunity."[13] Although it can only provide a limited window into the panorama of European experiences, the book is intended to contextualize the protest movements and cultures of "1968" within larger political processes and sociocultural transformations of postwar European history. Reflecting on the legacy of this year, German philosopher Hannah Arendt wrote from New York on June 26, 1968, to her colleague Karl Jaspers in Basel the following lines: "It seems to me that the children of the next century will once learn about 1968 the way we learned about 1848."[14] In this sense, the events of "1968" can be considered not only as a critical juncture in the history of the Cold War and the twentieth century but also as occupying a prominent place in the annals of transnational revolutionary projects. In both cases, their messages and reverberations are still with us today.

Notes

1. Participants included Tariq Ali (Great Britain), Daniel Cohn-Bendit (France), Lewis Cole (United States), Alan Geismar (France), Leo Nauweds (Belgium), Alberto Martin de Hijas (Spain), Yasuo Ishii (Japan), Jan Kavan (Czechoslovakia), Ekkehart Krippendorff (West Germany), Luca Meldolese (Italy), Dragana Stavijel (Yugoslavia), Karl-Dietrich Wolff (West Germany).

2. Most of the literature on 1968 in this respect focuses on the Western world and only rarely puts forward an integrative, transnational perspective. The very few decidedly transnational studies of 1968 to date are Massimo Teodori, *Storia delle nuove sinister in Europa, 1956–1976* (Bologna: Mulino, 1976); Ingrid Gilcher-Holtey, *Die 68er-Bewegung: Deutschland, Westeuropa, USA* (Munich: Beck, 2001); Gerd-Rainer Horn, *The Spirit of '68: Rebellion in Western Europe and North America, 1956–1976* (Oxford: Oxford University Press, 2007); Martin Klimke, *The "Other" Alliance: Global Protest and Student Unrest in West Germany and the U.S., 1962–1972* (Princeton, N.J.: Princeton University Press, forthcoming). However, pointing in this direction are Etienne Francois, *1968: Ein europäisches Jahr?* (Leipzig: Leipziger Universitätsverlag, 1997); Arthur Marwick, *The Sixties: Cultural Revolution in Britain, France, Italy, and the United States, c. 1958–c. 1974* (New York: Oxford University Press, 1998); Gerd-Rainer Horn and Padraic Kenney, *Transnational Moments of Change: Europe 1945, 1968, 1989* (Lanham, Md.: Rowman & Littlefield, 2004); Axel Schildt and Detlef Siegfried, ed., *Between Marx and Coca–Cola: Youth Cultures in Changing European Societies, 1960–1980* (New York: Berghahn, 2006). For other comparative or global approaches see Gianni Statera, *Death of a Utopia: The Development and Decline of Student Movements in Europe* (New York: Oxford University Press, 1975); George Katsiaficas, *The Imagination of the New Left: A Global Analysis of 1968* (Boston, Mass.: South End Press, 1987); Ronald Fraser, *1968: A Student Generation in Revolt* (New York: Pantheon, 1988); Jeremi Suri, *Power and Protest: Global Revolution and the Rise of Détente* (Cambridge, MA: Harvard University Press, 2003); Carole Fink et al., eds., *1968: A World Transformed* (New York: Cambridge University Press, 1998). For a chronology of the year itself, see David Caute, *The Year of the Barricades: A Journey through 1968* (New York: Harper & Row, 1988); Susan Watkins and Tariq Ali, *1968: Marching in the Streets* (New York: Free Press, 1998).

3. Eric Hobsbawm, "The Year the Prophets Failed," in: Eugene Atget and Laure Beaumont–Maillet, ed., *1968 The Magnum Photographs: A Year in the World* (Paris: Magnum Photos/Editions Hazan, 1998), 8–10.

4. Alain Touraine, *La Société post-industrielle* (Paris: Denoel, 1969); Daniel Bell, *The Coming of Post-Industrial Society. A Venture in Social Forecasting* (New York: Basic Books, 1973); Immanuel Wallerstein, "1968–Revolution im Weltsystem," in: Etienne François, et al., eds., *1968—Ein europäisches Jahr?* (Leipzig: Leipziger Universitätsverlag, 1997), 19–33.

5. See the chapter by Michael Frey in this volume.

6. C. Wright Mills, "Letter to the New Left," *New Left Review* 5 (September/October 1960): 18–23. Also see the chapter by Madeleine Davis in this volume.

7. For an illustration with respect to the Czechoslovakian reception of the West German, Italian, and Polish movements see Paulina Bren, "1968 in East and West: Visions of Political Change and Student Protest," in: Horn and Kenney, *Transnational Moments*, 119–135.

8. Dean Rusk to all European diplomatic and consular posts, "Student Unrest: Roundup of EUR Posts' Reporting," Department of State, January 14, 1969, 3, in: NSF, Intelligence File, National Archives, College Park, Maryland.

9. "Bonn Conference Of Embassy and USIS Officers On Youth and Change in Europe," Conference Report, Bonn, June 11–13, 1969, 3 f., in: RG 59, IAYC Records, NA. For more on official U.S. reaction to "1968" see Klimke, *The Other Alliance*, passim.

10. See the chapter by Philipp Gassert in this volume.

11. Kristin Ross, *May '68 and Its Afterlives* (Chicago: University of Chicago Press, 2002), 1.

12. The online and teaching guide to this book can be found at http://www.1968in europe.com and includes further information on sources, teaching aids, and related literature, as well as comprehensive chronologies prepared by Rolf Werenskjold on "1968" in various European countries. We are indebted to Rebekka Weinel and Marten Deuter for the creation and maintenance of this Web site. Furthermore, we especially want to thank Thea Brophy for her invaluable support, skill, and enthusiasm in completing this volume.

13. Horn, *The Spirit of '68*, 4.

14. Lotte Köhler and Hans Saner, ed., *Hannah Arendt–Karl Jaspers. Briefwechsel 1926–1969* (München: Piper, 1993), 715 f. (translation by the author).

Part 1

Transnational Roots
of the 1968 Protest Movements

1
Subcultural Movements
The Provos

Niek Pas

The Provo action group originated in Amsterdam in the spring of 1965; it existed for two years, until May 1967. The movement acquired worldwide fame following its involvement in events surrounding a controversial royal wedding and the June 1966 riots in Amsterdam. The term "Provo" was borrowed from Dutch criminologist Wouter Buikhuisen, who used it as an alternative to *nozem*, a sort of Dutch beatnik.

Social and Political Framework of the Country

Well before May 1968 the Netherlands experienced social revolt and political unrest. The country was relatively politically unstable; the government fell in October 1966 and new parties emerged, among them the Left-liberal D'66, who desired drastic change within the party system, and the rebellious New Left in the Social Democratic Party. Furthermore, alternative culture and the free press advocated an exuberant design culture, sexual permissiveness, and a libertarian lifestyle, placing the Netherlands in the vanguard of international counterculture. Together with "Swinging London," Amsterdam became a center of European youth activity and a place of pilgrimage for thousands of German, French or Italian youngsters. There was never a Dutch "1968," as it were, but there was a 1966.

Provo was at the forefront of this revolt. Politically it stemmed from anarchist currents, left-wing traditions, and pacifist movements that went back to the 1950s, such as the Pacifist Socialist Party. Provo was culturally rooted in the art scene that emerged in Amsterdam in the late 1950s, the multifaceted youth culture, and the Montessori school system. The handful of youngsters who constituted the Provo group were politically and culturally

13

engaged and were made up of a network of friends from different sociological and geographical origins.

Cognitive Orientation and Aims

In little more than two years, Provo developed from a local activist movement into an internationally debated phenomenon. Provo was incredibly diverse, spanning generations as well as social, cultural, and geographical groupings. The group was dominantly male, though the feminist action group Dolle Mina, which appeared in the summer of 1969, was inspired by Provo tactics. Provo proved to be an extremely open network, both liberal and libertarian. Aside from the core group of several dozen people in Amsterdam, the number of supporters that came and left was astonishing. The majority of youngsters associating themselves with Provo in late 1966 stayed for an average of three weeks.

The Provo movement aimed at provoking society through constant activity. The Provos presented a cocktail of ideas and ideals, a mix of seriousness and fun, all aimed at creating a better world. They believed that the classical proletariat had lost its vanguard role in the coming socialist revolution. This was not a new concept—it had been discussed by Dutch anarchists in the 1930s and again in 1964. Provo replaced "proletariat" with "provotariat," characterized as a coalition of students and beatniks that would lead the transformation of society. Provo also replaced the well-known dichotomy of proletariat and bourgeoisie with provotariat and *klootjesvolk. Klootjesvolk* included the bourgeois, common people, and workers, who were considered to be addicted to consumer society. Furthermore, Provo merged the concept of provotariat with that of *homo ludens,* a term originally coined by Dutch historian Johan Huizinga and later used by Dutch painter, sculptor, and International Situationist sympathizer Constant Nieuwenhuys. *Homo ludens* had previously been considered the ideal future man, living in a computer-dominated environment in New Babylon, where enjoying life was the most important aspect. *Homo ludens* was the Provo of the future.

Nineteenth-century ideological concepts such as Marxism and anarchism fused with twentieth-century ideas of futurology and utopianism to form an attractive, provocative mélange. This was partially meant as a gimmick, to shock established Marxist or anarchist thinkers whom the Provos viewed as taking themselves too seriously. Although this collage of ideas received some attention abroad, it is still unclear to what degree it influenced other movements. Traditional anarchist, Marxist, and Situationist groups debated this Provo Ideology from a classical political point of view but did not take it seriously; however, underground and alternative press figures favored this cultural, libertarian philosophy. Hence, the Provo Ideology was perhaps more a form of pop art than a serious contribution to social theory.

Although their social vision was ethically motivated, the form the Provos chose for expressing their ideas was primarily aesthetic. Their style was artistic and full of humor; as such, the movement broke with conventional politics and political parties. Formalism, assemblies, and function culture were neglected, and ritual and representation came instead to play an important role. In their provocations and appeal for social and political change they emphasized cultural identity.[1]

Organizational Structure

Provo was not a traditional political organization: it had no executive committee, party platform, or official membership. It can best be considered as a movement with a small, informal nucleus surrounded by several circles of sympathizers. For example, Provo Amsterdam gathered around a printing press, *Provo* magazine, and happenings, as opposed to an organization or a well-defined program. In the course of 1966, the group started meeting in specific locations, which included basements, a barge, and an abandoned cinema.

Eventually, a network spread domestically and abroad. In 1966, groups that identified with Provo emerged in several towns, primarily university locations. These groups did not form a united system but, rather, worked autonomously and had occasional contact with Amsterdam Provos. On an international level, groups and magazines associated with Provo appeared in Belgium, West Germany, Italy, France, and England.[2] Often these local groups and underground periodicals existed before Provo Amsterdam developed, but the emergence of the Dutch activists provided a strong sense of recognition of their own struggles, hopes, and ideals.

The transnational dimension of Provo cannot be explained by focusing on formal social or organizational structures but, instead, by exploring the idea of the "fabrication" of Provo. The group played with its own media image and with public opinion. Although the Provos had no fixed media strategy, they recognized the significance of representation in modern society. The emergence of this spectacular counterculture in the summer of 1965 was accompanied by waves of media hysteria. Provo was considered a problem by the media, authorities, and scholars;[3] its causes were simplified and its participants stigmatized as "folk devils," and new frames of debate were constantly created that perpetuated this panic.[4] Media reactions to Provo were not limited to popular or tabloid publications but entered into the serious press, where attention to the movement fluctuated between "dread and fascination, outrage and amusement."[5]

Media exposure can be considered an integral part of Provo's style and tactics. When, in 1968, the Dutch psychiatrist Frank van Ree considered Provo a "public-relations-affaire,"[6] he meant that Provo skillfully anticipated existing social topics such as housing problems, traffic, industrial and environmental pollution, and taboos related to sexuality. They boldly presented these topics to the media and public opinion in new formats such as the White Plans, the most famous being the White Bicycle Plan, which suggested free bicycles for all.

Provo also had an entrepreneurial dimension. The movement created its own, locally based small-scale economy as an alternative to both capitalism and Marxism. Income received from media interviews or the sale of material written about the movement was all invested in the group. For example, these monies might be used to purchase a new press or a barge, contributing to the emergence of organizational structure. This strategy both contributed to Provo's fame abroad and led to a growing materialization of the Provo image, which would ultimately contribute to its decline.

Forms and Tactics of Protest

As it was primarily an action group—as opposed to a group of intellectuals redefining the world through debate or theorizing—Provo manifested itself in public space: The street was its *agora*. There the Provos displayed their repertoire, including small-scale, theatrical street performances known as "happenings"; large-scale demonstrations; and sit-ins. This strategy contained similarities to techniques such as collage (usually associated with the classic twentieth-century international avant-garde, from the Futurists to the Situationists) or techniques used in Pop Art. Alternative ideas about society were published as White Plans, including the White Bicycle Plan. This was an idealistic, anarchist idea that called for the distribution of free white bicycles in Amsterdam—white being a reference to innocence and purity. These expressive actions accompanied participation in democratic elections for the Amsterdam council in June 1966. This form of politics was called Pol Art, or political art, in reference to Pop Art. The Provos also took part in debates and exhibits and appeared on radio and television programs in the Netherlands and abroad.

Only at a superficial level did the theatrical extravaganza of Provo appear trivial and ephemeral. On closer examination, an alternative cultural style is evident, accompanied by a set of values, assumptions, and ways of living that has been called the Expressive Revolution.[7] Political translation of expression, rituals, and symbolism was not an invention of the 1960s movement, although in retrospect this seemed to have been so. Recent studies have focused on the expressive action repertoire of nineteenth-century local movements.[8] Furthermore, several ethnological and religion studies have stressed the historical dimensions in processes involving representation, politics, and rituality.[9]

Through their bold presentation, Provo defied the hegemonic conventions of the dominant bourgeois social order to stretch its boundaries. Provos rebelled imaginatively and humorously at the symbolic level against conventions and taboos. Their attempts to explore and question boundaries, structures, and rituals align them with broader 1960s counterculture. Provo stood for a culture of revolt and a new aesthetic that was internationally articulated and that manifested itself in opposition to hegemonic ideology.[10] At the same time, however, Provo never became completely independent from "the larger culture involving parents, educational institutions, commercial companies, technology, and the mass media."[11]

The novelty of Provo lies in the combination of its awareness of (self-)representation, expressive style, and ideas. There was no blueprint for the fabrication of Provo: it occurred spontaneously when the media, political, and public spheres changed dramatically. Publicity was not generated solely by words in print but also through visuals; this meant widespread coverage that ranged from news headlines to talk shows, background programs to special reports, and even films. Media images also became implicated in the movement's self-representation. Media exposure had a profound effect on the movement and its leaders, who were transformed into activist celebrities.[12] While public spaces such as squares and streets were conquered, public opinion was also confronted by environmental issues, militarism, pacifism, city life, sexuality, housing, and education. With Provo, the personal became political in both theme and style.

Key Events

In 1966 the movement burst onto the international stage; this time period is typically understood as the second phase of the Provo movement. Two major events played a significant role in catapulting Provo to global attention. The first of these events was the royal wedding of Princess Beatrix and Claus von Amsberg. The Provos were displeased that the future Dutch queen was marrying a German diplomat who had fought in the Second World War. The war was still a sensitive topic in the Netherlands, especially in traditionally left-wing Amsterdam, which had lost almost its entire Jewish population to the German war effort. The wedding was the biggest media event in Dutch history to date and was a hegemonic event that legitimated authority and confirmed loyalty and the shared experience of *communitas*.[13] When Provos disturbed the event by throwing smoke bombs at the procession, it was considered an act of pure blasphemy and served as a catalyst for movement's growing international media reputation.

The second event occurred in June 1966 when Amsterdam witnessed a construction workers' revolt. Through its actions Provo had contributed to the climate that made the revolt possible. For the second time in several months, the Netherlands made international headlines. Special reports and extensive articles appeared in the press, and much attention was paid to the fact that Provo had won a seat in the Amsterdam council at the municipal elections of June 1966. International press and television coverage peaked during late summer of 1966. Belgian, French, British, German, and Italian companies sent radio and television crews to Amsterdam to interview Provo members, for which the Provos demanded large sums. For instance, Granada Television had to pay a sum of 3000 guilders (some 1400 euros), and a contract was made up that precisely dictated the interview conditions.[14]

What were the consequences of this media exposure for Provo? Apart from additional income, increasing appeal to youngsters, and growing infrastructure, the inner circle grew increasingly overcharged and in late 1966 reached its limits. Competition began to grow within the movement. Initially, the fame of the Provos was a result of their spectacular actions and media coverage of their repertoire, but during the course of 1966, such actions vanished, and their strategy reached a point where exposure and representations gained the upper hand.

The group could only control this extensive media coverage to a certain extent, and even such partial control was not always possible. This became clear in the case of the white bicycles. In 1967 the psychedelic band Tomorrow recorded the album "My White Bicycle." This is an excellent example of the process of commodification of an originally subversive style element that originated in counterculture and transformed into a consumer product. But Provo was never completely absorbed into "exploitative culture,"[15] because the group decided to end its activities in May 1967.

Influence on 1968 Protest Movements

Although Provo was locally rooted, its cognitive orientation had international dimensions. In addition to international anarchist movements, there were connections to the international avant-garde (Situationist International) and international peace movements such as the British Campaign for Nuclear Disarmament. Several movements and individuals, from the United States to Italy and from Sweden to Poland, were inspired by Provo. In France, Daniel Cohn-Bendit's anarchist group discussed Provo and met some of its members in December 1966 at an international anarchist conference in Milan. The

West German student leader Rudi Dutschke also visited Amsterdam.[16] There were various attempts to copy Provo tactics and ideas abroad, even behind the Iron Curtain.

Although Provo inspired other groups, there was a good deal of confusion and debate because international mass media and militant press alike were unable to reach a clear understanding of what Provo was truly about. For example, Ken Friedman, a young Fluxus artist living in Chicago, wrote, "Help us! What is Provo? All we hear is news-lies."[17] To a certain extent, this confusion was part of Provo tactics. For some newspapers, Provos and Beatniks were the same, whereas others confused Provos with Situationists. Although the comparison between Situationists and Provos was made frequently, the differences between them are more striking than their similarities. Encounters and meetings illustrated the distance in ideological concepts and intellectual sources between the movements. In its theoretical, neo-Marxist conception of society, the Situationist International was the opposite of the actionist and libertarian Provo.

The Situationist International also opposed the extremely publicized open network Provo represented with its sectarianism. Although the Situationist International originally showed some interest in Provo, as it appeared to be a revolutionary and radical movement, this enthusiasm soon disappeared. After the Amsterdam riots and the visit of a Situationist International delegation to Amsterdam in the summer of 1966, the avant-garde group distanced itself from Provo for good and took a more hostile stance.

Consequences, Narratives, and Politics of Memory

After 1967, Provo was increasingly glamorized and admired. With the events of 1968, they were recognized as an important transnational vector that prepared the ground for the students' revolt. All aspects that represented the particularity of Provo were downplayed or simply ignored, and the Dutch activists simply became an integral part of the myth of the Protest Movement of the 1960s. The ecologist movement particularly embraced Provo in the 1970s to 1980s, perhaps as a way of ideological self-legitimating. To French ecologist Yves Frémion, Provo was nothing less than one of the *soubresauts fondateurs* of May 68,[18] an opinion shared by Daniel Cohn-Bendit in his film *Nous l'avons tant aimée, la révolution* (1986).

The Provo movement presented numerous paradoxes. The movement had strong ties to a particular area (Amsterdam), yet it also had an element of universality. Its mentality of provocation appealed to many people, from Stockholm to Milan, as well as on both sides of the Iron Curtain. However, it became clear that it was difficult to put this mentality into practice in situations other than the Dutch one. Provo did not necessarily present unique ideas or repertoire, but the specific political and cultural circumstances in Amsterdam and the greater Netherlands made their success possible. Although the political and cultural significance of its action repertoire within the Netherlands and abroad should not be overestimated, Provo's inspirational function also should not be underestimated. Provo undeniably had its share in the transnational protest culture of the 1960s. Although U.S. cultural items such as Pop Art, music, and clothing, or protest techniques such as happenings, sit-ins, or teach-ins, dominated this transnational exchange process, the model must be refined and European particularities such as Provo taken into account.

Bibliography

For interpretations of media and protest movements see Cohen (1972) and Gitlin (1980). For studies on protest and rituality see Hall and Jefferson (1993), Hebdige (1979). For the religious dimension of protest movements see the outstanding work by Koenot (1997). Martin (1981) is an excellent sociological study of cultural change in the nineteenth and twentieth centuries. The perception of Provo abroad has been studied by Vassart and Racine (1968) and the activists Frémion (1988) and Guarnaccia (1997). The first historical analysis of Provo has been provided by Pas (2003).

Cohen, Stanley. *Folk Devils & Moral Panics: The Creation of the Mods and Rockers*. London: MacGibbon and Kee, 1972.

Frémion, Yves. "Les Provos, 1965–1967," in Geneviève Dreyfus-Armand and Laurent Gervereau, eds., *Mai 68. Les mouvements étudiants en France et dans le monde*. Nanterre: BDIC, 1988, 48–52.

Gitlin, Todd. *The Whole World Is Watching: Mass Media in the Making and Unmaking of the New Left*. Berkeley: University of California Press, 1980.

Guarnaccia, Matteo. *Provos. Amsterdam 1960–67: gli inizi della controcultura*. Bertiolo: AAA Edizioni, 1997.

Hall, Stuart and Tony Jefferson, eds., *Resistance through Ritual: Youth Subcultures in Postwar Britain*. London: Routledge, 1993.

Hebdige, Dick. *Subculture. The Meaning of Style*. London: Methuen, 1979.

Koenot, Jan. *Hungry for Heaven: Rockmusik, Kultur und Religion*. Düsseldorf: Patmos, 1997.

Martin, Bernice. *A Sociology of Contemporary Cultural Change*. New York: St. Martin's Press, 1981.

Pas, Niek. *Imaazje! De verbeelding van Provo 1965–1967*. Amsterdam: Wereldbibliotheek, 2003. Ph.D. Dissertation Utrecht University, 2003.

Vassart, Christian and Aimée Racine, eds., *Provos et provotariat: Un an de recherche participante en milieu provo*. Bruxelles: CEDJ, 1968.

Notes

1. Stuart Hall and Tony Jefferson, eds., *Resistance through Rituals. Youth Subcultures in Post-War Britain* (London: Routledge, 1993).
2. Niek Pas, "Images d'une révolte ludique. Le mouvement néerlandais Provo en France dans les années soixante," *Revue Historique* 634 (April 2005): 343–373; Niek Pas, "Die niederländische Provo–Bewegung und die Bundesrepublik Deutschland 1965–1967," *Zentrum für Niederlande–Studien* 15 (Münster, 2005): 163–178.
3. Christian Vassart and Aimée Racine, eds., *Provos et provotariat. Un an de recherche participante en milieu provo* (Bruxelles: CEDJ, 1968).
4. Stanley Cohen, *Folk Devils & Moral Panics. The Creation of the Mods and Rockers* (London: MacGibbon and Kee, 1972), 38–39.
5. Dick Hebdige, *Subculture. The Meaning of Style* (London: Methuen, 1979), 92–93.
6. Frank van Ree, *Botsende generaties. Een studie over sociopatie en ambivalentie* (Assen: Van Gorcum, 1968), 191.
7. Bernice Martin, *A Sociology of Contemporary Cultural Change* (New York: St. Martin's Press, 1981).
8. Dennis Bos, *Waarachtige volksvrienden. De vroege socialistische beweging in Amsterdam 1848–1894* (Amsterdam: Bert Bakker, 2001); Amanda Kluveld, *Reis door de hel der onschuldigen. De expressieve politiek van de Nederlandse anti–vivisectionisten, 1890–1940* (Amsterdam: AUP, 2000).
9. Gerard Rooijakkers and Ton Dekker and Herman Roodenburg, eds., *Volkscultuur. Een inleiding in de Nederlandse etnologie* (Nijmegen: SUN, 2000); Gerard C. de Haas, *De onvoorziene generatie. Essays over jeugd, samenleving en cultuur* (Amsterdam: Wetenschappelijke Uitgeverij, 1966).
10. Robert Lumley, *States of Emergency. Cultures of Revolt in Italy from 1968 to 1978* (London: Verso, 1990)
11. Arthur Marwick, *The Sixties: Cultural Revolution in Britain, France, Italy and the United States* (Oxford: Oxford University Press, 1998), 11.
12. Todd Gitlin, *The Whole World Is Watching: Mass Media in the Making and Unmaking of the New Left* (Berkeley; London: University of California Press, 1980).
13. Daniel Dayan and Elihu Katz, eds., *Media Events: The Live Broadcasting of History* (Cambridge, MA: Harvard University Press, 1992).
14. Letter from Michael Ryan, Amsterdam, October 15, 1966. Private Collection Lou van Nimwegen.
15. Stanley Cohen, *Folk Devils & Moral Panics*, 140.
16. Dieter Kunzelmann, *Leisten Sie keinen Widerstand! Bilder aus meinem Leben* (Berlin: Transit, 1998), 47.
17. Letter from Ken Friedman, San Francisco, March 1967. Amsterdam, International Institute for Social History. Collection CSD VRZ 002 box 1 map 1 "Kor 1965/1966."
18. Yves Frémion, "Les Provos, 1965–1967," in: Geneviève Dreyfus-Armand and Laurent Gervereau, eds., *Mai 68. Les mouvements étudiants en France et dans le monde* (Nanterre: BDIC, 1988), 48–52.

2
Situationism

Thomas Hecken and Agata Grzenia

Roots of the Movement

The Situationist International (S.I.) was one of many small groups of artists and bohemians in Europe who combined avant-garde points of view and revolutionary criticism of society. Founded in the 1950s, the S.I. was most influential between 1966 and 1968 when a number of important figures of the antiauthoritarian student movement adopted some of its radical principles.

The French Lettrists were one of the direct predecessors of the S.I. The Lettrists fit clearly within the tradition of the avant-garde, which included such trends as futurism, Dadaism, and surrealism. With the help of a new, sweeping cultural program, they wanted to fight against old values in politics and art. One of the defining Lettrist characteristics was the strategy of reducing literature to its smallest element—the letter. The sound and form of each letter gained importance and forced the meaning and content of words into the background. The Lettrists were also known for scandalous and disturbing actions, such as an event in 1950 when four of their followers proclaimed the death of God during a mass in Notre Dame.

Isidore Isou, the founder of the Parisian Lettrists, had a significant influence on Guy Debord, the central figure of the Situationists. In 1952 Debord founded the Lettrist International with some of Isou's other disciples, but there was no longer room for Isou himself. The Lettrist International spoke in an even more radical way against representative art, which degraded the recipient to a passive spectator. Under the editing of Guy Debord, the Lettrist International published the periodical *Potlatch*, in which some of the keywords that would play a central role in Situationist theory were introduced, such as unitary urbanism, situation, *dérive*.

The remaining elements of the Lettrist International drew international recognition to the Parisian Bohemians in 1957. S.I. was founded on July 27 during a conference in Alba. It was an alliance of former members of the Lettrist International, including artistic groups such as the International Movement for an Imaginist Bauhaus, the London Psychogeographical Committee (headed by Ralph Rumney), parts of CoBrA (painters from Copenhagen, Brüssel, Amsterdam), and later the German group SPUR.

Cognitive Orientation and Aims

"There is no such thing as situationism," Debord wrote in an issue of the *Internationale Situationniste*, the magazine of the S.I. Debord did not want to be attached to a recognizable style or cultural characteristic. He reproached existentialists and contemporary surrealists for their political opportunism and excessive connection to the fine arts. He believed that the S.I. struggle should take place on every front; in the view of the Situationists, cultural, political, economic, and social life all had to be changed. Their aim was the mobilization of the masses and the organization of many small subversive groups. Situationism was about freeing actions and a new everyday life that could no longer be negatively characterized by separation between the worlds of work and leisure.

The goal of the S.I. was that "the next form of society will not be based on industrial production. It will be a society of realized art."[1] However, the effect of art also needed to change: Rather than being limited to mere function of entertainment or instruction, or retiring to the position of *l'art pour l'art*, it needed to find its role in the transformation of everyday life. The primary goal of this expanded artistic view was the deliberate construction of newer, more intense situations through which a passionate playfulness would replace work.

Artists were to break down the divisions between individual art forms and to create situations, constructed encounters, and creatively lived moments in specific urban settings—instances of a critically transformed everyday life. They were to produce settings for situations and experimental models of possible modes of transformation of the city, as well as agitate and polemicize against the sterility and oppression of the actual environment and ruling economic and political system.[2]

Above all, Situationism demanded individual creativity and spontaneity and aimed to prevent a static, passive public. The "situation" would be constructed collectively; the audience would be led to action and eventually take over the direction itself. This concept was a clear refusal of the aesthetic that was previously effective, which S.I. viewed as increasing human passivity. In traditional art, the viewer stood in a contemplative way in front of the work of art, and any form of activity was suppressed. Situationists also believed that capitalism suppressed individual activity. In *The Society of the Spectacle*, published in 1967, Guy Debord criticized the modern phenomena of capitalism and Soviet and Chinese Socialism. The Situationists saw in the spectacle a negation of life and the principle of passivity. "Modern capitalism, which organizes the reduction of all social life to a spectacle, is incapable of presenting any spectacle other than that of our own alienation."[3] In the Situationists' opinion, in a society of consumption art existed only as a commodity of the spectacle. That is why the S.I. felt that art should be freed from institutionalized places such as the theater or art gallery.

Some of the key terms of Situationist theory were "unitary urbanism," *dérive*, and *détournement*. *Détournement* aimed at a turn, alienation, or placement of objects, signs, words, or gestures out of their traditional context; the Situationists believed this operation would reveal new, more exciting meanings. They intended to disappoint conventions of representation by attacking the order of certain genres or languages through this alienation. The term *détournement* also contained a political meaning: turning "ordinary goods and manufactured experiences" against the "requirements of the system."[4] *Dérive* meant to wander the city, by which the individual constantly discovered new, unknown surroundings or situations and thus transcended the routine of everyday life. *Dérive* was a "practice of a passionate uprooting through the hurried change of environments, as well as means of studying psychogeography and situationist psychology."[5] The city was a labyrinth that resulted in emotional disorientation, contained unexpected turns, and allowed meetings with known or unknown persons. In the Situationists' understanding, *dérive* was a game that allowed a sense of adventure that was excluded in the society of spectacle.

The concept of "unitary urbanism" aimed at the synthesis of art and techniques, especially in architecture and city planning. Unitary urbanism would permit experimental behavior on the part of citizens. For example, all separation between the spheres of life and work that formed the basis of modern, functional architecture had to be broken by this unitary urbanism. The new city landscape became a playground for the situational *Homo ludens*. The "New Babylon" project, a plan of the Situationist Constant (a Dutch artist), was based on the idea of the "design of an experimental utopian city with changing zones for free play, whose nomadic inhabitants could collectively choose their own climate, sensory environment, organization of space, and so on."[6]

In the early 1960s, a stronger reorientation toward politics took place. "Marx's thought is obviously the first which must be rediscovered," the S.I. wrote.[7] The S.I. especially advocated for the foundation of worker councils, which were viewed as a new democratic type of social organization that would lead to the end of exploitation.[8] The rejection of Lenin's or Stalin's

Communist Party went along with further anarchistic demands. For example, S.I. believed that students would emancipate themselves through rejecting state and family authority, and thus acquire real freedom. [9]

Organizational Structure

Guy Debord took over editing the journal *Internationnale Situationniste* and played a central role in the Situationist organization. He wrote fundamental theoretical essays and often personally decided the exclusion of members. In all, about seventy people belonged to the S.I. during the twelve years of its existence, but never more than twenty at any given time. Some of the most important members were Asger Jorn, Michèle Bernstein, Raoul Vaneigem, Ralph Rumney, and Constant.

Exclusions occurred for different reasons. In Debord's view, members were often seduced into cooperating too closely with the art business or leading a similarly bourgeois lifestyle, which violated the Situationist ideology. "The main issue at stake was the insistence of the theoretical group based around Debord in Paris that art could not be recognized as a separate activity with its own legitimate specificity, but must be dissolved into a unitary revolutionary praxis."[10] However, no consistent official party program was strictly adhered to. Inside the organization there were to be no "spectators," meaning students or disciples, but, rather, members who took up new issues and strived for cultural and social revolution by their actions.

Though the S.I. possessed several different centers in Europe, Paris always held supremacy. Until 1961, the main axis turned around Amsterdam and Paris. After the integration of new members, Belgium and Scandinavia also gained importance. In 1961, they decided that the S.I. would be led by a central council; soon after its formation, this council ordered the exclusion of the members of SPUR who wanted to continue production of table paintings. The S.I. was most active between 1958 and 1969. Following the exclusions, only Debord and the Italian Sanguinetti remained, and in 1972 the S.I officially disbanded.

Key Activities

After the exclusion of the artists, the main activity of the S.I. was the publication of articles and pamphlets against commodity-centered society. In addition, Situationist slogans were disseminated through the use of posters and comics. The S.I.'s platform was similar to other avant-garde groups, such as the surrealists, whom the S.I. fervently rejected. The radical Situationists also added verbal and violent attacks against critics and professors to their repertoire. Some of their more conventional activities included declaring solidarity with revolutionary groups all over the world and organizing international conferences. The most sensational action was not carried out by the S.I. itself but by students who read their magazine. Backed by school financing, elected representatives of students at the University of Strasbourg in 1966 distributed a radical essay written for them by the S.I. During an official university event, students delivered the pamphlet, "On the Poverty of Student Life," to the rector. The scandal was perfect, as the university students "were now encouraged by their elected representatives to occupy the university and steal books and food, whilst the campus psychiatric clinic was declared a centre for mind control."[11] For this reason the Strasbourg revolt, which received regional media attention, was the first clear precursor of the student demonstrations of 1968.

Consequences and Narratives

S.I. actions had very few direct consequences, and thus the group was viewed as a sect that concentrated on publishing theoretical texts. Only in May 1968 were they involved in the movement in a more direct way. During this period, they were organizationally involved in political debate, first during the occupation of the Sorbonne and then in the *Conseil pour le maintien des occupations*, which supported the wild demonstrations and factory occupations. This support turned against the trade unions, the Communist Party, and large parts of the students' movement.[12] The S.I. refused mere effort for reforms, causing the Situationists and their ideologies to remain unknown to the wider public. They were not recognized as political theorists, although the Situationists praised the events of May 1968 and suggested that those events followed Situationist tenets:

> The occupations movement was obviously a rejection of alienated labor—it was a festival, a game, a real presence of people and of time, and it was a rejection of all authority, all specialization, all hierarchical dispossession; a rejection of the state and thus of the parties and unions, a rejection of sociologists and professors, of medicine and repressive morality. All those awakened by the lightning chain reaction of the movement (one of the graffiti, perhaps the most beautiful, simply said, "Quick") thoroughly despised their former conditions of existence, and therefore those who had worked to keep them there, from the television stars to the urbanists. Many people's Stalinist illusions, in various diluted forms from Castro to Sartre, were torn apart, and all the rival and interdependent lies of an era crumbled.[13]

The hopes embedded in this statement turned out to be an illusion. An intensive reception of Situationism has taken place only in two quiet, unique fields since the late 1980s; namely, the art world and among anarchistic bohème groups and authors. In the history of art and the philological sciences, the Situationists found their place as well. They are described by avant-garde research as a group that continued the effort of the futurists, Dadaists, and surrealists to bridge the gap between life and art.[14] Moreover, in English-speaking arenas the influence of the Situationists has often been connected to elements of the punk scene.[15]

Above all, the Situationists received attention because of their participation in the events of 1968. Richard Neville describes them "as a mysterious radical cell whose ideas had infused the May Events."[16] The small group's opinions often flowed into the countercultural ideology without specifically being named. For example, there was a decidedly Situationist character to a number of countercultural watchwords. A report from Paris in 1968 stated, "The revolution which is beginning will call in question not only capitalist society but industrial society. The consumer's society must perish of a violent death. The society of alienation must disappear from history. We are inventing a new and original world. Imagination is a seizing power."[17] However, other counterculture theorists ignored the Situationists' ideological role, a phenomenon that Joseph Berke summed up canonically in 1968:

> According to the situationalists, a universally dominant system tending towards totalitarian self-regulation is being resisted, but only apparently, by false forms of opposition which remain trapped on the territory laid down by the system—a system which these illusions can thus only serve to reinforce. Bureaucratic pseudo-socialism is but the most grandiose of these guises of the old world of hierarchy and alienated labor. . . . The situationalists consider that the indivisible perspective of this opposition is the effective abolition of all class societies, of the commodity production system, of wage labor; the transcendence of art and of all cultural acquirements, by their re-entry into play through the free creation in everyday life.[18]

Influence on the 1968 Protest Movements

According to ideological history, the Situationists can be classified within the New Left, which focused on the alienation of human beings rather than on exploitation and considered new forms of both political and cultural action important.[19] However, the question still remains as to whether this small group of Situationists had a direct influence on the actors and organizations who determined the events of 1968. In France, the group was influential at the inception of student demonstrations at the University of

Nanterre. The *Enragés*, another group with a strong Situationist orientation, was also active in France in cooperation with Daniel Cohn-Bendit, one of the leading figures of the French May Movement. Their actions constantly provoked strong reactions from official institutions and decisively contributed to the escalation of events.[20]

King Mob was a group active in England that strongly adhered to Situationist ideas. More important, several Situationist writings supplied useful general buzzwords that intensified the radical discourse and protest.

The English translation of *De la misère en milieu étudiant*, translated as "Ten Days Which Shook the University," was beginning to have an important effect in America and particularly in Britain, where the Situationist-inspired outfits such as the Hornsey-based grouping King Mob were starting to make their voices heard. The hippie underground in London, which had heard the good news from Strasbourg, immediately seized on the term 'Situationist' as a catch-all term for aggressive and provocative actions.[21]

Although the term is hardly known in Germany, the Situationists' influence on parts of the 68 movement is probably the strongest. This is because of the Berlin Commune I, a countercultural, flat-sharing community founded in early 1967 by S.I. member Dieter Kunzelmann. Their joyful, provocative behavior at demonstrations, parades, and proceedings attracted special attention. "They sought to exemplify in their daily life exactly what they preached, to extend the possibilities of collective living and liberation from bourgeois values as far as possible."[22] An indictment written by Berlin public prosecutors against members of Commune I in June 1968 states that Commune I aimed for "general sexual fulfillment through the dissolution of the private relationships as private relationships," abolition of private property and state order, resolution of sexual frustration by unrestricted change of partners and through collective discussion of individual misconduct, and ending the difficulties of everyday living (housing, livelihood) by "actions" such as appropriation of empty houses, theft, and looting of shops and pubs.[23] Commune I specialized in sensational interviews and leaflets. They abolished the separation of art and life in a way that effectively influenced the public. In typical Situationist manner, they adopted critiques of consumption and radical rejection of all authorities.

Bibliography

A good overview of the organizational and artistic activities of the Lettrist International and the Situationist International is provided by Ohrt (1990), Kaufmann (2001), and Hussey (2001). Hollstein (1969), Marcus (1989), Briegleb (1993), and Hecken (2006a and 2006b) connect the aspirations of the Situationist avant-garde with other countercultural groups (such as the Provos and punks) and their ideologies and lifestyles. For a more philosophical analysis of Situationist theory, see Plant (1992). Essays about various Situationist subjects are offered by Ohrt (1999), McDonough (2002), and the French journal, *Archives & Documents Situationnistes* (2001ff.). A few former members of the Lettrist International—Brau (1968) and Mension (1998)—and the Situationist International—Zimmer (1984) and Kunzelmann (1998)—have recalled their past in historical and autobiographical sketches.

Brau, Eliane. *Le Situationnisme ou La Nouvelle Internationale*. Paris: Albin Michel, 1968.

Briegleb, Klaus. *1968: Literatur in der antiautoritären Bewegung*. Frankfurt: Suhrkamp, 1993.

Hecken, Thomas. *Gegenkultur und Avantgarde 1950–1970. Situationisten, Beatniks, 68er*. Tübingen: Francke, 2006.

Hecken, Thomas. *Avantgarde und Terrorismus. Rhetorik der Intensität und Programme der Revolte von den Futuristen bis zur RAF*. Bielefeld: Transcript, 2006.

Hollstein, Walter. *Der Untergrund. Zur Soziologie jugendlicher Protestbewegungen*. Neuwied: Luchterhand, 1969.

Hussey, Andrew. *The Game of War. The Life and Death of Guy Debord*. London: Jonathan Cape, 2001.

Kaufmann, Vincent. *Guy Debord. La révolution au service de la poésie*. Paris: Fayard, 2001.

Kunzelmann, Dieter. *Leisten Sie keinen Widerstand! Bilder aus meinem Leben*. Berlin: Transit, 1998.

Marcus, Greil. *Lipstick Traces. A Secret History of the Twentieth Century*. London: Secker & Warburg, 1989.

McDonough, Tom, ed. *Guy Debord and the Situationist International. Texts and Documents*. Cambridge, MA: MIT, 2002.

Mension, Jean-Michel. *La tribu*. Paris: Allia, 1998.

Ohrt, Roberto. *Phantom Avantgarde. Eine Geschichte der Situationistischen Internationale und der modernen Kunst*. Hamburg: Nautilus, 1990.

Ohrt, Roberto, ed. *Das grosse Spiel. Die Situationisten zwischen Politik und Kunst*. Hamburg: Nautilus, 1999.

Plant, Sadie. *The Most Radical Gesture: The Situationist International in a Postmodern Age*. London: Routledge, 1992.

Zimmer, Hans Peter. *Selbstgespräch. Bilder 1958–84*. München: Karl & Faber, 1984.

We thank Jessica Chronowski who assisted with the stylistic finish of this essay.

Notes

1. Situationist International, "The Bad Days Will End," [1962] in *Situationist International Anthology*, ed./trans. Ken Knabb (Berkeley, CA: Bureau of Public Secrets, 1981), 87.

2. Peter Wollen, "Bitter Victory: The Art and Politics of the Situationist International," in *On the Passage of a Few People through a Rather Brief Moment in Time: The Situationist International 1957–1972*, ed. Elisabeth Sussman (Cambridge, MA: MIT, 1991), 22.

3. Attila Kotányi/Raoul Vaneigem, "Elementary Program of the Bureau of Unitary Urbanism," [1961] in *Situationist International Anthology*, ed./trans. Ken Knabb (Berkeley, CA: Bureau of Public Secrets, 1981), 65.

4. Thomas Crow, *The Rise of the Sixties. American and European Art in the Era of Dissent 1955–69* (London: Weidenfels and Nicolson, 1996), 52.

5. Guy Debord, "Report on the Construction of Situations and on the Terms of Organization and Action of the International Situationist Tendency," in *Guy Debord and the Situationist International: Texts and Documents*, ed. Tom McDonough(Cambridge, MA: MIT, 2004), 46.

6. Wollen, "Bitter Victory," 25.

7. Situationist International, "The Bad Days Will End," 84.

8. Raoul Vaneigem, "Notice to the Civilized Concerning Generalized Self-Management," [1969] in *Situationist International Anthology*, ed./trans. Ken Knabb, 284.

9. Situationist International, "On the poverty of student life," [1966] in *Situationist International Anthology*, ed./trans. Ken Knabb, 323.

10. Wollen, "Bitter Victory," 25.

11. Andrew Hussey, *The Game of War: The Life and Death of Guy Debord* (London: Jonathan Cape, 2001), 204.

12. See René Vienet, *Enragés et situationnistes dans le mouvement des occpations* (Paris: Gallimard, 1968); Ingrid Gilcher-Holtey, *"Die Phantasie an die Macht." Mai 68 in Frankreich* (Frankfurt am Main: Suhrkamp, 1995).

13. Situationist International, "The Beginning of an Era," in *Situationist International Anthology*, ed./trans. Ken Knabb, 288.

14. Marcus (1989); Ohrt (1990); Hecken (2006b).

15. Jamie Reid, *Up They Rose. The Incomplete Works of Jamie Reid* (London: Faber and Faber, 1987), 37ff.; Jon Savage, *England's Dreaming. Sex Pistols and Punk Rock* (London: Faber and Faber, 1991), 30ff.; Fred Vermorel, *Fashion & Perversity. A Life of Vivienne Westwood and the Sixties Laid Bare* (London: Bloomsbury, 1996).

16. Richard Neville, *Hippie Hippie Shake. The Dreams, the Trips, the Love Ins, the Screw Ups . . . the Sixties* (London: Bloomsbury, 1996), 148. However, Situationists refused the well-known imperative "Power to the Imagination" as a slogan, "which did not know the means to put this power into practice, to reinvent everything; and which, lacking power, lacked imagination." Situationist International, "The Beginning of an Era," in Knabb, *Situationist International Anthology*, 226.

17. Theodore Roszak, *The Making of a Counter Culture. Reflections on the Technocratic Society and Its Youthful Opposition* (London: Faber and Faber, 1970), 22.

18. Joseph Berke, ed., *Counter Culture. Creation of an Alternative Society* (London: Owen, 1969), 197.

19. Cf. Ingrid Gilcher-Holtey, *Die 68er Bewegung. Deutschland–Westeuropa–USA* (München: Beck, 2001), 15ff.

20. Cf. Ingrid Gilcher-Holtey, *"Die Phantasie an die Macht,"* 126ff.

21. Hussey (2001, 212).

22. Berke, *Counter Culture*, 103.

23. Kuntze, Public Prosecutor, "Indictment," in Berke, *Counter Culture*, 108–110, 108f.

3
The International Peace Movement

Michael Frey

Although there has been a tradition of mainly religiously motivated conscientious objectors for many centuries, the origins of an organized peace movement can be traced back to two nineteenth-century ideologies: pacifism and antimilitarism. In this chapter, the *peace movement* is defined as a social movement that aimed to eradicate war as a means of policy and established itself between 1954 and 1963, following ideas originating in the pacifist, antimilitaristic, and socialist ideologies of the nineteenth century.[1]

Roots

The origins of pacifism can be found in middle-class liberalism. As early as the Napoleonic wars, middle-class liberals in numerous countries founded small clubs supporting human rights and rejecting military action on ethical and religious grounds. In many countries, these clubs finally came together in national *Peace Societies*, whose main objective was the limitation and reduction of national wars and the protection of the population from the effects of war. The Peace Societies worked at establishing an international court of arbitration and setting up an internationally binding code of law. They appealed to the governments and strove to achieve a modification of law—that is, they followed a legalistic course of action.

Antimilitarism, in contrast, was deeply rooted in the labor movement. Because of the labor movement's inner conflicts, however, it is impossible to give an exact definition of the term.[2] The majority of the Second Socialist International was heavily influenced by the German Socialists and believed that changes in society and the Socialists' seizure of political power would automatically stop any future wars, because the power over arms would lie in the hands of the proletariat. In contrast to those beliefs, revolutionary anarchism completely opposed the military and all forms of violence, including the "dictatorship of the proletariat." Organizations like the *Internationale Antimilitaristische Vereinigung* or the Industrial Workers of the World, founded in 1905 in the United States, were in favor of strategies against war that can be described by using key words like sabotage, objection, strike, and passive resistance. In short, the slogans "weapons to us" versus "weapons down" very pointedly describe the difference between Marxist and anarchist antimilitarism.

When World War I started in 1914, however, neither Peace Societies nor the labor movement was able to prevent the four years of slaughter. Both doctrines' lack of power finally led to the emergence of a new form of pacifism: "active pacifism." It presented a synthesis of "pacifism in favor of legal actions (organizational pacifism) and the revolutionary antimilitarism promoting direct actions"[3] and was trying to link the liberal middle-class pacifism of the peace societies with the antimilitarism of the anarchistic labor movement. One organization that followed the ideals of an "active pacifism" was the *War Resisters' International* (WRI). Founded in 1921 in the Netherlands, the WRI developed an antimilitaristic, political pacifism that saw its function not only in preventing wars through conscientious objections but also in setting further political and social aims. From then on, racial hatred and the removal of social setbacks also belonged to the range of action of the peace movement, because these were considered major reasons for armed conflicts.

The Second World War brought decisive changes in the quality of active pacifism because conscientious objectors (COs) in the United States started to realize these aims by using new methods of protest.[4] Many of them had successfully used nonviolent tactics, hunger strikes, and the mobilization of the public to end racial segregation in the American prison system. Learning from this fundamental victory, activists who left prison after the end of the Second World War started to use their methods of protest in other areas. Gandhi's nonviolent resistance became the leading philosophy in the fight for more civil rights, for disarmament, and against social setbacks; American COs, who now took an active part in the peace movement, were the pioneers of these new methods. However, the swiftly beginning Cold War soon put such a damper on the activities of the peace movement that there barely existed any movement at all at the beginning of the 1950s.

Cognitive Orientations and Aims

In the mid-1950s, the peace movement started its slow revival. Although the numerous groups of the resurrected peace movement had a clearly defined common goal, namely, the fight against the bomb and the nuclear arms race, they neither shared a common political agenda nor agreed on ideological questions. Furthermore, there was no consent on the means of how to reach their aims. Nevertheless, despite this heterogeneity there were two general ways of fighting that can be observed: liberal peace activists and radical pacifists.

Liberal peace advocates favored an international test ban and disarmament conferences. They believed that peace required a process of social and economic change, which was best promoted through support of international agencies and multilateral cooperation, through United Nations peacekeeping efforts instead of unilateral American intervention, and through technical and economic aid rather than military assistance. At most, peace liberals hoped for a reformed world order that might constrain national rivalries, temper Soviet–US antagonism, and open the way for orderly disarmament. They opposed continuing escalation of the nuclear arms race. Because of these beliefs, most of the liberal peace advocates were suspicious of ideologies and uninterested in mass movements and were inclined to use the means of persuasion and advocacy within established institutions. Liberal peace advocates were engaged in international peace organizations such as United World Federalists (UWF); Women's International League for Peace and Freedom (WILPF), an organization that had been set up by women during the First World War from several nations; and the Pugwash Movement, a movement including scientists from countries on either side of the Iron Curtain.

Although liberal peace activists kept criticizing the West's armament policy, many shared the official point of view that the aggressive ideology and foreign policy of the Soviet Union was responsible for the confrontation. The views of radical pacifists differed fundamentally. Radical pacifists believed that both sides of the Iron Curtain presented different manifestations of the same problem: "Whatever differences may exist between Communist and 'free world' regimes, in this decisive respect they are equal threats, two sides of the same threat to the survival of civilization," the American peace activist Abraham Muste wrote in the journal *Liberation*. "The H-bomb is not an instrument of peace in the hands of one and of war in the hands of the other. Nor is it a mere accidental excrescence in either of them but, rather, a logical outgrowth of their basic economic and social orders."[5] Consequently, radical pacifists like Muste supported a strategy of unilateral disarmament to solve the conflict between the two power blocks and suggested an independent worldwide movement against their binary policies. This concept of a "Third Camp" roused great hopes in countries without allegiance to either block:

> There are in Western Europe, Asia, Africa, and Latin America, peoples who live 'in between' the two atomically armed power blocks. Of necessity,

their prime objective is to keep from being drawn into either block and engulfed in the wars for which these leviathans are arming. . . . There are in non-committed areas groups seeking to deal with the problems of economics and politics in a broader way and at a deeper ethical level. They seek to build not another Military Force but a Third Camp or Third Way. They are striving not only to avoid war but to build a socio-economic order and culture different from both Communism and capitalism.[6]

This idea of a Third Camp also fundamentally differed with the strategies of liberal peace activists. In places where liberal peace advocates tried to achieve legal changes through reforms, radical pacifists sought to expose shortcomings through symbolic actions. As radical pacifist Ken Calkins wrote in 1958, "I have become convinced that direct action is the only way to reach the minds of men who have been morally benumbed by too many years of propaganda, fear and horror. I hope that my action will stir at least some of those who have so long remained silent to speak up and to act against what they know in their hearts is a hopeless and immoral policy."[7]

Organizational Structure

According to a rough estimate of the American peace organization SANE (the Committee for a SANE Nuclear Policy), the early 1960s saw approximately 100 nonaligned peace organizations (i.e., organizations without Communist support) in forty-four countries. The International Fellowship of Reconciliation alone counted 41,000 members in twenty-five countries. The WRI listed a similar number of members, and the WILPF had independent international sections in forty-one countries.[8] If all these groups had been internationally united, the peace movement would have had an influential voice in the Cold War. Because of the substantial political and strategic differences between these organizations, however, this was never an option. The greatest obstacle on the way to international cooperation was the attitude toward Communism. Most peace groups gave way to public pressure and presented a strictly anti-Communist ideology so as not to be suspected of Communist subversion. This led to conflicts with those (mainly radical pacifist) organizations that rejected Communism but were in favor of an open-door policy, or a line of policy that allowed for some dialogue with organizations from the Eastern Bloc. Because even these positions were hard to unite, cooperation with the World Peace Council seemed impossible, even though organization with a clearly Communist leadership had many sections all over Europe (in both West and East) and could have offered a good logistical base for international cooperation. However, as a result of these unbridgeable differences, the early 1960s saw not only a deeply divided nonaligned peace movement but also a competing Communist-led movement.

Despite these unfavorable preconditions, limited networks started to unite some of the groups of the nonaligned movement in the late 1950s. The initial step was taken by smaller groups who found common aspects in their programs or activities. One example is the cooperation of the nonviolent peace activists of the British Direct Action Committee with the American Committee for Non-Violent Action (CNVA). Similarly, the *Sozialistische Deutsche Studentenbund* corresponded with like-minded students of the U.S. Student Peace Union and the Japanese *Zengakuren*. Although limited by geographical distance, their cooperation still resulted in simultaneous demonstrations of all three student organizations against atmospheric nuclear testing on April 27, 1962. Inspired by these efforts, larger organizations also began creating transnational networks. One of the first was the Pugwash Movement, launched during a July 1957 conference that united famous scientists from both hemispheres. In 1959, the European Federation Against Nuclear Arms established yet another, albeit very selective, international organization. It was limited to Western Europe and specifically excluded pacifist groups and organizations using direct action. But when forty peace groups from eighteen countries met in Oxford in 1963 to found the International Confederation for Disarmament and Peace (ICDP), an organization open to all nonaligned peace groups was finally created. By 1967, fifty-six nonaligned peace groups had become members of the ICDP, including not only the three pacifist internationals but also direct action, unilateralist, multilateralist, student, and women's groups.[9] Despite the common trend toward networking and cooperation between the nonaligned groups, the numerous differences among the single groups still prevented an effective, unified policy. The bigger the organization, as in the case of the ICDP, the harder it was to define common aims that could be supported by the various national groups. In addition, as the different interests often prevailed, the peace movement can hardly be called transnational.

Transnationalism can be found within the two pacifist Internationals, the WRI and the International Fellowship of Reconciliation. Both Internationals understood themselves as being transnational networks, as seen within the organizational structure of the WRI. Contrary to international organizations like the ICDP, which tried to unite the positions of numerous national umbrella organizations by discussion, the WRI saw itself as a movement of individual members without a central administration or rigid hierarchy. Membership was obtained simply by agreeing to a common declaration of principles. This way, it was possible to accept groups or individuals with differing ideologies and even support their ideas, as long as the basic principles remained untouched. In that respect, the WRI rather resembled a pluralistic debate club than an organization, because it was not so much an instrument to execute common political aims as a turntable for new ideas, which were presented during its international conferences or published in WRI publications.[10] The WRI thus became an "international transmission belt which helped to spread regionally limited discussions of theory and action into different countries."[11]

Members such as Bayard Rustin were mainly responsible for spreading nonviolent action in numerous movements and countries during the 1950s and 1960s. As a member of the American section of the WRI, the War Resisters League, and the American Fellowship of Reconciliation, Rustin came across Gandhi's philosophy of nonviolent resistance in the 1940s and successfully practiced it as a war resister in World War II and as a protestor against racial segregation in American prisons.[12] During the Montgomery Bus Boycott in 1955 and the first spectacular success of the modern Civil Rights Movement through the means of nonviolent action, Rustin was one of the most important advisors of Martin Luther King Jr. By 1963, when Rustin organized the March on Washington, he had taken part in organizing countless international peace projects.[13] His experiences became as much a part of the network of the WRI as the experiences of activists of other countries. Peace activists such as the American Abraham Muste, April Carter and Michael Randle from Great Britain, or the German Hans-Konrad Tempel, who initiated the German Easter March, were thus responsible for two important preconditions: On the one hand, they helped spread new ideas such as Gandhi's ideas of nonviolence and the concept of a Third Camp or the Easter March as a new form of protest against the nuclear armament to other countries. On the other hand, they created the transnational network of the WRI, which was mainly based on personal contacts (the Fellowship of Reconciliation was organized along similar lines). This transnationalism was lacking in other international peace organizations but left a deep impression on people who took part in activities such as the Easter March movement.

Key Activities

Because the threatening effects of the atmospheric nuclear tests had prepared the breeding ground for a new awareness, the peace movement started to grow considerably in the late 1950s. At the same time, increasing numbers of people were attracted by the broad activities of numerous peace groups that had seized public attention through their innovative forms of protest. Probably the most important innovation of the late 1950s was made by the Campaign for Nuclear Disarmament (CND) in Great Britain in 1958 in the march from Aldermaston to London, and subsequently the whole Easter March movement.[14] At first, it was the special status of Great Britain as an atomic power that helped spur the movement: The British H-bomb tests scheduled for May 1957 on the Christmas Islands prompted such massive opposition that the National Council for the Abolition of Nuclear War Tests was founded. Because public opinion in Great Britain gradually turned against nuclear weapons and the policy of both blocks, the National Council for the Abolition of Nuclear War Tests changed its name to the Campaign for Nuclear Disarmament on January 27, 1958. Because of the prominent support of the movement, 270 local groups were founded by the end of 1958 with the aim of unilateral disarmament of Great Britain.

Despite this large number of participants, the CND's goal was not a membership drive but a moral mission, which became especially obvious during the Aldermaston march. Scheduled for Easter 1958 and originally organized by the Direct Action Committee, the march secured CND's support and participation. The artist Gerald Holtom convinced the organizers to adopt a new symbol: a circle encompassing a broken cross. The cross contained, as the artist explained, the semaphore signals for the *n* and *d* of "nuclear disarmament." In April of that year, almost 5800 marchers gathered for a rally in Trafalgar Square and began the fifty-two mile walk to the nuclear weapons facility at Aldermaston. During this four-day march, large numbers of serious and well-dressed citizens carried the new disarmament symbol in chilling rain and astounded the British public with a powerful demonstration to halt the nuclear arms race. The march was so impressive that CND immediately adopted the new symbol and continued these demonstrations. In 1960, an estimated 100,000 peace advocates gathered in London under the nuclear disarmament banners—a number that rose to 150,000 at the culminating rally in 1962. This development was paralleled by constant growth of the CND. By 1961, the organization could point to more than 800 chapters. *Sanity*, CND's monthly newspaper, soon had 45,000 subscribers, and in Great Britain the CND symbol became as recognizable as the Union Jack.

Other countries adopted the British model. Within a few years, similar organizations were founded in Denmark, Norway, Sweden, and Finland.[15] Other Easter Marches could be found in Germany, the Netherlands, Italy, and Greece, where people marched from Marathon to Athens. The CND also proved to be a successful model outside Europe: Activists in Canada, Australia, and New Zealand followed the group's lead and sometimes even adopted the name for their own organizations. Similar movements in Africa, the Middle East, and Asia (especially in Japan, with its recent memories of Hiroshima and Nagasaki) made the CND activities a global success story. The CND symbol crossed the globe as a symbol of peace and was adopted by many of the newly founded peace organizations. At times it seemed as if during the Easter holidays, a worldwide movement was on the march. As a result of these growing numbers and rising public attention, the objective of the Easter Marches—to ban the bomb—was slowly becoming a politically accepted demand.

Although far less influential in terms of public opinion and number of supporters, the movement of radical pacifism and its enrichment, since 1957, of the protest repertoire of the peace movement turned out to be equally decisive for the protest cultures of the 1960s. The American pacifists who had founded the CNVA in May 1957 (until 1959 it was known as Non-Violent Action Against Nuclear Weapons) were pioneers of this development.[16] Contrary to most other peace organizations, CNVA was not a card-carrying membership organization, but like the WRI, it, rather, was a network originating from other peace groups. It included members of the American Friends Service Committee (a Quaker organization); activists from the anarchist War Resisters League, the American branch of the WRI; and the Christian pacifists of the Fellowship of Reconciliation. Hence, the CNVA was not a mass movement but a small disciplined vanguard of sixty to seventy radical pacifists who championed Gandhi-like techniques of direct action and civil disobedience.

This became obvious in 1958–1959, during the highly dramatic CNVA actions against the testing and deployment of intercontinental ballistic missiles. The most widely covered action occurred in 1958 when activists tried to sail their ships *Golden Rule* and the *Phoenix of Hiroshima* into the Pacific Ocean bomb-testing area. Although both crews were arrested, CNVA did not stop protesting and received broad news coverage in the American media. Another protest action at the construction site of a strategic missile base in 1958 in Cheyenne, Wyoming, went a step further to more confrontational tactics and acts of obstruction. Participants aimed to block base construction by sitting in front of trucks carrying construction material. The only way to remove the protestors was to drag or carry them off—or run them over. Similar activities took place in New York, when activists of CNVA tried to board Polaris submarines (the first nuclear-powered ballistic missile–launching submarines the U.S. Navy acquired) when they were about to leave the harbor. Although the activists could not stop the submarines from leaving, they still managed to make it to the front page of the *New York Times*.

Almost all actions of the CNVA ended similarly, with the activists' arrests. Imprisonment and physical injuries (such as in Cheyenne) were part of the plan. These drastic methods were designed to raise awareness about nuclear overkill and to demonstrate a new, morally justified unwillingness to compromise with which the pacifists pursued their ideals. Pacifist networks like the WRI or the Fellowship of Reconciliation therefore contributed to the spread of Gandhi-like techniques of direct action and civil disobedience of protest.[17] Although these protest techniques mostly met with ignorance in the early 1960s, a young generation of protesters would avidly accept and act on these very impulses of radical pacifists only a few years later.

Consequences and Narratives

Although the Atmospheric Test Ban Treaty of August 5, 1963, banned tests of nuclear weapons in the atmosphere, in outer space, and underwater, it at the same time marked a substantial lessening of the activities of the nuclear disarmament movement. Although the treaty did not lead to peace, disarmament, or an end of the Cold War, nearly all campaigns for nuclear disarmament saw a reduction in both members and enthusiasm. In particular, the liberal elements of the movement, which were content with the moderate aims of controlled disarmament and détente, almost completely stopped their activities. Some organizations even collapsed, such as American Student Peace Union in 1964, or were absorbed by other movements.

However, fewer activities did not mean the end of the international peace movement. The organizational cores stayed alive even after the Test Ban Treaty. More important, the escalation of the Vietnam War both rejuvenated and transformed the movement. As a result of the influence of a youthful New Left, the peace movement experienced further politicization and radicalization. Former radical pacifists began to include anti-imperialism and anti-capitalism in their rhetoric and started to identify with Third World revolutionaries. In the late 1960s, many peace activists followed the arguments of the New Left, thus changing the peace movement into an antiwar movement.[18] The end of the Vietnam War in 1974 brought a spell of rest for the peace movement after long years of massive protests, but the organizations continued to exist. When in 1977 the development of the neutron bomb caused as severe worldwide protests as the NATO Double-Track Decision did, the cores of the peace movement, which still existed, passed on their knowledge to a new generation of protesters.[19] Thus, protest forms developed in the late 1950s experienced a resurrection. Marches under the CND symbol took place, as well as nonviolent actions like sit-down strikes or the so-called "Die-Ins," where demonstrators lay down on a signal as if they were dead.

Influence on the 1968 Protest Movement

Historical research has hardly noticed the role and effect of the international peace movement on the New Left and the protest movements of 1968. This gap seems to be unjustified, especially when considering the plethora of personal and intellectual links between the two movements. The tremendous influence of the peace movement can be summarized in three points.

First, as early as the 1950s, the peace movement developed and anticipated many of the central ideas and protest methods later to be considered typical of the protesters of 1968. Even if innovations such as decentralized organizations, transnationality, solidarity with Third World countries, and nonviolent resistance are credited to protagonists of the 1968 movement, these elements had already been developed and used by the peace movement in the 1950s. Groups like CND and CNVA, the "shock troops" of the movement, managed to break the ice in the political culture of the Cold War with ideas like the Third Camp and new protest methods. They acted as a loose network that spread their ideas internationally and laid the foundation for later protest movements.

Second, the peace movement was present in the late 1950s when a young generation of protesters started to form a New Left. Activists of the peace movement played a crucial role in creating student-led New Left organizations. They were able to offer organizational help and cognitive orientations. Whether lecturing on the war in Algeria, conveying a Third Camp perspective, or teaching nonviolent tactics, activists of the peace movement almost always provided substantial impulses to New Left thinking. The American Student Peace Union, the Students for a Democratic Society, or the Student Nonviolent Coordinating Committee would hardly have been as successful without the help of the experienced protesters of the War Resisters League.

More important than these direct political and strategic influences, however, were the personal experiences the young generation made in the peace movement. Casual manners and unorthodox role models observed during the Easter Marches influenced the lifestyle of the young generation as well as the action-based ideology exhibited in direct actions. "Putting your body on the line" to display personal commitment to the cause, even if it involved physical dangers, was the way the older peace activists behaved, and they were subsequently imitated by the rising New Left.

Third, in the heyday of the 1960s, the peace movement was not only striding side by side with the student movement but played an important role in the protest movements of 1968. Although student protestors often dominated media coverage, studies analyzing protests against the Vietnam War show that the antiwar movement was mainly made of loosely connected liberal and radical organizations, with student groups playing only a minor role.[20] Therefore, it seems appropriate to interpret the protest movement of 1968 as a "movement of movements" in which, apart from the student movement, the peace movement played an essential part.[21]

Bibliography

A comprehensive overview of the history of the international nuclear disarmament movement is provided by Wittner (1993, 1997, and 2003). For a comparative perspective on the peace movements in the United States and Great Britain, see Young (1977). For studies on the American peace movement, turn to Wittner (1984) or to DeBenedetti (1990), who concentrates on the Vietnam War. For studies on the peace movements in Great Britain and Germany, see Taylor (1988) and Cooper (1996). On radical pacifism and nonviolence, see Tracy (1996). For an analysis of the WRI, see Prasad (2005).

DeBenedetti, Charles, and Charles Chatfield. *An American Ordeal. The Antiwar Movement of the Vietnam Era*. Syracuse: Syracuse University Press, 1990.

Cooper, Alice Holmes. *Paradoxes of Peace: German Peace Movements Since 1945*. Ann Arbor: University of Michigan Press, 1996.

Prasad, Devi. *War is a Crime Against Humanity. The Story of War Resisters' International*. London: War Resisters' International Press, 2005.

Taylor, Richard. *Against the Bomb: The British Peace Movement, 1958–1965*. Oxford: Clarendon Press, 1988.

Tracy, James. *Direct Action: Radical Pacifism from the Union Eight to the Chicago Seven*. Chicago: University of Chicago Press, 1996.

Wittner, Lawrence S. *Rebels Against War: The American Peace Movement, 1933–1983*. Philadelphia: Temple University Press, 1984.

Wittner, Lawrence S. *The Struggle Against the Bomb*, vols. 1–3. Stanford, CA: Stanford University Press, 1993, 1997, and 2003.

Young, Nigel. *An Infantile Disorder? The Crisis and Decline of the New Left*. Boulder: Westview Press, 1977.

Notes

1. On the international peace movement, see the comprehensive study provided by Lawrence S. Wittner, *The Struggle against the Bomb*, 3 vols. (Stanford, CA: Stanford University Press, 1997).
2. For the following, cf. Wolfram Beyer, ed., *Widerstand gegen den Krieg. Beiträge zur Geschichte der War Resisters' International* (Kassel: Weber, Zucht und Co., 1989), 8ff.
3. Franz Kobler and Bart de Ligt, "über die Taktik des aktiven Pazifismus," in Franz Kobler, ed., *Gewalt und Gewaltlosigkeit. Handbuch des aktiven Pazifismus* (Zürich: Rotapfel-Verlag, 1928), 346 (translation by the author).
4. Cf. James Tracy, *Direct Action. Radical Pacifism from the Union Eight to the Chicago Seven* (Chicago: University of Chicago Press, 1996), 12ff.
5. Abraham J. Muste, "Tract for the Times," *Liberation* 1, no. 1 (1956):6.
6. Ibid.

7. Ken Calkins, "An Appeal to the Conscience of Cheyenne," August 1958, Swarthmore College Peace Collection, CNVA Records, Box 11.

8. For statistical reference see Wittner, *The Struggle Against the Bomb*, vol. 2, 291.

9. Ibid., 303ff.

10. See Beyer, *Widerstand gegen den Krieg*, 35.

11. Ibid. (translation by the author).

12. See Tracy, *Direct Action*, 1–11.

13. On Bayard Rustin, cf. Daniel Levine, *Bayard Rustin and the Civil Rights Movement* (New Brunswick, NJ: Rutgers University Press, 2000).

14. On the Campaign for Nuclear Disarmament, see Paul Byrne, *The Campaign for Nuclear Disarmament* (London: Croom Helm, 1988); Richard Taylor, *Against the Bomb: The British Peace Movement, 1958–1965* (Oxford: Clarendon Press, 1988).

15. Cf. Wittner, *The Struggle Against the Bomb*, vol. 2, 210ff.

16. On the following see Maurice Isserman, *If I Had A Hammer. The Death of the Old Left and the Birth of the New Left* (New York: Basic Books, 1987), 125–69.

17. Beyer, *Widerstand gegen den Krieg*, 33ff.

18. For the process of transformation, cf. Nigel Young, *An Infantile Disorder? The Crisis and Decline of the New Left* (Boulder, CO: Westview, 1977), 163–88.

19. On the development of the peace movement in the 1970s and 1980s, cf. Lawrence S. Wittner, *Toward Nuclear Abolition. A History of the World Nuclear Disarmament Movement, 1971 to the Present* (Stanford, CA: Stanford University Press, 2003).

20. C.f. Nancy Zaroulis and Gerald Sullivan, *Who Spoke Up? American Protest Against the War in Vietnam, 1963–1975* (Garden City, NY: Doubleday, 1984); Charles DeBenedetti and Charles Chatfield, *An American Ordeal. The Antiwar Movement of the Vietnam Era* (Syracuse, NY: Syracuse University Press, 1990).

21. This opinion is supported by Van Gosse, "A Movement of Movements: The Definition and Periodization of the New Left," in *A Companion to Post-1945 America*, ed. Jean-Christophe Agnew and Roy Rosenzweig (Malden: Blackwell, 2002), 277–302.

4

The Origins of the British New Left

Madeleine Davis

The political development of the British New Left followed a somewhat unique trajectory in comparison with the broad international New Left of the late 1960s. It was in its early phase, from 1958 to 1962, that the group's style and preoccupations most closely paralleled or, more accurately, anticipated key elements of late '60s radicalism in its antibureaucratic—even anarchic—spirit, its participatory ethos, and its experimentation with direct action. This "movementist" phase was brief, its energies exhausted by 1962, and thereafter the New Left in Britain was a predominantly intellectual tendency without a unified political or activist agenda. Therefore, 1968 was not as defining a moment for the British New Left as it was in the United States, France, or Germany. This chapter focuses on the movementist phase of the British New Left as one of the earliest manifestations of an intellectual and activist New Left in Europe.

Roots

The New Left had its origins amid the dual crisis of 1956. The twin shocks of that year, Khrushchev's denunciation of Stalinism, contradicted by his own suppression by force of Hungary's effort to forge an alternative model, and hubristic British and French imperial aggression over the Suez Canal, created the conditions for rethinking and recomposition of socialist means, ends, and values. The common depiction of the New Left[1] as a response to these events through an attempt to occupy a third space between Stalinism and social democracy, rejecting the moral and political bankruptcy of both, is corroborated by participants. Stuart Hall, for instance, has called 1956 "the break up of the political Ice-Age," which "defined for people of my generation the boundaries and limits of the tolerable in politics."[2] However, the

45

New Left did not spring fully formed from this conjuncture. Indeed, the term "New Left" was not taken up among its key protagonists in Britain until 1958, and what we refer to as the "first" or "early" New Left in fact encompassed a range of very different responses, impulses, and influences, in which the distinction between the Old and New Lefts was never completely clear.

Two major factions gradually came together between 1956 and 1958 to form a self-conscious New Left current. One was composed of dissident Communists, who in July 1956 published the first issue of a discussion journal, *The Reasoner*, to debate the implications of the Khrushchev speech for world and British Communism in the face of the British Communist Party (CPGB) leadership's refusal to sanction open debate. Produced by two Communist historians, Edward Thompson and John Saville, who were then adult educationalists based in the north of England, the journal ran for three issues until November 1956, when, already under threat of suspension for breaking Party rules, its editors resigned their Communist Party membership in protest at the leadership's refusal to condemn Soviet actions in Hungary. It continued in a new form, outside the Party and with a larger editorial board of ex-Communists, as the quarterly *New Reasoner* from summer 1957 until its merger with *Universities and Left Review* on the cusp of the 1960s. The second group was made up of young independent socialists, based out of Oxford University, who established the thrice-yearly *Universities and Left Review* in spring 1957 as a platform for experimental, nonaligned student politics that embraced more eclectic political and cultural influences than the existing Oxford Labour Club magazine, *Clarion*.[3]

Collaboration between these two nonaligned groupings, which shared a commitment to bringing into being a new movement of socialist ideas, began almost immediately, although the influences and preoccupations of each were somewhat distinct.[4] The *New Reasoner* group was primarily concerned to revive and reaffirm, as they saw it, a libertarian and humanist communist tradition as an alternative to Stalinism—a project articulated most eloquently by Edward Thompson as socialist humanism.[5] Rather than looking to other humanist Marxist currents abroad, they drew primarily on British radical traditions, particularly literary and romantic radicalism and English traditions of cultural and moral critique, with William Morris being a key influence. Such influences were not viewed as antithetical but as complementary to the Marxist and Communist traditions. The Reasoners, several of whom had joined the CPGB during the Popular Front period, also took a close and sympathetic interest in British working class and labor movement politics. The younger group around *Universities and Left Review*, in contrast, were politically formed and preoccupied by the changing conditions of postwar Western capitalism and were particularly concerned about analyzing the implications for socialism of changes in culture and consciousness being wrought by consumerism and the affluent society. Convinced that "socialist intellectuals should face the damage which Stalinism and welfare capitalism have done to socialist values," this group was were less concerned with reviving older radical traditions than with generating new concepts and strategies to remake socialism for contemporary conditions.[6] They were also organizationally experimental, sponsoring a wide variety of activities and enterprises including a *Universities and Left Review* club and associated coffeehouse that became the nucleus of a rapidly expanding network of clubs and reading groups. This emergent, activist New Left lent its support to the newly formed Campaign for Nuclear Disarmament (CND), and with both journals' editorial teams sensing the possibility of shaping a new kind of intellectual–political intervention outside existing political channels, the decision was taken to merge in 1959. The resulting publication, *New Left Review*, launched in 1960, was intended to give shape and direction to this unstable, diverse entity—"a mood rather than a movement"—that became the New Left.[7]

Cognitive Orientation

The early British New Left conceived of itself primarily as an arena and platform for a fundamental, open debate about the aims, values, and strategies of socialism. Four key themes are relevant here: its attitude toward Marxism; its position in relation to domestic politics, especially those of the Labour Party; its pioneering analysis of culture; and its attempt to articulate a positive neutralist position internationally.

Marxism

Ideologically, the New Left was diverse and experimental, with a broadly revisionist, creative, and nonsectarian attitude toward Marxism coexisting with a strong orientation to native traditions of ethical socialism.[8] The *Universities and Left Review* grouping acknowledged that Marxism itself required reappraisal: "Marx's work itself," Stuart Hall argued, "is a body of analytic concepts and not a sealed house of theory."[9] The Reasoner group, in contrast, thought of themselves as Marxist humanists and were interested in the wider rediscovery of the early Marx, yet their engagement with Marxism was not particularly sophisticated theoretically, and they paid little sustained attention to currents of humanist Marxism developing elsewhere in Europe, such as the Frankfurt school.[10]

There were important parallels between the British and French experiences. Indeed, the adoption of the term "New Left" was inspired by the French example. The *New Reasoner* was founded at the same time as Henri Lefebvre's revisionist Marxist journal *Arguments*, which was also staffed by disillusioned Communists, whereas *Universities and Left Review*'s opposition to the bureaucracy of both capitalism and communism had some similarities to the *gauchiste* position associated with Cornelius Castoriadis and the journal *Socialisme ou Barbarie*. Later, *New Left Review*, under Perry Anderson's editorship from the mid-1960s on, was to draw self-consciously on the style of Sartre's *Les Temps Modernes*. In both countries, there occurred a turn to humanism, subjectivity, experience, and culture and a rejection of economism, dogmatism, and scientism. Despite some dialogue between French and British New Left strands, there were also crucial distinctions reflecting the different intellectual traditions of the two countries. Whereas French revisionism was explicitly philosophical and theoretically sophisticated, its British counterpart was expressed through moral and political critique, its sources literary and historiographical rather than philosophical. Only after 1963 and the transition to a restyled *New Left Review* was serious attention devoted to the nuances of the theoretical debates.

In the meantime, the early New Left's primary orientation was to a distinctively British brand of socialist humanism best expressed in Thompson's 1957 essay of the same name: "One of the cardinal falsehoods of Stalinism" he asserted, was "the attempt to derive all analysis of political manifestations directly . . . from economic causations, the belittling of the part played by men's ideas and moral attitudes in the making of history."[11] Economism for Thompson was a distortion of Marx and Engels' thought, which involved a "dialectical interaction between social consciousness . . . and social being." This interaction was unfortunately expressed in Marxism as "base-superstructure," a metaphor taken up and used by Stalin as "a mechanical model, operating semi-automatically and independently of conscious human agency."[12]

Fundamental, then, to the reconstitution of a rational and humane Marxist and Communist tradition was the reassertion of morality and agency. However, the sources for this were primarily domestic and not necessarily Marxist. "The insights of William Morris, his discoveries about man's potential moral nature," Thompson said, "were not icing on the Marxist gingerbread but were complementary to the discoveries of Marx."[13] Thus, British socialist humanism essentially expressed a moral and political rejection of Stalinism that was not fully worked through in theoretical terms.

Challenging "Labour Revisionism"

On the domestic political scene, the early New Left was closely involved in debates over the direction of Labour Party policy and strategy. They challenged the Labour revisionism encapsulated most famously in Tony

Crosland's *The Future of Socialism* (1956), which asserted that "the intellectual framework within which most pre-war socialist discussion was conducted has been rendered obsolete."[14] The widespread assumption that underlay Crosland's thesis was that postwar capitalism had solved the problem of production and that the mixed economy could ensure material well-being for all. The Labour revisionists, therefore, advocated a shift in Labour and socialist priorities: nationalization of the economy was to be deemphasized and attention shifted to issues of welfare, personal freedom, culture, and leisure, reflecting a conviction that rising social mobility and working-class affluence would undermine the traditional class basis of British party politics. The New Left offered a creative and critical response to this prospectus, positioning itself to the left of Labour and insisting on the indispensability of common ownership to socialism, yet recognizing the limitations of the bureaucratic public corporation model hitherto dominant. It attempted to advance novel arguments for an alternative model of common ownership that encompassed genuine democratic workers' control, adhering to a vision of socialism as fundamentally a project to extend human control and capacities on the basis of democratic and egalitarian values.[15]

"Culturalism"

Much early New Left writing addressed itself to the immediate political situation, especially the 1959 general election, and to an effort to push the Labour Party to the left on issues such as economic policy and unilateral nuclear disarmament. However, its interventions were underpinned by a sophisticated

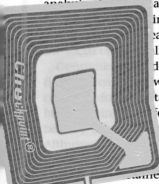

analy_____ and social change. Key contributions by Stuart Hall and in particular laid the basis for an important body of theo-ated culture as constitutive and not simply reflective of llenging traditional Marxist assumptions.[16] d the rise of mass communications were early on identi-with the potential to reshape consciousness in ways that talist dominance. As this "culturalist" project developed, espan of the early New Left as a movement, it gradually theoretical sources including Gramsci, Marcuse, and alism. However, British cultural studies retained some istinguished it somewhat from developments elsewhere, _____ed interest in the potential of class-based or non-class-based agencies to subvert and challenge capitalist dominance.

"Positive Neutralism"

Although the early New Left was a formation with deep roots in British traditions and addressed itself primarily to domestic debates, its agenda was shaped by a broader internationalist orientation. In common with other New Left currents, a major animating factor was opposition to Cold War bipolarity, against which it articulated a position it described as positive neutralism, or active neutrality. This position viewed unilateral nuclear disarmament as a first step in the creation of an alternative, independent international politics, in which British withdrawal from the North Atlantic Treaty Organization would open the way for alliances with other actively neutral countries, especially in the Third World. Such alliances could advance moves toward political self-determination in decolonizing nations and help break the grip of superpower politics, improving the prospects for socialism everywhere.[17] This was the strategic position that underlay the early New Left's active support for the CND, which it sought to push in the direction of socialism, and of a sharper political analysis. Reflecting the persistence of the ex-Communist influence, the New Left was also, especially early in its lifespan, interested in the prospects for de-Stalinization in the Eastern bloc. This orientation was complemented by an emerging interest in decolonization, postcolonialism, and Third World revolutions. The 1959 Cuban revolution was described in an early *New Left Review* editorial as "the most important event in the history of the international socialist movement."[18] Before 1963, however, the politics of the Third World were mainly viewed in the context of socialist internationalism, and specifically positive neutralism.

Organizational Structure

The novel organizational politics of the early New Left were one of its most distinctive features. Its self-conception as a movement of ideas saw its publishing enterprises, first *Universities and Left Review* and then *New Left Review*, as the hub of a broader grassroots New Left movement comprising semiautonomous local clubs, reading groups, or other centers of cultural and political activity. At its height in 1960–1961, the New Left clubs network extended to some fifty organizations with a paid-up membership of around three thousand individuals.[19] The success of the clubs, together with the rapid growth of CND, which attracted thousands to its regular demonstrations and in 1960 secured a majority in favor of unilateral disarmament at the Labour Party Conference, seemed for a time to hold out the chance of building a real grassroots New Left movement that would unite protest politics, youth and student revolt, and elements of the traditional labor movement behind an expanded socialism conceived of as the full liberation of the human individual within a community. The New Left also tried to adopt a novel organizational position in relation to the Labour Party, one it described as "parallelism" or, less grandly, "one foot in, one foot out"—meaning that it remained outside party structures (though a number of New Left activists were simultaneously members of the Labour Party) yet closely attuned to its debates and more than prepared to collaborate with sympathetic figures on the Labour Left.[20]

Yet, as would happen with student movements of the late 1960s, the strengths of the early New Left as a movement—its spontaneous and participatory nature, its refusal to bureaucratize and adopt traditional positions on questions of organization and leadership—reduced its own lifespan. The energies it invested into CND failed to transform that organization from a basically single-issue, moral, and middle-class campaign into a broader based leftist movement. The New Left's strategy of parallelism in relation to Labour was equally unsustainable and became a source of confusion, frustration, and disagreement. In practice, this strategy pushed the New Left into a role as more or less a pressure group or think-tank to the left of Labour while simultaneously discouraging it from seizing opportunities to form or support autonomous New Leftist electoral initiatives. In the absence of strategic direction from the center, the clubs network suffered from a lack of overall purpose and fell into decline. At the heart of these difficulties was an unresolved tension between the political and intellectual ambitions of the New Left: Was it first and foremost a journal? Or a grassroots movement? The pressure to be both exhausted *New Left Review*'s first editor, Stuart Hall, and exacerbated tensions on a large editorial board, among whom there was in any case no real agreement on some fundamental issues. By the end of 1961, this early model of the New Left was in crisis: Hall resigned as editor, the clubs fell away, and the editorial board began to break up.

Consequences and Narratives

The early British New Left was a diverse and ambiguous entity. Even among its participants there was no consensus on how to interpret it. Thus, although Stuart Hall in 1987 could largely concur with a common view that sees the movement as having played a role in the reorientation of left conceptions of agency, away from class-based analyses and toward a recognition of complex and differentiated social identities, Raphael Samuel could argue that it retained much of the content of preexisting socialist thought, aiming at a revival rather than a fundamental rethinking of a socialism whose basic assumptions were hardly questioned. For him, "the New Left marked an end rather than a beginning. It came at possibly the last moment when a new politics could be thought of in terms of a resumption of Labour's forward march."[21] In his comparative study, Nigel Young interprets it rather teleologically as an early false start in the progress of 1960s radicalization, whereas others have focused primarily on its pioneering of cultural studies.[22] Beyond the left, the significance of the New Left has tended to be conflated with the wider cultural legacy of the 1960s, and though the work of individuals in their specialist areas (Thompson as a social historian, Williams and Hall as cultural critics, etc.) is generally respected by the liberal media and in academe, the broader political project of the New Left has not been treated as being of much interest. In the best account to date of the early New Left, Mike Kenny locates it at a turning point in postwar politics and culture as some Old Left assumptions were questioned or undermined and new issues emerged. Kenny argues that the early New Left is most to be valued for the "directions in which its work pointed."[23]

In a similar vein to Kenny, I see the early New Left's significance as arising from its early articulation of difficult issues for the left—especially concerning agency, culture, the status of Marxism, and political organization—outside traditional organizational structures and without deference to ideological orthodoxies. Its manifestation as a movement of ideas was novel and significant but was ultimately unsustainable. After its disintegration, many of the questions it raised and the tensions that broke it up were addressed by its successors, but in formats that were less organizationally experimental. Many commentators have seen the takeover of *New Left Review* by a more theoretically inclined cohort committed to a wholesale makeover of British intellectual culture via the importation of continental Marxist ideas as a radical shift in priorities, with some even denying that this "second New Left" was really New Left at all. However, although Anderson and his associates were sharply critical of the early New Left's movementist ambitions, and took their influences from elsewhere, there remained important overlaps, continuities, and collaborations between the different New Left cohorts. Nor was *New Left Review* the sole vehicle for a New Left politics through the 1960s and 1970s. Other mediums with a direct lineage back to the 1958–1962 period included the *Socialist Register*, an annual book-length publication set up by Ralph Miliband and John Saville; the Birmingham Centre for Contemporary Cultural Studies, established in 1964 by Richard Hoggart and Stuart Hall; and the History Workshop, founded by Raphael Samuel at Ruskin College, Oxford, in 1966.[24] Individuals not necessarily linked to all or any of these, including Raymond Williams and Edward Thompson, also contributed to the creation of an impressive and important corpus of New Left work in history and historiography, cultural studies, Marxist theory, and analysis of the state. There were also some more directly political interventions with a New Left lineage: In 1967, the May Day Manifesto initiative brought senior figures from the early New Left together to debate the possibility of forming an extra-parliamentary opposition movement. This movement was overtaken by the student radicalization of 1968, in which some New Left intellectuals also played a role. Collaboration continued intermittently between New Left figures and other left currents, including the Labour Left (especially in the early 1980s around Tony Benn's program for the Labour Left) and the Communist Party as it became influenced by Gramscism in the mid- to late 1970s. Economists associated with the early New Left, including Michael Barratt-Brown and John Hughes, helped found the Institute for Workers' Control, which developed early New Left proposals around income policy and worker self-management from 1968 to the mid-1970s. Thus, although there existed in Britain no one unified New Left current after 1963, the term "New Left" may still be used to denote a range of projects operating in a space that the early New Left had opened up—a space for a politically independent, (generally) nonsectarian, critical interrogation and reworking of socialist and Marxist ideas.

Influence on 1968 Movements

It is obvious that in Britain the New Left and the student radicalization of 1968 were in many ways quite distinct phenomena. Unlike several other countries in which the term "New Left" is regarded as synonymous with the campus revolts or, even more broadly, with the wider phenomenon of 1960s radicalism and the counterculture, the term in Britain has a more restricted currency. However, very broad usages can tend to deemphasize the real political and ideological issues at stake, and it may be more useful to reserve the term "New Left" for particular segments within or alongside the 1968 movements that sought to give them theoretical coherence and political direction.[25] Even with this narrower definition, the New Left in Britain is not directly comparable to counterparts elsewhere. In its movementist phase from around 1958 to 1962, it may be seen as having played an analogous role in relation to CND that, for example, the SDS did in relation to the American student movement. However, as we have seen, thereafter it became a fragmented, primarily intellectual force, and there existed no straightforward correspondence between its perspectives and those of a domestic student movement that was in any case relatively weak and separate from other movements of the British left. The student activists who participated in strikes and sit-ins at the London School of Economics; Essex, Hull, Leicester, Warwick, and Birmingham Universities; and Hornsey Art College in general had no prior connection with the New Left and were inspired mainly by causes and movements abroad. In fact, some New Left figures, including Thompson, saw student revolt through rather Old Left eyes as irrational, essentially middle-class radicalism with barely any roots in

British radical traditions. In contrast, a number of New Left intellectuals did play prominent roles in student activism. Robin Blackburn was dismissed from the London School of Economics for his support of the student occupation, and Saville, Miliband, Hall, and Nairn were all active supporters of student actions in their workplaces. Tariq Ali was a prime mover of the Vietnam Solidarity Campaign—the single most important British 1968 organization. Members of the *New Left Review* editorial board were also involved in a short-lived effort to provide political direction to the student movement via the Revolutionary Socialist Student Federation, which was committed to "the revolutionary overthrow of capital and imperialism and its replacement by workers' power."[26] New Left influence competed, however, with that of other far left groups as well as with countercultural and anarchist tendencies, and it failed to establish any lasting presence in student politics. However, the 1968 revolts, especially the Paris May event, did encourage a general radicalization of New Left perspectives, reinvigorating revolutionary aspirations. British New Leftists also cultivated links with counterparts elsewhere, visiting Paris, Vietnam, and other centers of radical activity.

If the British New Left stood somewhat in the role of an enthusiastic spectator in relation to broader 1968 radicalism, it can nevertheless take some credit for having pioneered or experimented with the tactics and style that would help define later currents. Its emphasis on grassroots activism, direct action, and spontaneity; its anti-bureaucratic spirit; and its loose, experimental organizational structures prefigured some key characteristics of the later movements. Moreover, it allied these to a sophisticated and novel analysis of contemporary capitalism and culture while retaining links to older radical traditions of communism and ethical socialism.

Bibliography

The most comprehensive study to date of the early British New Left is Kenny (1995). Lin Chun (1993) covers both early and later New Left currents. Dworkin (1997) focuses on the analysis of culture. Archer (1989) is a useful collection of assessments and recollections by protagonists. Studies of the work of individuals include Newman (2002), Higgins (1999), and Elliott (1998). There is a notable lack of studies comparing the British New Left with counterparts elsewhere: Young (1977) does so to some degree but in my view misunderstands the nature of the British New Left. For the New Left's attitude toward Marxism, see Forgacs (1989) and Davis (2006).

Archer, Robin, et al., eds. *Out of Apathy: Voices of the New Left Thirty Years On*. London: Verso, 1989.

Chun, Lin. *The British New Left*. Edinburgh: Edinburgh University Press, 1993.

Davis, Madeleine. "The Marxism of the British New Left," *Journal of Political Ideologies* 11, No. 3 (October 2006): 335–58.

Dworkin, Dennis. *Cultural Marxism in Postwar Britain: History, the New Left and the Origins of Cultural Studies*. Durham, NC: Duke University Press, 1997.

Elliott, Gregory. *Perry Anderson: The Merciless Laboratory of History*. Minneapolis, MN: University of Minneapolis Press, 1998.

Forgacs, David. "Gramsci and Marxism in Britain," *New Left Review* 176 (July/August 1989):70–88.

Higgins, John. *Raymond Williams: Literature, Marxism and Cultural Materialism*. London: Routledge, 1999.

Kenny, Michael. *The First New Left: British Intellectuals After Stalin*. London: Lawrence and Wishart, 1995.

Newman, Michael. *Ralph Miliband and the Politics of the New Left*. London: Merlin, 2002.

Young, Nigel. *An Infantile Disorder? The Crisis and Decline of the New Left*. London: Routledge and Kegan Paul, 1977.

Notes

1. The two most widely cited accounts are Lin Chun, *The British New Left* (Edinburgh: Edinburgh University Press, 1993), and Michael Kenny, *The First New Left: British Intellectuals after Stalin*, (London: Lawrence and Wishart, 1995).
2. Stuart Hall, "The First New Left: Life and Times," in *Out of Apathy: Voices of the New Left Thirty Years On*, ed. Robin Archer, et al. (London: Verso, 1989), 13.
3. The four editors were Stuart Hall, Gabriel Pearson, Raphael Samuel, and Charles Taylor. The first three were PhD students, and Taylor was a philosophy fellow, at Oxford University.
4. See Edward P. Thompson, "Socialism and the Intellectuals," *Universities and Left Review* 1 (Spring 1957): 34.
5. Edward P. Thompson, "Socialist Humanism," *New Reasoner* 1 (Summer 1957): 105–43.
6. Editorial, *Universities and Left Review* 1 (Spring 1957): 2.
7. "Letter to readers," *New Reasoner* 6 (Autumn 1958): 137.
8. For a fuller discussion of the ambiguity of New Left Marxism, see Madeleine Davis, "The Marxism of the British New Left," *Journal of Political Ideologies* 11, No. 3 (2006): 335–58.
9. Stuart Hall, "A sense of classlessness," *Universities and Left Review* 5 (1958): 32, note 3.
10. See Douglas Kellner "The Frankfurt school and British Cultural Studies: The Missed Articulation," available at http://www.uta.edu/huma/illuminations/kell16.htm
11. Edward P. Thompson, "Socialist Humanism," *New Reasoner* 1 (1957): 108.
12. Ibid, 113.

13. Ibid, 125.
14. C. A. R. Crosland, *The Future of Socialism* (Jonathan Cape, 1956), 41.
15. See Ralph Miliband, "The Transition to the Transition," *New Reasoner* 6 (1958); Charles Taylor, "What's Wrong With Capitalism?" *New Left Review* 2 (1960): 5–11; and the *Universities and Left Review* pamphlet *The Insiders*, 1958, for discussion of these themes.
16. For analysis of the British New Left contribution to cultural studies, see Dennis Dworkin, *Cultural Marxism in Postwar Britain: History, the New Left and the Origins of Cultural Studies* (Durham, NC: Duke University Press, 1997).
17. See Edward P. Thompson, "NATO, Neutralism and Survival," *Universities and Left Review* 4 (1958).
18. Editorial, "Siege of Cuba," *New Left Review* 7 (1961): 2–3.
19. Dworkin, *Cultural Marxism*, 69.
20. See John Saville, "Apathy into Politics," *New Left Review* 4 (1960): 8–9.
21. Stuart Hall, "The First New Left: Life and Times," in *Out of Apathy*, ed. Robin Archer (London: Verso, 1989), 38; Raphael Samuel, "Born Again Socialism," in *Out of Apathy*, ed. Robin Archer, 57.
22. Nigel Young, *An Infantile Disorder? The Crisis and Decline of the New Left* (London: Routledge and Kegan Paul, 1977); Dworkin, *Cultural Marxism*, passim.
23. Kenny, *First New Left*, 48.
24. These are the four "institutional tendencies" identified by Lin Chun, *British New Left*, 64.
25. See Richard Flacks, "The New Left and American Politics After Ten Years," *Journal of Social Issues* 28 (1976): 23–24.
26. RSSF Manifesto, *New Left Review* 53 (1969): 21–22.

5

Music and Protest in 1960s Europe

Detlef Siegfried

Roots of the Connection between Music and Political Protest

The social relevance of music does not emerge from melody or sound. Rather, as a system of signs, music exhibits individually specific characteristics of form and content that are loaded with assigned meanings by fans and critics, governmental bodies, and the media; these assigned meanings include political ones that vary according to point of view and circumstance. The assigned meanings can yield information on the shifting values and standards of particular social groups. In the 1950s, jazz music frequently carried idealistic connotations of democracy, civil society, and anti-racism among its followers, whereas rock 'n roll fans associated their music with a vague concept of rebellion. Beginning in the early 1960s, cultural critics of various political stripes attributed a subversive potential to "beat" music. East of the Iron Curtain, beat music was seen as the sound of the Western capitalist lifestyle; in the West, it was sometimes seen as a vehicle for communist egalitarianism. However, those who saw no threat in jazz and beat music would eventually prevail. Meanwhile, political subcultures tried to extensively harvest the rebellious potential of rock music.

The end of the 1960s saw the emergence of political rock bands that explicitly sought to change society, and fast and aggressive rock music emerged as both the expression of an outspoken lifestyle and an ideal medium for the transmission of revolutionary messages. Even in the early days, it was especially the proponents and artists of the counterculture who recognized the revolutionary potential of beat music. It could be consumed, but it could also contribute to the shaping of consciousness. In the politicization of beat music, a significant role was played by folk and *chanson* music, which, inspired by influences from the labor movement and left-wing intellectual circles, often carried political messages across the United States and through much of Europe. The electrification of folk music, as seen in Bob Dylan's 1965 transition from the acoustic to the electric guitar, also brought a political element to electrically amplified music. However, it was kept vague by the anarchosurrealist elements that accompanied this shift in *Lebenswelt* (the "life-world" of direct experience). Attempts to recodify protest songs toward the right, as seen in the "Sing Out" movement, which was related to the right-wing Christian organization Moral Re-Armament and promoted by both the American and some European governments, remained unsuccessful.

The transnational youth culture that spread all across Europe in the late 1950s was based above all on music; electrically amplified popular music was perceived as being left wing because it presented a particularly democratic form of media expression and represented cosmopolitanism, a do-it-yourself activity, and shared participation. Musical tastes were traditionally divided according to social class, but beat music and rock music were increasingly produced and consumed across class boundaries. It was only through the achievement of equal rights that a fertile ground for individualization could be created.

Rock bands, vinyl records, live music clubs, magazines, and radio stations: the whole material ensemble of pop culture could only emerge because the golden years of economic prosperity had broken out in the mid-twentieth century. This worldwide swell in prosperity peaked in the long 1960s, accompanied by a cultural revolution. In Europe, this era began in the 1950s and ended with the economic crisis of the mid-1970s. Cultural and political upheavals came to a worldwide peak in 1968, not only because of global shifts in power but also because internal social changes were building up an enormous potential for conflict and forcing a decisive change of course. Beat, pop, and rock music emerged directly from these altered living conditions.

An independent youth culture could only emerge during the 1950s, when young people had their own spending money. In Western Europe, these youth were targeted by a consumer goods industry specially geared toward this market demographic. They could spread out and differentiate themselves because increased leisure time and extended years of primary through postsecondary education allowed for the development of a distinct generation between childhood and adulthood.

The surge in material prosperity resulted in a shift in the fundamental attitudes and values of society, starting in Western European countries in the early 1960s. Traditional values such as order and obedience were replaced by ideals such as self-actualization and social engagement; it was no longer about saving for future happiness in later years but, rather, about enjoying life here and now—as was forcefully promoted in advertisements. These new ideals were particularly present in pop music because young people, particularly the better educated, made up the population group that was most enthusiastic about transforming society's values. The manifestations, courses of development, and consequences of this transformation varied greatly.

A significant difference between the various countries of Europe could be traced to the fact that traditional values were longer able to retain their binding character in the still strongly agrarian countries of Southern Europe and the industrial zones of Eastern Europe. Meanwhile, Northern and Western Europe saw the growth of a service economy that provided a fertile ground for pop culture, as particularly evidenced by the media, the record industry, and the cultural events sector. Eastern Europe had no privately owned enterprises that could popularize new ideas by using market forces, thus overcoming the resistance of established tradition. Young people who were interested in developing an independent youth culture were therefore missing an important ally.

Cognitive Orientation and Aims

Music is fundamentally open to accepting all types of cognitive injections, which is precisely why it is especially appropriate for expressing the particular spirit of an era. Its special characteristic consists not of its verbal content, or even of its political goals, but of its sensitive and emotional quality. It is not the text, but rather the sound, that forms the primary basis of music's power to connect and mobilize. Beat music was therefore described by contemporaries as "unspoken opposition"—representing the least articulate form of social criticism on the broader spectrum of possible protests but, on the level of symbolism and habitus (understood as a system of internalized basic approaches), simultaneously providing the accompaniment to the approaching political upheavals.[1] From the mid-1960s onward, electrically amplified music further progressed to become a medium of explicit political messages. Sources for this politicization could be found in folk music, *chanson*, and performance art and among the beatniks and the hippies. To some extent, these types of music continued to exist independently and also to connect with commercial pop music, producing a multifaceted cultural expression of the political protest movements.[2] At first, musically articulated protest linked itself particularly to pacifist traditions, aligning itself against rearmament and military deployments (especially against the U.S. war in Vietnam), but also in general against the oppression of the individual in a technocratic society. As the protest movements became further radicalized, the rhythms and lyrics became increasingly aggressive—turning against the capitalist system as a whole and frequently using militant expressions.

In the years around 1968, a significant element of rock music was the aura of "authenticity," which was even less verbally articulated and more based on habitus. The more music displayed artistic originality, the more authentic it seemed. There emerged a stark contrast between the singer created by the culture industry, who interpreted the compositions of others in a "beautiful" voice, and the artists or groups who were far distant from the consumer industry and who demonstrated individualism and an independent streak. The role models of "authentic" rock music were frequently African-American blues musicians, who as representatives of a marginalized and persecuted ethnic group seemed to illuminate everyday problems more deeply and more directly—and therefore more convincingly—than the interchangeable mannequins of the culture industry.[3] This transcultural interest in apparently less-alienated role models and systems of perception was a reflection of the increasing criticism of the Western way of life. Rock music's aura of authenticity was part of a critical self-reflection among European societies, which were transitioning toward a postindustrial modernity.[4]

Organizational Structures

The connection between popular music and protest movements was especially motivated by the grassroots organizations. They were founded on amateur movements represented by jazz, skiffle, beat, and rock bands, in which youth of all social classes had been articulating themselves artistically since the late 1950s. At the same time, of all the forms of expression available to protest movements, popular music was the one most dependent on the culture industry's infrastructure for production and distribution. The politically oriented part of the music scene frequently tried to set up cooperatives and independent business structures to provide an alternative to the established record companies and broadcasting corporations. At the same time, clubs, radio stations, magazines, record companies, and concert agencies were taking up musical trends from below, even if they were colored by political agendas. It is particularly apparent in the success of the "underground," seen as the cultural counterpart of the political protest movements, that politically coded music could be successfully marketed by the established players of the culture industry, too.

Places such as the Cavern Club (Liverpool) and the Star-Club (Hamburg), two of the original venues of beat music, offered an ambience of deviance from social conventions that could also be seen as protest. The 1960s saw the emergence of other venues such as the Club Voltaire (Frankfurt), which offered jazz and beat music, art exhibitions, film screenings, readings and political events, thereby merging oppositional culture and politics into a new kind of events concept. The rise of discotheques after 1967 saw the establishment of dance clubs like Grünspan (Hamburg), Sound (Berlin), and Klub 27 (Copenhagen), where psychedelic music, recreational drugs, and a vaguely political opposition formed a diffuse alliance.

Televised music programs played a pivotal role in global youth culture; though initially apolitical, such programs did offer a space for the articulation of an independent youth culture. The United Kingdom had an early start with programs like *Six-Five Special* (1957), *Oh Boy!* (1958), and *Ready, Steady, Go!* (1963). France soon followed with *Salut Les Copains* (1959). It was not until 1965 that Germany brought *Beat-Club* to the small screen, but this show soon became the best of the bunch on the European continent, reaching an average of seventy-five million viewers in 1968. Later, talk segments were also mixed in, sometimes with political content.[5] After 1968, a whole series of programs emerged that attempted to connect pop with politics, but most survived only until the early 1970s. Pop music became far more widespread in radio than in television, especially in the programs of American and British soldier stations such as AFN and BFBS, and taking over completely at pirate stations. Their steep rise began in 1960 with Radio Veronica in the Netherlands and with Radio Nord off the coast of Sweden. Radio Caroline and Radio London were launched in 1964, both off the British coast with programming entirely based on pop music and financed by advertising. Radio Caroline broadcast daily from six o'clock in the morning until six o'clock in the evening and could be heard in southern England, southern Scandinavia, and on the European continent all the way to northwest Germany. On January 22, 1967, as ten pirate stations were broadcasting mostly pop music across the continent, the Council of Europe brought an end to the movement. Certainly the most popular radio station among youth remained Radio Luxembourg, which broadcast programs in various languages. Although these radio stations mostly stayed away from explicit politics, their youth-specific, frequently unconventional, and at times subversive aura helped ensure that contemporary ideals ranging from individualism to rebellion would reach a large number of European youth.

In addition to radio stations and televised youth programs, there were also youth magazines; these became increasingly important over the course of the 1960s as mediators of consumer culture and political standards. In West Germany, major mass-market magazines like *Twen* (1959–1971) and *Konkret* (since 1955) connected popular culture with politics alongside newly established specialist magazines like *Song* (1966–1970) and *Sounds* (1966–1983), which served the then-emerging underground market. The youth market in France was served by the magazine *Salut les Copains*, which was founded in 1962. It was followed as early as 1963 by the communist-leaning magazine *Nous les Garçons et les Filles*, which combined pop culture with politics, similar to publications in Italy (*Nuova Generazione*) and West Germany (*Elan*). The Catholic Church in France and West Germany also tried to keep up with the latest developments in youth culture by relaunching their own magazines.

Pure music magazines like *Melody Maker*, and later others like *Pop* and *Popfoto*, also served the ever-expanding market of pop music consumers. In addition, a completely separate market emerged with the numerous underground magazines, which shot up like mushrooms in the second half of the 1960s, including titles like *International Times* and *Oz* (both from the United Kingdom), *Hotcha* (Switzerland), *Peng* (West Germany), and *Superlove* (Denmark), some of which commanded respectable circulation figures.

Although political *chansons* and protest songs were achieving some success on established record labels, American record companies such as CBS and Liberty and the Swedish company Metronome were establishing themselves on the European market with English-language popular music that occasionally included political content. In particular, CBS was developing the "underground" into a musical trademark that was marketed in Europe as the sound of the "counterculture."[6] Developing in parallel were those sometimes locally based record labels that were either independently self-managed or that oscillated between the culture industry and the left-wing scene. Over the course of the 1960s, there developed within the youth-oriented sector of the culture industry a new type of manager, who regarded artists not simply as interchangeable mannequins but, rather, as autonomous producers. The fact that these new music managers took seriously those professional and ethical criteria that were considered most important to the audience being served can be seen in the early example of the Frankfurt concert agency Lippmann + Rau. Lippmann + Rau organized the American Folk Blues Festival from 1962 to 1969, facilitating direct encounters between African-American blues musicians and the social protagonists of many European countries. They did not appeal just to the current musical tastes of young white Europeans but also to their rising demand for identification with the oppressed and marginalized of the whole world, their criticism of the alienation within Western consumer societies, and their protest against racism and colonialism.

Key Events

Festivals were events of pan-European importance and were seen as manifestations of counterculture. They were supposed to demonstrate on a short-term and exemplary basis the ideal of coming together as an alternative to compartmentalized and alienated modernity—at least according to the proclamations of the organizers and the expectations of many fans. Held together by the bonding agent of music, the festivals frequently reached a much larger crowd of young people than did political events like mass protest demonstrations or the international Vietnam Congress in West Berlin in February 1968.

A variation on the American hippie movement developed under various labels in Europe, too, as seen for the first time in June 1965 with the Underground Poetry Festival at London's Royal Albert Hall, which was attended by 7,000 young people. From 1964 to 1969, there existed at Burg Waldeck in southern Germany a European nucleus for the folk and protest song movement. This festival, formulated on the American model as a German Newport, became a site of transnational exchange between diverse musical styles combined with a socially critical viewpoint. The spectrum ranged from political protest songs to anarcho-surrealist *chanson* to psychedelic rock music. Even as folk and protest songs were achieving commercial success and reaching the upper regions of the hit parades in 1966, discussions were held at Burg Waldeck about how to maintain the sociopolitical relevance of music despite its consumer industrial potential. Some younger activists saw a possibility in the development of a "young culture" (Rolf–Ulrich Kaiser), which could be seen in many artistic fields, but which found its most pointed expression in June 1967 at a festival in Monterey, California. Monterey Pop, where artists like Jimi Hendrix, The Who, Janis Joplin, and Jefferson Airplane first became known to a wider audience, presented a new form of pop music that articulated a generational consciousness, social criticism, and the desire for an alternative lifestyle.[7] From the impulses of Burg Waldeck and the American underground scene emerged the *Internationale Essener Songtage* in September 1968. This festival, at that point the largest European pop festival, pulled in 40,000 visitors, mostly from West Germany, but also from across Europe, and presented around 200 artists of the most diverse musical genres, including Alexis Korner, Franz Josef Degenhardt, Tangerine Dream, and the American bands Mothers of Invention and The Fugs.

After the big musical events of 1969, with the Woodstock Festival and the Rolling Stones concert in Altamont symbolizing the light and dark sides of pop music, respectively, 1970 became the year of regional festivals in Europe, which was an indication that rock music, although still frequently marketed under the label of counterculture, was now diffusing across the breadth of society. In West Germany that year, some 500,000 young people attended the festivals, which only partially fulfilled their inflated hopes for a community of solidarity among all the "beautiful people."

Consequences and Narratives

It was precisely because pop and rock music were not explicitly political that they could synchronize a great number of youth with political protest movements; these movements contemporaneously and similarly encompassed abstract ideals such as freedom, rebellion, social responsibility, and international reconciliation. In later years, too, the aura of the rebellious and revolutionary would attach itself to rock music, regardless of its contents. Bands like The Fugs, coming from the beat scene in New York; Floh de Cologne, originally a cabaret troupe in Cologne; and Savage Rose, founded as a hippie band in Copenhagen, used rock music as a medium for political messages. The extreme radicalization of certain elements among left-wing protest movements was mirrored by bands like MC 5 (Detroit), Edgar Broughton Band (Warwick), and Ton Steine Scherben (West Berlin), which used militant lyrics to underline the "more assaulting"[8] character of rock music.

Alongside musicians like Frank Zappa and Joe McDonald, who saw themselves as specifically political artists, there were also numerous other protagonists in the overall groundswell of rock music and left-wing protest movements who were perceived as being political without any explicit effort on their part, such as Jimi Hendrix and the Rolling Stones. "Progressive" rock music, along with other signifiers and style elements such as long hair, unconventional clothing, drugs, and freewheeling sexuality, was regarded as a cultural expression of the counterculture, which was to be defended against the encroachments of the mainstream, and particularly against commercial interests. Some musicians resisted being conscripted to this cause. Thus, Mick Jagger declared on behalf of the Rolling Stones that the band was rebelling "against nothing at all" and that he and his colleagues did not in the least aspire to be the "political leadership" that the youth looked for from them.[9] When Led Zeppelin singer Robert Plant spoke about West German fans, who more than others expected a sense of direction, Plant said, "the German audience is okay in and of itself, but it's far too political."[10] Political demands and forms of action, such as protests against overpriced tickets and collective storming of pop concerts, were to be found to differing degrees in various European countries, but they were more common in West Germany than in the United Kingdom or Scandinavia, where the connection between rock music and political protest was looser and the respective scenes remained more separate.

Transnational movements such as the Rock Against Racism campaign founded in the United Kingdom in 1976 exploited music's potential for political mobilization. However, with the rise of a right-wing youth scene, rock music also became used as a medium for racist and nationalist messages, so that the idea of an everlasting association between rock music and left-wing protest yielded to the realization that the "kids" could also be "not alright."[11] Beyond that, the commercial exploitation of rock music was continuously and repeatedly posing the question of how it could retain its nonconformist character. As a reaction against the perceived domestication of originally rebellious styles, an innovative potential pushed itself further and further, putting out new material and feeding the culture industry with these impulses too.

Because of stronger governmental controls, anti-Western resentment, and the lack of an independent culture industry in the countries of Eastern Europe, the possibilities for young people to articulate musical and cultural protests were more strictly limited than in the western half of the continent. The shift from an industrial to a postindustrial society, which significantly influenced the political and cultural transformation of Western Europe, occurred in Eastern Europe only after a substantial delay. Official reactions to beat and rock music varied greatly in Eastern European countries. In East Germany, for example, it oscillated in the 1960s and 1970s between phases of tolerance and repression. However, Eastern Europe also saw a process of generational separation, which on a rudimentary level allowed the formation of something like a "generation of '68." However, 1968 did not have the effect of a banner that united a generation, such as that which emerged in Western Europe amid the whirlwind of phenomena that played out in public discourse: political events, a social movement, and subcultural points of projection and convergence such as Kommune I in West Berlin, the Essener Songtage, the Kabouter movement in the Netherlands, and Freetown Christiania in Copenhagen. This discrepancy was partly attributable to cultural authoritarianism and political repression, which increased again in Eastern Europe after the suppression of the "Prague Spring." This suppression in Prague occurred just at the moment that youth cultures were spreading there, too, although they were much more restricted to their private niches than were their Western counterparts. Nonetheless, a liberating effect is frequently attributed in hindsight to transnational pop music because it also connected the youth of Eastern Europe to the West, thus facilitating the internal erosion of state socialist systems.

Influence on the 1968 Protest Movements

In the 1960s, popular culture and social movements merged together to a certain degree. Music largely defined the emotional character of protest movements while also lowering the entrance threshold for those youth who did not start out politically interested. Because certain aspects of rock music, such as spontaneity, physicality, activism, violating the rules, and questioning authority, corresponded with the formal aspects and content of the protest movements, pop and politics became closely intertwined in the everyday lives of many participants. In the early 1960s, in demonstrations from the Campaign for Nuclear Disarmament that were originally initiated by older left-wing intellectuals, the guitar and banjo began to play an increasingly important role as more and more youth with a taste for folk and underground music started taking part. In 1966, the German *Ostermarsch* (an annual protest march during Easter) was enhanced by the participation of American folk star Joan Baez. Because the leaders of the student movements often regarded electrified popular music with skepticism, it tended to be the younger members and activists who opened the door for new sounds to enter the cultural arena of the protest movements. Emotionally, they stood especially close to beat music as an expression of the very youngest generations and imbued it with political meaning. The Liverpool subculture activist Mike Evans saw "a relationship to what the Provos are doing Amsterdam, Frankfurt and elsewhere" in the political happenings at the Cavern Club, the British nucleus of beat music.[12] Music contributed substantially to the participants imagining themselves as part of a transnational revolution. In 1967, the Frankfurt Provos regarded beat music not only as a "cultural revolution for show business," particularly benefitting the young, but also hoped that the Beatles, Bob Dylan, and other stars would found an "international beat party" to combat racism and colonialism.

In contrast to established left-wing cultural critics who interpreted music brokered by the culture industry as the medium of alienation, certain younger intellectuals saw modern mass culture as the medium of liberation. They created a theoretical hero out of Walter Benjamin, who had proclaimed the transformation of society through the politicization of art. In his book *Swinging Benjamin* (1973), Helmut Salzinger stated that mass media such as photography, television, and electrically amplified music took away the aura of uniqueness from art, making it accessible to everybody and thus expressing its revolutionary potential.[13]

Around 1968, protest movements could hardly escape from the new musical tastes of the young. This is largely because they often positioned themselves explicitly as movements of the young. At the beginning of 1968, the German Students for a Democratic Society defined itself as part of a "revolutionary youth movement." At the same time, the underground Danish paper *Superlove* called for "a new class struggle between the older and the younger generations" and set the objective of transforming "unarticulated youth culture into an articulated youth uprising."[14] The previous year in the United States, Abbie Hoffman and Jerry Rubin had already founded a Youth International Party, which sought to connect the hippie counterculture with the New Left and placed all its faith in the revolutionary role of the younger generation. The generational focus of the rebellions around 1968 found its symbolic anchor points in the musical tastes of young people; however, it focused only on very particular tastes, which should ideally be commercially unexploited. Anti-commercialism was an important criterion, taken as proof of the "authentic" character of the music. Only that music that was initiated "from below," produced and marketed under the direct control of the artist, could defend itself against appropriation by the culture industry and maintain its rebellious potential; at least, that was the ideal scenario.

This is why many protagonists of the protest movements distanced themselves from pop and rock music as it attracted an ever-increasing audience. Their doubts were fed primarily by the fact that this music was being mediated by the culture industry. The breakthrough came with the "underground" campaign of the record giant CBS from 1968 to 1970. This campaign marketed numerous bands under the banners of "pop revolution" and "underground" and thus was interpreted by many as robbing a central countercultural element of its rebellious potential. This cultural–industrial process was regarded as "cultural imperialism" and helped to push forward the radicalization that was sweeping the disintegrating student movements. In reaction to the dominance of American-driven pop music, countries like Sweden and Greece were rediscovering local music as a form of non-alienated national culture. However, this historical self-affirmation under the banner of "people" and "nation" did not negate the preferences of many young people for electrically amplified pop music but, rather, complemented it.[15] Ideas of unalienated purity, prevailing in some Maoist groups, could not keep away many of their young members and sympathizers from rock music. In Germany, for example, they could listen to Eric Clapton and The Doors as well as to African-American Blues performers and political singer-songwriters like Franz Josef Degenhardt and the communist singer Ernst Busch, a longstanding partner of Bertolt Brecht and Hanns Eisler.

The diversification of pop and rock music shows how little this mass culture can be explained by conventional conceptions of politics and revolution. Ideas that were diametrically opposed to the rational ideals of Marxist-Leninist categorization played a significant role in the rock music of the late 1960s and early 1970s. Far Eastern music, drug experiences, and new religious models were brought into play, all to be rejected by those subcultures that considered themselves rational. The relationship between pop and politics could be diffuse, contradictory, and fluctuating, as seen in the example of the 1968 Beatles song "Revolution," which referred to the May revolts in Paris but did not say whether the revolution could count on the Beatles. The lyrics of the first version of the song stated, "We all want to change the world / But when you talk about destruction / Don't you know that you can count me out." However, because of the skeptical popular reaction to the song, John Lennon later tried to please all listeners in a second version that left it completely open, with a reformulated line that read, "Don't you know that you can count me out/in." As seen in a controversy between Lennon and John

Hoyland in the British Marxist magazine *Black Dwarf*, the Beatle had to endure fierce attacks from the radical wing of the protest movements.[16] Other bands were seen as being more consistent. The German left-wing magazine *Konkret* declared at the end of 1968, "When it finally gets going— in Paris, Mexico City, Prague, Chicago, Columbia University and in Berlin, Frankfurt, Hamburg—then the music of the Stones will withstand the realities far better than that of the Beatles."[17] However, the Rolling Stones would also soon lose their revolutionary aura, just like many other artists who were unable to extricate themselves from the mechanisms of the culture industry.

The praxis of those youth cultures that were critical of consumerism also displayed such ambivalences. Even the American hippies and their European counterparts, who made the conspicuous rejection of consumerism a central element of their agenda, could not completely escape their environment, which was marked by the culture industry. Not only did their stylistic inventory include drug consumption and particular kinds of pop music but they also went to movies and pop concerts and bought records, stereo systems, buttons, posters, and blue jeans. They travelled, too, and drove particular brands of cars. Their consumption included "alternative" demands such as authenticity, sustainability, or fair trade and could therefore be arranged in accordance with a fundamental criticism of consumerism. The attraction to American Indians and Far Eastern religions, as well as an overall interest in the Third World and the romanticism of the simple life, were also a reaction to the unthinking consumerism of the Western world that would soon solidify into a movement for critically conscious consumption. So it was that rock music, in transporting such concepts, became an expression of the "reflexive modern" (Ulrich Beck), bringing forth a critique of the unintended consequences of modernity—a critique that emerged from modern society itself.

Bibliography

For in-depth material on the role of pop music in the social transformation of the United States, the United Kingdom, France, and Italy, see Marwick (1998); for Northern and Western Europe, see Schildt/Siegfried (2006). For the United Kingdom, cf. Osgerby (1998) and Green (1999); for Denmark, Martinov (2000) and Jenson/Jørgensen (2007); for East Germany, Rauhut (1993); for West Germany, Siegfried (2006); for insight into France, Yonnet (1996). For an overview of the history of rock music between 1954 and 1971, cf. the still valid Gillett (1996); on the relationship between pop music and politics, see Street (1986). For theoretical and social-historical criticism, see Eyerman/Jamison (1998) and Leggewie (1998). For the social relevance of pop music as mass culture and its relationship to political protest, see Frith (1978), Chambers (1983), Frith/Home (1987), and Wicke (1990 and 2006).

Chambers, Iain. *Urban Rhythms. Pop Music and Popular Culture.* London: Macmillan, 1984.

Eyerman, Ron and Andrew Jamison. *Music and Social Movements: Mobilizing Traditions in the Twentieth Century.* Cambridge: Cambridge University Press, 1998.

Frith, Simon, *The Sociology of Rock.* London: Constable, 1978.

Frith, Simon and Howard Horne. *Art into Pop.* London: Methuen, 1987.

Gillett, Charlie. *The Sound of the City. The Rise of Rock and Roll,* 2nd ed. New York: Da Capo, 1996.

Green, Jonathon. *All Dressed Up: The Sixties and the Counterculture.* London: Pimlico, 1999.

Jensen, Steven and Thomas Ekman Jørgensen. *1968—og det der fulgte.* Copenhagen: Gyldendal, 2008.

Leggewie, Claus. "A Laboratory of Postindustrial Society: Reassessing the 1960s in Germany." In *1968: The World Transformed,* edited by Carole Fink, Philipp Gassert, and Detlef Junker, 277–94. Cambridge: Cambridge University Press, 1998.

Martinov, Niels. *Ungdomsoprøret i Danmark. Et portræt af årene, der rystede musikken, billedkunsten, teatret, litteraturen, filmen og familien.* Copenhagen: Aschehoug, 2000.

Osgerby, Bill. *Youth in Britain Since 1945.* Oxford: Blackwell, 1998.

Rauhut, Michael. *Beat in der Grauzone: DDR–Rock 1964 bis 1972—Politik und Alltag.* Berlin: Basis Druck, 1993.

Schildt, Axel and Detlef Siegfried, eds. *Between Marx and Coca–Cola: Youth Cultures in Changing European Societies, 1960–1980.* New York: Berghahn Books, 2006.

Siegfried, Detlef. *Time Is on My Side: Konsum und Politik in der westdeutschen Jugendkultur der 60er Jahre.* Göttingen: Wallstein, 2006.

Street, John. *Rebel Rock: The Politics of Popular Music.* Oxford: Basil Blackwell, 1986.

Marwick, Arthur. *The Sixties: Cultural Revolution in Britain, France, Italy, and the United States, c.1958–c.1974.* Oxford: Oxford University Press, 1998.

Wicke, Peter. *Rock Music: Culture, Aesthetics and Sociology.* Cambridge: Cambridge University Press, 1990.

Wicke, Peter. "Music, Dissidence, Revolution, and Commerce: Youth Culture between Mainstream and Subculture." In *Between Marx and Coca–Cola: Youth Cultures in Changing European Societies, 1960–1980,* edited by Axel Schildt and Detlef Siegfried, 106–23. New York: Berghahn Books, 2006.

Yonnet, Paul. *Jeux, Modes et Masses: La Société Française et la Moderne 1945–1985.* Paris: Gallimard, 1996.

Notes

1. Dieter Baacke, *Beat—die sprachlose Opposition* (Munich: Juventa, 1968).
2. On American folk music, see Ronald D. Cohen, *Rainbow Quest. The Folk Music Revival and American Society, 1940–1970* (Amherst: University of Massachusetts Press, 2002).
3. Moritz Ege, *Schwarz werden. "Afroamerikanophilie" in den 1960er und 1970er Jahren* (Bielefeld: Transcript, 2007).

4. Charles Taylor, *The Ethics of Authenticity*, (Cambridge, MA: Harvard University Press, 1991).

5. *New Musical Express*, February 3, 1968.

6. Detlef Siegfried, "'Underground': Counter-Culture and the Record Industry in the 1960s" in *Mass Media, Culture and Society in Twentieth-Century Germany*, ed. Karl Christian Führer and Corey Ross (Basingstoke: Palgrave Macmillan, 2006), 44–60.

7. Joel Selvin, *Monterey Pop* (San Francisco: Chronicle Books, 1992).

8. Dieter Baacke, *Jugend und Subkultur* (Munich: Juventa, 1972), 95. "More assaulting" in comparison to pop music, which was considered less of an intervention.

9. *Konkret* 1968;1:45; *Der Spiegel* September 21, 1970, 222ff.

10. *Sounds* 1974;2:20.

11. According to Diedrich Diederichsen 1992, inverting a 1965 song title from The Who, reprinted in Diedrich Diederichsen, *Freiheit macht arm* (Cologne: Kiepenheuer & Witsch, 1993), 253–283.

12. This and the following in *Peng* 3 (May 1967).

13. Helmut Salzinger, *Swinging Benjamin* (Frankfurt: Fischer, 1973).

14. *Superlove* 1968;5:4.

15. Thomas Ekman Jørgensen, *Transformations and Crisis. The Left and the Nation in Denmark and Sweden 1956–1980* (New York: Berghahn Books, 2007).

16. Cf. Wicke (2006).

17. *Konkret*, December 16, 1968, 49.

6
Motions and Emotions

Jakob Tanner

Imaginative Explosions - Explosion of Imaginations

With the final scene of *Zabriskie Point*, Michelangelo Antonioni made film history. The main character Daria drives away from the villa into the desert. Fantasy is overheating. Daria stops, gets out, and looks back angrily at this stronghold of consumerism and commerce, now engulfed in a ball of fire. Then the villa reappears and the spectacle repeats itself over and over again. The embellishments of modern prosperity go up in the burning mushroom cloud. The detonation of the outside world is the explosion of the imaginary. Antonioni shows himself to be a resourceful "blaster," staging a slow-motion aesthetic of destruction. Freezer and television, clothes and whole interiors disintegrate in one surreal movement. Through Daria's eyes, the audience experiences the transformation of functional objects into useless fragments, which rearrange themselves in bright spaces into wonderful images with instinctive precision. The explosive effect is sublimated into an immaculate execution of colors and forms. Several minutes later, the time-suspended apocalypse reverts back to the desert landscape. Daria glances at the smoking ruins, turns, starts the motor, and drives away into a red sunset.

Zabriskie Point was released in spring 1970 and was supposed to be Antonioni's commercial triumph in the United States. Instead, it was a complete disaster. It came to a conflict after the Metro Goldwyn Mayer film company intervened in the soundtrack—which was especially important for the director—adding the sugary Roy Orbison song "So Young" to the final scene, with the car driving away against the red horizon. The contrast to Antonioni's original intention to show an airplane writing "Fuck You America!" in the sky at the end could not have been greater. In addition to this artistic nightmare, the film was also a commercial flop. In 1968, at the start of filming, the images had been in tune with the current mood, but by 1970 they no longer were. The film encountered a wave of rejection and ridicule among the counterculture and New Left, whose psychographics Antonioni had wanted to express in emotional images. The accusation that Antonioni had copied elements of avant-garde films and commercialized the counterculture's aesthetic potential for Hollywood cut deep. The establishment also reproached the film for its anti-American statements and filed several lawsuits, albeit unsuccessfully.[1]

Counterculture, Authenticity, and Bodily Experience

Today, in hindsight, one recognizes an attempt in *Zabriskie Point* to artistically visualize the emotional framework of the 1968 movement and the often contradictory mindset of its participants. Because of this, the film has become a historical source. The interpretation of such visual documents could enable historiography to adequately portray the emotional quality of the 1960s, which has barely been considered up to this point. For this process, it is be important that nostalgia, heroization, and sentimentalizing are not clouding the perspective from the very start. In 2000, the essayist and feminist Ellen Willis published a review of the film "Steal this Movie," Robert Greenwald's portrait of Abbie Hoffman. She commented: "What's missing . . . is the 60's as emotional experience. . . . For my generation, the pursuit of happiness was not a slogan; it turned our guts inside out and left us with a bone-deep sense of loss. 'Steal This Movie' makes a stab at expressing this dimension, but in the end it sentimentalizes."[2]

A story of emotions trying not to fall into the trap of self-mythologization has to start with the self-descriptions and subjectifications of the participants themselves, who argued that the private was political and vice versa. The intellectual model of "self-realization," equally popular among both the European and American counterculture, was to abolish bourgeois modes of differentiation. Capitalist society was perceived as an arsenal of manipulative methods and external forces of subordination to be fought against for the altruistic culture of feelings and an appreciation of things not calculable in terms of mere profit. This attitude was reflected in the catchword "solidarity." Instead of rivalry and Social Darwinism, people sought new forms of peaceful coexistence: "Make love not war." They were searching for authenticity, and the body seemed to promise this. Flower power aimed for an activation of the senses. The hippies and the yippies were in pursuit of the truth "about Who We All Really Are."[3] This "Really" was something concrete. The slogan "Sex, Drugs and Rock 'n' Roll" stood for a broad range of cultural practices that involved people physically and appealed to their sensory sensitivity.

The goal was to transform the body from an object of conformist consumerism into a creative subject.

Physical forms of action, as promoted by the Civil Rights Movement, strengthened the emotional identification of the New Generation with campaigns for rights and justice as sit-ins, go-ins, and involvements required a physical presence. After their marriage in 1969, John Lennon and Yoko Ono's "honeymoon bed-in for peace" in Amsterdam and Montreal hotel suites contributed to the sexual revolution and political contestation with a sensation-stirring "body performance" with the motto "John & Yoko meet the opposition."[4]

The loss of critical self-reflection, as well as a regressive schematization of thought patterns could sometimes be associated with this close attention to the body. In the years following 1968, West German terrorists showed their solidarity with those fighting in the Third World in a narcissistic way on the basis of their physical commitments.[5] These violent activists were consumed less by a distant desire for liberation than by incorporating the habitus of the "armed fighter" and his moral innocence. Over time, it became apparent that the terrorists met in a paradoxical contrasting way, as part of this physical self-investment, with hippies who had had enough of the abstractions of modern life and now wanted to enjoy their liberated physicality—regardless of their loss of social status—with flowers in their hair, listening to pop songs, living in a colorful world, and taking drugs. This was often meant less harmlessly than it appeared. Protagonists of alternative culture also used warlike metaphors. For them, rock 'n roll was "a weapon of cultural revolution." As John Sinclair, manager of the politicized rock band MC5, wrote in 1968, "Rock 'n' roll music . . . blows people all the way back to their senses and makes them feel good, like they're alive again in the middle of this monstrous funeral parlor of western civilization." Timothy Leary's dropout slogan, "turn on, tune in, and drop out," was politicized to give "turn on, tune in, and *take over!*"[6]

Rejection and Anti-achievement: The Navigation of Feelings in the 1960s

Historiography must not reproduce this physical "short-circuit" and sensuality cult when examining the emotional dimension of the '68 movement. Mark Oppenheimer writes that the counterculture of the Sixties was "what Nietzsche would call a Dionysian irruption of music, poetry, and sexual experimentation into an Apollonian world of serenity and rectitude,"[7] yet this leads the analysis up the wrong track. It could just as well be said that the Vietnam War was a Dionysian orgy of unleashed technological destruction, which the protest movement opposed with its Apollonian criticism. These oppositions do not lead anywhere. Emotions do not stand in contrast to rationality; furthermore, they change in the same way as people's mental instruments and intellectual perceptions. Far from constituting an anthropological constant of the *Homo sapiens*, they are subjected to a variety of transformations.

The counterculture created a new emotional attitude and lifestyle, stabilizing its basic orientation through refusal and an impertinent attitude of opposition ("anti-"). Chelsea Cain, publisher of an anthology recounting the experiences of children of American hippies, stated, "For my parents and her friends, the idea at the heart of the counterculture was simple: rejection. Rejection of the Establishment's war, its social mores, its institutions, its hang–ups, its corruption and its pursuits."[8] The result of this was nonparticipation as the dominant form of social protest. From this point of view, participation in demonstrations was a manifestation of individual refusal. Hippies wanted to be seen as "anti–achievers."[9]

The communication barriers built up during the 1960s between the counterculture and the establishment escalated into bitter conflicts in the years around 1968 but can only in a small part be attributed to the incompatibility of cognitive orientation and practical action; the *pursuit of happiness* marked the one aspiration connecting all camps, and after 1945, it also led the way for economic reconstruction and consolidation in Europe. The Civil Rights Movement fought for the validity and realization of human rights, and the New Left also championed a normative universalism that could be traced back to the Enlightenment. Confrontation and contestation resulted from the different emotional connotations of these values. Irreconcilable emotional regimes between generations, social groups, and the sexes generated the moment of conflict, and both revolt and repression gathered momentum from a mutual interdependency of emotion and motion.

Classificatory logic and cognitive models were central to the New Left. This was apparent not only in theoretical concepts such as class society, capitalism, and cultural industry but also in more diffuse fighting vocabulary such as "overconsumption" and "Establishment." In all its forms and facets, the emotional mobilization capacity of the counterculture remained bound to intellectual models of reason; people wanted to know what it was about. Even *Underground*, a booming loose network of innovative magazines that started in 1966 in Zurich, London, and San Francisco, had a pronounced theoretical self-conception, which expressed itself in poetical language and avantgarde forms. Similarly, the Situationists turned well-established systems of order into chaos with their actions. The dynamic of the '68 movement generally relied on synergies that could only be established through a concurrence of innovative cognitive categories and emotional models.

Overall, it can be said that the argumentative habitus depends on an emotional background "noise," which allows categorically functioning reason to reach meaningful thoughts in the first place. In the *stream of consciousness* (William James), the burning interest of the present coexists and interacts with accumulated knowledge from the past and a cloudy anticipation of the future. Knowledge bases the relevance of its actions on an emotional charging, on which memory also depends. Therefore, it is unproductive to see the revolts of the '68 movement as a raging emotional rebellion against a cold, calculating, capitalist society. Emotions also ran high on the side of the establishment, and without these, it would be almost impossible to understand the exaggerated reactions of the government and police in response to the cultural-revolutionary challenges.

Transatlantic Circuits and Emotional Resistances

The attitude of refusal that constituted one of the main features of the '68 movement was not an American specialty but was also the quintessence of the West European counterculture and the New Left. In the 1960s, an intercontinental cultural exchange began as a counterpart to the transatlantic alliance, one of the foundations of the Cold War. It intensified the reciprocal adoption of forms of protest and lifestyles on both sides of the Atlantic. Although the '68 movement cannot be reduced to a generational conflict, the self-positioning of "youth" as belonging to the future was decisive in stabilizing an emotional regime, which made the expressions of the counterculture extremely penetrable across all national boundaries. The new ways of dressing, musical preferences, and modes of expression, as well as demonstration techniques and forms of action, proved to be variable and flexible in their implementation. The permissive society, more tolerant toward all things new, eased this cultural transfer and acculturation process.

Especially in music, one recognizes a variety of reciprocal effects; in the 1950s, it was the United States in particular that spread a new attitude toward life with Rockability. Soul music, a development from rhythm and blues and gospel, was synonymous with African American "black" pop music in the 1960s and marked an important emotional resource in the Civil Rights Movement's fight against racial segregation and social equality. The blues also had large emotional potential. The beginning of the sixties then was Britain's finest hour, most visibly with Beatles-mania from 1963 and a considerable number of successful new groups (Rolling Stones, Kinks, The Who, The Animals), who triggered a positive shock and sketched out a new image of a youth oscillating between rebellion and hedonism. Since the end of the 1960s, U.S. rock groups, above all from California (The Grateful Dead, Jefferson Airplane, Mother Earth) began to reemerge.

Concerning lifestyles and emotional attitudes, the year 1969 was a peripeteia for which the hippie festivals were symptomatic. These huge media events had a considerable vibe, generating feelings and intensifying emotions, and therefore contributing to the communal experience of the dropout generation. In August 1969, two years after the Monterey Festival, Woodstock took place, marking the highlight of this type of event. In December of that same year, extreme acts of violence occurred at the Altamont festival. The murder of the Manson family in August 1969 and the cluster of terrorist attacks in West Germany (the West Berlin Tupamaros attacked the Jewish community center in Berlin in late 1969; the founding of the Red Army Faction in 1970) and Italy (the founding of the Brigate rosse in 1970) contributed to a change in public opinion that ushered in the "no future" attitude of the 1970s. The lost generation had left its drugged-up state of creativity behind and now threatened to give in to the bleak state of addiction. This breakdown was strengthened by the drug-related deaths of pop and rock stars (Jimi Hendrix, September 18, 1970; Janis Joplin, October 4, 1970; Jim Morrison, July 3, 1971). Politically, the disintegration of the counterculture triggered the foundation of a large number of left-wing parties. In the preceding period, from the early 1960s onward, the protest forms of the Civil Rights Movement and the participatory democracy approach of the New Left had been well received by the student movements in the urban centers of Europe. Now, a rigid party development dominated in the Old World that had no counterpart in the United States. If one agreed with Barry Mills that "the Sixties began in black & white and ended in color," it must also be said that in the seventies, Manichean black-and-white schemes dominated people's take on the world.[10]

Yet even during the Summer of Love, there was remarkable resistance against the free circulation of countercultural forms of expression, and not only between the United States and Western Europe. The Iron Curtain, serving as the political–military line of demarcation in the Cold War, was also a big hurdle for the international diffusion of countercultural practices. But the infiltrating powers of the counterculture, and especially pop music, supported by mass media, proved to be so strong that they even reached a wide audience in Eastern Europe, and in East Germany they provoked phenomena such as "rowdies," long–haired youths, and "loafers." Although the SED regime that took power after the erection of the Berlin wall in 1961 attempted to coopt the numerous new rock groups for political ends, for example, the "fight against imperialism," live music performances under party authority, as was the case in Eastern and Central Europe, remained a permanent source of annoyance; the rock 'n roll rhythm and associated gestures continuously clashed with the system's demand for order.

Simulacrum in an Age of Wonders
and Tasks for Historical Analysis

Central to the lifestyle and emotional attitudes of the 1960s was the notion that times would change on a global scale. Bob Dylan's 1964 song, "The Times, They Are A'Changin" found its equivalent in the title simultaneously adapted by the Rolling Stones, "Time is on My Side." Expectations for the future also intensified in the 1960s. The changes seemed to close in on the present, and were supposed to put society out of its misery. For many exponents of the counterculture, political prognoses merged with religious prophecies. The "futurum"—the open future that can be shaped through present actions—fused with the "adventum"—the unstoppable future approaching the spectators. Many sensed a "storm from paradise" (Walter Benjamin), which intensified the feeling of absolute urgency among many activists. The *a–venir* developed immense suggestive powers. Later critics of the '68 movement deprecatingly spoke about an "age of wonders," nurtured by a "belief in epiphanies" and the anticipation of a "new Jerusalem."[11]

As differentiated and heterogeneous as the cultural production of the '68 movement was, in terms of lifestyles and emotional attitudes, it was a homogenous simulacrum. This reality arose from an appearance of simultaneousness generated by mass media and consolidated itself in a mythology of a revolutionary passage on a global level. The powers of change seemed to be at work and on the brink of a breakthrough everywhere: Vietnam, China, Cuba, the Third World, socialist countries, and capitalist regions of Italy and France. This imagined synchronicity made it possible to perceive the many "small" refusals and contestable actions as part of one fantastic "Great Refusal" with structure-breaking violence. Detlev Claussen therefore justifiably speaks of the "metropolitan self-misconception of the revolts as a revolution."[12] That the "chiffre 68" was in a position to unite the emotional dispositions, motives, hopes, and disappointments of all those who considered themselves part of the social awakening in the 1960s, however, can only be understood when taking into account the effect of mass media. Newspapers, magazines, radio, film, and above all, television boosted the belief that people shared events with each other on a global scale: "The Whole World is Watching" (Todd Gitlin). Participants of 1968 failed to consider the dependency of their feelings, experiences, and aspirations on a technical mediatization of the senses, an omnipresent media infrastructure, and a significant increase in spending power. The manipulative culture industry and criticism of an alienated appropriation of the world was all too rapidly reproached. It is obvious today to what extent the counterculture's common lifestyle and the divided horizon of time depended on miniaturized everyday technical equipment (transistor radios, record players, television sets), fabricated cultural products (especially records), the fashion industry, and the media apparatus and sociotechnical systems that kept these systems of circulation and proliferation in operation.[13]

In *Zabriskie Point*, the now-legendary love scene in the white desert and rugged, sandy landscape of Death Valley, with its hallucinatory multiplication of sexual acts, also acquired its sensory intensity through Jerry Garcia's (of The Grateful Dead) melodic-crystalline solo improvisation. His (third) wife, Deborah Koons Garcia, explained that Jerry had described the collaboration with Antonioni as "the best of his upside" and added: "Still, watching *Zabriskie Point* now has made me fall in love with my generation all over again. We were all so young and beautiful, and time was on our side."[14] Today, Antonioni's film generates those magic moments, which did not emerge in theaters after its release, even more powerfully. In contrast, there are studies written by authors who feel the need to come to terms with their own involvement in the counterculture. They conclude that the sixties were simply a "nostalgic artifact," with which a "destructive generation" attempted to cheat itself.[15]

However, the coming to terms with the emotional dimension of the past can also be more differentiated. Moon Unit Zappa, born in 1967 to Mothers of Invention leader Frank Zappa, describes the added personal value of comprehending her origins in the hippie milieu: "Understanding and accepting fringie life helps me to better navigate the waters of the normie world."[16] Here the experience of the '68 protesters, who did not consider the aspiring counterculture as a marginal phenomenon, is set straight. Many hippies and yippies had been transformed from bearers of hope to lonely figures on the brink of lunacy all too soon, and their children were forced to shuttle between the two worlds. In addition, in areas in which the counterculture was culturally and commercially particularly successful, it was not immune to normalization and spawned new uniformities. Any history of emotions of the '68 movement has to take into account these nuances and differentiations. We are still looking forward to an analysis of the structure of feeling and the grammar of emotional expressions of the sixties; without such an approach, we will continue to misconceive the atmosphere of that decade that set new emotions in motion.

Bibliography

Because every social phenomenon has an emotional dimension, it is extremely difficult to draw up an overarching analysis of the moods, feelings, and affects of the counterculture, pop music, and movements surrounding

1968. For a broad view of the American counterculture and its effect on Europe, see Braunstein/Doyle (2002) and McConnell (2004). An emotional dissociation from 1968, resulting in an affective acting-out against the movements, is provided by Collier/Horowitz (1996). Different aspects of emotional identification in Europe are discussed in Kraushaar (2000) and Giles/Oergel (2003). For cross-country and transatlantic transfers of emotional styles and affective patterns, see Marwick (1999) and DeKoven (2004). The religious dimension is analyzed by Oppenheimer (2003) and Kießling (2006). For interesting insights into the personal experience and biography, see Cain (1999).

Giles, Steve and Maike Orgel, eds. *Counter-Cultures in Germany and Central Europe. From Sturm und Drang to Baader-Meinhof.* Bern: Lang, 2003.

Braunstein, Peter and Michael Doyle, eds. *Imagine Nation. The American Counterculture of the 1960s and '70s.* New York: Routledge, 2002.

Cain, Chelsea. *Wild Child. Girlhood in the Counterculture.* Seattle: Seal Press, 1999.

Collier, Peter and David Horowitz, eds. *Destructive Generation: Second Thoughts about the Sixties.* New York: Free Press, 1996.

DeKoven, Marianne. *Utopia Limited. The Sixties and the Emergence of the Postmodern.* Durham, NC: Duke University Press, 2004.

Frank, Thomas. *The Conquest of Cool: Business Culture, Counterculture, and the Rise of Hip Consumerism.* Chicago: University of Chicago Press, 1997.

Gitlin, Todd. *The Whole World is Watching: Mass Media in the Making and Unmaking of the New Left.* Berkeley: University of California Press, 2003.

Kießling, Simon. *Die antiautoritäre Revolte der 68er: Postindustrielle Konsumgesellschaft und säkulare Religionsgeschichte der Moderne.* Köln: Böhlau, 2006.

Kraushaar, Wolfgang. *1968 als Mythos, Chiffre und Zäsur.* Hamburg: Hamburger Edition, 2000.

Marwick, Arthur. *The Sixties: Cultural Revolution in Britain, France, Italy, and the United States, c.1958–c.1974.* Oxford: Oxford University Press, 1999.

Oppenheimer, Mark. *Knocking on Heaven's Door. American Religion in the Age of Counterculture.* New Haven, CT: Yale University Press, 2003.

McConnell, William, ed. *The Counterculture Movement of the 1960s.* San Diego: Greenhaven Press, 2004.

Swingrover, Elizabeth, ed., *The Counterculture Reader.* New York: Pearson/Longman, 2004.

Notes

1. See, e.g., David James, "'The Movies Are A Revolution': Film and the Counterculture," in: Peter Braunstein and Michael Doyle, ed., *Imagine Nation. The American Counterculture of the 1960s and '70s* (New York: Routledge, 2002), 275–303; Thomas Frank, *The Conquest of Cool: Business Culture, Counterculture, and the Rise of Hip Consumerism* (Chicago: University of Chicago Press, 1997).

2. Ellen Willis, review of *Steal This Movie*, New York Times, 20 August, 2000, I, 18f., quoted according to Marianne DeKoven, *Utopia Limited. The Sixties and the Emergence of the Postmodern* (Durham, NC: Duke University Press, 2004), 289f.

3. Moon Unit Zappa in Chelsea Cain, ed., *Wild Child. Girlhood in the Counterculture* (Seattle: Seal Press, 1999), xvii.

4. Title of Al Capp footage, May 26, 1969, http://archives.cbc.ca/IDC-1-68-195-997-10/arts_entertainment/montreal_bed_in/

5. Jamie Trnka, "The West German Red Army Faction and its Appropriation of Latin American Urban Guerilla Struggle," in Steve Giles and Maike Oergel, ed., *Counter-Cultures in Germany and Central Europe: From Sturm und Drang to Baader-Meinhof* (Oxford: Peter Lang, 2003), 315–332.

6. Quoted according to Elizabeth Swingrover, ed., *The Counterculture Reader* (New York: Pearson/Longman, 2004), 43, 45.

7. Mark Oppenheimer, *Knocking on Heaven's Door. American Religion in the Age of Counterculture* (New Haven: Yale University Press, 2003), 213.

8. Cain, *Wild Child*, xxii.

9. Jesse Pitts, in: William McConnell, ed., *The Counterculture Movement of the 1960s* (Sand Diego: Greenhaven Press, 2004), 66ff.

10. Barry Miles, *In the Sixties* (London: Jonathan Cape, 2002), 1.

11. Peter Collier and David Horowitz, eds., *Destructive Generation: Second Thoughts about the Sixties* (New York: Free Press, 1996).

12. Detlev Claussen, "Chiffre 68," in Dietrich Harth, ed., *Revolution und Mythos* (Frankfurt: Fischer, 1992), 219.

13. Todd Gitlin, *The Whole World is Watching: Mass Media in the Making & Unmaking of the New Left* (Berkeley: University of California Press, 2003).

14. http://www.phinnweb.org/links/cinema/directors/antonioni/zabriskie/, 13.

15. Collier/Horowitz, *Destructive Generation*.

16. Moon Unit Zappa, in Cain, *Wild Child*, xviii.

Part 2

**Protest Histories
in Different European Countries**

7
Italy

Jan Kurz and Marica Tolomelli

For international comparative studies, the importance of the Italian case cannot be stressed enough. In hardly any other country did the events of 1968 lead to such a similarly comprehensive *rivoluzione antropologica*, and no other country can so clearly differentiate the before and after in historical time. Only in Italy did the protest mobilization of 1968 directly carry over into a new social movement, the Extra-parliamentary Opposition. This constitutes the distinctiveness of the Italian case, the causes of which are analyzed in this chapter.[1]

Social and Political Framework of the Country

In the late 1960s, Italy was a nation that had been profoundly transformed by the peculiar dynamics of a period of considerable economic, social, cultural, and political development; this era entered the annals of history as the "economic miracle." These developments did not represent an anomaly within the European context, as they were fully integrated into a trend of extraordinary economic growth in the world system. However, the suddenness of the developments that took place in Italy stands out. The speed is particularly noticeable if we consider that during the early 1950s, Italy was still a prevalently agricultural nation that had not yet been integrated into productive cycles and international markets and had also maintained a highly traditional social-cultural profile. In spite of symptoms of economic development and transformation recognizable in the late 1940s, the radical structural transformation of the nation, following which Italy would enter into the rankings of the most highly industrialized nations in the world, took place almost entirely during the five-year period between 1958 and 1963.[2] The rapidity of this transformation had a devastating effect on society, including massive migration from southern to northern regions, evolution of a mass proletariat in leading Fordist industries, dismantling of structures and traditional family and gender roles, and affirmation of a secular culture defined by consumption and affluence.[3] These factors eventually led to an increase in the generation gap between young people—who had grown up on the crest of the wave of affluence, with prospects of social mobility and access to an ever-increasing range of public and private consumption[4]—and adults, who had grown up amidst Fascism, war, resistance, and reconstruction and who were still firmly anchored in an ethic of sacrifice and moderate consumption with limited leisure activities.[5]

The social elements that least identified with the declining social structure and that were more sensitive in grasping and becoming protagonists of this ongoing development—primarily young people, but also open-minded politicians and intellectuals—began manifesting critical attitudes toward the national government. Institutional life in Italy rotated around two main political parties, the *Democrazia Cristiana* (Christian Democrats, or DC) and the *Partito Comunista Italiano* (Communist Party, or PCI). After 1947, only the DC could legally govern, and the PCI was relegated to the opposition.[6] Political imbalances changed following the "earthquake" of 1956 when the PSI *(Partito Socialista Italiano)* veered down a path that diverged drastically from Soviet platforms. At the same time, within the government realm, the foundation of the liberal-moderate consensus on which Christian-Democratic centrism had been constructed from 1948 to 1958 experienced increasing difficulties in dealing with problems and tensions caused by ongoing industrialization. These difficulties culminated in the government crisis of spring 1960 and the dramatic epilogue of July 1960.[7] During the early 1960s, amidst a climate of attenuated Cold War tensions inaugurated by the election of John F. Kennedy in the United States and the abandoning of hard-line anti-Communist rhetoric by the Vatican Council (1962/65), the formation of a center-left government based on a DC–PSI coalition became possible for the first time. The entry of socialists into the administration was perceived as a turning point and generated high hopes for social renewal and reforms. Following its initial years (1962–1964), however, it became increasingly evident that the DC and conservative factions were determined to block any reform policies that might have given rise to undermining political stability.[8] Both the center-left's disregard of growing disappointment and the difficulties demonstrated by all the main political factions in dealing with problems arising from Italy's modernization spurred an attitude of critical social analysis and a search for innovative solutions among some political–intellectual and student circles.

Organizational and Social Structure of the Protest Movement

Until 1968, the UNURI (*Unione nazionale universitaria rappresentativa italiana*) existed as a central organization committed to the interests of the student body.[9] UNURI was the representative organ of the student body and was structured on both a national and local level in the form of student parliaments. The political student organizations (the Catholic *Intesa*, Socialist UGI, *Unione goliardica italiana*, and many others) delegated representatives to these parliaments. However, from the 1950s on, these organizations began to lose their political independence and became pure transmission conduits for the interests of their mother parties. In effect, the student parliament became a mere reflection of the country's party politics. As a result, both UNURI and the political student organizations completely lost legitimacy. The logical consequence was the end of this type of representation in 1968.

The counter-concept of the student movement initially consisted of the attempt to create a new organization with the help of basic democratic instruments. It was an attempt to move away from the unity prescribed by UNURI and toward a unity through the movement. The student activists tried to make all-important decisions through goals and actions in the plenum, the *Assemblea*. Contemporary observers noticed that the plenum quickly became "an essential reference point above the traditional institutions, regardless of whether they were those of the university or those of the students' representative organs."[10] With the delegation of all decisions to the *Assemblea*, the students created an ambience that was functional for collective living, debating, and the division of work. All important decisions were made by general conventions, and commissions were created to examine political and didactic problems, with the participation of several professors. As early as 1963, the search for basic democratic decision-making processes defined a topic that would become a characteristic of the student movement of 1968. Its climax was reached with efforts to integrate local plenums into the national conferences in 1968. Here the attempt was made to create uniform politics for all participants in the movement. However, it quickly became clear that it would be extremely difficult to reach such a consensus.[11]

Despite all basic democratic models, certain supporting groups of the 1968 movement formed within the student body as a result of long occupations at several universities beginning in January 1966. Catholic Socialist students Marco Boato, Renato Curcio, and Paolo Sorbi, along with Socialist-oriented students such as Guido Viale, Mauro Rostagno, and Adriano Sofri, stepped into the spotlight and remained prominent figures for several years. Without tying themselves to traditional organizational models of student interest groups and by partially positioning themselves in direct contrast to them, these groups mobilized previously spontaneous protest, turning it into a continuous protest movement on a broader basis than the 1968 "student" movement.

Cognitive Orientation

The activists derived their demands and goals from a heterogeneous mesh of approaches and interpretations that cannot be precisely defined by the term "New Left." It is necessary to distinguish between at least two directions, the Italian *Nuova Sinistra* and the international New Left. Further intellectual approaches flanked these core elements of the 1968 movement ideology.

The important organs for the development of the *Nuova Sinistra* were, among many others, the *Problemi del Socialismo* (since 1958), the *Quaderni Rossi* (since 1961), and later the *Classe Operaia*. The ideas and beliefs of *Operaismo* represented by the *Quaderni Rossi* and its successors constituted a main element of the Italian 1968 movement's cognitive orientation. Here authors developed new interpretations of classical Socialist theory and established a basic framework for their criticism of Italian society and the "Old Left" (the PSI, the PCI, and the unions).

The Old Left's bureaucratic, centralized, and hierarchical socialism stood at the center of criticism. The *Quaderni Rossi* opposed the Old Left with the demand for completely new workers' organizations, "in which socialism must be realized as autonomy and liberation."[12] The ideal model was the workers' internal basic democratic organization, the *"Controllo Operaio"*—a concept that was also discussed in France with the *"Gestion Ouvrière."* The "renewal of the socialist movement" should be the consequence of the new organization itself. Only by consequently doing away with outdated party and union concepts would it be possible "to achieve the concrete anticipation of the new civil society."[13] For the *Quaderni Rossi*, establishing socialism initially meant establishing organizations there and then through which society could be transformed. The responsibility for social change was thus put back in the workers' hands. The political actions of every individual interested in socialist change were to be understood as the first utterance by the new socialist society and not as just another step in the capitalist system. This characterized the intellectual attraction of *Operaismo*.

In addition to the theory offered by *Operaismo*, active interest in the international New Left was unfolding. The exemplary model and most important organ of the student movement in Italy was the *Quaderni Piacentini*. Founded in 1962, the *Quaderni Piacentini* quickly transformed from a culturally critical to a political organ. Its publishers were students and artists who grew up without connections to the left. The content of *Quaderni Piacentini* was structured around analyses of the left-wing situation in China, North and South America, and Europe. Cooperation with magazines such as the *Monthly Review, Studies on the Left, Revue Internationale du Socialisme*, and *Les Temps Modernes* further ensured the diffusion of the New Left in Italy.

Attitudes toward the Superpowers

During the 1960s, Italy presented a distinctly heterogeneous political culture. Although a liberal-democratic and moderate orientation undoubtedly prevailed and revolved politically around the DC, it contrasted strongly with the vast, articulate, and socially rooted Communist subculture that centered on the PCI.[14] In very schematic terms, at least until the end of the 1950s, the American Dream and the Soviet Myth coexisted and interacted within the universe of Italian social values, giving rise to criticisms and heated controversies concerning the model of social growth that Italy decided to follow— or had been driven into following.[15] With the events of 1956, the situation became even more complex. The Soviet intervention in Hungary was interpreted by the anti-Communist culture as yet another demonstration of the inherently repressive nature of Socialism while giving the PSI a motive for breaking the alliance with their Communist "big brother" and narrowing the gap with the governing majority. PCI leaders instead worked to maintain strong fraternal relations with the Soviet Union, although never fully confronting the critical debate that was unfolding within the party itself.[16]

The positions that emerged at least a decade later during the formation of the student movement were very different. It was evident that both major world powers were rejected because of the model of social organization that each proposed. The Soviet model faded in 1956 and definitively fell into decline after the events of August 1968. In spite of criticism directed toward its consumer society, a negative perception of the United States did not dramatically increase until the Vietnam War.[17] In this context, a deeply rooted Communist tradition that condemned American imperialism from the early postwar years offered students a useful argumentative support network. In addition, the interpretation of U.S. policies as imperialism allowed Italian students to consolidate relations with social and cultural exponents of the so-called *Altra America* (Other America) that they had come to know in the literary, political, and social arenas.[18]

Key Events

The 1968 movement in Italy stemmed from no particular center or background. It unraveled in a chain of events that intensified, culminating in

March 1968. The country got its first impression of protest potential and speed of mobilization in university settings after April 27, 1966. On this day, during a dispute between left-wing and neofascist students at the University of Rome, the socialist student Paolo Rossi tragically died in a fall. Within a few days, this accident sparked a wave of protest that led to occupations at academic institutions across Italy. Ultimately, nothing resulted from the protests, as the left-wing quickly established student and party organizations, took charge of shaping opinions, and steered the protest back into traditional institutional channels.[19]

However, this strategy was unsuccessful at the small university in Trento. From early 1966, students there had adopted a new form of interest representation, the plenum, which shut out traditional student organizations. On January 24, 1966, Trento students occupied their institution to demonstrate for the establishment of a diploma in sociology. The occupation of the University of Trento rapidly catalyzed the process and led to the recognition of the diploma within only a few days. "Non-traditional forms of political action had scored a victory over politics as usual."[20] The opportunity to influence political processes through direct actions was wide open.

The explosive nature of the developments in Trento was apparent just a few months later during demonstrations following the death of Paolo Rossi in Rome. Only in Trento did the protests escalate into violence; it was only there that Rossi's death was understood not as the result of right-wing extremism (according to official interpretations by the country's left-wing parties) but, rather, as an expression of society's repressive structures. In Trento, students reached this interpretation based on their analysis of the American protest movement, according to which protest against Paolo Rossi's death was simultaneously protest against the existing social order.[21] From their perspective, which is illustrated by the "Manifesto for a Negative University," one of the key documents of 1968 in Italy, both theory and forms of actions of the American New Left were applicable to the situation in Italy.[22]

In early 1967, protests intensified across Italy, and two developments collided. Protests against the plan for a large university reform climaxed, while massive protests against the Vietnam War began to spread throughout the entire country. In this situation, an autonomous student group occupied the University of Pisa for the first time on February 6, 1967, which resulted in the *Tesi della Sapienza*, another key document of the Italian New Left. The most important theoretical foundations for the student movement were thus laid between 1966 and the first half of 1967. However, the fiercest protests, which would change the student movement from something associated with only a few faculties and universities into a national political phenomenon, began with the start of the 1967/68 academic year.[23]

For the public, the cycle began on November 18, 1967, when the students at the Catholic University in Milan voted for the occupation of their institution. Even though police evacuated the university just a few hours later, the occupation became an important symbol for later occupations. Inspired by the actions of the students in Milan, Trento, and Turin, an increasingly concentrated chain of occupations and protest movements took place throughout Italy in the months following November 1967. Large student centers such as Florence, Genoa, Rome, and Naples were just as affected as the smaller faculties in places such as Sassari, Lucca, Macerata, Lecce, Urbino, Carrara, and Catania.

By late February 1968, tens of thousands of students were on strike, and hundreds of thousands of students were unable to continue their studies in a regular fashion. The universities were blockaded, besieged, or occupied; professors faced locked or empty lecture halls. Instruction took place on an irregular basis, and exams were postponed or cancelled. For all practical purposes, there was no contact between students and teaching staff. Counter-courses, general assemblies and commissions, discussions, occupations, and demonstrations had replaced the daily study routine for activists. In the various protest actions, ideological divisions made way for common action, which targeted the common enemy of authoritarianism.[24]

The turning point in the nationwide movement occurred on March 1, 1968 in a battle around the Architecture Faculty in the Valle Giulia in Rome. For the first time, students did not retreat from the approaching police but, instead, directly attacked them. Violence thus became an option for students, and they pursued this option over the following days and weeks. From March 1968 onward, formerly peaceful protests often ended in open street battles with police. For a few weeks, the student movement became the most important political player outside of parliament. Their protests began to take place more frequently outside of the universities, some in streets and squares to give their concerns as much public exposure as possible, some in front of large industrial factories in Northern Italy to strengthen joint mobilization with the working class. In exchange, they had to pay the price of giving up their terrain at the universities, where occupations decreased and nearly normal operations resumed in the autumn of 1968.

Forms and Tactics of Protest

With documents like the "Manifesto for a Negative University" and the "*Tesi della Sapienza*," students developed an analysis of society that contained new models for interpreting reality and strategies for overcoming it. However, to overcome existing conditions, it was first necessary to "arrive at a realization" about one's own situation. This arrival at a realization is reflected in numerous activities that became the unifying elements of the Italian movement. A core element of this strategy was the "active strike." The special characteristic of the active strike was that, in contrast to a "hot strike," it was carried out parallel to ongoing university operations. Its goal was not to forcefully blockade lectures but, rather, to shed light on the authoritative nature of the institution. During the strike, demonstrative-appellative actions served to plainly show the students their own situation while simultaneously awakening their consciousness for change within universities and society. Various types of events served to express the active strike, such as the so-called *Controlezioni*, meaning "more or less planned forms of open discussion that scandalize university indoctrination and which take place during or outside of official lectures and attempt to expose political content taught by the university in a pseudo-academic disguise." These counter-seminars, which took place parallel to regular lectures (in terms of schedule and content) to put students in the situation of deciding for or against the movement, were supplemented by the *Occupazioni bianche*, or "interventions with the goal of radically demystifying the political significance in teachings." The third element of action involved the *Controcorsi*, in which society and the movement were fundamentally analyzed. "For part of the student body, the *Controcorsi* are an adequate tool for analyzing capital and class and have the goal of bringing about organized political socialization, which builds the indispensable foundation for any political discussion."[25] A new organizational concept, centered on the plenum, supplemented this strategy. The *Assemblea* thus became the highest entity for representing student interests.

New organizational models borrowed from the United States, such as sit-ins and teach-ins, served to connect the student movement to international protests in public perception. Passive resistance was initially the main instrument used in direct confrontations with the police. Over the course of the mobilization in 1967/68, student commissions on topics such as "Connections between the student movement and the workers' movement" and "Connections between society and universities" soon marked a significant change in the student movement's identity and objectives. With the increasing integration of sociopolitical topics into the movement and the adaptation of demonstrative-appellative forms of action outside the universities, the students' strategy of action changed.

Since the battle in the Valle Giulia, violence against both property and people became a course of action. In the months following March 1, the key players attempted more direct forms of violence based on the concept of "Limited Rule-breaking," developed by the German New Left. Conscious escalation arose from protest with the goal of finally leading the movement out of the universities and into the center of society. "The offensive of the student movement," prominent student leader in Milan Mario Capanna judged at the time, "cannot be seen as anything other than general . . . [so that] the metropolis can become a powder keg in the heart of capitalism."[26] However, the radicalization reflected most strongly in the biographies of individual protagonists. For Mara Cagol and Renato Curcio—initially contributors to the Negative University, then to the Marxist–Leninist magazine *Lavoro Politico*—it was the beginning of a new form of political militancy much more determined to intervene on the workers' conflicts that had been escalating since the spring of 1969. In 1969, both of them moved to Milan, one of the epicenters of labor unrest, where they were among the initiators of the *Collettivo Politico Metropolitano*, a radical Marxist–Leninist group interested in the radicalization of class struggle. This was the particular context— marked by a surprising escalation of the workers' conflicts, as well as by the offensive activation of neofascist organizations[27]—in which Cagol and Curcio, together with Alberto Franceschini and other radical militants, founded the root of the Red Brigade in 1970–1971 in Milan. This became the largest left-extremist terrorist group that used political violence as the principal instrument of their strategy over the next several years. Although the path seemed to be paved from 1968 to the post-1968 period and to extra-parliamentary opposition, this was not an inevitable development.[28]

Transnational Relations

During the years that preceded the formation of the movement, exchanges and comparisons with intellectual currents of the New Left—especially Anglo-American, German, and French—took place mostly in the printed media or were centered on periodicals that served as hotbeds for international debate. In Italy, such magazines were represented by *Problemi del Socialismo, Quaderni Piacentini*, and the Italian edition of the *Monthly Review* (first published in 1968), the aim of which was to open dialogue with partners from other nations.

Personal ties also played an important role, such as the friendship between West German student leader Rudi Dutschke and Italian activist and publisher Giangiacomo Feltrinelli, which was an important connection to the German movement; certain types of historic-cultural traditions, such as the particular reception of the German language culture at the University of Trento (which partially explains the reception of the critical theory at this site); or yet again, the existence of consolidated ties between students of bordering regions, as in the case of Turinese students and their French colleagues.

In addition to promoting the dynamics for communication, sharing and merging of issues, and organizational structures, strategies, and forms of action, transnational relations also served to stimulate critical afterthoughts or the defining of specific strategies, according to the peculiarity of the national context in which the movements operated. In this regard, the debate that opened within the Turinese movement following the rapid decline of Parisian mobilization in May 1968 was highly significant. Despite great admiration for the revolutionary situation in Paris, some members of the Turinese movement soon grasped the incisive effect of a movement based on spontaneity. By the end of the month, Turinese students began reflecting on what could be learned from May in France—resulting first in the need to be equipped with coordination structures that would convey the revolutionary drive of students and workers within a wide-ranging and possibly longer-lasting social transformation strategy.[29] Turinese students attempted to meet this need through the creation of the *Lega studenti e operai* (Student and Worker League), an organizational structure on which the existing interaction between the two social groups could be potentially and permanently developed over the long term. Although the experience was actually somewhat bland and only slightly relevant, the Italian students' efforts to elaborate their own action strategy, prompted by the critical observation of similar movements in other nations, were significant.[30]

Consequences, Narratives, and Politics of Memory

In the case of Italy, as for others, much has been written on the effects of 1968, despite the fact that the problem of ascribing consequences to a complex social phenomenon that interacted with numerous other areas and forces (namely, institutional and cultural) is often too easily neglected. Although until the late 1980s the literature was completely in the hands of those who were the protagonists at that time,[31] the studies that emerged for the occasion of the thirtieth anniversary of 1968 recorded some new elements, including a significant effort to manage historical data through interdisciplinary methodological approaches aimed at going beyond personal testimonies. The Bologna convention promoted by the Istituto Gramsci Emilia-Romagna and by John Hopkins University of Bologna (autumn 1998) was important for the Italian case, as there was a sort of methodological–generational comparison of the interpretations of 1968.[32] However, many older historians also began to free themselves from the memoirs to give space to an authentic historiography of 1968.[33] The major contributions of the historiography resulting from this process are apparent in the deconstruction of the 1968 myth based on an effort of historical contextualization, research, analysis, and reconstruction of the movement as an event and of the main factors of continuity and break-up between the movement and its past as well as its future. The controversy regarding the political interpretation of the movement was, however, not quelled, particularly with regard to the question of connections between 1968 and the emergence of anti-Establishment terrorism in the 1970s. Nonetheless, further research being done in this area and the desire to understand those years that were so crucial for Italian history is strong.

The legacy of 1968 for Italian history can best be expressed by an *ex post* reflection by one of the main exponents of the 1968 events in Italy, Guido Viale, a university student in Turin during the years of the movement, and his personal, yet significant and shareable opinion:

> From the point of view of the things that [1968, *author's note*] has left us and that have remained, there was undoubtedly a liberalization and modernization of customs, of interpersonal relations . . . between the sexes . . . between parents and children, of the family structure that was radical and irreversible, in spite of all the attempts at restoration carried out with particular virulence afterwards and even today. From a point of view of political change, there was one immediate and one that continued throughout the 1970s and that was very strong: it corresponded to a recovery, also to an electoral comeback of the left, but above all in the field of labor, in labor relations, in the workers' movement that was undoubtedly triggered by the students' revolt. From a point of view of learning; something that we can still strive for, but which has hardly reached today's younger generation, is a life experience and a collective practice founded on a daily invention of the way we interact with others, our peers and the rest of society. It was an experience directed at liberalisation that is re–proposed, in unequal forms, every time a collective movement seeks to resume the initiative and break away from codified social relations which otherwise prevail during moments of calm and lack of protest.[34]

Therefore, 1968 is recalled neither as a myth nor an unavoidable point of reference but simply as an experience that reflects how those past aspirations to transform the world are again perceived with such intensity as to trigger a new but necessarily diverse process of social mobilization.

Bibliography

An excellent overview of the Italian case of 1968 in English is provided by Horn (2007) and Lumley (1990). For a closer look at the student movement, see Kurz (2001), Ortoleva (1988), Agosti (1991), and Cavalli (1997). For studies on the workers' movement and its dimension in 1968, turn to Tolomelli (2001) and Giachetti (2002). An entrée to the spirit of the movements is offered by autobiographic texts such as Boato (1979), Capanna (1988), Viale (1978), and Passerini (1996). For the theoretical framework and perception of New Left thought, turn to documents and analysis in Università (1968) and Rossanda (1968). For researching the Italian New Left, see Panzieri (1972).

Aldo, Agosti, Luisa Passerini, Nicola Tranfaglia. *La cultura e i luoghi del '68.* Milan: F. Angeli, 1991.

Boato, Marco. *Il 68 è morto. Viva il 68!* Verona: Bertani, 1979.

Capanna, Mario. *Formidabili quegli anni.* Milano: Rizzoli, 1988.

Cavalli, Alessandro and Carmen Leccardi. "Le culture giovanili," in Francesco Barbagallo, ed. *Storia dell'Italia repubblicana.* Torino: Einaudi, 1997.

Giochetti, Diego. *Anni Sessanta comincia la danza. Giovani, capelloni, studenti ed estremisti negli anni della contestazione.* Pisa: BFS, 2002.

Horn, Gerd-Rainer. *The Spirit of '68. Rebellion in Western Europe and North America, 1956–1976.* Oxford: Oxford University Press, 2007.

Kurz, Jan. *Die Universität auf der Piazza. Entstehung und Zerfall der Studentenbewegung in Italien 1966–1968.* Cologne: SH-Verlag, 2001.

Lumley, Robert. *States of Emergency. Cultures of Revolt in Italy from 1968 to 1978.* London: Verso, 1990.

Ortoleva, Peppino. *Saggio sui movimenti del 1968 in Europa e in America.* Roma: Editori Riuniti, 1988.

Panzieri, Raniero. *La ripresa del marxismo–leninismo in Italia.* Milano: Sapere, 1972.

Passerini, Luisa. *Autobiography of a Generation: Italy, 1968.* Hanover, NH: University Press of New England, 1996.

Rossanda, Rossana. *L'anno degli studenti.* Bari: Bari De Donato, 1968.

Tolomelli, Marica. *"Repressiv getrennt" oder "organisch verbündet." Studenten und Arbeiter 1968 in der Bundesrepublik Deutschland und Italien.* Opladen: Leske & Budrich, 2001.

Università. *L'ipotesi rivoluzionaria. Documenti delle lotte studentesche. Trento, Torino, Napoli, Pisa, Milano, Roma.* Padova: Marsilio, 1968.

Viale, Guido. *Il sessantotto. Tra rivoluzione e restaurazione.* Milano: G. Mazzotta, 1978.

Notes

1. Eric Hobsbawm, Giorgio Napolitano, *Auf dem Weg zum "historischen Kompromiss"* (Frankfurt: Suhrkamp, 1977), 73; Alessandro Cavalli, Carmen Leccardi, "Le culture giovanili," in Francesco Barbagallo, ed., *Storia dell'Italia repubblicana*, vol. 3/2 (Torino: Einaudi, 1997), 762; Marco Revelli, "Movimenti sociali e spazio politico," in Francesco Barbagallo, ed., *Storia dell'Italia repubblicana*, vol. 2/2 (Torino: Einaudi, 1995), 454.

2. Guido Crainz, *Storia del miracolo italiano. Culture, identità, trasformazioni tra anni cinquanta e sessanta* (Roma: Donzelli, 1996).

3. Silvio Lanaro takes these changes fully into account. See idem, *Storia dell'Italia repubblicana. L'economia, la politica, la cultura, la società dal dopoguerra agli anni '90* (Venezia: Marsilio, 2001).

4. Simonetta Piccone-Stella, *La prima generazione: Ragazze e ragazzi nel miracolo economico italiano* (Milan: FrancoAngeli, 1993).

5. Marica Tolomelli, "Giovani anni Sessanta. 'Sulla necessità di costituirsi come generazione'," in Paolo Capuzzo, ed., *Genere, generazioni, consumi. L'Italia negli anni Sessanta* (Rome: Carocci, 2003), 191–216.

6. Fundamental for the understanding of the Italian political system is the study of Paolo Farneti, *Il sistema dei partiti in Italia. 1946-1979* (Bologna: Il Mulino, 1983).

7. To resolve the government crisis during the spring of 1960, the Christian Democrats were obliged to form a government (Tambroni) with votes of confidence from the Fascist party, or MSI. The political climate was very tense; the anti-Fascist paradigm on which the Italian Republic was founded was given new value. In early July, the numerous protests that took place against the legitimization of the MSI were dramatically repressed, to the point that the government was forced to relinquish its hold. Cf. Fabrizio Loreto, "1960: La 'lunga' crisi," in Luca Baldissara et al., ed., *Un territorio e la grande storia del '900. Il conflitto, il sindacato e Reggio* Emilia, Vol. 2 (Roma: Ediesse, 2002), 117–78.

8. The events related to the summer 1964 government crisis are emblematic of this profile. See Paul Ginsborg, *Storia d'Italia dal doppoguerra a oggi. Società e politica 1943–1988* (Turin: Einaudi, 1989), 373.

9. On student organizations, clubs, associations and the representative forms of political representations, see Carlo Oliva, Aloisio Rendi, eds., *Il movimento studentesco e le sue lotte* (Milano: Feltrinelli, 1969).

10. Rinascita; 9 (1963), 8 (translated by the authors).

11. Cf. Jan Kurz, *Die Universität auf der Piazza. Entstehung und Zerfall der Studentenbewegung in Italien 1966-1968* (Cologne: SH-Verlag, 2001).

12. Raniero Panzieri, *La ripresa del marxismo-leninismo in Italia.* (Milano: Sapere, 1972), 91 (translated by the authors).

13. Ibid., 104 (translated by the authors).

14. Stephen Gundle, *I comunisti italiani tra Hollywood e Mosca. La sfida della cultura di massa (1943–1991)* (Firenze: Giunti, 1995).

15. Pier Paolo D'Attorre, ed., *Nemici per la pelle: sogno americano e mito sovietico nell'Italia contemporanea* (Milan: F. Angeli, 1991).

16. Claudio Pavone, "Le contraddizioni del dopo Ungheria. 'Passato e Presente' (1958–1960)," *Classe* 17 (1980): 109–36.

17. The first student protest against the Vietnam War was organized by students of the University of Trento in March 1967. Armando Vadagnini, *Trento città del '68* (Trento: L. Reverdito, 1988).

18. The intellectuals of the Quaderni Piacentini closely followed American developments. The birth of the Italian edition of the *Monthly Review* and the *New Left Review* is also important. The writings of C. Wright Mills were soon translated in Italy.

19. Jan Kurz and Marica Tolomelli, "Gli studenti. Tra azione e mobilitazione," in Carmelo Adagio, Rocco Cerrato, Simona Urso, eds., *Il lungo decennio. L'Italia prima del '68* (Verona: Cierre, 1999), 51–71.
20. Gerd-Rainer Horn, *The Spirit of '68. Rebellion in Western Europe and North America, 1956-1976.* Oxford: Oxford University Press, 2007, 77.
21. *L'Adige*, April 30, 1966, 4.
22. For the only discussion of the Manifesto available in English see Horn, *Spirit of '68*, 77–85.
23. "Pisa—le tesi sull'Università," in: *Lavoro Politico* 2 (1967), 26–30.
24. Kurz, *Universität auf der Piazza*, 213.
25. Citations see "Università negativa," in: *Lavoro Politico* 2 (1967), 20–22 (translated by the authors).
26. "Un anno di lotte: i limiti del tatticismo," (II) in: *L'Astrolabio* 38 (1968), 32 (translated by the authors).
27. This brings to mind the bombing at the Piazza Fontana in Milan on December 12, 1969, which marked the beginning of the *Strategia della tensione* practiced throughout the 1970s until the attack at the Central Station in Bologna on August 2, 1980. Cf. Ugo Maria Tassinari, Fascisteria. *I protagonisti, i movimenti e i misteri dell'eversione nera in Italia, 1965–2000* (Roma: Castelvecchi, 2001).
28. For outcomes and aesthetics cf. Horn, *Spirit of '68*, 190–228; see also the chapter by Dorothea Hauser in this volume.
29. Cf. Bozza preparatoria per l'assemblea dei quadri del 24.5.1968, Fondazione Vera Nocentini (Turin), Marletti (F3-3A), Fondazione Vera Nocentini (Turin), 4.
30. Cf. Marica Tolomelli, *"Repressiv getrennt" oder "organisch verbündet." Studenten und Arbeiter 1968 in der Bundesrepublik Deutschland und in Italien* (Opladen: Leske und Budrich, 2001), 215–18.
31. Mario Capanna, *Formidabili quegli anni* (Milano: Rizzoli, 1988); Marco Boato, *Il '68 è morto. Viva il '68!* (Verona: Bertani, 1979); Guido Viale, *Il Sessantotto. Tra rivoluzione e restaurazione* (Milano: Mazzotta, 1978); Luigi Bobbio, *Storia di Lotta Continua* (Milan: Feltrinelli, 1988).
32. "Gli atti," in Luca Baldissara, ed., *Le radici della crisi. L'Italia tra gli anni Sessanta e Settanta* (Rome: Carocci, 2001).
33. Marcello Flores and Alberto De Bernardi, *Il Sessantotto* (Bologna: G. Mazzotta, 1998); Diego Giachetti, ed., *Per il Sessantotto. Studi e ricerce* (Bolsena: R. Massari, 1998); Marco Revelli, "Movimenti sociali e spazio politico," in Francesco Barbagallo, ed., *Storia dell'Italia repubblicana*, vol. 2/2 (Torino: Einaudi, 1995), 385–476.
34. Guido Viale interviewed by Fabio Pelini in Rome on October 30, 2002, in Giovanni Orsina, Gaetano Quagliariello, eds., *La crisi del sistema politico italiano e il Sessantotto* (Soveria Mannelli: Rubbettino, 2005), 542 (translated by the authors). Viale was the author of *Contro l'Università*, one of the manifestos of the Italian student movement, published in *Quaderni Piacentini*, 33, 1968.

8
West Germany

Martin Klimke

On June 2, 1967, West German police officer Karl-Heinz Kurras killed twenty-six-year-old student Benno Ohnesorg with a shot to the head during a demonstration in West Berlin against the Shah of Persia. A photograph of the dying Ohnesorg lying on the street, with his head bleeding and a helpless woman in an elegant fur coat leaning over him, was to become one of the most iconic images of the German student movement and the 1960s in West Germany. The events of June 2, 1967, marked the transformation of the West German New Left into a nationwide student revolt; until then, it had largely been centered in Berlin and Frankfurt. After that day, the largest student organization on the Left, the Socialist German Student League (*Sozialistischer Deutscher Studentenbund*, or SDS), experienced a rapid increase in sympathy and support, jumpstarting a broad movement whose participants would go down in West German history as the "68ers."

Social and Political Framework of the Country

The Federal Republic of Germany was founded in 1949 as a merger between the French, British, and American occupation zones after the Second World War. The reconstruction period that followed was closely associated with the name of the first West German chancellor, Konrad Adenauer, who led the country from 1949 to 1963 and firmly anchored it in the Western alliance. In contrast to its East German counterpart, the Federal Republic soon established a liberal parliamentary democracy, a federal state system, and a capitalist "social market economy." Internationally, the country's membership in the North Atlantic Treaty Organization (NATO) cemented its alignment with the West. However, the division of Germany and the permanent stationing of Allied troops on its territory made the country one of the hot spots of the Cold War, with the divided city of Berlin being in the limelight of global attention.

Domestically, the first steps of the young West German democracy in the early 1950s were flanked by an unprecedented economic boom (*Wirtschafts-wunder*), which brought material wealth and prosperity to the country. On the political scene, the conservative Christian Democratic Party (CDU) and Christian Social Union (CSU) led all governments between 1949 and 1966, sometimes in coalition with the liberal Free Democratic Party (FDP). In 1966, the conservative parties formed a grand coalition with the second largest political force, the Social Democratic Party (SPD), the chief representative of values such as anti-fascism, anti-militarism and socialism in the country's early years. In 1959, however, the Social Democrats had given up their Marxist heritage with the Godesberg program to broaden their political appeal.

In an atmosphere of anti-Communism, economic reconstruction, and the establishment of a stable democratic system, however, the political culture in West Germany was only slowly coming to terms with its National Socialist legacy.[1] The questionable past of many members of the political and administrative elites, the ban of the Communist Party in 1956, and the "Spiegel scandal" of 1962 (in which Defense Minister Franz-Josef Strauss initiated the unlawful arrest of journalists residing abroad) provoked fears of an erosion of democracy. This mood came to a climax in discussions about the so-called emergency laws of the mid-1960s, which threatened to expand the powers of the executive branch at the expense of constitutional rights in the event of an internal or external state emergency.[2]

Organizational and Social Structure of the Protest Movement

In purely quantitative terms, the 1960s protests were less intensive than those of the previous decade, when Adenauer's Western alignment and the question of rearmament caused large numbers of people to take to the streets.[3] Thus, when the Socialist German Student League (SDS) emerged as the main representative of the New Left, it built on the organizational and personal networks of the Easter March campaign, a movement for peace and nuclear disarmament supported by the German trade unions, which had gathered momentum at the beginning of the 1960s.[4]

Although part of a longer socialist tradition, the German SDS was newly founded in 1946 and closely associated with the SPD. At the beginning of the 1960s, however, this close relationship came to an end when the SDS moved further to the left and positioned itself closer to the "Critical Theory" of the Frankfurt School and the burgeoning international New Left movement.

Outraged by this leftward turn, the SPD officially disassociated itself from SDS on November 6, 1961, by declaring membership in the two organizations mutually exclusive. SDS subsequently came to understand itself as an avant-garde organization, focusing exclusively on workers as agents for social change, but also looking toward the growing technical and scientific elite at the universities and in society to provide alternatives to the existing order.[5]

In the second half of the decade, SDS was forging alliances with the ongoing Easter March campaign and emerging public opposition against the government plan to install emergency laws. Naturally, the common goals of this heterogeneous alliance of pacifists, liberals, trade unions, and socialist students were limited. With its push for a more democratic university, its opposition to the war in Vietnam, and the charismatic personality of Berlin student activist Rudi Dutschke, SDS quickly began to set the pace of events. With chapters all over the country, it took the leading role in this extra-parliamentary opposition (*Ausserparlamentarische Opposition*, APO), but was frequently joined in its actions by other student or trade union organizations, discussion clubs (e.g., the Republican Club), and later on even leftist high school student associations. The most prominent of these various groups was the *Kommune I*, founded as an anti-authoritarian commune in West Berlin in January 1967 by Dieter Kunzelmann, Fritz Teufel, and Ulrich Enzensberger and later joined by Rainer Langhans. The commune very successfully orchestrated its political actions and agenda of sexual liberation in the mass media and, because of its blend of Situationist provocation, political existentialism, and alternative lifestyle, soon advanced as the countercultural representative of the movement.

However, the sudden nationwide growth of the student movement after June 2, 1967, transformed its organizational and social structure. Although growing on the local level, SDS was beginning to slowly disintegrate as a national organization in the second half of 1968. After the ratification of the emergency laws by the German parliament on May 30, 1968, and the summer break, a unified national strategy could no longer be found. Ideological infighting, local idiosyncrasies, and the emerging women's movement contributed to the end of SDS as a national organization. In 1969–1970, various ideologically exclusive and hierarchical splinter groups subscribing to Maoist, Communist, or Leninist ideologies emerged. In addition, the counterculture had begun to spread and diversify itself throughout the country, creating numerous communes and subcultural scenes, out of which a movement based on spontaneous political action (*Sponti–Bewegung*) emerged, with one center in Frankfurt. At the same time, self-described groups of "armed struggle" dedicated to terrorism such as the Movement June 2 (*Bewegung 2. Juni*) or the Red Army Faction (*Rote Armee Fraktion*, RAF) entered the scene and would dominate the public picture for years to come. A mixed gathering of SDS members ratified the dissolution of the organization on March 21, 1970, in Frankfurt.

Cognitive Orientation

The German SDS was one of the main representatives of the international New Left movement in the early 1960s. In its rejection of orthodox Marxism and anti-Communism and its dissatisfaction with the Cold War, materialism, and apathy in society, it found a connecting point to similar movements in France, Great Britain, the United States and elsewhere. Although particularly influenced by a tradition of theoretical Marxism, SDS was equally inspired by the theories of American sociologist C. Wright Mills and saw the role of students or the intellectual elite as a catalyst for social change.

At the same time, the issue of university reform was at the forefront of SDS's efforts, the long-term goal being a fundamental structural change and democratization of the academy.[6] Beyond university issues, SDS had also taken on larger problems affecting West German society. To showcase the continuing legacy of the National Socialist past in the Federal Republic, SDS had compiled lists of Nazi perpetrators still active in the legal branch and in 1959 organized an exhibition on the issue entitled "Unredeemed Nazi Justice" (*Ungesühnte Nazijustiz*). While continuing to pursue these subjects, SDS experienced a voluntaristic and anti-authoritarian turn in 1965–1966 because of the influx of a new group of people. The most prominent among these was Rudi Dutschke, a refugee from East Germany and student of sociology at the Free University of Berlin. Based on his roots in the Situationist artist group *Subversive Aktion*, Dutschke had developed a characteristic amalgam of revolutionary theory.[7] For him, any revolutionary politics had to be perceived on a global level, as both financial forces and imperialist policies were operating internationally, suppressing national liberation movements worldwide. Consequently, national protest organizations had to reach out to other revolutionary movements around the world to respond to this "counterrevolutionary challenge," which could no longer be grasped within the confines of nation states.

In addition to this internationalism, Dutschke sought a way to translate the analysis of critical theory into political action to activate the revolutionary masses. Inspired by the works of Herbert Marcuse, Dutschke assumed that society's minorities and marginalized remained the only potential forces for social change since the working class was completely manipulated and their revolutionary potential absorbed by the system.[8] For students and intellectuals to initiate the "emancipation" of the masses, Dutschke drew on the works of the Hungarian Marxist philosopher George Lukács and advocated a voluntaristic concept of revolution, in which revolutionary consciousness and theory was created through action.[9] In contrast to Lukács, however, Dutschke discovered potential revolutionary agents in social minorities and the liberation movements of the Third World. In his mind, the liberation movements formed part of an international class struggle, which had long replaced Cold War confrontations of East and West with a North–South divide between wealthy industrialized societies and countries stricken by poverty. For Dutschke, the liberation movements and their techniques were prime models to create revolutionary consciousness. Che Guevara's foco-theory as well as Frantz Fanon's liberation concepts thus formed prominent ingredients in his thinking and work for revolutionary change from within the "European periphery."[10]

The gradual implementation of these theoretical models coincided with a topical shift toward opposition to the war in Vietnam. Since 1965, SDS resolutions and congresses had described the conflict as a model case for colonial liberation movements and interpreted it in a larger framework of U.S. imperialism. SDS activists increasingly began to feel that, through its alliance with the United States, the West German government indirectly supported the war and, given its National Socialist past, thus shared responsibility for what was happening in Vietnam.[11] Alongside calls for university reform and fundamental socialist transformation of society, the war in Vietnam therefore became one of the central mobilizing and radicalizing issues of the German SDS in the years 1967–1968. At the 1967 national convention, Rudi Dutschke and Hans-Jürgen Krahl, the leading theoretician of the Frankfurt SDS, jointly demanded that SDS should move toward a "propaganda of action" in the metropolis, complementing the "propaganda of bullets" in the Third World.[12] Inspired by Che Guevara's foco-theory, the goal was to discover the "subjective factor" by personally experiencing the abstract repression of the system through direct actions confronting the established powers. This process of "revolutionizing the revolutionaries" was not only the precondition for Marcuse's "Great Refusal" but also the basis for a global alliance of revolutionary forces to defend Vietnam against internationally operating imperialist forces. As Dutschke argued in February 1968, "The globalization of revolutionary forces is the most important task of the whole historical period that we live in and in which we are working towards human emancipation. . . . In the world-wide demonstrations lies, in an anticipatory sense, something like a global revolutionary strategy."[13] Turning the seemingly distant Vietnamese revolution into a test case for social change and revolution worldwide, SDS called for a comprehensive coordination of revolutionary protest to counter global imperialism and achieve the long-term goal of creating a new human being liberated from capitalist and bureaucratic repression.

When this global revolutionary strategy did not seem to materialize in the course of the late 1960s, activists shifted their attention to other venues such as local grassroots or labor organizing, carrying their ideas into West German society. Here the countercultural concepts of the *Kommune I* developed the strongest appeal. Liberalization in fashion and lifestyle, and new ideas about communal living, individual freedom, democratic structures, and gender relations, helped to substantially transform West German culture in the following decade. Nonetheless, the outward failure of the desired political objectives drove a minority of activists into a continuation of their struggle by means of violence and terrorism, thereby drawing their own consequences from the cognitive orientation and theoretical framework developed in the student movement.[14]

Attitudes toward the Superpowers and the Cold War

As a result of the central role of the Federal Republic in the Cold War and its close political, economic, and cultural association with the United States, the student movement's attitude toward the country's most important ally was ambivalent. On the one hand, it held U.S. imperialism responsible for the suppression of national liberation movements worldwide and the discrimination of its ethnic minorities at home. In consequence, its actions were frequently aimed at American military, cultural, and political representation in West Germany; for example, during an infamous anti-war demonstration in February 1966, when demonstrators threw several eggs at the America House in West Berlin, or in the so-called Custard-Assassination (*Pudding-Attentat*), when members of the Kommune I were arrested during preparations to attack American Vice President Hubert Humphrey with butter tarts during his visit in West Berlin in April 1967. These attacks against NATO and U.S. representations became increasingly violent in the 1970s, especially when the Red Army Faction chose American military personnel and installations as targets for their terrorist attacks. In contrast, West German students were greatly inspired and in close touch with their American counterparts, the nonofficial "other America." Because of the great number of exchange programs, a massive influx of American (counter)culture, and the presence of about 80,000 American soldiers within the Federal Republic, West German students often engaged American citizens and soldiers residing in the country in their protest.[15]

Student opinion on the Soviet Union was largely marked by a refusal of what was perceived as a failed Communist experiment sharing imperial ambitions equal to the other superpower. Although financial and logistical support was occasionally accepted from East Germany, the Soviet invasion into Czechoslovakia in August 1968 crushed any hopes for Socialist experiments in the Eastern bloc. It was only in the 1970s after SDS had disintegrated that groups such as the Communist League West Germany (*Kommunistischer Bund Westdeutschlands*, KBW) or other Marxist-Leninist factions sought closer ties to the Soviet model again.

Key Events

The major event for "1968" in West Germany actually occurred on June 2, 1967, when the Persian head of state, Rehza Pahlewi, visited West Berlin. During a demonstration against this visit organized by the Berlin SDS, a group of Iranian agents acting as pro-Shah demonstrators attacked protesting students and others in front of the police.[16] As a result, several thousand demonstrators gathered for an unauthorized demonstration around the Berlin opera house that evening. The brutal police strike against the demonstrators climaxed in the killing of twenty-six-year-old Benno Ohnesorg, who for the first time in his life had taken part in a demonstration.[17] For students and intellectuals, this fatal shooting suddenly seemed to confirm their analysis of West German society as authoritarian and already in a state of "emergency." A SDS congress on June 9 in Hanover on how to respond to the situation saw a verbal clash between Rudi Dutschke and the philosopher Jürgen Habermas, who feared the escalation of violence and characterized Dutschke's voluntaristic strategies of direct action as "left fascism."[18]

Nonetheless, the wheel of protest was in full swing and spread from Berlin to the whole country. The national SDS convention from September 4 to 8 in Frankfurt launched a campaign against the media power of Axel Springer's publishing house, which the students perceived to be primarily responsible for negative media coverage of the protest. The convention's ambition was not only to show the manipulative techniques of Springer's newspapers but also to produce a critical public sphere and independent, alternative media structures. To reveal the manipulative and repressive character of existing institutions and create a counterforce to them, a Critical University (KU) offering an alternative curriculum was also established in Berlin on November 1.

Another important step was the Vietnam Congress of February 17 to 18, 1968, at the Technical University (TU) Berlin, which attracted roughly 5,000 students and anti-war activists from Europe and overseas.[19] Having achieved at least part of their goals (the West Berlin police president and the mayor had both resigned in August/September 1967), the students displayed confidence and showed solidarity with the Vietnamese people. The closing demonstration saw about 12,000 people marching through the streets of West Berlin, carrying posters of Che Guevara, Rosa Luxemburg, and Leo Trotsky, and chanting "Ho Ho Ho Chi Minh" and "We are a small radical minority!"

A counterdemonstration of about 60,000 people organized by the Senate three days later illustrated the pervasive anti-Communism and the growing frustration of Berlin's citizens with the student protesters. In this heated atmosphere, student leader Rudi Dutschke was assassinated on April 11, 1968, by the twenty-three-year-old painter Josef Bachmann. Dutschke survived the initial attack but suffered from brain damage; resulting severe health problems eventually led to his untimely death in 1979. SDS blamed the Berlin senate and the Springer media as spiritual agitators of the attack and demanded the resignation of the Senate and the expropriation of Springer. The same night, students unleashed their anger at the Springer publishing house by smashing windows and overturning delivery cars and setting them on fire. The following week saw protests across the whole country. On Easter Sunday alone, 45,000 demonstrators in more than twenty cities tried to obstruct the delivery of Springer papers by blocking entrances or other actions. Two people died and more than 400 were left injured after these Easter riots.

Although encouraged by the French May, the movement suffered a harsh blow when, despite a march on Bonn with 60,000 participants in May and numerous campus actions such teach-ins, student strikes, and occupations of university buildings all over the country, the emergency laws were ratified by the German parliament on May 30, 1968. With the coalition of extra-parliamentary forces crumbling and SDS unable to counter a feeling of resignation and frustration, the unity of the organization was shattered, and the movement began to diversify in different directions, increasingly resorting to more drastic measures. In Berlin, the "Battle at the Tegeler Weg" on November 4, 1968, saw a mixed group of about 1,000 demonstrators attack policemen with cobblestones, signaling a new level of confrontation and an increasing use of violence. At Frankfurt University, the SDS occupied the sociology department on December 9, renaming it "Spartacus–Seminar" after various professors such as Theodor W. Adorno and Jürgen Habermas had refused to use their seminars for discussions on the anti-authoritarian revolt and student participation in university bodies. On December 18, the director called the police, who cleared the house.[20] From the students' perspective, this action demonstrated a fear of discussion and retreat to authoritarian methods, whereas the other side was unwilling to tolerate any attack on the autonomy and freedom of science; these two views could no longer be reconciled.

The departure from previous contents and forms of protest was already signaled when Thorward Proll, Horst Soehnlein, Gudrun Ensslin, and Andreas Baader committed an arson attack on two department stores in Frankfurt on April 3, 1968, inspired by a *Kommune I* flyer.[21] In November 1969, they were sentenced to three years in prison, whereupon Andreas Baader and Gudrun Ensslin fled to France. After Baader was arrested again following his return, Ensslin and the well-known journalist Ulrike Meinhof planned Baader's successful liberation on May 14, 1970, which marked the foundational act for the creation of the Red Army Faction and the West German terrorism of the 1970s.[22]

Forms and Tactics of Protest

Protest techniques and actions of West German activists were inspired by American examples but received their distinctiveness through their fusion with the movement's unique cognitive orientations. Debates about "direct action" and the examples of both the African American Civil Rights movement and the Free Speech Movement in Berkeley in 1964 characterized the anti-authoritarian transformation of SDS and caused a renaissance of the idea of civil disobedience.[23] The first shift into a West German context took place with a sit-in at the Free University of Berlin on June 22, 1966, when a bipartisan student coalition demanded the democratization of both university and society.[24] Subsequently, the limited but open and symbolic overstepping of conventional boundaries in the form of direct actions gradually turned into a distinctive component of West German student protest. Students held sit-ins against budget cuts at university and teach-ins about the war in Vietnam or disturbed public discussions and academic lectures by go-ins, attempting to monopolize the events for their purposes.

In contrast to their SDS peers, the protest of *Kommune I* members already lay in their exotic and colorful way of dressing, their informal communication style, and their open celebration of their sexuality. Their actions were designed as happenings undermining social conventions and belief systems. Blowing soap bubbles toward policemen or masking a demonstration as an afternoon stroll to confuse the police (December 1966) were calculated attempts not only to generate widespread media response but also to transform the public sphere and society at large through these unique Situationist provocation techniques.[25] The nature and satirical quality of their protest often brought the *Kommune I* in conflict with the ideological agenda of the Berlin SDS, which after a particularly sharp series of provocative flyers ridiculing university officials and politics in May 1967 excluded the members of the commune from its organization.

Transnational Relations

From the very beginning of the 1960s, the West German New Left had a strong transnational orientation. Already in 1961, German SDS initiated and spear-headed a New Left nucleus in the International Union of Socialist Youth (IUSY), published English newsletters, and was well-connected to other student movements and youth organizations worldwide. Because of the significant impact of the Cold War and the presence of a sizable number of foreign students in West Germany, global issues such as the problems of the Third World or the Algerian war formed an integral part of SDS's outlook. In addition, there existed close contacts to artistic avant-gardes such as the German branch of the Situationist International, the *Subversive Aktion*, or the Dutch *Provos*. As a result of transatlantic exchange programs, the association with the American movement was also particularly close, with German SDS member Michael Vester even taking part in the writing of the Port Huron Statement of the American SDS in 1962. Throughout the decade, a global *lingua franca* of protest dominated by cultural exports from the United States, thus combined with the example of Third World liberation movements to exert a significant influence on West German students, as can be seen in their inspiration by and cooperation with the Black Panther Party.[26] Beyond this, student activists also began to rediscover the works of German Marxists who had emigrated to the United States in the 1930s, of whom Herbert Marcuse, with his frequent speeches at German SDS congresses and close friendship with Rudi Dutschke, was only the most prominent and personally active inspiration.[27]

The Vietnam congress in February 1968 in West Berlin was therefore only the climax of SDS's transnational orientation, which found its ideological equivalent in the "revolutionary global strategy" put forward by Rudi Dutschke and took on an institutional form in a short-lived International News and Research Institute (INFI) in West Berlin dedicated to inform and coordinate revolutionary movements worldwide. In 1968 alone, German SDS members were present at the French May events, visited the Prague Spring and witnessed the Soviet invasion, and participated in the International Assembly of Revolutionary Student Movements at Columbia University in September 1968.[28]

Consequences, Narratives, and Politics of Memory

The events of "1968" in West Germany profoundly liberalized the cultural fabric of the Federal Republic and its society in terms of individual lifestyles and value systems but were embedded in longer historical processes of reform and democratization reaching back into the preceding decade. The signum "1968" should therefore not only comprise the actions of the New Left or student movement but also include a social departure that was experienced by all parts of West German society.[29] It was, nonetheless, the young generation that provided both the catalyst and utopian moment of this transition period. With their radical political demands and actions, they challenged social conventions, generated new forms of cultural expression and alternative spaces, and created the impression of an accelerating cultural transformation. Through dissent and new forms of protest, young activists extensively used and changed the public sphere and were inextricably intertwined with the rise of an international youth and consumer culture.[30] Although all plans for a socialist revolution faltered, politically, "1968" paved the way for the emergence of the Green Party, the enlargement of the transnational sector, and as a transcendence of the mental and geopolitical stalemate of the Cold War, a fundamentally different outlook on global issues.

In public memory, "1968" in West Germany has therefore taken on the status of a caesura in postwar history similar to the foundation of the Federal Republic in 1949 or the fall of the Berlin wall in 1989. This is not to say that "1968" has lost any of its polarizing and controversial qualities, as to date it is still partly overshadowed by the terrorist movements that succeeded it. However, "1968" as a label only emerged in the 1980s in the middle of the culture wars about how to interpret the events that shook the country in the late 1960s, when a new generation of peace activists wanted to distance themselves from their predecessors, who were about to celebrate the twentieth anniversary of their revolt. Today, as memoirs, movies, and monographs on the decade are produced in abundance, the legacy and memory of "1968" remains heavily contested among both academics and the public at large.

Bibliography

To this date, Thomas (2003) provides the first history of West German protest movements in English. For further contextualization of "1968" in West German history, see Gilcher-Holtey (1998), Schildt (2000), and Hodenberg (2006). Klimke (2007) provides an overview of various aspects of the cultural and media history of "1968," and Siegfried (2006) examines links of youth and student cultures to consumer society. The history of German SDS itself is chronicled by Lönnendonker (2002), and its connection to the Frankfurt school is examined by Kraushaar (1998). Gassert (2006) integrates the student movement in further efforts to come to terms with the National Socialist past. Herzog (2005) frames the student movement and the *Kommune I* into a larger history of sexuality in Germany, and Markovits

(1993) provides a longer narrative leading up to the foundation of the Green Party. Klimke (2008) analyzes the transnational dimensions and establishment response, whereas Schmidtke (2003) and Varon (2004) offer a comparative perspective with respect to the United States and Juchler (1996) highlights the relationship to Third World liberation movements.

Gassert, Philipp, and Alan E. Steinweis. *Coping with the Nazi Past: West German Debates on Nazism and Generational Conflict, 1955–1975.* New York: Berghahn Books, 2006.

Gilcher-Holtey, Ingrid, ed. *1968—vom Ereignis zum Gegenstand der Geschichtswissenschaft.* Göttingen: Vandenhoeck & Ruprecht, 1998.

Herzog, Dagmar. *Sex after Fascism: Memory and Morality in Twentieth–Century Germany.* Princeton, NJ: Princeton University Press, 2005.

Hodenberg, Christina von, and Detlef Siegfried. *Wo "1968" liegt: Reform und Revolte in der Geschichte der Bundesrepublik.* Göttingen: Vandenhoeck & Ruprecht, 2006.

Juchler, Ingo. *Die Studentenbewegungen in den Vereinigten Staaten und der Bundesrepublik Deutschland der sechziger Jahre: Eine Untersuchung hinsichtlich ihrer Beeinflussung durch Befreiungsbewegungen und -theorien aus der Dritten Welt.* Berlin: Duncker & Humblot, 1996.

Klimke, Martin. *The "Other" Alliance: Global Protest and Student Unrest in West Germany and the U.S., 1962–1972* Princeton, NJ: Princeton University Press, in press.

Klimke, Martin, and Joachim Scharloth. *1968: Handbuch zur Kultur– und Mediengeschichte der Studentenbewegung.* Stuttgart: J.B. Metzler, 2007.

Wolfgang Kraushaar, ed. *Frankfurter Schule und Studentenbewegung: Von der Flaschenpost bis zum Molotowcocktail.* 3 vols. Hamburg: Rogner & Bernhard, 1998.

Lönnendonker, Siegward, Bernd Rabehl, and Jochen Staadt, eds. *Die antiautoritäre Revolte. Der Sozialistische Deutsche Studentenbund nach der Trennung von der SPD.* Wiesbaden: Westdeutscher, 2002.

Markovits, Andrej S., and Philip S. Gorski. *The German Left. Red, Green and Beyond.* New York: Oxford University Press, 1993.

Schildt, Axel et al., ed. *Dynamische Zeiten. Die 60er Jahre in den beiden deutschen Gesellschaften.* Hamburg: Christians, 2000.

Schmidtke, Michael. *Der Aufbruch der jungen Intelligenz: Die 68er Jahre in der Bundesrepublik und den USA.* Frankfurt: Campus, 2003.

Siegfried, Detlef. *Time is on My Side: Konsum und Politik in der westdeutschen Jugendkultur der 60er Jahre.* Göttingen: Wallstein, 2006.

Thomas, Nick. *Protest Movements in 1960s West Germany: A Social History of Dissent and Democracy.* Oxford: Berg, 2003.

Varon, Jeremy. *Bringing the War Home: The Weather Underground, the Red Army Faction, and Revolutionary Violence in the Sixties and Seventies.* Berkeley: University of California Press, 2004.

Notes

1. See Philipp Gassert and Alan E. Steinweis, eds., *Coping with the Nazi Past: West German Debates on Nazism and Generational Conflict, 1955–1975* (New York: Berghahn, 2006).
2. For a general overview, see Konrad Jarausch, *After Hitler: Recivilizing Germans, 1945–1995.* (Oxford: Oxford University Press, 2006).
3. Wolfgang Kraushaar, ed., *Die Protest-Chronik 1949–1959: Eine illustrierte Geschichte von Bewegung, Widerstand und Utopie* (Hamburg: Rogner & Bernhard, 1996).
4. See also the chapter by Michael Frey in this volume.
5. For SDS' early phase, see Willy Albrecht, *Der Sozialistische Deutsche Studentenbund (SDS), Vom parteikonformen Studentenverband zum Repräsentanten der Neuen Linken* (Bonn: Dietz, 1994). For the impact of the Frankfurt school, see Wolfgang Kraushaar, ed., *Frankfurter Schule und Studentenbewegung: Von der Flaschenpost bis zum Molotowcocktail* (Hamburg: Rogner & Bernhard, 1998).
6. See the SDS memorandum "University in the Democracy," originally published in 1961: Wolfgang Nitsch, *Hochschule in der Demokratie* (Berlin: Luchterhand, 1965).
7. Frank Böckelmann and Horst Nagel, ed., *Subversive Aktion. Der Sinn der Organisation ist ihr Scheitern* (Frankfurt: Neue Kritik, 2002).
8. See Herbert Marcuse, *One-Dimensional Man. Studies in the Ideology of Advanced Industrial Society* (Boston: Beacon Press, 1964), 256–57.
9. See Gyèorgy Lukács, "Reification and the Consciousness of the Proletariat," in idem, *History and Class Consciousness. Studies in Marxist Dialectics* (Cambridge, MA: MIT, 1971), 83-222.
10. Hans Magnus Enzensberger, "Europäische Peripherie," *Kursbuch* 2 (1965):154–73.
11. Wilfried Mausbach, "Auschwitz and Vietnam: West German Protest Against America´s War During the 1960s," in *America, the Vietnam War, and the World: Comparative and International Perspectives*, ed. Andreas Daum, et al. (New York: Cambridge University Press, 2003), 279–98.
12. Rudi Dutschke and Hans-Jürgen Krahl, "Organisationsreferat auf der 22. Delegiertenkonferenz des SDS," in *Geschichte ist machbar*, ed. Rudi Dutschke (Berlin: Wagenbach,1980), 89–95.
13. SDS Westberlin, *Der Kampf des vietnamesischen Volkes und die Globalstrategie des Imperialismus: Internationaler Vietnam-Kongress 17./18. Februar 1968* (Berlin: SDS, 1968), 107, 117.
14. See the chapter by Dorothea Hauser in this volume.
15. Martin Klimke, *The 'Other' Alliance: Global Protest and Student Unrest in West Germany and the U.S., 1962–1972* (Princeton, NJ: Princeton University Press, in press).
16. The great number of participants was partly the result of a speech given the night before by Bahman Nirumand, an Iranian in exile and massive critic of the Iranian leader. See Bahman Nirumand, *Persien. Modell eines Entwicklungslandes oder Die Diktatur der Freien Welt* (Hamburg: Reinbek, 1967).
17. Knut Nevermann, ed., *Der 2. Juni 1967: Studenten zwischen Notstand und Demokratie. Dokumente zu den Ereignissen anlässlich des Schah-Besuchs* (Köln: Pahl-Rugenstein, 1967).

18. Habermas apologized for the term soon afterwards. See Bernward Vesper, ed., *Bedingungen und Organisation des Widerstandes. Der Kongreß in Hannover* (Frankfurt: Edition Voltaire, 1967), 42–48, 78–82 ff.

19. SDS Westberlin and INFI, ed., *Der Kampf des vietnamesischen Volkes und die Globalstrategie des Imperialismus* (Berlin: Internationales Nachrichten-und Forschungs-Institut, 1968).

20. For a detailed view, see Kraushaar, *Frankfurter Schule und Studentenbewegung*, vol. 2, 502 f., 512–527.

21. Wilfried Mausbach, "'Burn, ware-house, burn!' Modernity, Counterculture, and the Vietnam War in West Germany," in *Between Marx and Coca-Cola: Youth Cultures in Changing European Societies, 1960–1980*, ed. Axel Schildt and Detlef Siegfried (New York: Berghahn Books, 2006), 175–202.

22. See the chapter by Dorothea Hauser in this volume.

23. See Michael Vester, "Die Strategie der direkten Aktion," in *neue kritik* 1965;30:12–20; Martin Klimke, "Sit-In, Teach-In, Go-In: Die transnationale Zirkulation kultureller Praktiken in den 1960er Jahren," in *1968. Ein Handbuch zur Kultur- und Mediengeschichte*, eds. Martin Klimke and Joachim Scharloth (Stuttgart: Metzler, 2007), 119–135.

24. Siegward Lönnendonker and Tilman Fichter, ed., *Hochschule im Umbruch, Teil IV: Die Krise. 1964–1967* (Berlin: FU Berlin, 1975), 333 f.

25. For participants' perspective, see Ulrich Enzensberger, *Die Jahre der Kommune 1. Berlin 1967–1969* (Muenchen: Goldmann, 2006). For historical contextualization, see Alexander Holmig, "Die aktionistischen Wurzeln der Studentenbewegung: Subversive Aktion, Kommune I und die Neudefinition des Politischen," in *Handbuch zur Kultur- und Mediengeschichte*, eds. Klimke/Scharloth, 107–18.

26. For the role of American examples see Martin Klimke, The 'Other' Alliance; idem, "Black Panther, die RAF und die Rolle der Black Panther-Solidaritätskomitees," in *Die RAF und die Reformzeit der Demokratie*, ed. Wolfgang Kraushaar (Hamburg: Hamburger Edition, 2006), 562–582.

27. Claus-Dieter Krohn, "Die Entdeckung des 'anderen Deutschland' in der intellektuellen Protestbewegung der 1960er Jahre in der Bundesrepublik und den Vereinigten Staaten," *Kulturtransfer im Exil* 13 (1995): 16–51; Peter-Erwin Jansen, ed., *Herbert Marcuse: Die Studentenbewegung und ihre Folgen, Nachgelassene Schriften, Bd.4* (Springe: Zu Klampen, 2004).

28. See, for example, Sibylle Plogstedt, *Im Netz der Gedichte. Gefangen in Prag nach 1968* (Berlin: Chr. Links, 2001).

29. For contextualization, see Christina von Hodenberg and Detlef Siegfried, eds., *Wo "1968" liegt: Reform und Revolte in der Geschichte der Bundesrepublik* (Göttingen: Vandenhoeck & Ruprecht, 2006).

30. Detlef Siegfried, *Time is on My Side: Konsum und Politik in der westdeutschen Jugendkultur der 60er Jahre* (Göttingen: Wallstein, 2006).

9
France

Ingrid Gilcher-Holtey

Social and Political Framework of the Country

The May movement in France did not start until international developments had reached their peak. Within a few weeks, however, it caught up with other movements in terms of mobilization and then surpassed the German and American protest movements in its political explosiveness. What began as a revolt by a small minority of students in the Parisian suburb of Nanterre quickly developed into a general strike that paralyzed the entire country. It also caused a political crisis that threatened to topple the Gaullist System. How could this happen?

The protests were not a reaction to an economic or political crisis. The mobilization of the student movement in France happened spontaneously as the result of an essentially self-generating process of action. Indeed, the French student movement emerged against the background of a general crisis in the university system that directly affected the learning environment, career outlook, and life prospects of the students. However, the student movement was more than simply a reaction to these deficiencies. Since the mid-1960s, the student union, *Union Nationale des étudiants de France* (UNEF), had been criticizing the structural weaknesses of the university and of government reform plans without receiving much support from the students. The student strike that UNEF helped to organize in Nanterre at the beginning of the 1967–1968 academic year faded after a few weeks. The mobilization process that led to the May movement in France was not triggered until small core groups of students began undertaking limited unconventional actions in the spring of 1968 and noticeably upsetting university operations by breaking rules, violating taboos, and committing other provocations.

Organizational and Social Structure

The student groups that initiated the protest, the Enragés and the Movement of March 22, perceived themselves as anti-dogmatic, anti-bureaucratic, anti-organizational, and anti-authoritarian. For both groups, the university represented only a forum for action and the starting point for a comprehensive, socio-cultural transformation process; the Enragés[1] aimed to abolish the university, whereas the protagonists of the Movement of March 22[2] strove instead to transform it into a "critical university." The Movement of March 22 was an alliance that emerged out of and was geared toward action. It emanated from the occupation of the administrative building of the University of Nanterre on March 22, 1968, and it comprised Trotskyites, Maoists, and Anarchists, who elsewhere acted separately or even against each other. Their highest maxim was that the revolutionary combat unit arose directly out of action and was not a result of a certain policy or ideology. This maxim was aimed against the sectarian mentality that had disrupted the left-liberal groups and made them incapable of forming alliances, thereby robbing them of almost any political influence. The negation of action along a political line or ideology was a result of the rejection of the Leninist organizational and action strategy and its replacement by a new strategy, organizational concept, and theoretical program. The theory of a proactive minority constantly played the role of ferment and called for action without claiming leadership.[3]

Their success in mobilizing large numbers of students was initially limited to the Nanterre campus. It might easily have subsided in the manner of the UNEF strike had the student protest not spilled over to the Sorbonne, which was responsible for disciplinary actions against eight students from Nanterre. Repressive measures were used against the small core of student activists at the Sorbonne, including the use of massive police force in the inner courtyard. These events caused the previously inactive student majority to demonstrate its solidarity with the active student minority. In a matter of days, the mobilization accelerated in alternating student actions and government repression into a series of violent clashes between demonstrators and police around the Sorbonne and in the streets of the Latin Quarter. The events' dynamics brought more and more high school students, youths, and a few young workers onto the university students' side. From May 3 to 10, merely a week after the beginning of the conflict, France caught up with the developments in other Western nations. Within another twenty-four hours, the French student movement surpassed the other movements. A large part of the organized working class showed solidarity with the students. Within a few days, an estimated 7.5 to 9 million workers went on strike without a call from union headquarters. The workers' mobilization process followed the same spontaneous action strategy as the student movement. The parallel movements were united by common values and practices.

Cognitive Orientation

The protest movements of 1968 saw themselves as movements of the New Left and were preceded by the formation of an intellectual *Nouvelle Gauche* in France, the New Left in Great Britain and the United States, and the *Neue Linke* in Germany. Intellectual dissidents from traditional leftist parties were their founding members. By the late 1950s and early 1960s, this intellectual New Left emerged internationally in publications, discussion circles, journals, and actions. French developments best exemplify the systematic evolution of the new cognitive orientation, or cognitive praxis, of the New Left. The intellectual New Left in France constituted itself around the journals *Socialisme ou Barbarie* (1949–1966), *Arguments* (1956–1962), and *International Situationniste* (1958–1969). The cognitive orientation with which the free-floating intellectuals of the New Left confronted the traditional Left consisted of the following five elements.[4]

First, the new orientation centered on a reinterpretation of Marxist theory. Referring to the early writings of Marx, the New Left accentuated the aspect of alienation rather than exploitation. It attempted to open the theoretical interpretation by combining Marxism with existentialism and psychoanalysis to free the former from its sclerotic paralysis and identification with institutionalized Marxism. Second, the New Left envisioned a new model of socialist society that would not be restricted to political and social revolution, seizure of power, and nationalization of means of production. Rather, it would eliminate the alienation felt by the individual human being in everyday life. Third, partisans of the New Left embraced a new transformation strategy. They believed the individual should be freed from subordination to the collective. The premise was that changes in the cultural sphere must precede social and political transformation. New lifestyles and modes of communication had to be developed along with an anticipatory, experimental basis by creating new cultural ideals, applying them in subcultures, and testing them as alternatives within existing institutions. Fourth, the new cognitive orientation required a new organizational concept. The maxim was action, not organization. The New Left understood itself as a movement, not a party. As a movement, it used the full spectrum of direct action strategies, from the demonstrative-appellative to the direct-coercive action. It sought to generate awareness through action and agitate the public by provocation while simultaneously using action to change those participating in it. Finally, the New Left also called for redefinition of the leaders of social change. The proletariat was no longer seen as the leader of social and cultural change; instead, the New Left believed that the impetus for social transformation came from other groups such as the new (skilled) working class, young intelligentsia, and social fringe groups.

The interrelationship of individual and collective emancipation, social and cultural criticism, and cultural and social revolution inherent in New Left thought gave rise to internal tension in the movement of 1968. It also explains the plethora of categories with which researchers label the movement: As expression of a generational conflict, as Neo-Marxist and anti-bureaucratic, or as a movement of cultural revolution or sexual emancipation. Its overarching social utopia combined these diverse threads and places the movement in the tradition of social utopias, such as those espoused by Saint-Simon, Fourier, Proudhon, Marx, and Bakunin. However, its utopian content was not limited to the expectation of a collective emancipation of labor from outside control. It articulated themes and individualistic values that we now call post-materialistic and represented a transition between old and new social movements.

Attitudes toward Superpowers and the Cold War

The separation of the New Left from the Old Left resulted in part from contemporary occurrences, such as the events in Prague in 1948, the Twentieth Party Congress of the Communist Party of the Soviet Union, the suppression of the Hungarian Uprising, the Cold War, and the lack of public debate about nuclear arms in the East and West. However, this separation also had systemic causes that unfolded during a critical debate about the development of socialism and communism since the 1920s. The New Left was convinced that the self-imposed restriction of democratic socialism to a welfare-state model, as well as the perversion of communism under Stalin, had undermined the emancipatory content of the socialist and communist movement. This loss of the utopian perspective resulted in an incapacity of traditional left-wing parties to offer a real alternative to the status quo. They appeared to be imprisoned by *realpolitik*, unable to overcome the current political and social situation and unwilling to address present problems or to mould the future. They stagnated materially, as measured by their numerical strength, and philosophically, as measured by their capacity to solve problems.

With their anti-capitalist, anti-Communist orientation, the intellectual and student New Left in France emphasized their distance from both the United States and the Soviet Union. The quarrel with the Soviet Union was voiced through criticism of the Communist Party of France (PCF), from whose student association *Union des étudiants Communistes* (UEC) the New

Left's left-radical supporter groups had separated in the early 1960s.[5] Criticism of the United States was expressed in protests against the Vietnam War organized by the *Trotskyite Comités Vietnam Nationaux* (CVN) and the *Maoist Comités Viétnam de Base* (CVB), and in commitment to Third World liberation movements. The latter found a forum in two groups around the publisher François Maspero through the magazine *Partisans* and the readers' club *La joie de lire*.[6] Although the Algerian War sharpened attention for Third World problems, the 1961 Bay of Pigs invasion became the decisive event that ignited their willingness to actively support the attacked party.

In 1966 the young French philosopher Régis Debray, a member of both of these groups around Maspero, departed for Cuba with the intention of supporting Castro's socialist experiment and foreign policy project—the foundation of the *Organización Latinoamericana de Solidaridad* (OLAS). This organization was intended to coordinate and reorient the fight of the liberation movements of Latin America. Debray became the writer and theorist of Castro's strategy of the Latin American armed fight, which was opposed to Moscow-oriented guidelines that claimed the supremacy of the party against the guerilla and tried to block guerilla warfare. Debray's *Revolution dans la révolution*[7] became worldwide canon of the 1968 movement and decisively helped convey the Cuban approach toward Latin American social problems and diffuse the guerilla strategy of Ernesto Che Guevara. The Cuban Model was considered as the Third Way to socialism until 1968; the French Movement of March 22 derived its name from Castro's Movement of June 26.

Key Events

Student protest was conveyed to the workers by means of a "critical event"[8]—the Night of Barricades—which synchronized the perception of different social groups. During the night of May 10–11, students and youths occupied an enclave in the Latin Quarter after a peaceful demonstration. In a spontaneous and playful manner, they built barricades within the occupied area. They were determined to leave this area only after the government had met their demands, which included release of students arrested during a protest march, reopening the Sorbonne—which had been closed by order of the university president and was being guarded by police—and the withdrawal of police from the Latin Quarter. The barricading of Paris during the night of May 10–11 was a historic allusion to the barricades of the Paris Commune in 1871 and the liberation of Paris from German occupation in 1944. Erected by high school and university students, the barricades evoked memories of those earlier examples without merely imitating them; they were expressive rather than instrumental in nature. Only later in the course of this provocative action and subsequent police deployment was the student protest politicized by media response, public reaction, and the steps taken by the government and labor unions.

The students' activism attracted mass media attention. The effect of the movement on the outside world grew as a result of broadcasts from two radio transmitter vans driven into the occupied area immediately after the first barricades were erected. This spread the news not merely outside the Latin Quarter but beyond the limits of the capital itself. The media reports created an audience that attentively registered events and formed its own opinion of them. Thus, the flames of student protest jumped from Paris to the provinces.

The government was faced with a loss of reputation regardless of whether authorities reacted in a lenient or repressive manner; observers eagerly awaited a reaction. Finding itself under increasing pressure to act, the government lacked a convincing plan of action and decision-making capabilities. In the prime minister's absence, the cabinet ministers had difficulties coordinating their actions, and after mediation attempts failed, the ministers resorted to an interpretation of the situation that was strongly influenced by the president's opinion. They saw demonstrating students as rebels and the demonstration for the three demands as an *emeute* (riot). After much hesitation, the Minister of the Interior had the barricades removed by police and security forces in the early morning hours of May 11. Police brutality led to vociferous and immediate public protest. A "critical event" had occurred.

The Night of Barricades was neither determined by socio-structural factors nor planned by the groups or individuals involved. Rather, it was a result of uncoordinated decisions by the government, situational decisions by individual groups within the movement, and repressive police behavior. In other words, it resulted from contingencies and created an entirely new situation. This critical event disturbed the routine of everyday life and formal, unquestioned order. It synchronized the perception of different social groups and transformed a moment into a public event that was identical for everyone and measured by the same points of reference. It led the French labor unions to enter into solidarity with the student movement in its demands. To protest repression and emphasize student demands, the labor unions called for rallies and a 24-hour general strike.

The situation changed, however, after a second political intervention. Returning from Afghanistan on the evening of May 11, Prime Minister Pompidou granted all the students' demands in a television address just fourteen hours after the brutal clearing of the Latin Quarter. The prime minister's decision contributed greatly to the transformation of the critical event into Bourdieu's "critical moment." "If the government submitted to the students, why shouldn't it submit to us?" the workers argued.[9] A situation was created wherein anything seemed to be possible. The horizon of possibilities also expanded for other groups, and new forms of action increased their willingness to act.

Forms and Tactics of the Protest

The cognitive orientation of the New Left served as the integrative element of the socially heterogeneous movements. Again, the movement began with a single action by a small, proactive minority. On May 14, after the 24-hour general strike organized by the unions in solidarity with the students and in protest against police repression, young workers in an airplane factory near Nantes refused to go back to work. Instead, they occupied the factory workshops, sealed off the plant, and took the plant manager into custody. The occupation of a provincial factory, barely noticed at first by actors in the capital, triggered a chain reaction in the following days. The spontaneous strike spilled over to the Renault car factories, and from there to other plants. Within just a few days, about 7.5 to 9 million workers were on strike without a call from union headquarters. What was their motivation?

There was no economic crisis on the eve of the May events. There were conflicts over distribution of wealth and a rising unemployment rate, but the French economy had suffered far less from the recession of 1966 than had Germany's, and it was therefore less subject to economic fluctuation and breakdown. The protest can therefore not be imputed solely to socioeconomic causes. Rather, it was the result of an increasing discontent with authoritarian structures in industry. In May 1968, this latent dissatisfaction turned into collective willingness to act and an attitude of protest that could not be controlled, even by union leaders.

The workers in state-owned industries triggered the strike movement. Among them, the young workers were the driving force and activated the rest of the workers. Their goal was to force the *état patron* to submit by means of direct action. The direct action unleashed a dynamic force for mobilization. It was based on traditions within the labor movement and caused a collective willingness to act without directing it toward a specific goal. For example, the occupation of factories could be viewed as a means of exerting pressure on the government and industry to force them to negotiate or make concessions, a way to demonstrate the independence of the local rank and file from the Old Left labor union apparatus, or the beginning of a comprehensive transformation in the structure of industry, business, and economy based on either the anarcho-syndicalist strategy or the concepts of the New Left. It all depended on the actors' intentions. The goals of the workers' strike movement evolved as a result of the process of societal interaction, as had the goals of the student movement.

The strike committees' initial demands were not fundamentally different from union requests made before May 68; however, a social movement is more than its printed words. The orientation of the non-Communist French workers union, *Confédération française et démocratique du travail* (CFDT), was closest to that of the New Left, and they created a new term expressing the workers' expectations: *autogestion* (self–administration). Just two days after the first spontaneous strike, the slogan added a new dimension to the movement. With its demand for *autogestion*, the CFDT was calling for reforms in the management and decision-making structures of business and industry, reduction of hierarchies and concentration of power, and opportunities for workers to release their creative potential through self-determination and self-administration. Although the institutional and legal details of how *autogestion* would be implemented remained unclear, the anti-hierarchical and anti-authoritarian component was sufficient to unite the student and worker movements in their goals. The democratization of the universities was to be followed by the democratization of industry: *"A la monarchie industrielle et administrative, il faut substituer des structures démocratiques à base d'autogestion"* (The industrial and administrative monarchy must be replaced with democratic structures based on self-administration). Worker and student movements formed a community united by common endeavors, hopes, and expectations.[10]

The Old Left used its organizational power to crush New Left action strategies and goals. The conflict was channeled into institutionalized mechanisms of the collective bargaining system. The Communist-oriented General Workers Union, or *Confederation generale du travail* (CGT), did not support *autogestion* as a goal of fundamental social change. It dismissed the concept of *autogestion* as a hollow formula that was primarily oriented toward changing power and decision-making structures rather than the distribution of wealth. The CGT fought the alliance formed between the student and worker movements. Wherever possible, it tried to prevent direct contact between students and workers at the plants and vehemently distanced itself from the figurehead of the student movement, Daniel Cohn–Bendit. Furthermore, it did everything within its organizational power to transfer this social movement, which had paralyzed economic life and had the potential of triggering a revolutionary situation, into the well-established system of collective bargaining. It was the driving force behind a hasty collective bargaining agreement with representatives of government and industry the Grenelle agreements of May 27, which offered wage settlements and represented the first time that French business officially recognized the labor unions' right to engage in activities on plant territory, the right of union members to assemble, the right to post union announcements on plant bulletin boards, and the right to distribute union newspapers. For the time being, however, the CGT was unable to enforce its strategy and goals effectively at the grassroots level. The general assemblies of workers in the plants protested against the wage settlements. Work did not resume.

The strike at the universities also continued, and the Sorbonne remained occupied. In the big auditorium, the Amphitheatre, endless debates dragged on. The walls of the Parisian Odéon theater, which was also occupied by students, read: "L'avenir est à prendre, car l'avenir est perdu par un gouvernement viellard. Inventer—c'est prendre le pouvoir de demain." (The future is at our disposal, because it has been lost by an aged government. To invent means to take the power of tomorrow into one's own hands.)

Thousands came daily to watch the process of the creation of a new world and to take part in it. The debates in the packed theater, whose balconies would almost bend under the influx of the masses, unleashed the spontaneous collective latent discomfort and reflected long-suppressed hopes, wishes, and desires. Creative excitement characterized the atmosphere. The theater offered a stage for the permanent self-production of the audience. Did the imagination come to power? "In May 68," the philosopher Michel de Certeau wrote, "people took hold of the word as if they took hold of the Bastille again." [11] What counted was not the spoken word but the word's capture as a symbol of the cultural revolution that was on the verge of being unveiled with this movement: the revolution of perception.

Most strikers in the plants supported a political solution to the social crisis. They considered their opponent to be not the *pouvoir patronat* but the Gaullist regime itself. They demanded a change in political power as a prerequisite for social structure reforms. This meant a shift in the movement's goal orientation and means of conflict resolution. After the failure of the Grenelle agreements, they retreated from the stage, and political parties took their place. The social movement entered a new arena, where, because of its spontaneous and anti-party character, it did not enjoy a firm structural foundation, and for which its core groups were conceptually unprepared. The non-Communist New Left was unsuccessful in its attempt to use the situation to define its own political standpoint. The Old Left used its organizational power to crush the action strategies and goal orientation of the New Left. By deciding to hold new parliamentary elections, the government reestablished a strategy of action based on the institutions of the Fifth Republic.

Transnational Relations

Before, during, and after May 1968, a boundary-transgressing diffusion of ideas and slogans, types of actions, and strategies had taken place between the French 1968 movement and other 1968 movements. This phenomenon enabled a connection of student support groups in Berkeley, Berlin, Paris, London, and Turin. This is true not only for synchronization of perception of the Vietnam War and coordination of protest activities against this war but also for types of action within the framework of criticism of the university system and working conditions in the plants. If one differentiates two types of international diffusion of "ideas" and "tactics" of social movements—direct relational ties and non-relational channels—one can state that processes of exchange took place through direct personal contacts and networks, as well as through indirect channels such as the media.[12] For example, Alain Krivine and Daniel Bensaïd, members of the Trotskyite group *Jeunesse Communiste Révolutionnaire* (JCE), brought the principle of "limited rule violation" to Paris as *stratégie escalade-provocation*. They became acquainted with this particular principle during a demonstration at the International Vietnam Congress in Berlin and did not realize that Rudi Dutschke, the figurehead of the German student movement, had borrowed it from the Situationists around Guy Debord. Another example is the German author Hans Magnus Enzensberger, who adopted the magical formula of *autogestion* and demanded the creation of "French conditions" in the Federal Republic of Germany.[13] *Autogestion* became a keyword that transgressed inner European boundaries and promised to link the dual emancipation strategy of the New Left: the demand for self-determination and self-administration through the transformation of steering and deciding mechanisms on the one hand, and self-experiencing and self-realization through the testing of new types of communication in all fields of society and emancipation of the individual from subordination to the collective on the other.

Consequences, Narratives, and Politics of Memory

The stability of the institutional system steered New Left impulses toward subculture experimentation with new lifestyles and cultural forms that dealt with institutional problems by withdrawing from them. Being both individualistic and socialistic, the New Left rebelled against alienation in the realm of production and everyday life. In the struggle against alienation they broke taboos, norms, and traditional values. They violated rules to provoke and to delegitimize institutions of authority. Most activists felt a subjective emancipation in violating rules and disregarding established structures of organization and power. They perceived their experiences as progress toward individual self-determination and self-actualization. Subcultures developed that preserved the atmosphere of awakening present in New Left origins, but the political program gave way increasingly to a cult of individual affliction. Thus, the awakening of 1968 ended for many people as the shaping of alternative lifestyles and individualization of life's opportunities and risks, but also as political retreat into the private realm.

Individual emancipation based on eliminating alienation in everyday life and personal relationships was inherent in New Left strategy. However, its concept of transformation did not end with individual self-actualization but included political and social emancipation through collective self-determination and self-administration. The essential goal was to escape from the *"stahlharten Gehäuse der Hörigkeit"* (iron cage of bondage)[14] that blocked individual actions by means of the power wielded over human beings by the need for consumer goods and the dependence on hierarchically organized bureaucracies that govern all aspects of an individual's life in modern society. It was a program that questioned not only the secular tendencies of the drive for efficiency in Western capitalist society but also the modern way of life and the political, economic, social, and cultural structures that produced it.

May 1968 in France has undergone diverse interpretations. The first analyses were offered by sociologists; according to their different approaches, their theses about May 1968 and their constructions of the social phenomenon behind it varied greatly. So the events were interpreted as "a new social conflict" (Touraine), as "generational conflict" (Morin), as "general crisis of institutions" (Crozier), or as a "critical moment" (Bourdieu) in the societal development of France. The overall evaluation showed the same variety as the construction of the phenomenon. The events were classified as "revolt" (Touraine), "quasi-revolution" (Morin), "breach of culture" (Crozier), "carnival" (Aron), and "crisis of the mode of reproduction," which developed into a "general crisis" (Bourdieu). As in other countries, the recollection of May 1968 in France was dominated by the autobiographies, monographs, essays and interviews, novels, and movies of the protagonists, which were published decades after the events took place.

Two narratives can be differentiated: modern and postmodern. Both try to integrate May 1968 into the history of postwar France and to determine the effects of the events. Perceiving the French May as "cradle of a new bourgeois society," Régis Debray claimed that these events have opened France "to the American way of life and to American-style consumption habits." Ten years after the events, Gilles Lipovetsky attributed to May 1968 the acceleration of "the arrival of contemporary narcissistic individualism" and stated that the movement was a central element in the rise of postmodernism. Both were convinced that the effects of the events were not intended by the protagonists but could be considered the result of a "ruse of history."[15] In 1987–1988, Hervé Hamon and Patrick Rotman attempted to influence the struggle about collective memory of May 1968. To the central representatives of the New Left's supporting groups, they offered the chance to publish their retrospective opinions about activities in May 1968. According to literary scientist Kristin Ross, the successful television and book project of Hamon and Rotman was able to fuel the myth of the "generation" as the mainstay of the May movement by emphasizing the generational aspect, whereas the central role of the working class was almost completely left aside. The most refined analysis of the effects of May 1968 has been published by Luc Boltanski and ève Chiapello (2003), who argue that the criticism of hierarchical structures and demand for self-administration and self-responsibility that were voiced by avant-garde groups of the 1960s had been taken up by employers in the 1970s. However, the authors opine that granting a higher degree of autonomy in the plants and offices weakened the collective protection system of the workers (unions, collective bargaining, regulations, contracts). It thereby led to precariousness and individualization of the labor conditions.

Bibliography

The first analyses and evaluations were carried out by sociologists: Morin/ Lefoirt/Castoriadis (1968), Touraine (1969), Lacroix (1981), and Bourdieu (1984). Historical accounts focus on May 1968 in an international context, such as Dreyfus-Armand/Gervereau (1988); the depiction of the cognitive constitution, formation, mobilization, and demobilization of the 1968 movement by Gilcher-Holtey (1994/2001); the position of the protest movement within the context of political reforms and the processes of modernization of the 1960s by Dreyfus-Armand/Frank, Levy, Zancarini (2000); and the concept of *autogestion* by Georgi (2003). Regarding the longtime effects and the representation of May 1968 in public memory, see Boltanski/ Chiapello (2003) and Ross (2002).

Boltanski, Luc and Eve Chiapello. *Le nouvel Esprit du Capitalisme*. Paris: Gallimard, 1999.
Bourdieu, Pierre. *Homo academicus*. Paris: Seuil, 1984.
Dreyfus–Armand, Geneviève and Laurent Gervereau, eds. *Mai 68: Les mouvements en France et dans le monde*. Nanterre: BDIC, 1988.
Dreyfus–Armand, Geneviève and Robert Frank et al., eds. *Les Années 68: Le temps de la contestation*. Brussels: Complexe, 2000.
Georgi, Frank, ed. *Autogestion: La dernière utopia*. Paris: Editions de l'Atelier: 2003.
Gilcher–Holtey, Ingrid. *'Die Phantasie an die Macht'. Mai 68 in Frankreich*, 2nd ed. Frankfurt: Suhrkamp, 2001.
Hamon, Hervé and Patrick Rotman, eds. *Génération, vol. 1: Les années de rêve, vol. 2: Les années de poudre*. Paris: Seuil: 1987–1988.

Lacroix, Bernard. *L'utopie communautaire. Mai 68. Histore sociale d'une révolte*, 2nd ed. Paris: PUF, 2006.

Morin, Edgar and Claude Lefort et al. *La brèche: Première réfléxions sur les événements*. Paris: Fayard, 1968.

Ross, Kristin. *May '68 and its Afterlives*. Chicago: University of Chicago Press, 2002.

Touraine, Alain. *Le Communisme utopique: Le mouvement de mai*. Paris: Seuil, 1968.

Notes

1. For a history of "The Enraged," see René Viénet, *Enragés et situationnistes dans le mouvement des occupations* (Paris: Gallimard, 1968).

2. For a history of the Movement of March 22, see Jean-Pierre Duteuil, *Nanterre 1965–66–67–68. Vers le mouvement du 22 mars* (Mauléon: Acratie, 1988); or Daniel Cohn-Bendit and Gabriel Cohn-Bendit, *Linksradikalismus: Gewaltkur gegen die Alterskrankheit des Kommunismus* (Hamburg: Rowohlt, 1968).

3. Sic Daniel Cohn-Bendit in a dialogue with Jean-Paul Sartre, published in Jacques Sauvageot, Alain Geismar, and Daniel Cohn-Bendit, *Aufstand in Paris oder Ist in Frankreich eine Revolution möglich?* (Reinbek: Rowohlt, 1968), 77.

4. Compare regarding formation and cognitive orientation of the New Left Ingrid Gilcher-Holtey, *'Die Phantasie an die Macht'. Mai 68 in Frankreich*, 2nd ed. (Frankfurt: Suhrkamp, 2001), 44–104; idem, *Die 68er Bewegung. Deutschland, Westeuropa, USA*, 3rd ed. (München: Beck, 2007), 11–24.

5. See Richard Gombin, *Les origienes du gauchisme* (Paris: Seuil, 1971).

6. François Maspero, *Les Arbeilles et la Guêpe* (Paris: Seuil, 2003).

7. Régis Debray, *Révolutions dans la révolution*, (Paris: Maspero, 1967).

8. According to Bourdieu, a critical event synchronizes perceptions of heterogeneous protagonists, causes a breach with everyday routines, forces people to comment the event, and evokes and projects expectations and claims. Comp. regarding the terms "critical events" and "critical moment" Pierre Bourdieu, *Homo academicus* (Paris: Seuil, 1984); Ingrid Gilcher-Holtey, "La nuit des barricades," in *La Nuit. Société & Représentations*, vol. 4, ed. Véronique Nahoum-Grappe and Myriam Tsikounas (Paris: CREDHESS, 1997), 165–84.

9. Quoted according to Philippe Gavi, "Des ouvriers parlent," *Les Temps Modernes* (Paris: Gallimard, 1968), 82–83.

10. See *Albert Detraz et les militants de la CFDT, Positions et actions de la CFDT en mai 1968*, Syndicalisme, Numéro spécial 1969, 53 ff.

11. Michel de Certeau, *La prise de parole: Pour une nouvelle culture* (Paris: Desclée de Brouwer, 1968), 16.

12. Comp. Doug McAdam and Dieter Rucht, "The Cross National Diffusion of Movements Ideas," in *Annals of the American Academy of Political and Social Sciences* 528, (Thousand Oaks: Sage, 1993), 56–59.

13. Comp. Grass, Günter (1968c), *Französische Zustände*, Grass-Archiv (Archiv der Akademie der Künste: Berlin), 1594.

14. Max Weber, "Parlament und Regierung im neugeordneten Deutschland," in *Gesammelte politische Schriften*, ed. Johannes Winkelmann (Tübingen: J.C.B. Mohr, 1971), 331–332.
15. Régis Debray, *Modest contribution aux discours et cérémonies officiels du dixème anniversaire* (Paris: Maspero, 1978); Gilles Lipovetsky, *L'ère du vide. Essais sur l'individualisme contemporaine* (Paris: Gallimard, 1983).

10
Great Britain

Holger Nehring

As in other countries, "1968" in Great Britain was more than simply a historical date. It has served as a cipher for a variety of protest movements, protest events, and processes of sociocultural change, mainly in the period from around 1965 to the early 1970s. Yet, in Britain, the year has not obtained quite the iconic status of the long 1960s in other countries around the world. Because of the diversity of issues discussed at the time and the lack of overarching reference points, such as the Nazi past in Germany or the legacy of fascism in Italy, historical time in Britain never appeared as synchronized as it was in the experiences of "1968" elsewhere. Historians of "1968" in Britain would be well advised to analyze these phenomena as processes of societal communication and self-observation in a highly complex, differentiated society, in which mass media played a key role.

Social and Political Framework of the Country

British activists encountered a social and political framework similar to that of other Western nations. The 1960s were years of growing affluence, especially among younger people, after a period of austerity in the immediate postwar years.[1] The 1960s in Britain also saw the spread of mass consumption to embrace young people. This coincided with the development of a network of youth and activist subcultures, particularly in London, Manchester, and other major cities.[2] Secondary and higher education was significantly expanded, and new universities were built, including the University of Warwick in Coventry and the University of Exeter. Whereas there had been 82,000 students in 1954–1955 and 118,000 in 1962–1963, this number had almost doubled to 235,000 by 1970–1971.

Unlike elsewhere, however, protesters remained connected to mainstream politics in Britain's two-party system, in which the Labour Party and the Conservatives competed for power. The British Communist Party (CPGB) remained an important reference point of far-left politics, though its membership remained rather small.[3] Outside Parliament, loose networks of New Left activists and anarchists continued to attract some support, especially on the local level.[4]

Labour Prime Minister Harold Wilson (1964–1970) sought to integrate dissenting voters on the political left through radical political language, but he followed a pragmatic approach in everyday politics.[5] Wilson's government became known for its reformist drive, its scientific approach toward governance, and the modernization of social and economic planning, thus centralizing political and governmental power even further around the civil service and special advisory committees in London. The issues of decolonization and immigration continued to play an important role in British domestic politics. Although Wilson campaigned on a platform of dramatic foreign policy changes, his government maintained British nuclear weapons capabilities and continued to support American involvement in Vietnam.

Organizational and Social Structure of the Protest Movement

It was within this political and social context that movement organizations developed. They were frequently embedded in local cultures of radicalism. Only a few of these organizations knew formal membership, and support for these various groups often overlapped. The first organizational networks emerged around the issue of nuclear weapons and British security policy. The Campaign for Nuclear Disarmament (CND) and pacifist networks played an important role, both in London and beyond.[6] From 1965 onward, the Vietnam War became the most salient issue of extra-parliamentary politics. The British Council for Peace in Vietnam (BCPV) was founded in May 1965 to campaign for a rapid end to the war. Yet the pacifist BCPV was soon overtaken in size and importance by the more radical Vietnam Solidarity Campaign (VSC), founded in June 1966.

A second set of organizations comprised anarchist, other far-left networks and, most importantly, the New Left. The groups had a focus in London, but were equally strong in regional cities and towns with strong radical traditions. The British New Left had two distinct roots. One lay in the dissident Communist movement in northern England, centered on the historians Edward P. Thompson and John Saville. Thompson and Saville had been expelled from the British Communist Party (CPGB) in 1956 after their vocal criticism of its Stalinist heritage in the wake of Soviet leader Nikita

Khrushchev's speech at the Twentieth Party Congress of the Soviet Communist Party in spring 1956 and of the Soviet invasion of Hungary in autumn 1956.

The British New Left's second root lay in the more metropolitan movement around the journal *Universities and Left Review* (ULR). It primarily appealed to students at the universities of Oxford and London, who sought to develop an ideological alternative to both classical political Marxism and reformist approaches within the Labor Party. Both groups converged in their concern for the renewal of socialism in an affluent age, their emphasis on authenticity and individuality, and their rejection of bureaucratic rule; they merged their publishing activities in the *New Left Review* after 1960.[7]

Other movement organizations that represented specific strands of broadly socialist ideas emerged from the mid-1960s onward. This led to the organizational fracture of the broad New Left movement. Perhaps the most prominent of these groups in the first half of the 1960s was the Vietnam Solidarity Campaign, founded by Pakistani Trotskyist Tariq Ali, who had come to Oxford as a student in the early 1960s. Other far-left organizations such as International Socialism (IS) and the International Marxist Group (IMG) had some influence through their publications, such as the IMG's *Red Mole*, but their official membership hovered between 450 and 500 members (IS) and a mere forty members (IMG) in 1968.[8] The Revolutionary Socialist Students' Federation (RSSF) was particularly influential at the London School of Economics (LSE), where its supporters campaigned for the revolutionary overthrow of capitalism and imperialism. More important than the movement organizations were the journals they produced, such as the countercultural *IT* (*International Times*, launched in October 1966), the Trotskyite *Black Dwarf* (founded in March 1968 and edited by Ali), and the *New Left Review*.[9] From the mid-1960s, groups concerned with student-related issues gradually emerged at some universities, although they never formed one national student movement because many in the National Union of Students (NUS) rejected radical political engagement.

Toward the end of the 1960s Britain saw the rise of organizations that addressed issues of black immigrants from an anti-racist viewpoint. One important example is the Campaign Against Racial Discrimination (CARD), founded in 1964. Increasingly, however, this took the form of championing essentialist views of ethnic identity, namely in the Racial Adjustment Action Society (RAAS) under Michael de Freitas, also known as Michael Abdul Malik or Michael X. The Universal Coloured People's Association (UCPA) was established after Stokely Carmichael's visit to Britain in 1967.[10] In both their self-perception and contemporary interpretations, these black power movements remained distinct from the mainstream movement, yet their links to certain groups of the American student movement and their cognitive orientations suggest that they should be seen as part of the British "1968."

Politically, the overwhelming majority of activists classified themselves as supporters of the Communist Party or the Labour Party. Socially, these organizations were dominated by middle-class academics and students. Although many activists were younger than thirty years old by the late 1960s, there were hardly any protest organizations run by pupils, unlike in France or West Germany. Also, unlike in France or Italy, there were no groups that transcended the boundaries between the student and labor movements, although Britain saw a parallel wave of industrial protests in 1968 and 1969.

Cognitive Orientation of the Movement

Mass media reception and internal movement communications never managed to turn these different organizations into one coherent extra-parliamentary movement. Only for a brief period in 1968—and in the context of global protests—did interpretations of a united extra-parliamentary movement emerge. The cognitive orientations of the British movements were never fixed, and it is difficult to locate a point of consensus. There were, however, a number of key issues that were debated both within and among various movement organizations.

The first issue that British activists debated was the issue of Britain's nuclear weapons and their function in foreign policy. However, beginning in the mid-1960s, this issue was eclipsed by campaigns against the Vietnam War. What is remarkable in this context is that many activists failed to engage with the heritage of British colonialism in Northern Ireland. Only a small minority of VSC activists drew on the more radical proposals for violent protests by Frantz Fanon and Mao Tse Tung.

Most university activists initially focused on issues of student representation in the fabric of universities' self-governance structures and on specific local phenomena that the activists then connected to international developments, such as housing and living conditions in halls of residence. For example, LSE students were concerned with the appointment of a new director with links to the racist government of Rhodesia in the late 1960s. There were also protests against the visit of a Conservative member of parliament to Leeds University on May 3, 1968, and issues of student participation on university disciplinary committees arose from the consequences of the demonstrations.

Only Bristol University allowed student to sit on its Senate, and no university allowed students to be represented in their councils. Until 1970, the age of majority in Britain was twenty-one, and students were concerned about the need to gain their parents' consent to attend late-night functions at certain universities and about the prohibition of visitors from other halls of residence.

British activists' cognitive orientations were united in their contribution toward a new definition of "democracy" that transcended the focus on parliaments, parties, and elections that had dominated the 1950s and 1960s in most of Western Europe. They championed a more direct form of democracy from below that began with the acknowledgment of inalienable rights at the local level and that focused on democratic processes and debate rather than on generating solutions. Activists sought to realize their subjectivity and their personhood. They strove for a more authentic, concrete form of democracy in the economic, political, and cultural realms. As New Left activist Stuart Hall summarized, "We raised issues of personal life, the way people live, culture, which weren't considered the topics of politics on the Left. We wanted to talk about the contradictions of a new kind of capitalist society in which people didn't have the language to express their private troubles."[11]

In framing their concepts of democracy, British New Left activists drew on the writings of C. Wright Mills and Herbert Marcuse as well as a number of French theorists, most notably Louis Althusser and Regis Debray, to give their arguments theoretical credibility. However, only very few activists advocated setting up "Red Bases" on British campuses to emulate Regis Debray's suggestions for Latin America.[12] The only prominent native influence was R. D. Laing, a Scottish psychiatrist, who was interested in exploring alienation and sexuality.[13]

Specifically engaging with what they regarded as regressive Labor Party policies, some New Left activists revived ideas for independent and more direct workers' control in the late 1960s. This was demonstrated most famously in the May Day Manifesto (which was jointly drafted by New Left veteran Edward P. Thompson, sociologist and founder of *Universities and Left Review* Stuart Hall, British cultural theorist and literary critic Raymond Williams, and a large group of mostly academic contributors).[14]

Attitudes toward the Superpowers and the Cold War

These cognitive orientations resulted in a distinctive set of attitudes toward the superpowers and the general Cold War framework. Some activists displayed elements of the traditional ideologically framed anti-Americanism of the British Left within which the United States appeared as a war-prone capitalist–imperialist power. They rejected American consumerism as potentially totalitarian and regarded the American intervention in Vietnam as a novel form of colonialism that would pacify powerful capitalist interests in the United States. Some civil rights groups, particularly those involving minorities, also pointed to the prevalence of racial discrimination in the United States. Some protesters expressed their anger at U.S. policies by burning American flags; one such example occurred at Sheffield University in early 1968 during a demonstration against Prime Minister Harold Wilson.[15] Yet, in general, criticism of American foreign and defense policy was far more important for the general shape of British protest discourses than anti-Americanism.

Apart from the small number of CPGB supporters among the activists, anti-American sentiments were not matched by pro-Soviet sentiments. New Left and Trotskyite activists sought to establish new forms of socialism that purposefully diverged from the centralistic models championed by the Soviet Union. Although activists had engaged with the Cold War framework during the late 1950s and early 1960s, they now highlighted the function of the Cold War as a new form of colonialism across the world, practiced by the superpowers as well as by China. Support for Maoism in general and for China's stance in the Cold War in particular was rare in Britain. The effect of anti-colonial networks on attitudes toward the Cold War has not been examined in greater detail for the late 1960s.

Key Events

Protests events at which movement organizations presented their ideas to a wider audience and demonstrated their commitment were central elements of movement communication. The first anti–Vietnam War protests were held in 1965 and primarily took the form of traditional walking demonstrations, but there were also occasional sit-ins and teach-ins. Britain did not see iconic turning points in extra-parliamentary protests, such as the shooting of Benno Ohnesorg on June 2, 1967, in Germany or May 1968 in France. If there was a series of key events in the protest landscape of 1960s' Britain, it was the anti–Vietnam War demonstrations in London during 1968.

Large-scale demonstrations that resulted in clashes between the police and protesters had already taken place in 1967. On July 2, 1967, around five thousand activists marched in London, and around thirty-one arrests were made as a result of confrontations between protesters and the police. A demonstration on October 22, 1967, attracted between four- and eight thousand participants. March 17, 1968, saw the largest and most violent demonstration in post-1945 Britain so far. Between 10,000 and 20,000 activists gathered in front of the American Embassy on London's Grosvenor Square, resulting in three hundred arrests and around thirty-one people injured.[16]

The mass demonstration that was scheduled to take place in London on October 27, 1968, attracted more than 100,000 activists, yet only a small group broke away to march on Grosvenor Square. Violent clashes ensued, but they were far smaller than the mass media had predicted in the run-up to the protests.[17] Most protest events took place in London, though there were some examples of protests in university towns and cities, usually when politicians passed through on visits.

In addition to the anti–Vietnam War demonstrations, a series of sit-ins and small-scale demonstrations at universities took place in 1968 and early 1969. The most famous of these confrontations with university authorities was the series of protests, sit-downs and occupations at the LSE, which arose from conflicts over the appointment of a new director who had links to the racist Rhodesian government. Other famous sit-ins and protests that were primarily concerned with issues of students' political representation within the university took place at Leeds, Hull University, the recently founded universities of Sussex and Warwick, and the Colleges of Art at Hornsey and Guildford.[18]

Forms and Tactics of Protest

The two main forms of protest were demonstrations and sit-ins; there were also occasional teach-ins that followed American examples. Although demonstrations were held in London and greater cities, sit-ins dominated local protests. The first teach-in took place at the Oxford Union debating society in mid-June 1965.[19] Many university campaigns organized exhibitions and debates, mostly about students' participation within the university, but occasionally also about the war in Vietnam and the heritage of British colonialism.[20] Most protesters rejected the use of violence; in general, both the protesters and the police authorities prided themselves on their self-control and restraint and on their peaceful and rational conduct, thus tapping powerful tropes of British national identity that had been first established in the political debates of the 1920s and 1930s.[21]

Transnational Relations

Protesters' cognitive orientations and the forms of protests they employed have to be interpreted in the transnational context created through the mass and movement media, rather than through direct personal contacts. Within the movements, most transnational discussions took the form of mutual observations. For example, *New Left Review* published a number of influential theoretical pieces by French and American activists during the later

1960s.[22] Mainly during 1968, the British mass media began to embed both the anti–Vietnam War protests and the local student protests within a broader narrative of global student rebellion. The tabloid press stirred rumours about an invasion of foreign revolutionaries, whereas more liberal voices still criticized activists for unthinkingly copying examples of French, German, and American students by trying to conjure up grievances that did not really exist in Britain.[23]

Personal links between British protesters and activists and other countries were rare. Tariq Ali, a leading figure in the British 1968 who had established close contacts to New Left activists during his time as a student at Oxford University, had close links to the continental European movements and participated in the International Vietnam Conference in Berlin in 1968. The historian and activist Sheila Rowbotham, who was strongly influenced by the New Left historian Edward Thompson, spent some time in Paris during the mid-1960s.[24] Foreign students, concentrated mainly at the three top universities (Oxford, Cambridge, and LSE) played important, yet so far unexplored, roles as conduits of information.[25] It is likely that students from the Commonwealth in general and India in particular opened the British movements toward the practice of nonviolent ways of protesting.[26] Transnational relations to the American civil rights movement were particularly strong among British Black Power activists. Interestingly, direct and indirect contacts between British and Northern Irish protesters appeared to have remained rather weak.

Consequences, Narratives, and Politics of Memory

As in countries across the world, the British 1968 resulted in a pluralization of extra-parliamentary politics that remained contained within the framework of mainstream politics. Apart from the largely ineffectual protests of the Angry Brigade, an anarchist grouping that was loosely connected to some of the 1968 protests, the United Kingdom did not see widespread political violence during the 1970s.[27] However, it did suffer from the violent consequences of the civil rights movement in Northern Ireland.[28]

Most prominently, the British "1968" gave rise to the Women's Liberation Movement that emerged from the fallout of the 1968 protests, as male protesters had failed to acknowledge the specificity of female experiences. The various grassroots groups expressed anger at the discrimination against women's movement politics and highlighted the gendering of many of the key cognitive orientations of the 1960s movements.[29] The Gay Liberation and Black Power movements made analogous points.[30] There were also important continuities from the New Left and CND of the late 1950s to protests against town planning and road-building and other "green" forms of protests in the 1970s and 1980s.[31]

Because of the lack of any sustained historical research on the social history of protest in 1960s Britain, it would be too soon to speak of historiographical narratives that structure historical research. There are, however, a number of key interpretations that historians and sociologists have used to make sense of 1968 in Britain. They usually follow certain contemporary interpretations that emerged during the 1970s.

One interpretative strand that already emerged during the mid- and late 1960s can be traced back to the Marxist cultural theorist Perry Anderson, editor of the *New Left Review* from 1962 to 1982. He described Britain as the only major industrialized society that had not seen widespread student unrest and interpreted this as the result of specific British bourgeois culture that had not generated radical concepts of society.[32] Another strand conceptualizes the protests as a generational revolt, driven by a group of affluent students who followed postmaterial values.[33] Another interpretation neglects the political debates even more and focuses on the emergence of a "permissive society" in Britain on an entirely sociocultural level, highlighting the emergence of new sexual norms and the emergence of youth subcultures.[34]

Despite the activist past of many members of the current British Labor government, 1968 fails to engender as much political debate in Britain as in the United States, France, and Germany. It was only against the background of the diverging views on the benefits of "1968" under Margaret Thatcher's Conservative government of the 1980s that the politics of memory of the British 1968 played an important role. In the British politics of memory, 1968 has been overshadowed by more specific issues of direct concern to former activists, such as the nature of the Labour Party and the nature of British colonialism.

Bibliography

Research on extra-parliamentary movements in Britain during the 1960s is still in its infancy. There is no reliable archived-based historical study on the British protests in the later 1960s and early 1970s. Most of the literature on the British "1968" is unsophisticated from a conceptual point of view and unquestioningly adopts contemporary interpretations. Nick Thomas (2002) offers a good inroad into the British debates in the 1960s. For social change in Britain during the 1960s, see Donnelly (2005). Nick Thomas (1997) provides a rare study of the protests in the later 1960s. Despite its rather unstructured nature, Sandbrook (2006) offers numerous useful anecdotes and details. A rather generic sociological perspective on British social movements can be gleaned from Lent (2001). Nehring (2005) embeds the protests of 1968 in the general history of protest in post–World War II Britain, and Nehring (2006) highlights the importance of pacifist traditions for British extra-parliamentary protests. The politicization of popular culture and consumerism still awaits its historian, however. Dworkin (1997) offers a succinct analysis of the interaction between New Left thought, history writing, and the emergence of cultural studies in Britain during this period. Anecdotal evidence on the "long 1960s" can be gleaned from Green (1988 and 1998) on subculture, and from relevant passages in Marwick (1998). Rowbotham (2001) and Ali (2005) present memoirs that offer an excellent inroad into the cognitive orientations, networks, and experiences of activists.

Ali, Tariq. *Street-Fighting Years: An Autobiography of the Sixties.* London: Verso, 2005.

Donnelly, Mark. *Sixties Britain: Culture, Society and Politics.* London: Pearson, 2005.

Dworkin, Dennis. *Cultural Marxism in Postwar Britain. History, the New Left and the Origins of Cultural Studies.* Durham, NC: Duke University Press, 1997.

Green, Jonathon. *Days in the Life: Voices from the English Underground 1961–1971.* London: Pimlico, 1988.

Green, Jonathon. *All Dressed Up: The Sixties and Counterculture.* London: Pimlico, 1999.

Lent, Adam. *British Social Movements: Sex, Colour, Peace and Power.* London: Macmillan, 2001.

Marwick, Arthur. *The Sixties: Cultural Revolution in Britain, France, Italy, and the United States, c. 1958–c.1974.* Oxford: Oxford University Press, 1998.

Nehring, Holger. "The Growth of Social Movements," in *A Companion to Contemporary Britain, 1939–2000,* ed. Paul Addison and Harriet Jones. Oxford: Blackwell, 2005, 389–406.

Nehring, Holger. "The Politics of Security. The British and West German Protests against Nuclear Weapons," Ph.D. diss., Oxford University, 2006.

Rowbotham, Sheila. *Promise of a Dream.* London: Penguin, 2001.

Sandbrook, Dominic. *White Heat: A History of Britain in the Swinging Sixties.* London: Little, Brown, 2006.

Thomas, Nick. "The British Student Movement from 1965 to 1972." Ph.D. diss., University of Warwick, 1997.

Thomas, Nick. "Challenging Myths of the 1960s: The Case of Student Protest in Britain," *Twentieth Century British History* 13, no. 3 (2002): 277–97.

Notes

1. For data cf. London and Cambridge Economic Service, *The British Economy: Key Statistics 1900-1970* (London: HMSO, 1971), tables 6 and 10.

2. Cf. Bill Osgerby, *Youth in Britain Since 1945* (Oxford: Blackwell, 1998).

3. John Callaghan, *Cold War, Crisis and Conflict: The History of the Communist Party of Great Britain 1951–68* (London: Lawrence and Wishart, 2003).

4. For an example of the strength of mainstream political adherence among LSE students cf. Tessa Blackstone, et al., *Students in Conflict: LSE in 1967* (London: Weidenfeld & Nicolson, 1970), 205–207.

5. For a general evaluation cf. Glen O'Hara and Helen Parr, eds., *The Wilson Governments 1964–1970 Reconsidered* (London: Routledge, 2006).

6. Richard Taylor, *Against the Bomb: The British Peace Movement, 1958–1965* (Oxford: Oxford University Press, 1988).

7. On the New Left cf. Michael Kenny, *The British New Left. British Intellectuals After Stalin* (London: Lawrence and Wishart, 1995).

8. Cf. John Callaghan, *British Trotskyism: Theory and Practice* (Oxford: Blackwell, 1984); and Avishai Zvi Ehrlich, "The Leninist Organisations in Britain and the Student Movement 1966–1972," Ph.D. diss., University of London, 1981, 52.

9. Cf. Jonathon Green, *All Dressed Up. The Sixties and Counterculture* (London: Pimlico, 1999), 153–155.

10. Cf. Paul Gilroy, *There Ain't No Black in the Union Jack* (London: Routledge, 1987).

11. Stuart Hall, quoted in Ronald Fraser, et al., *1968. A Student Generation in Revolt* (London: Chatto & Windus, 1988), 30.

12. Cf. "RSSF Manifesto," *New Left Review*, no. 53 (1969): 21–22.

13. Cf. Robert Boyers and Robert Orrill, eds., *R. D. Laing and Anti-Psychiatry* (Harmondsworth: Penguin, 1972).

14. Raymond Williams et al., eds., *May Day Manifesto* (Harmondsworth: Penguin, 1968).

15. *Darts*, February 7, 1968, 7.

16. *VSC Bulletin*, July–August 1967;6:1; *Guardian*, March 13, 1968, 1, 3 and 16.

17. For accounts cf. *Guardian*, October 28, 1968, 1; *The Times*, October 28, 1968, 1; as well as J. D. Halloran et al., *Demonstrations and Communications: A Case Study* (Harmondsworth: Penguin, 1970).

18. Cf. The Staff and Students of the Hornsey College of Arts, *The Hornsey Affair* (Harmondsworth: Penguin, 1968); and MRC MSS.280, box 52/HG on Guildford.

19. *Guardian*, June 16, 1965, 1.

20. *Manchester Independent*, May 23, 1967, 1; *Union News*, May 5, 1967, 1.

21. Sylvia Ellis, "'A Demonstration of British Good Sense?' British Student Protest during the Vietnam War," in *Student Protest: The Sixties and After*, ed. Gerard J. de Groot (London: Longman, 1998), 54–69.

22. Cf. Lin Chun, *The British New Left* (Edinburgh: EUP, 1993), ch. III.

23. *Sun*, March 19, 1968, 16. See also *The Times*, September 5, 1968, *Guardian*, June 13, 1968, 8.

24. Sheila Rowbotham, *Promise of a Dream* (London: Allen Lane, 2001).

25. For an earlier period cf. Stuart Hall, "The 'First' New Left: Life and Times," in *Out of Apathy Voices of the New Left Thirty Years On*, ed. Oxford University Socialist Discussion Group(London: Verso, 1989), 13–38.

26. Cf. Holger Nehring, "National Internationalists: British and West German Protests against Nuclear Weapons, the Politics of Transnational Communications and the Social History of the Cold War, 1957–1964," *Contemporary European History*, 14, no. 4 (2005): 559–82.

27. Cf. Gordon Carr, *The Angry Brigade. The Cause and the Case* (London: Gollancz, 1975).

28. Cf. Simon Prince, "The Global Revolt of 1968 and Northern Ireland," *Historical Journal* 49, no. 3 (2006): 851–75.

29. Sheila Rowbotham, *Woman's Consciousness, Man's World* (Harmondsworth: Penguin, 1973), especially 1–25.

30. Cf. Lisa Power, ed., *No Bath But Plenty Of Bubbles: An Oral History Of The Gay Liberation Front 1970–73* (London: Cassell, 1995).

31. Cf. Malcolm MacEwen, *The Greening of a Red* (London: Pluto, 1991).

32. Perry Anderson, "Origins of the Present Crisis," *New Left Review* 1964; 23:26–53; idem, "Components of the National Culture," *ibid*, 1968;50:3–57.

33. Cf. Thomas, "Challenging Myths"; Arthur Marwick, *The Sixties. Cultural Revolution in Britain, France, Italy, and the United States, c. 1958–c.1974* (Oxford: Oxford University Press, 1998).

34. Cf. Green, *All Dressed Up*; Christopher Booker, *The Neophiliacs: The Revolution of English Life in the Fifties and Sixties* (London: Collins, 1969).

11

Northern Ireland

Niall ó Dochartaigh

Social and Political Framework of the Country

Northern Ireland as a political unit came into existence in 1920 to 1921, when an autonomous parliament and government were established in Belfast with jurisdiction over six northern Irish counties. When the rest of Ireland secured independence from the United Kingdom in 1921, Northern Ireland remained under British sovereignty but enjoyed an exceptionally high level of autonomy. The Ulster Unionist party, institutionally linked to the British Conservative party and dominated by business interests and the local aristocracy, enjoyed overwhelming support from the Protestant majority of the population, winning every election and forming every government. The Unionist party maintained Protestant working-class support by emphasizing the danger to the state's existence posed by any breach in Protestant solidarity and supporting the extension of British welfare provisions to Northern Ireland after the Second World War. The Catholic minority, forming a third of the state's population, was almost completely excluded from the exercise of power at all levels.[1]

Catholics tended to be concentrated at the bottom of the social scale, dominating unskilled jobs and the ranks of the unemployed, whereas Protestants were heavily overrepresented in skilled industrial employment, in business, and in the professions. One of the principal aims of civil rights activists starting from the mid-1960s was to provoke British government intervention to pressurize the Unionist government at Stormont to put an end to widespread discrimination against Catholics in the allocation of public housing and public employment.

A series of deep economic and social changes after World War II helped to create the conditions for the mobilization that began in the mid 1960s and culminated in the civil rights campaign of 1968 and 1969. The north of Ireland had been the most industrialized and prosperous part of Ireland since the late eighteenth century, but by the 1960s, Northern Ireland was one of the most economically depressed areas in the United Kingdom. When the new Labor government in Britain began building the British welfare state in the late 1940s, the Ulster Unionist party sought and received British government funding to provide the same services in Northern Ireland, fearful that a widening gap in services between Northern Ireland and Britain would erode their working-class Protestant support.[2] The consequent expansion in public services in Northern Ireland had direct political implications.

A major program to build new public housing improved the material conditions of tens of thousands of people but also created new grievances and new opportunities for collective action. Before the 1940s, very little public housing had been built in Northern Ireland. The tens of thousands of new houses constituted a novel public resource. Some Unionist-controlled local authorities systematically discriminated in the allocation of these houses, at least partly to maintain political control in places such as Derry, where even minor population movements would endanger Unionist political control of the city.[3] The growth in public housing also facilitated collective action. Before this, tenants in working-class areas were isolated and atomized in their dealings with private landlords. In public housing estates, tenants had a landlord in common—a landlord susceptible to political pressure. By the mid-1960s, tenants' associations had been established across the north. The experience of the tenants' associations in achieving small local gains demonstrated that collective action could be effective and helped to create a corps of activists.[4]

At the same time, the expansion of the public health service and the education system created thousands of new middle-class service jobs for health professionals and teachers, creating a large new Catholic middle class strongly connected with the working class communities many of its members served. Catholic teachers and doctors would play a prominent role in the civil rights mobilization of the mid- and late 1960s.

Alongside this expanded Catholic middle class, the postwar introduction of free university education dramatically expanded the student population and opened up the universities to students from working-class backgrounds. This new student generation played a central role in the mobilization of the late 1960s. At the same time, the ranks of the unemployed and unskilled Catholic population had also increased with economic decline, and this marginalized population provided mass support for the movement.

Since the foundation of Northern Ireland, the politics of the Catholic minority had been dominated by the consensus that the state was illegitimate and that Ireland should be reunited. By the mid-1960s it seemed that the Catholic minority was finally accepting the permanence of partition. When the civil rights movement began, focusing on the need for reform rather than on the ending of partition, it seemed that the issue of the border had been successfully "parked" and that debate could now focus on internal reforms.

However, it proved impossible to separate internal issues from the disputed external boundary. Unionists resisted moderate demands for internal reform on the basis that these demands masked a plot to destroy the state itself, whereas Irish Republicans argued that repression of the movement proved that the state could not be reformed—that only in a united Ireland could the divisions between Catholic and Protestant be resolved.

Organizational and Social Structure of the Protest Movement

Beginning in the early 1960s, a variety of new political forces began to emerge to challenge the Unionist government in Northern Ireland. Members of the newly expanded Catholic middle class began to search for ways to become politically involved while avoiding the moribund Nationalist party. For example, one of the earliest civil rights organizations, the Campaign for Social Justice (CSJ), established by Con and Patricia McCluskey in 1964, was dominated by Catholic professionals and deliberately avoided being identified with the Nationalist party.

In the mid-1960s, the Northern Ireland Labor Party (NILP) scored some notable electoral successes while never presenting a serious challenge to the ruling Unionist party. Some of the radicals in the NILP forged strong working relationships with younger and more radical elements in the Republican movement and began to take part in joint protests. "The Republican movement" was a deliberately ambiguous term encompassing the political party Sinn Féin, associated political initiatives, and the Irish Republican Army (IRA) while avoiding the admission of any institutional link between them. The core aim of the Republican movement was the political reunification of Ireland. Left-wing Republicans had been staging protests on social issues from 1963 onward in an attempt to forge a new direction for the movement in the wake of the failure of the IRA's border campaign of 1956–1962. By 1967, they were cooperating closely with leftist activists in both Belfast and Derry and were centrally involved in agitation on housing and unemployment issues.

In the midst of this changing political landscape, the Republican movement organized a meeting in Maghera, County Derry, in August 1966 to discuss the establishment of a civil rights organization as a way to build alliances beyond the narrow confines of the movement while also providing a novel way to exert pressure for change. By this stage, the Republican leadership, influenced by a small number of Marxist intellectuals, had decided that reform of Northern Ireland and working class unity in the north was a necessary prelude to a united Ireland. The civil rights campaign was to be part of a Marxist strategy to reform the north with the ultimate goal of reuniting Ireland.[5]

Republicans played a central role in the establishment of the Northern Ireland Civil Rights Association (NICRA) in Belfast in February 1967, but the association also included a wide range of opinion, including Communists, leftists, Catholic reformists, and initially, at least one Unionist. Modeled on the British National Council for Civil Liberties while invoking the terminology of the U.S. civil rights movement, NICRA was initially focused primarily on the legal system, calling for reform of the repressive legislation deployed by the Unionist government. Housing and employment discrimination were very much secondary concerns.

Many of the more radical activists on the ground saw NICRA as an excessively cautious and conservative organization, fearful of confrontation. Catholic moderates and conservatives, in contrast, distrusted it because of the heavy involvement of Marxist Republicans. Although NICRA launched the civil rights campaign, it did not retain control for long, and the civil rights movement was characterized by its ideologically fractured nature.

In August 1968, NICRA held its first civil rights march from Coalisland to Dungannon in County Tyrone. There was a surprisingly large turnout. Republican and left-wing members of the Derry Housing Action Committee (DHAC) who had taken part in the march decided to invite NICRA to stage a march in Derry. The DHAC activists saw themselves as actively manipulating NICRA to force a cautious leadership in Belfast to follow them down a confrontational route.[6] When the march was banned and baton-charged, intense rioting broke out in Derry and lasted for three days. It was the first violence of the Troubles. In the wake of the march, local moderates and conservatives in Derry moved to take control of the mass mobilization provoked by these events. The local radicals found themselves incorporated into a Derry Citizens Action Committee (DCAC) that eschewed links with NICRA and was dominated by reformist Catholics. Its leadership was described by prominent radical activist Eamonn McCann as "Middle-aged, middle-class and middle of the road."[7] The DCAC subsequently presided over the largest and most politically important civil rights marches, stressing the local dimension to grievances in Derry and keeping NICRA as far as possible away from proceedings.[8]

As the civil rights campaign got underway in Derry, students in Belfast established People's Democracy (PD). PD was more radical than either

NICRA or the DCAC, but it too was a wide coalition, described by Eamonn McCann as "a loose organization without formal membership and with an incoherent ideology comprising middle-class liberalism, Aldermaston pacifism and a Sorbonne-inspired belief in spontaneity. At its core was a small group of determined left-wingers."[9] Although it was a tiny organization, it played a key role in forcing the pace of events at key moments, and some of its leaders consciously saw themselves as part of a wider European and international protest movement.[10]

Although some of the most prominent civil rights leaders were Protestant, and the movement enjoyed the support of significant numbers of Protestant students and middle-class liberals, the Catholic minority—and working-class Catholic communities in particular—provided the bulk of the movement's support on the streets. The Protestant working class reacted fearfully, and support for extreme reactionary Unionism grew in the Protestant community.

By early summer 1969, the mass civil rights campaign was effectively over, and the DCAC in Derry had practically dissolved. NICRA was taken over by the Marxist Republicans, but the organization would never again enjoy the central leadership role it had briefly enjoyed at the beginning. PD remained in existence, briefly enjoying limited electoral success in Belfast in the mid 1970s, having moved much closer by then to the Provisional Republican movement. When Provisional Sinn Féin began to contest elections in the early 1980s, PD was eclipsed.

Two powerful opposing forces emerged from the civil rights campaign. On the one hand was the Social Democratic and Labor Party (SDLP), uniting the new middle-class activists in the civil rights movement with independent Labor figures from Belfast and the more active elements of the old Nationalist party. For decades they would enjoy the electoral support of a majority of northern Catholics but attract minimal Protestant support. On the other hand was the Provisional Republican movement, established in 1970, which mounted a sustained campaign of violence aimed at reuniting Ireland. Many of those on the left of the civil rights movement ultimately ended up closer to the Provisional Republicans than to the SDLP, as the Provisionals came to embody the most radical and determined opposition to the state.

Cognitive Orientation of the Movement

The civil rights movement was an uneasy and ideologically fractured alliance, drawing in support that ranged from the conservative Catholic through the liberal center and center left to Labor, Republican, Marxist, and New Left elements of varying degrees of radicalism. This broad front was the secret of the movement's success and its mobilization of mass support among the Catholic minority in the North, but it was also its greatest weakness. All elements of the movement could unite in their opposition to discrimination and to the Unionist party and on the need for major reforms in housing, employment, policing, and political structures. Beyond this, there were fundamental disagreements.

Moderate reformist elements in the movement were concerned from the beginning about restraining and controlling the mass mobilization, seeking a negotiated compromise and relatively modest reforms, and fearful of a breakdown of order. Many of the moderates were perfectly content to work within the framework of British sovereignty and saw the British Labor government as an ally to be courted in attempts to force reform on Stormont.

Marxist Republicans saw both reform within the North and the issue of a united Ireland as part of a larger, long-term revolutionary struggle. They emphasized working-class solidarity in opposition to sectarian or ethnic allegiances, as well as anti-imperialist opposition to Britain's control of the North. As sectarian violence increased, they placed less emphasis on anti-imperialism, and within a few years they had become more supportive of the state and state security forces than even the moderate reformists, on the basis that an end to violence was a prerequisite for the building of working-class unity. At the same time, however, their popular support dwindled, and they moved to the political margins. Some of the most prominent radical activists saw themselves very consciously as part of a wider international movement, emphasizing working-class unity as Marxist Republicans did, but placing more emphasis on Britain's imperial role and on state repression.

As reformists, Marxist Republicans, and left-wing radicals struggled for control of the civil rights movement, a new political current was gathering strength in the background. Traditional Republicans dissatisfied with the Marxist turn taken by the leadership, young Republicans frustrated by the cautious conservatism of the leadership, and new recruits to the Republican movement radicalized by the violence surrounding the civil rights campaign were beginning to coalesce into a powerful new force. In late 1969 and early 1970, the Republican movement split into two factions as the new Provisional Republican movement was established, including the political party Provisional Sinn Féin and the Provisional IRA. The Provisionals emphasized their opposition to Marxism, their allegiance to "democratic Socialism," and their central focus on ending British sovereignty and achieving Irish unity. At least some of the Provisional leaders saw the escalating violence around the civil rights movement as providing a unique historical opportunity to launch an armed campaign to reunite Ireland.

Attitudes toward the Superpowers and the Cold War

The civil rights movement united active supporters of the Soviet Union with conservative admirers of the United States, New Left critics of both Soviet and U.S. power, and almost every variation in between. Student activists identifying with the New Left condemned U.S. action in Vietnam and the Soviet invasion of Czechoslovakia in the same breath. Reformist and conservative elements in the movement were much less critical of the United States, and some conservative supporters of the movement harshly condemned "lefties and weirdies" who "harped and howled over Vietnam."[11] Certain civil rights leaders strongly emphasized their anti-Communist credentials, and speakers at civil rights marches in 1968 regularly drew parallels between police repression of the civil rights movement and Soviet action in Czechoslovakia.[12] This was a much more comfortable analogy for conservative supporters of the movement than the parallels drawn by radicals with student protest in Europe and the United States.

When the Republican movement split in early 1970, the Marxist Official Republican leadership went on to build strong and direct links to the Soviet Union. The Official Republican analysis of conflict in Northern Ireland, arguing that the Provisional IRA's armed campaign was a sectarian campaign to be opposed rather than an anti-imperial struggle, helped to shape the Soviet Union's policy on the conflict for much of the 1970s.[13]

Forms and Tactics of Protest

Left-wing, Republican protestors in Northern Ireland deployed slogans and tactics borrowed directly from the U.S. civil rights movement in protests on housing and employment issues from 1963 onward.[14] When moderate reformists established the CSJ in 1964, they too deployed the rhetoric of discrimination and civil rights. In the year of the march on Washington, 1963, the U.S. movement provided a frame, an analogy, and a vocabulary that were enthusiastically adopted by the movement in Northern Ireland and by journalists covering the events. It also provided a set of tactics.

Reformist civil rights leaders such as John Hume emphasized the commitment to nonviolence of the U.S. movement, regularly invoking the name of Martin Luther King, Jr., and emphasizing the moral superiority that nonviolence could confer on the movement. In addition to protest marches, civil rights protestors in Northern Ireland used sit-downs, pickets, disruption of local government meetings, and the squatting of empty houses in protesting housing allocation policies. In many cases, they openly cited the example of the U.S. civil rights movement but were also influenced by radical action in Great Britain and elsewhere in Western Europe.

A key tactic of more radical elements in the movement was to provoke confrontation by challenging the official allocation of public space—a tactic that caused uneasiness among more moderate activists. Marches and demonstrations associated with the Catholic community had customarily been permitted to take place in Catholic residential areas but had been forcibly prevented from proceeding into civic centers. Civil rights protestors insisted on marching into urban centers and occasionally on marching through or past Protestant areas to symbolically reject the identification of the movement with the Catholic community alone and to challenge the convention that oppositional protest should not be allowed into civic centers. They also did so to provoke police repression that would increase popular mobilization and attract external sympathy. This tactic carried the danger of providing occasions for sectarian violence. The intense disagreement within the movement over the PD's Belfast–Derry march of January 1969 arose from the fear of many that marching through mainly Protestant rural areas "would cause nothing but fucking sectarianism," as Derry activist Dermie McClenaghan put it.[15]

Escalating violence surrounding civil rights marches in 1969 brought violent protest tactics to the fore. As early as October 1968, barricades had been built at the edge of the working-class Catholic Bogside area of Derry in an attempt to keep the police out of the area. By January 1969, the first local "defense committees" had been established in Derry, organized by Republicans who would later be central to a revived IRA campaign.

In the atmosphere of wider radicalization created by the excesses of the security forces, some Republicans began to engage in more organized violence. Thus, as protestors battled the police in Derry in April 1969, the IRA in Belfast petrol-bombed post offices throughout the city in the first distinctively organized and concerted tactical use of violence in relation to the disturbances surrounding the civil rights campaign.

Transnational Relations

A central achievement of the civil rights movement was to attract sympathetic media coverage and outside attention, forcing the British government to impose reform on the Unionist regime. Some of the elements in the civil rights movement had existing international links before the movement began, but these connections would expand rapidly as the movement took off. The Republicans, for example, had links to the left-wing Connolly Association in Great Britain, were organizationally linked to the Republican *Clan na Gael* organization in the United States, and also had extensive informal networks linking them to Irish-born Republican emigrants in the United States.

Support for the civil rights movement outside Ireland was at its strongest in Great Britain and the United States, but there were also notable clusters of support in Australia and New Zealand and in several European countries. Support networks were based on varying blends of emigrant activism, internationalist solidarity, and ethnic solidarity, taking very different forms in different locations.[16]

Support for the movement in Great Britain was strongly institutionalized in mainstream British politics. The Campaign for Democracy in Ulster (CDU) was established in 1965 by British Labor party activists, many of them Irish immigrants in Britain. It forged links with the CSJ and Gerry Fitt, the Republican Labor member of parliament for West Belfast, and enjoyed the support of over 100 British parliamentarians.[17] The fact that Britain was the sovereign power ensured that much activism in Great Britain was focused on directly influencing the detail of British government policy.

Support networks in the United States were the site of intense struggles between reformists, Marxist Republicans, leftist radicals, and those who would go on to support the Provisional Republican movement. Both reformists and Provisional Republicans feared that Marxist and radical leftist rhetoric would alienate potential supporters among the large ethnic Irish urban communities. The radicals and Marxist Republicans sought to build links in the United States with minority groups, the anti-war movement, and the radical left. On her visit to New York in 1969, the prominent PD activist Bernadette Devlin had been presented with the key to New York City by the mayor. In a gesture that dramatized the sympathies of radical left-wing activists in Northern Ireland, Eamonn McCann brought the key back to New York in 1970 and presented it to the Black Panthers.[18] As violence escalated in Northern Ireland, leftist support groups in the United States withered, and reformists focused their attention on Congress, seeking to gain influence with elected representatives. Ultimately, only the Provisional Republicans would build an extensive and influential grassroots support network in the United States.[19]

Consequences, Narratives, and Politics of Memory

The civil rights campaign petered out in early summer 1969 as violence on the streets escalated. After the deployment of British troops in August 1969, the British government became deeply involved in the affairs of Northern Ireland. Initially the British government applied strong pressure on the Unionist government to implement major reforms to resolve minority grievances. In the face of popular Protestant resistance to the reforms and an escalating IRA campaign, the British government diluted the reforms and moved toward active support of the Unionist government.

In August 1971, internment without trial was introduced, aimed at ending the violence by removing key IRA activists. Over 300 people were detained on the first night, and over the following years, almost 2,000 people would be detained without charge in internment camps. Internment provoked an abrupt escalation of violence, but it also brought NICRA back on the scene and reawakened the rhetoric of civil rights. Internment without trial was a clear-cut issue that reunited Catholic moderates, left-wing radicals, and Republicans of all varieties in opposition to repression. NICRA launched a new marching campaign toward the end of 1971. One of the first marches took place in Derry on January 30, 1972. NICRA was dominated at the time by the Official Republicans, whose leadership was trying to steer the movement away from violence. The marches were, at least in part, an attempt to provide an alternative form of opposition to state repression, to move away from armed violence. Despite the leading role of the Official Republicans, the NICRA march in Derry attracted support from a broad range of forces in the city, and several thousand people turned out to march. It was the first large-scale civil rights march in the city since 1969. The march was banned from the city center and rioting broke out. As the rioting petered out, more than a hundred British Paratroopers surged forward into the thinning crowds. In the space of the following twenty minutes, they shot dead thirteen unarmed civilians. A fourteenth died later of injuries received.[20]

For many Irish republicans and nationalists, this provided proof that the British government was prepared to ruthlessly crush dissent and that peaceful protest was not a viable tactic. It put an end to NICRA's attempt to revive the civil rights approach of the late 1960s. The events of Bloody Sunday, as it became known, are the subject of a major British government inquiry due to report in 2008.[21]

Anniversaries and commemorations of key events provide a focus for ongoing struggles to claim the legacy of the civil rights movement. Characterizing the movement primarily by its nonviolent tactics, reformist elements in the movement, now continued in the SDLP, present themselves as its true inheritors. They emphasize the fact that several of the most prominent leaders of the movement were founder members of the SDLP. Provisional Republicans for their part emphasize the involvement of their future activists at grassroots levels, as squatters, demonstrators, and housing activists from the early 1960s onward, and as marchers and stewards during the civil rights protests. They characterize reformist involvement as opportunist, aimed at seizing leadership from more radical forces as the movement gathered popular support. The Provisionals argue that the repression of the movement proved that the state could not be reformed, exposing the true character of the state. They present the struggle for a united Ireland as the logical continuation of the civil rights struggle.

Marxist Republicans laid direct claim to the legacy of the civil rights movement, holding on to the "title deeds" of the movement through their control of NICRA from 1970 onward. They argued that a combination of irresponsible New Left elements and what they characterized as the right-wing Catholic sectarianism of the Provisionals recklessly stoked up sectarian violence through a combination of ignorance and design. They quickly declined in importance however.

In the political struggle between Provisional Republicans and the SDLP, many of the former student radicals in PD offered tacit, and sometimes explicit, critical support to the Provisional Republicans, characterizing the British state as a repressive and imperialist force. As violence escalated, they devoted energy to opposing state repression in a variety of ways. Although some of them were portrayed as fellow travelers of the Provisional Republicans, they retained a distinctive perspective and voice. Prominent radical leaders such as Bernadette Devlin (now McAliskey) and Eamonn McCann remain active political commentators and activists, involved in issues ranging from civil liberties, support for immigrants, opposition to the invasion of Iraq, and workers rights.

Key Events

January 1964: CSJ established in Dungannon, County Tyrone.

April 1964: Short-lived Working Committee on Civil Rights in Northern Ireland established by left-wing students at Queen's University, Belfast.

February 1965: CDU established in London by British Labor party activists.

1966: Tension and violence surrounds commemoration of the 50th anniversary of the Republican Easter Rising of 1916.

August 1966: Meeting of Republican Wolfe Tone Societies in Maghera, County Derry, discusses the establishment of a civil rights organization.

February 1967: NICRA established in Belfast.

November 1967: DHAC established.

November 1967: First large-scale student protest in Belfast as 1,500–2,000 march to protest the government banning of Republican Clubs.

June 20, 1968: Austin Currie, Nationalist minister of parliament at Stormont, squats a house in Caledon, County Tyrone, in protest at housing discrimination.

August 1968: First NICRA civil rights march, from Coalisland to Dungannon in County Tyrone.

October 5, 1968: Police baton-charge a small march in Derry organized by DHAC and sponsored by NICRA; 400–600 take part. Three days of rioting follow. DCAC established in the wake of the march.

October 9, 1968: Student march in Belfast to protest police violence in Derry; about 3,000 take part. The first of several student marches, sit-downs, occupations, and pickets in Belfast.

October 19, 1968: First DCAC demonstration in Derry; 4,000–5,000 take part in sit-down.

November 2, 1968: DCAC retrace steps of October 5 march; 3,000–4,000 take part.

November 13, 1968: Unionist government imposes one-month ban on marches within Derry's city walls.

November 16, 1968: DCAC retrace steps of October 5 march again, and marchers proceed into the center of the walled city. Over 15,000 take part.

November 22, 1968: Unionist government announces a modest reform package.

November 30, 1968: Civil rights demonstration in Armagh fails to reach the town center because of a loyalist counterdemonstration.

December 4, 1968: Violent clashes between loyalists and civil rights marchers follow a march in Dungannon.

December 9, 1968: Unionist Prime Minister Terence O'Neill makes his "Ulster stands at the crossroads" speech, appealing for restraint. In response, NICRA and the DCAC suspend all protests for a month.

January 1–4, 1969: PD marches from Belfast to Derry. The march is attacked at Burntollet Bridge on the last day. Followed by severe rioting in Derry and the establishment of the first "Free Derry," lasting a few days.

January 11, 1969: Civil rights march in Newry organized by PD ends in rioting.

January 1969: British government establishes the Cameron Commission to investigate the causes of the violence.

February 24, 1969: Stormont elections. Several civil rights leaders elected to the Northern Ireland parliament.

March 1969: A new Public Order bill outlaws a range of protest tactics including sit-downs. The civil rights movement launches a new campaign to oppose this bill, but protests are marked by increasing violence.

April 1969: Major rioting in Derry after an aborted civil rights march. Police beat a middle-aged man, Sammy Devenney, who dies several weeks later—the first fatality of the increasing violence. NICRA and PD hold protests around the north to divert police resources from Derry, some of which end in riots. IRA petrol bombs Belfast post offices. The loyalist Ulster Volunteer Force (UVF) plants bombs that are attributed to the IRA.

April 17, 1969: PD activist Bernadette Devlin elected as Westminster MP for Mid-Ulster as an anti-Unionist "Unity" candidate.

April 28, 1969: Prime Minister Terence O'Neill resigns. His successor finally grants "one man one vote," a key civil rights demand, and announces a sweeping amnesty.

July 1969: Violence and sectarian rioting intensify in Belfast and Derry as the loyalist marching season begins. Two men die in the rioting. The DCAC in Derry dissolves.

July 20, 1969: DCDA established by Republicans to prepare for possible violence on August 12.

August 12, 1969: Intense rioting breaks out at a loyalist Apprentice Boys march in Derry.

August 14, 1969: British Army deployed to Derry to restore order after three days of rioting.

August 15, 1969: British army deployed to Belfast, where seven people had been killed and 1,800 had fled their homes.

Bibliography

Purdie (1990) remains the most detailed and comprehensive study of the Civil Rights movement in Northern Ireland, whereas Arthur's book on People's Democracy (1974) is still the most important study of the student contribution to the movement. The extended debate between Hewitt and O'Hearn (with a contribution from Kovalcheck) in the *British Journal of Sociology* between 1981 and 1987 addressed some of the key debates around the character of the movement. Some of these issues are also addressed in a key article by Whyte (1983). More recently, several scholars have begun to apply social movement theory to the movement and to the dynamics of conflict surrounding it, among them Bosi (2006), Ellison and Martin (2000), and Maney (2000). Mulholland's (2000) analysis of the Unionist government response to the movement provides a useful account of official responses, while ó Dochartaigh (1997) analyses the process by which the civil rights movement was superseded by increasing street violence and paramilitary violence.

The University of Ulster's *Conflict Archive on the Internet* (CAIN) hosts an extensive collection of publications, primary materials and background materials on the Civil Rights campaign (http://cain.ulst.ac.uk/events/crights/). The Political Collection of the Linenhall Library in Belfast also holds a large collection of primary materials relating to the movement, including the archives of NICRA. The full text of much of this collection is available on a series of *Northern Ireland Political Literature* microfiche collections.

Arthur, Paul. *The People's Democracy 1968–73*. Belfast: Blackstaff, 1974.

Bosi, Lorenzo. "The Dynamics of Social Movement Development: Northern Ireland's Civil Rights Movement in the 1960s," *Mobilization* 11, no. 1 (2006): 81–100.

Ellison, G. and G. Martin. "Policing, Collective Action and Social Movement Theory," *British Journal of Sociology* 51, no. 4 (2000): 681–99.

Hewitt, Christopher. "Catholic Grievances, Catholic Nationalism and Violence in Northern Ireland During the Civil Rights Period: A Reconsideration," *British Journal of Sociology* 32, no. 3 (1981): 362–80.

Hewitt, Christopher. "Discrimination in Northern Ireland: A Rejoinder," *British Journal of Sociology* 34, no. 3 (1983): 446–51.

Kovalcheck, Kassian A. "Catholic Grievances in Northern Ireland: Appraisal and Judgment," *British Journal of Sociology* 38, no.1 (1987): 77–87.

Maney, Gregory M. "Transnational Mobilization and Civil Rights in Northern Ireland," *Social Problems* 47, no. 2 (2000):153–79.

Mulholland, Marc. *Northern Ireland at the Crossroads: Ulster Unionism in the O'Neill Years 1960–9.* New York: St. Martin's, 2000.

ó Dochartaigh, Niall. *From Civil Rights to Armalites: Derry and the Birth of the Irish Troubles.* Basingstoke: Palgrave Macmillan, 2005.

O'Hearn, Denis. "Catholic Grievances, Catholic Nationalism: A Comment," *British Journal of Sociology*, 34, no. 3 (1983): 438–45.

Purdie, Bob. *Politics in the Streets: The Origins of the Civil Rights Movement in Northern Ireland.* Belfast: Blackstaff, 1990.

Whyte, John. "How Much Discrimination Was There Under the Unionist Regime, 1921–68?" in *Contemporary Irish Studies*, edited by Tom Gallagher and James O'Carroll. Manchester: Manchester University Press, 1983.

Notes

1. See, for example, Paul Bew, et al., *Northern Ireland 1921–1994: Political Forces and Social Classes* (London: Serif, 1995) or Michael Farrell, *Northern Ireland: The Orange State* (London: Pluto, 1980).

2. Bew et al., *Northern Ireland*, 99–106.

3. Niall ó Dochartaigh, "Housing and Conflict: Social Change and Collective Action in Derry in the 1960s," in Gerard O'Brien ed., *Derry and Londonderry: History and Society* (Dublin: Geography Publications, 1999), 625–45. For contrary analyses, see Christopher Hewitt, "Catholic Grievances, Catholic Nationalism and Violence in Northern Ireland during the Civil Rights Period: A Reconsideration," *British Journal of Sociology* 32, 3 (1981): 362–80; Paul Kingsley, *Londonderry Revisited: A Loyalist Analysis of the Civil Rights Controversy* (Belfast: Belfast Publications, 1989) or Tom Wilson, *Ulster: Conflict and Consent* (Oxford: Oxford University Press, 1989).

4. ó Dochartaigh, "Housing and Conflict," 632–35.

5. Bob Purdie, *Politics in the Streets: The Origins of the Civil Rights Movement in Northern Ireland* (Belfast: Blackstaff, 1990), 127–30. Also, see Bob Purdie, "Was the Civil Rights Movement a Republican/Communist Conspiracy?" *Irish Political Studies* 3 (1990): 33–41.

6. Eamonn McCann, *War and an Irish Town* (London: Pluto, 1993), 92–97.

7. McCann, *War and an Irish Town*, 101.

8. Niall ó Dochartaigh, *From Civil Rights to Armalites: Derry and the Birth of the Irish Troubles* (Basingstoke: Palgrave Macmillan, 2005), 20–23.

9. McCann, *War and an Irish Town*, 106.

10. See Simon Prince, "The Global Revolt of 1968 and Northern Ireland," *The Historical Journal* 49, no.3 (2006): 851–75; and Liam Baxter, Bernadette Devlin,

Michael Farrell, Eamonn McCann, and Cyril Toman, "Discussion on the Strategy of Peoples Democracy," *New Left Review* 55 (1969), 3–19.

11. According to an editorial in the *Derry Journal* on June 11, 1968. The *Journal* strongly supported the civil rights protests.

12. Purdie, *Politics in the Street*, 136–37.

13. Chris Skillen, "Pravda's Provos: Russian and Soviet Manipulation of News from Ireland," *Irish Political Studies* 8 (1993), 73–88.

14. ó Dochartaigh, "Housing and Conflict," 630. Brian Dooley, *Black and Green: The Fight for Civil Rights in Northern Ireland and Black America* (London: Pluto, 1998), 29–30.

15. ó Dochartaigh, *From Civil Rights to Armalites*, 35.

16. Gregory M. Maney, "Transnational Mobilization and Civil Rights in Northern Ireland," *Social Problems* 47, 2 (2000),153–79.

17. Purdie, *Politics in the Streets*, 107–12.

18. Dooley, *Black and Green*.

19. See Dooley, *Black and Green*; Brian Hanley, "The Politics of Noraid," *Irish Political Studies* 19, no.1 (2004):1–17; ó Dochartaigh 1995; and Andrew J. Wilson, *Irish America and the Ulster Conflict* (Washington, DC: CUA, 1995).

20. Eamonn McCann and Shiels, Maureen, eds., *Bloody Sunday in Derry: What Really Happened* (Dingle: Brandon, 1992).

21. For more information, see http://www.bloody-sunday-inquiry.org/

12
Belgium

Louis Vos

Social and Political Framework of the Country

The Belgian state emerged through the national and liberal revolution of 1830 and the breaking off of the Southern Netherlands from the Dutch Kingdom. Belgian national identity was affirmed both in the northern part of Belgium (Flanders), where Dutch was the popular language, and in southern areas (Wallonia), where people spoke French. However, three major conflicts dominated Belgian society and political life. The first was between Catholics and non-Catholics, resulting in the formation of the first two political parties: the Liberals and the Catholics. The second, between capital and labor, caused the rise of both social democracy and Christian democracy, which eventually took over the Catholic party. The three major political parties gradually built a network of organizations for every aspect of social life, as instruments of both protection and mobilization of their members, and Belgium became a "pilarized" country. People lived within a Catholic, Liberal, or Socialist subculture or "pilar" without social contact with people from "outside."

The third conflict was between Francophones and Dutch speakers, which resulted in the emergence of a Flemish movement. In 1831, the Francophone upper class in power declared French the sole official language in Belgium. This in turn fostered a movement beginning in the 1870s for equal recognition for Dutch and bilingualism in Belgium. Next, as Francophones rejected bilingualism in Wallonia, Dutch monolingualism was realized in Flanders in the 1930s. Until the mid-twentieth century, the Belgian political system was divided into various networks along these Catholic, liberal, and socialist groups.[1]

It was only in the 1950s that the political elite managed to neutralize the split between Catholics and non-Catholics and later reduce the capital/labor conflict. In the early 1960s, they also wanted to solve the Francophone–Flemish divide. As the Southern economy declined and a new socialist Walloon regionalism emerged, dissatisfaction increased in the Flemish North regarding Francophones unwilling to respect Dutch monolingualism in Flanders. To resolve territorial disputes involving Flanders, Wallonia, and Brussels, in 1963 the government fixed linguistic borderlines within Belgium and adjusted the administrative structure of provinces and municipalities to them, thereby creating two monolingual territories and a bilingual Brussels.

On the eve of 1968, there were four major universities in Belgium; two were state universities (one Dutch-speaking in Gent, one French-speaking in Liège), and two were free universities. The free university in Brussels was primarily French-speaking, whereas the Catholic free university in Leuven had both a Francophone and Flemish section. As a result of the postwar baby boom, the number of first-year students at Belgian universities rose from 29,150 in 1960 to 81,024 in 1972. The university was becoming a mass institution, providing highly qualified personnel needed in industrial consumer society. However, this new university character caused frustrations among both staff and students.

The linguistic situation complicated this process. Brussels University was traditionally French speaking but began offering courses in Dutch in 1955. The number of Dutch-speaking students increased from 6.9 percent in 1960 to 13.1 percent by 1968. Although by 1967 all courses were also available in Dutch, the institution itself remained French-speaking. In Leuven, the situation was even more complicated. Leuven was a monolingual, Dutch-speaking town, but the university included both a Dutch and French section. Francophone professors and staff members felt threatened by the new language legislation and in 1963 demanded bilingual status for the city. Flemish public opinion rejected this idea and wanted to maintain a homogeneous Flemish Leuven in accordance with the recent language legislation. This "Leuven Question" became the major catalyst for separation between the two linguistic communities in Belgium, in which the protest movement of 1968 played a major role

Organizational and Social Structure of the Protest Movement

Since the late nineteenth century, Flemish students had found their mission in the Flemish movement and passed on loyalty to its goals from generation to generation. In the 1950s, a new generation of students combined this traditional Flemish nationalism with social commitment and attempted to provide university access to students from the lower social classes. By mobilizing numerous Flemish students, the Flemish national student association became the main promoter of student trade unionism and a democratic university of the Flemish community.

At other universities, the goals of student activities were limited to student issues. In Gent, despite some Flemish nationalist student organizations, there was significant ideological diversity, representing a mixed student body consisting of Catholics and non-Catholics, Socialists, and Liberals. This prevented a strong, lasting, unified student movement. At French-speaking universities like Liège and Brussels, there was almost no tradition of activism, and only small, left-wing groups emerged with limited support among professors and staff members. In the 1960s, the only political actions of the Francophone student body of Leuven were directed against Flemish demands, and a concerted student movement was nonexistent.

In Leuven, the 8,000 Flemish students considered themselves of a lower social background and therefore more democratic than their Francophone counterparts, whom they perceived as privileged and patronizing. Despite the fact that they attended classes in the same buildings, these two student bodies lived in completely separate social spheres. Moreover, the Flemings felt at home and saw French-speakers as foreigners; however, the Francophone academic community insisted on staying in Leuven.

Key Events

The Belgian bishops were the highest authorities of the Catholic University in Leuven. Trying to solve the Leuven Question, the bishops issued a proclamation on May 13, 1966, stating that the Francophone section of the university would remain. The proclamation's content and authoritarian tone drew massive protest from Flemish students, the academic staff, and the Flemish community. This Flemish student revolt of May 1966 strengthened their determination to expel the Walloons while also causing bitter anti-clericalism and anti-authoritarianism. Surprised by this reaction, the bishops decided to leave the solution to politicians, in the meantime enhancing the autonomy of the university's two language sections. In January 1968, the Francophone academic authorities revealed elaborate plans for staying in Leuven. Again, the Flemish students and community revolted. Their protest lasted three weeks and eventually put the government under such pressure that it was forced to resign.[2] New elections brought victory for proponents of relocating the French-speaking university. The Organic Charter of November 19, 1968, officially announced the transfer of the now-autonomous Francophone university to Wallonia. Following the second revolt, New Left analysis developed by student leaders since 1966 was now gradually adopted by the majority of student activists.

The French May served as a role model for protest movements at other Belgian universities. At Brussels University, for example, students contested the traditional university leadership, demanded student and staff participation in democratic decision-making processes, and occupied several administrative buildings for almost fifty days. Their demands also inspired actions elsewhere in Brussels, in high schools, in the theatre academy, and among actors and artists. In the aftermath of the revolt, and with pressure from Flemish staff and students, the existing French-speaking university split, and a new Flemish university was founded alongside it in the same (bilingual) city. Throughout the next academic year, student protest reemerged at the Francophone university and was directed against the new technocratic order and at gaining more democracy.

In Francophone Leuven, the example of Paris triggered similar student actions. Here authorities quickly capitulated to student demands, promising student and staff participation in decision making, organizing university-wide "Days of Reflection and Dialogue," and setting up reform committees. In Liège, a student strike in the winter of 1968–1969 included a week-long occupation of a central university building and established contacts with Walloon Socialist trade union leaders and political activists, broadening the strike program to demands for Socialist political and economic reforms in Wallonia. In Gent, censorship measures taken by the university authorities in March 1969 resulted in the occupation of a faculty building, which eventually led to reforms providing increased student participation.

From 1968 to 1974, the New Left student movement in Belgium thus experienced a breakthrough with ramifications throughout Flanders, Wallonia, and Brussels that had a deep effect on an upcoming generation of high school students.[3] Starting with mobilization around student-related issues, the movement quickly expanded its goals and supported workers' strikes and Third World liberation movements. Despite their differences, Flemish and Francophone students of all universities also worked together in some protest actions. They demonstrated against the 1970 military coup in Greece, governmental measures restricting foreign students, increasing college fees and cuts in university funding in 1972, plans to abolish military service facilities for students in 1973–1974, and subsequent plans for a professional Belgian army.

Cognitive Orientation of the Movement

The May 1966 revolt against the Leuven bishops' decision was initially experienced as liberation from ecclesiastical authority: Flemish Catholics simply stopped obeying the bishops' political orders. Second, the revolt marked the beginning of a turn away from pure Flemish nationalism among student activists. For example, the Flemish nationalist anthem no longer served as the student's battle song and was instead replaced by "We Shall Overcome," indicating strong identification with the African American civil rights movement. Third, students and Catholics began to question whether the university's Catholic label, implying power for the authoritarian ecclesiastical hierarchy, should be dropped.

The real New Left turn, however, took place in the January 1968 revolt, when a large group of Flemish Catholic students became convinced of the fragile character of Belgian democracy through their confrontation with the police and the establishment. The result was a radical questioning of established society, a loosening of ties with the Flemish nationalist movement, and a move to the left. Students wanted to make societal contradictions visible through a strategy of conflict but gradually concluded that class antagonism was the main contradiction and the key for understanding society. Substituting their New Left analysis for a Marxist perspective, a radical core of student activists started studying Lenin's *What To Do* (1902) in the summer of 1968. Although Marxist-Leninists remained the minority in Brussels, large photographs of Marx, Lenin, and Che Guevara gradually appeared in May 1968, and red and black flags were flown at occupied buildings. Everywhere the spontaneous, anti-authoritarian utopia that originally mobilized the majority of students was eventually paralyzed by the manipulative actions of the "revolutionary" segments of the movement. In Leuven, Maoists formed a new Marxist-Leninist Communist party, encouraging activists to give up university and go to factories as workers to spread revolutionary spirit among the working class. However, this Leninist turn was not followed by the majority of student activists, who maintained New Left ideals and became wary of extremist manipulation.

Attitudes toward the Superpowers and the Cold War

Belgian public opinion was predominantly pro-American through the mid-1960s; Vietnam was initially not a major topic of protest. Apart from two small demonstrations in Brussels and Gent in 1965, a 1967 teach-in on Vietnam in Leuven, and two demonstrations against the movie "The Green Berets" in 1968, the topic did not lead to any significant display of dissent. In Belgium, the protest movements of the 1960s were mainly triggered by domestic problems. It was only after 1968 that an anti-American atmosphere emerged in New Left and radical left-wing circles. Sympathy for the Soviet Union or Eastern Bloc Communist regimes manifested itself in the small Belgian Communist party, which attracted only a few students in Brussels,

Liège, and Gent. New revolutionary groups like the Trotskyites and Maoists were both anti-American and anti-Soviet, considering both nations to be imperialistic powers.

Forms and Tactics of Protest

Before the revolts of 1966 and 1968, the forms and tactics of protest in Belgium were rather traditional. Students were mobilized through journals and meetings. Mass demonstrations had police permission, and there was little confrontation. This changed completely after the revolts. In 1966, Flemish Catholic students performed an unedited mockery of religious symbols, complete with Gregorian chants, in front of bishops and academic authorities, and clergy puppets in cassocks hung from student houses. At the opening of the 1966 academic year, Flemish students turned their back to the academic procession, loudly demonstrating their disdain for church and authority.

Illegal demonstrations and confrontations with the police became a daily ritual in 1966 and 1968, although violence comparable to that seen in Germany or Italy remained absent. Protesters generally followed the line of nonviolent resistance, and arrested demonstrators were usually released the same day. Property destruction occurred only twice in Leuven in January 1968. In a provocative action, Flemish student leaders threw the furniture and dossiers of the Francophone vice-rector on the square in front of the main university building and burned them in a bonfire. A week later, there was an unsuccessful nocturnal attempt to set an auditorium on fire.

Among new forms of action in 1968, the sit-in or occupation of university buildings became a regular occurrence. "Wall papers" appeared in the streets, an illegal daily newspaper was distributed, and a mass *Volksvergadering* (People's Meeting) was held. Action committees multiplied, and students formed permanent "study and action groups" around specific themes or academic disciplines. As the democratic spirit grew, students organized bus trips to distribute leaflets at provincial factory gates, explaining to workers that students were demanding a "university for the people." In Brussels an *Assembleé libre* (free meeting) continued uninterrupted for over a month, attended by Belgian and foreign students, professors, staff, administrative, and technical personal. Some considered this a means to obtain more democratic structures at the university, whereas others saw it as a symbolic reality, prefiguring the free, democratic society to come. Still others experienced the endless discussions as a sort of psychodrama through which participants learned to express themselves freely and independently.[4] Occasionally teach-ins or information meetings were organized. In Leuven, the "Active

University" was launched, inspired by the German example, and encouraged students to take active roles in their education by organizing their own courses or staging critical interventions in classes to unmask the "bourgeois" ideology of the course.

Transnational Relations

In 1950, both Flemish and Francophone Belgian student organizations left the pro-Soviet International Union of Students (IUS) and joined the pro-Western International Conference of Students (ICS). However, neither international organization had much effect on the student groups.

In the mid-1960s, some European student leaders advocating New Left student trade unionism rejected the Cold War approach of IUS and ICS, along with student movements only dealing with specifically student problems. They started a series of international student conferences that met from 1966 to 1968 in Genève, Gent, Brussels, and Berlin, discussing one another's national experiences and movement orientations.[5] The effect was striking; only shortly after discussion at such a conference of Berlin's Critical University in 1967, the concept was introduced in Belgium and the Netherlands.

Consequences, Narratives, and Politics of Memory

The major political results of the 1968 Leuven revolt were the fall of the government, the later Catholic University split, and the transfer of the Francophone institution to Wallonia. The Leuven Question led to growing antagonism between Flemings and Francophones, waning Belgian national identity, linguistic division of all political parties, and the transformation of the unitary Belgian state into a federal entity based on language regions. The year 1968 also marked the end of the Leuven student movement's long-standing tradition as vanguard of the Flemish nationalist movement and the beginning of a New Left movement that also emerged at other universities, advocating participatory democracy and new forms of political action that emphasized grassroots involvement. The Belgian student movement also experienced a Leninist turn that was strongest in Leuven, where the new Marxist-Leninist (Maoist) political party founded in the early 1970s still remains under the leadership of the former students of 1968.

For Belgian society, 1968 came to signify a shift in mentality that included four aspects. The most crucial consequence was the waning of the unquestioning acceptance of authority. Second, a mental depilarization delegitimized the ideology of the pilarized social organizations. Third, there was an increase in grassroots action groups and new social movements dealing with various social issues.[6] Finally, and perhaps most lasting, "the spirit of 1968" was the generational event of those who participated in the movement, and it deeply affected their later role in society.

The Belgian memory of 1968 has changed substantially over time. In the first decade, it served as a reference point for subsequent student generations, and the tenth anniversary was celebrated by student leaders in 1978 as a milestone for what they considered to be their mission as the heritage of 1968: the democratization of the university. That living tradition vanished in the next decade, when economic hardship and neoliberalism brought the next student generations to an apolitical defense of the material conditions of student life. In 1988, the twentieth anniversary was celebrated by academics, former student leaders, and publishing houses, resulting in often-partisan publications. Although this bias disappeared in 1998 in favor of a more scientific approach, the events of 1968 in Belgium and the transformations they initiated seem to have been erased almost completely from public memory. For some, 1968, seen as a reduced image of the flower power children, is even considered the starting point for a growing individualism and egoism that has replaced the commitment to community.

Bibliography

For a theoretical approach to the history of student movements, see the introduction in Gevers and Vos (2004). A chronicle of student protest in Belgium between 1958 and 1976 including important events from abroad is provided by Vos (1988). On the problem of the splitting of Leuven University, see Laporte (1999) and Gevers (2006). On the history of Leuven University and its student movement, see Rogiers and Lamberts (1995) and Vos (1993, 2006). On Brussels University and the contestation there, see Govaert (1990) and Tyssens (1995). On the student movement in Gent, see Simon-Vandermeersch (1988), and in Francophone Leuven, see Gevers and Vos (2001). A general view on Belgium in 1968 is provided by Horn (2005).

Despy-Meyer, Andrée ed. *Mai 68: 20 ans déjà*. Brussels: Université Libre de Bruxelles, 1988.

Gevers, Lieve and Louis Vos. "Le mouvement estudiantin Flamand et Wallon à Louvain (1836–2000)." In *Leuven/Louvain–la–Neuve. Aller Retour*, edited by Jan Roegiers and Ignace Vandevivere, 160–73. Leuven: Leuven University Press, 2001.

Gevers, Lieve and Louis Vos. "Student Movements," in Walter Rüegg, ed., *A History of the University in Europe. Vol. 3: Universities in the Nineteenth and Early Twentieth Centuries (1800–1945)*. Cambridge: Cambridge University Press, 2004, 269–361.

Gevers, Lieve. "Neither Prince nor Church: The Battle for Independence." In *The City on the Hill: A History of Leuven University: 1968–2005*, edited by Jo Tollebeek and Liesbet Nys, 32–49. Leuven: Leuven University Press, 2006.

Govaert, Serge. *Mai 68: C'était au temps où Bruxelles contestait* Brussels: CRISP, 1990.

Horn, Gerd–Rainer. "The Belgian Contribution to Global 1968," *Revue Belge d'Histoire Contemporaine/Belgisch Tijdschrift voor Nieuwste Geschiedenis* 35 (2005): 597–635.

Lamberts, Emiel and Jan Roegiers. *Leuven University: 1425–1985*. Leuven: Leuven University Press, 1990.

Laporte, Christian. *L'affaire de Louvain: 1960–1968*. Paris: De Boeck Université, 1999.

Simon-Vandermeersch, Anne-Marie, ed. *20 jaar RUG–studenten in Actie: 1968–1988*. Gent: Archief Rijksuniversiteit Gent, 1988.

Todts, Herman and Willy Jonckeere. *Leuven Vlaams: Splitsingsgeschiedenis van de Katholieke Universiteit Leuven*. Leuven: Davidsfonds, 1979.

Tyssens, Jeffrey. "Zaaien in de tuin van Akademos. Over het ontstaan van de Vrije Universiteit Brussel op het einde van de jaren zestig." In *De tuin van Akademos. Studies naar aanleiding van de 25ste verjaardag van de Vrije Universiteit Brussel*, edited by Els Witte and Jeffrey Tyssens, 23–133. Brussels: VUB, 1995.

Vos, Louis, et al. *Studentenprotest in de jaren zestig: De Stoute Jaren*. Tielt: Lannoo, 1988.

Vos, Louis. "Van Vlaamse Leeuw tot rode vaan . . . en verder. De naoorlogse Leuvense studentenbeweging," *Onze Alma Mater* 47 (1993): 223–42.

Vos, Louis. "Student Politics. Contestation, and Participation," in Jo Tollebeek and Liesbet Nys, eds. *The City on the Hill: A History of Leuven University. 1968–2005*. Leuven: Leuven University Press, 2006, 65–81.

Vos, Louis. "Student Movements." In *A History of the University in Europe. Vol 4: Universities since 1945*, edited by Walter Rüegg. Cambridge: Cambridge University Press, in press.

Notes

1. For more information on Belgian history, see J. C. H. Blom and Emil Lamberts, eds., *History of the Low Countries* (New York: Berghahn Books, 1999); Kas Deprez and Louis Vos, eds., *Nationalism in Belgium. Shifting Identities. 1780–1995* (Houndmills: Macmillan Press, 1998); Theo Hermans, Louis Vos, and Lode Wils, eds., *The Flemish Movement. A Documentary History. 1780–1990* (London: Athlone, 1992).

2. See *De Januarirevolte te Leuven* (Antwerpen: De Galge, February 1968).

3. This history remains to be written. The effect on the Catholic youth movement for high school students is discussed in Louis Vos, "Traditie als bron van vernieuwing. De katholieke studentenactie in Vlaanderen. 1955–1975," *Bijdragen tot de Eigentijdse Geschiedenis* 8 (2001): 133–79.

4. For an extensive discussion of Assemblée Libre see Micheline Créteur, "Le mouvement de contestation à l'Université libre de Bruxelles," *Res Publica* 3 (1968): 433–64.

5. There were participants from Belgium, England, France, Germany, Ireland, Luxemburg, the Netherlands, Portugal, Spain, and Switzerland.
6. On the history of new social movements in Belgium, see Staf Hellemans and Marc Hooghe, eds., *Van 'Mei 68' tot 'Hand in Hand.' Nieuwe sociale bewegingen in België. 1965–1995* (Leuven: Garant, 1995); and Marc Hooghe and Jaak Billiet, eds. *Historische en sociologische benaderingen van nieuwe sociale bewegingen*. Special issue of *Revue belge d'Histoire Contemporaine* 2004;34:3.

13
Czechoslovakia

Jan Pauer

The "Prague Spring" of 1968 was the first peaceful attempt at reform "from above" and marked the beginning of the transformation of the whole system in former Eastern bloc countries. It was significant because it did not result in a dramatic split between society and the Communist-controlled state, military, and police bodies, similar to the situation in Hungary in 1956 or Poland in 1980/81. On the contrary, interdependence developed between the successful reform wing of the party, led by the then-unknown Slovakian Communist Alexander Dubček, and the activities of the emerging civil society that expressed itself within an independent public sphere.

The experiment in reform, which evolved in March 1968, was named "Prague Spring" by the Western Media after the music festival of the same name. It lasted only eight months. Hopes of a modern, democratic "Socialism with a human face" were relinquished with the military invasion on August 21, 1968; this marked the second military occupation of the country in thirty years. In the largest military maneuver in postwar Europe and the only military intervention by troops from the Warsaw Pact countries—with the politically motivated abstention of Romania—Czechoslovakia was occupied by a half million soldiers on the pretext of saving it from an anti-Socialist counter-revolution. State and party leaders were arrested and transported from the country. On August 26, the reformers—half prisoners and half national representatives—signed a political dictate at the Kremlin, bringing about the political restoration of Czechoslovakia. It took just one more year, until August 1969, until Gustav Husák, the new party leader, turned the country's own police force on Czech and Slovak demonstrators, thus single-handedly suppressing the last traces of freedom. A second wave of Sovietization, known as "normalization policy," spread through the country and transformed it into one of the most repressive Neo-Stalinist regimes in the former Eastern bloc.

Social and Political Framework of the Reform Movement

As a result of its high industrialization, Czechoslovakia, established in 1918, had one of the most political and union-organized labor movements. In the 1920s, the Czech Communist Party, KPČ, was the second most powerful in the Comintern and during the interwar years frequently gained around 10 percent of votes. However, thanks to the global economic crisis, it enjoyed the support of a considerable number of workers, intellectuals, and artists.

The 1938 Munich Dictate, disappointment by the Western powers, disenchantment over democracy's failure to protect national sovereignty in the First Republic, the consequences of the Nazi occupation, and the end of World War II, were all factors that led to the political realignment of leading figures among the population. In an atmosphere of political and national retribution from 1945–1947, the Czechoslovak President Edvard Beneš initiated a conscious turn to Eastern and Slavic-oriented postwar policies linked to dependence on its Soviet protector, thereby preparing the gradual transition to Communism. The status of the pro-Moscow Communist Party increased, thanks to the Red Army's liberation of the country and capital city, the respect for the enormous number of Soviet victims in the Second World War, and the fact that the Soviet troops immediately withdrew after liberating the country, leaving Czechoslovakia as the only unoccupied Central European country. The Communist party gained 38 percent in the 1946 elections; this figure was 40 percent in the Czech part of the country, making it the highest vote a Communist party ever achieved in European free elections, and making it the most powerful party in Czechoslovakia. The Stalinist core of the party was masked by its parliamentary tradition and the slogan declaring a "specific path to socialism," befitting the country's needs. Anti-capitalist sentiments in postwar Europe also eased the nationalization process of large-scale industry and banks in Czechoslovakia. Almost 80 percent of the electorate opted for Socialism. The beginnings of the Cold War, the division of Europe, and Czechoslovakia's renunciation of the Marshall Plan in 1947 all facilitated the KPČ's "short march" to power in February 1948.[1]

The bloodless Communist takeover was immediately followed by the violent Sovietization of the whole country. The Social Democrats' forced annexation with the KPČ, the revocation of party pluralism, the complete nationalization of all commercial enterprises, even including tradesmen and a rigorous, enforced collectivization, were all accompanied by a policy of widely enforced political repression. Numerous labor and penal camps existed, and the legal system was transformed into a tool of oppression. Show trials were held with 233 political death sentences, 250,000 political prisoners, three times as many victims of social or work-related persecution, and 500–750,000 victims of religious discrimination. In total, two million people were politically persecuted or discriminated against during the Stalinist period. During this "catch-up" phase in Sovietization, Czechoslovakia experienced the most intense repression per head in all of Eastern Europe. The existing structures of civil society were eliminated and the potential of democratic resistance crushed.

After the twentieth party conference of the Soviet Communists, Czechoslovakian party leadership reacted reservedly to Chruščev's revelations of Stalin's crimes. The suppression of the Hungarian revolution and pacification of the agitators of the Polish October 1956 enabled the "de-Stalinization" of Czechoslovakia without political crisis. Despite the tentative rehabilitation and release of the first show trial victims, the rehabilitation of most victims of the legal system did not materialize. Those released from prison contributed substantially to the disillusionment of KPČ members in the 1960s. Despite party purges and repression in the 1950s, the KPČ, with its 1.5 million members, remained a party of the masses, in which 10 percent–12 percent of the population was actively involved—almost twice as many as in Hungary or Poland. This made it easier for social tensions to penetrate power structures. In trying to overcome the identification crisis caused by de-Stalinization, an ideological need to modernize emerged and materialized as the concept of a "scientific and technical revolution." The impetus of this historical progress was no longer class struggle; instead, the entire nation was involved in the development of productive strength within society. A side effect of this ideology was the acknowledgment of intellectuals who were vitally important within society. Empirical social research was endorsed, providing convincing evidence of system shortcomings. With party leadership approval, research teams were appointed to deal with the consequences of scientific and technical advancement, the advancement of the political and legal system, and economic reform.[2]

Meanwhile, the visible crisis surrounding Stalinist ideology strengthened tendencies toward the disintegration of Marxism in Czechoslovakia. Intensified discussions of non-Marxist theories (existential philosophy, structuralism, psychoanalysis) and Western Marxism (Frankfurt School, Yugoslavian Praxis School, Antonio Gramsci) occurred, and Marxist philosophy became increasingly polymorphic, corresponding to the contemporary worldwide renaissance of Marxism. In addition, the rigid aesthetic norms of Socialist realism were being bypassed and subverted in the fine arts, literature, theater, and film. In almost all of these areas, the 1960s marked a "golden decade" of Czech and Slovak culture. At the Kafka conference in 1963, the party's right to make political allegations in the domain of art and literature was disputed. The conflict between artists and party bureaucrats culminated at the fourth Writers' Congress in 1967, when there was an open clash with the party apparatus.[3] Simultaneously, generational conflicts became noticeable, and the youth began to rebel. October 1967 saw the first student demonstration, which was followed by hard-line police and political repression.

The disrespect of any national features was a distinguishing mark of the Communist regime. Despite acknowledging the basic principle of equality for both nations, Slovak aspirations were not honored during the Communist rule. The Communists did not exert as strong an influence in Slovakia as in the Czech part of the country. This was illustrated in the 1946 elections, where in Slovakia the Communist Party gained only 30.6 percent of votes to the Democratic Party's 62.5 percent. Without support from Prague, the takeover of power in Slovakia would never have been possible. Stalinism and the Sovietization of the whole country marked the end of any kind of Slovakian autonomy and was often seen in Slovakia as a new form of Prague centralism. The show trials for "Slovak bourgeois nationalists" (V. Clementis, G. Husák, L. Novomeský), which still took place a year after Stalin's death, symbolized the absence of national participation. Although Slovakia made the most progress in terms of modernization in its recent history during Communist rule, the Slovak Communist Party's power was reduced to a regional level. In the new constitution of 1960, the powers of the Slovak National Assembly were officially transferred to the ministries in Prague. For Slovakia, there was no sign of the general liberalization seen in politics, the economy, and society. Nonetheless, from 1963, Alexander Dubček, leader of the Slovak Communist Party, succeeded in establishing a power base against the wishes of party leader Antonín Novotný. He pleaded for the rehabilitation of convicted Slovak Communists and created a liberal climate in Slovakia.[4]

The inconsistent de-Stalinization and visible deficiencies in politics and the economy contributed to the emergence of informal publications and strategic groups within the power structure. This critical potential combined forces with the Slovak national opposition to form a reform wing in the party, gaining the upper hand in the corridors of power at the turn of the year 1967–1968.

Organizational and Social Structure of the Reform and Democratization Process

The Prague Spring was a process with three aspects: a self-led reconfiguration and modernization of power structures, a social movement striving toward democratization and modernization of the country, and a movement for national emancipation in Slovakia. Far from being the product of a sudden international, economic, or political crisis, this experiment was the result of a cumulative process, preceded by a period of disillusionment among large numbers of the Communist elite concerning the nature of the Soviet Union and their own regime. Its relatively unified reform objectives, favorable economic terms, initial efforts at easing political tension between East and West, and most notably, system-changing rather than system-disrupting nature seemed to indicate favorable conditions for democratization and the loosening both of Czechoslovakia's satellite status and of the rigid bloc formation in Europe. The eight months of the Prague Spring were shaped by the internal struggle between reformist and conservative forces within the party, the cultivation of an independent public sphere producing decisive democratic incentives, and the backdrop of Soviet menace.

Documents of the reform process such as the "action program of the KPČ"[5] and the government program from April 1968 illustrate the goal of extensively reorganizing the extant system. The reformers aspired to a program that connected central planning to the market, including the stemming of heavy industry in favor of innovative economic sectors and a consumer industry identifying with the needs of society. Businesses were supposed to introduce employee participation and self-administration. The reform of the political system was aimed at democratizing the party, state, and society based on pluralism of interests. The Communist Party wanted to maintain its leading role while reducing its previous dirigisme to functions related to programmatic and conceptual tasks. The government would gain more autonomy from the party leadership and be controlled by parliament. The state security service (Stb) was no longer to be used as an instrument in domestic conflicts, and the Department of the Interior would be controlled by parliament. The National Front, the traditional transmission belt of the party with which non-Communist parties and organizations were kept under party control, would be modernized to become a place for dialogue with the non-Communists. Labor unions, trade organizations, and pressure groups were to become more autonomous.

The principle of the separation of powers was acknowledged, and the theory of a uniform character of state power factually revised. Courts were to become independent of political power, and the position of judges and lawyers strengthened. The powers of the Prosecuting Attorney's Office, which simultaneously acted as a legal control, would be curtailed and replaced by the creation of a constitutional and administrative court. The new attorney general initiated public discussions on the humanization of the penal system, the abolition of the death penalty, and the importance of human rights. The rehabilitation of victims of political persecution was a matter of prime importance, regulated by law and institutionalized. The freedom of religion and the rights of national minorities were guaranteed.

Amendments to the right of assembly and association, as well as an electoral law, were announced. The relationship between Czechs and Slovaks led to a comprehensive reform of the constitution and transformation of the country into a federation. The most far-reaching decision of 1968, however, was the abolition of censorship, which permitted the existence of an independent public and in turn became the driving force behind democratization, allowing the rebirth of civic society.

The devotion to pre-ecological growth and technology supported the widely believed prospect of a long-term convergence of the Eastern and Western systems; a position that seemed to be confirmed by the development of the welfare state in the West and democratization in the East. Contemporary reform notions assumed that nationalization and social revolution after 1948 led a new, unchangeable social structure. Because of this belief, the reformers also dared to "risk more democracy."

International Policy and Attitudes toward the Superpowers

In the domain of foreign and security policy, there was no radical turning point; rather, it was a series of qualitative steps that led to liberation from ideology and the opening up and modification of Czechoslovakian foreign policy. Reformers strove toward an equal partnership within the Soviet alliance. According to Italian Communist Party leader Palmiro Togliatti's saying, "unity through diversity," both relations within the bloc as well as international relations were to be pluralized under the Communist parties and movements. The UN Charta became an integral part of the notion of sovereignty and non-interference, even among the Socialist states. Each country was to take "exclusive" responsibility for its own Socialism. This was the exact opposite of the duty of all Socialist countries as declared by Moscow, East Berlin, Warsaw, and Sofia—the collective defense of Socialism in every country, which later went down in history books as the Brežnev Doctrine. The Czechoslovakian reforms strove toward improved contact with Socialist and Social-Democratic parties and went to great efforts to overcome the ostracism of Yugoslavia.

A focus on European affairs was the core of the new foreign policy, with the motto for future relations between East and West being cooperation, not confrontation. Future plans included improvement in relations with West Germany and Austria and signing non-aggression pacts with various West European countries or nonviolence pacts with potential adversaries (West Germany, France, and Austria). In international conflicts such as the Vietnam War, the official policy remained consistent with the Soviet stance. The reformers did not attempt any rapprochement with the U.S. administration and entertained no hope of aid from the West if a conflict arose with the Soviet Union.

Key Events

The practical execution of reform proposals largely failed to materialize. Only two important laws were passed before the military invention in August 1968: the abolition of censorship and the rehabilitation law. Other laws such as the introduction of the five-day week, the increase of the minimum pension, the extension of maternity leave, and the first increase in real wages, negotiated in the first collective bargaining between trade unions and the government, showed that the slogan of "Socialism with a human face" was not just empty talk. The freedom of movement granted was expressed in an almost unrestricted possibility for citizens to travel out of the country and into Western European countries.

The power structure, along with the party itself, remained largely unchanged during these eight months; only the highest organs underwent a partial reorganization. The conservatives even enjoyed a nominal majority in the party executive committee. At no point was party leadership homogenous. Only around 100 leading functionaries were replaced from the 250,000 nomenklatura posts. New faces appeared most of all in the regional and district committees of the KPČ after secret elections in June and July 1968, in which 71 percent of the party cadre was substituted.[6] The party committees became more autonomous and began to link horizontally to each other. They acted as a counterbalance to the central committee, dominated by conservatives, and forced the convening of the emergency party conference of the KPČ. Insufficient political protection of the reforms resulted from initial aspirations for an integrationist course and rejection of reformers' undemocratic methods. The party conference was supposed to bring about democratic modernization. After an internal census, approximately 80 percent of party members pledged their support for the official party line. The general trend toward democratization was also expressed within the party structure. New statutes stipulated lifting the ban on parliamentary parties.

The strongest political and moral burden of guilt during the regime was, however, the brutal repression in the 1950s. The debate surrounding the Stalinist terror (1948–1955) became a central topic of the Prague Spring. The "K–231" action group founded by former political prisoners was named after the notorious law that legalized political terror (no. 231/1948 Sb). The group had 100,000 members and extended a hand to the Communist Party for discussions. Because many prominent Communist reformers were also political victims of the show trials, a common language in the rehabilitation process was found and reconciliation seemed possible.

The forming of a new and independent public sphere demanded the development of independent and political initiatives. The "Club of Committed Non–Party Members" (KAN), a discussion forum of non-Communists, organized itself as an independent political power alongside the KPČ. In the spirit of voluntary self-restraint in the face of Soviet threats, this action initiative did not seek to question the system but wanted to politically influence the forthcoming elections based on human rights. A newly formed Society for Human Rights lobbied for the establishment of human rights in the constitution. The reestablishment of social democracy posed a challenge for the Communist reformers; however, external pressure stemmed this process of political differentiation. Even the bloc parties, the People's Socialists and the Christian People's Party, revised their political objectives and recruited new party members. The Catholic Movement for the Reformation of the Synod attempted to give impetus to the Second Vatican Council. In Slovakia, the previously banned Greek Catholic church was authorized. The trade unions aspired toward autonomy, and worker and employee councils were formed with the aim of implementing self-management. Intellectuals, artists, and journalists adapted the formal autonomy of their pressure groups to create one intrinsic group. The writers' association's journal, *Literární noviny*, reemerged following a temporary ban as *Literární Listy* and, with a circulation of 130,000, proved to be an independent cultural and political factor in society. Magazines such as *Reportér* or *Student* became a mouthpiece for radical criticism of Communist reform policy's half-measures. Even the official party newspaper *Rudé právo* no longer wanted to be exclusively the voice of the party executive committee and the central committee, but that of the whole party. From the beginning, radio and television positioned themselves behind Dubček's reform policies and became the medium of critical public opinion.

It was democracy and not democratization that characterized the radical democratic criticism postulated by intellectuals with completely different worldviews, such as the Marxist philosopher Ivan Sviták or the non-Communist dramatist Václav Havel. The most spectacular expression of this independent public opinion was the June 1968 manifesto "2,000 Words," in which renowned intellectuals and artists appealed to citizens for moral courage, self-organization, and mobilization against the threat of political restoration. The reform policy was welcomed and the Communist Party harshly criticized, but at the same time, in light of political interference and external threats, the signatories pledged to "our government . . . that we will stand behind it, if necessary with arms, for as long as it is doing the things

for which we have given it our mandate."[7] As no truly democratic representation of the citizens existed at any point during the Prague Spring, wishful
thinking and reality became confused in this case. Nonetheless, the political
hegemony of the reform Communists corresponded to overriding public
opinion. Socialism was not questioned, and the KPČ was held in much
esteem, despite its past. In April 1968, between 42 percent and 53 percent of
voters put their trust in the KPČ, a figure that rose to 82 percent in times of
direct threats from outside. Only 5 percent of citizens argued for the restoration
of capitalism; 89 percent were for the continuation of Socialist development.[8]

In Slovakia, the situation evolved differently. After the election of the first
Slovak as party leader (Alexander Dubček), the dogmatic Stalinist Vasil Bilak
took over leadership of the Slovakian Communist Party and succeeded in
curbing the reform process. The Slovak party program was configured along
conservative lines and distinguished itself nationally. Gustav Husák, a victim
of the 1950s political campaign against Slovak "bourgeois nationalism," was
entrusted with preparations for the federalization of the country, which was
supposed to restart the lapsed national equalization process between the
Czechs and the Slovaks. Husák's biography made him the natural choice as
spokesman for the Slovak Communists. The Slovaks pressed for the adoption
of a federation with equal representation and the establishment of national
sovereignty linked with a ban on outvoting for the numerically stronger
Czech nation. The federation was proclaimed on the fiftieth birthday of the
foundation of Czechoslovakia on October 28, 1968. The dissent between
Czechs and Slovakians was, however, temporarily obscured by the military
occupation of the country on August 21, 1968. The week of civil resistance
against the occupation in which both nationalities were involved was
recorded as the most Czechoslovakian week in the history of their common
statehood. Never before had Czechs and Slovaks acted so concertedly as in
these few days. The national debate flared up again in autumn 1968, as
Husák succeeded in ousting Josef Smrkovský—a leading reformer and thorn
in the Kremlin's side—from his post with arguments based on the national
issue. By late 1968, federalization was the only reform plan to have survived
the year. However, as part of the "normalization policy," only a formal
national equality within a centralistic regime of oppression was established,
and not national equal rights.

Despite the half-measures of the Communist reform concept of the pluralism of interests, a rationalization of conflicts of interests was in progress.
Basic constitutional rights were intended to guarantee citizens legal cer-
tainty. The creation of the framework for establishing freedom of opinion,
assembly, and association led to a transformation of the system, despite the
Communist Party retaining its claim to leadership in its own logic. On this

course, conflicts between the party and society were not only possible but probable. However, Dubček rejected the use of violence in domestic conflicts. The reformers found a realistic political and institutional transition to bring about a transformation of the whole society, aimed at reforming and modernizing the system without disrupting it. A division in society along the line of party affiliation was no longer critical in the 1960s and was weakened further in 1968. The pluralization and democratization process already in progress amounted to a transformation of the system that went far beyond the reformers' original goals.

Forms and Tactics of the Student and Youth Movement

The Prague Spring took place in the context of the 1960s, in an atmosphere of optimism toward progress, and reflected the surge of modernization in both East and West. The success of electronic devices and synchronic spread of music, film, and cultural trends, tastes, and fashion promoted the convergence of lifestyles and a youth culture that transgressed bloc divisions. Miniskirts, jeans, and the Beatles became symbols of simultaneously experienced global events that did not stop at the borders of Eastern Europe.

Students formed an autonomous factor of the movement in civil society. Their protest against poor living conditions in 1967 on the eve of the Prague Spring, using the popular slogan "We want light!" gained political significance and increased criticism of the old Novotný regime. During the reform process, student leaders concentrated on building an independent student organization that remained outside the Communist Party–controlled National Front. Despite contacts to student movements in the West and West German student leader Rudi Dutschke's visit to Prague, there were no comparable antiauthoritarian revolts with generation-specific features as seen in Western countries. The student movement in Czechoslovakia was also not as ideologically influenced but had a distinct national profile in Slovakia and was, in both parts of the country, integrated into society and free from violence. After 1948, the most important student action was the November strike in 1968, directed against the Communist Party leadership's quiet abandonment of the reform policy. For this reason, student Jan Palach decided to make the nation and responsible politicians take action against the political restoration by setting himself on fire on January 16, 1969. His act, inspired by the self-immolation of Buddhist monks in Vietnam, seemed out of place in the Central European cultural context, yet his very realistic demands testified to his astonishing political rationality.[9] His burial was attended by around 100,000 people and became a huge national manifestation of silent and increasingly powerless protest against the political auto-restoration that was taking place. When Alexander Dubček, by then acting without any concept, was replaced in April 1969 by Gustáv Husák, who intensified the pro-Soviet party line, the August 1969 mass protests on the anniversary of the military occupation were no longer directed against the external aggressor but against the internal regime. An above-average number of young demonstrators took part in these largest mass protests in 1968–1969, during which five people died and hundreds were injured.

Consequences: The Intervention and Restoration

The reformers' political realism was primarily concerned with domestic factors, although the Soviet security policy toward its satellite countries was based on their identity with the Soviet system. Whereas the reformers emphasized bloc loyalty in their foreign policy and never considered the possibility of neutrality or leaving the Warsaw Pact, party and state leaders in the brother nations interpreted Socialism with a human face as a peaceful counter-revolution and violently brought it to a halt. The realistic estimate in the Kremlin that the Communist Party–aided system change in Czechoslovakia could no longer be turned back finally led to military intervention on August 21, 1968.

The first large-scale criticism of the Prague leaders' reform policies occurred at the first collective meeting of party leaders (with the exception of Romania) in Dresden in March 1968. Even before the democratic breakthrough became publicly visible and the KPČ's action program was accepted, Brežnev, Gomulka, Živkov, and Ulbricht condemned the events in Czechoslovakia as a counterrevolution. An anti-reform alliance was formed by five of the Warsaw Pact countries—the Soviet Union, the German Democratic Republic, Poland, Bulgaria, and Hungary. Romania was again excluded because it was considered a problem country. From May 1968, this coalition developed a concerted restoration strategy that simultaneously aimed to put Dubček's leadership under pressure, prepare a military approach, and force the search for a group willing to collaborate from within the KPČ leadership. The open rupture between Prague and the coalition in mid-June 1968 in Warsaw marked the beginning of a new phase of Soviet escalation policy. Now the military option became the focus of the Soviet restoration strategy. The bilateral negotiations in Cierná and the ensuing collective meeting in Bratislava at the beginning of August 1968, at which the "common duty" of the participating countries to "defend Socialism" was announced, were a last attempt by the anti-reform alliance to put a stop to the system reform from within Czechoslovakia. The absence of a radical turnaround after this meeting led to the decision by the Soviet Communist

Party Politburo to undertake military action. The original plan of a quasi-legal putsch, carried out by the conservative majority of the party leadership and the central committee of the KPČ, followed by legalization of this "brotherly aid," however, failed as a result of civil and institutional resistance in Czechoslovakia.

Civil resistance in August 1968 was one of the most successful such actions in the twentieth century. The national and peaceful resistance plunged the military occupation into a deadlock. Tanks and divisions were in the country but were unable to gain control over the mass media. Their presence was simply ignored after a few days. The counterrevolution could not be localized because it was everywhere: It was an occupied country without an occupation regime. The Polish party leader Gomulka summed it up: "We surprised them with our intervention and they surprised us with their resistance."[10] For the first time in the history of Soviet military intervention and "brotherly aid," legitimization of aggression failed. However, the unmasking of the Soviet Union in the court of world public opinion was of historical importance. The political planning of the intervention failed and came to a dead end.

An integral part of the existence of the Prague Spring is its end, which began with the reformers signing the Moscow dictate as a result of blackmail, reminiscent of the political show trials in the 1950s. The reformers—with the exception of František Kriegel—all signed their "confessions" in Moscow. They returned home to much jubilation, declaring that they had been able to rescue the substance of the reforms. The pro-Soviet collaborators retained their posts, as did most of the reformers. The press remained uncensored at first, and there were no feelings of fear in the country. Following the intervention, the illusion continued to grow, and admiration for the reformers reached its peak. The auto-restoration instigated by Communist reform heroes lasted a whole year. Because they had legalized the military occupation of the country by signing the dictate in Moscow, the reformers transformed the conflict's character. Whereas in August a military occupation power and the almost closed ranks of the national resistance front stood up against each other, the reformers, after returning from Moscow, found themselves in a conflict of loyalty between their own reform leadership and the defense of the freedoms already gained. The blackmailed reformers asked for support in every crisis and every further restriction to democratic freedom to prevent a bloodbath from taking place. This meant a program of demobilization and demoralization for the whole nation. The defeat of the Prague Spring therefore did not come about suddenly but, rather, little by little, with the most difficult part carried out by the reformers themselves.

The twenty years of Husák's subsequent regime were characterized by resignation, cynicism, emigration, escape into the private sphere, and outward collaboration with the regime, which itself was Neo-Stalinist, repressive, and primitive and transformed the country into a cultural wasteland. The former ideology of the revolutionaries had long since become a doctrine of the party functionaries in which nobody believed anymore. All notions of reform were banished from the party, and in contrast to neighboring countries, up until 1989 Czechoslovakia resembled a museum of Communism.

Narratives and Politics of Memory

After 1989, parts of the new political elite and spin doctors in the Czech Republic treated the Prague Spring with disrespect. Although the rest of Europe considered the defeat a Czechoslovakian national tragedy, after 1989, some voices in the Czech Republic interpreted the Prague Spring as a struggle primarily between different Communist factions. Alexander Dubček, celebrated throughout the whole world as a symbol of the will to freedom, was compared with a likeable and humane "penal camp custodian" by the Czech head of parliament. Younger journalists believed that only historians would be interested in the bloody and bloodless ideological conflicts led by Hitler, Goebbels, Strasser or Trotzky, Stalin, Dubček, and Tito. More differentiated voices attested the reformers an effort for more humanity while at the same time declaring policies illusionary, inconsistent, feeble, and beyond August 1968, even a betrayal of national interests. They considered failure the most significant part of the Prague Spring, as it marked the end of the illusion of any possibility of reform of the Communist system and of the utopian idea of a third way between capitalism and Communism.

The Prague Spring was used as a political tool in the Czech Republic. With Václav Klaus' provocative bon mot that "all third ways in the economy lead to the third world,"[11] social democratic concepts of transformation and the legacy of 1968 were heavily contested. In contrast to neoliberal criticisms, however, the Czech population regards the Prague Spring mainly as an attempt to reform democracy (47 percent) and less as a struggle between the various Communist factions within the KPČ (21 percent); three quarters of those questioned considered the process of reform and democratization a matter concerning the majority of the population.[12] In Slovakia, there is a more positive attitude to the legacy of the 1968 reform process. Alexander Dubček is considered the world's most well-known Slovak and has long since been inducted into the national pantheon. His political authority was recognized after 1989 across the party spectrum, although his political influence remained moderate in Slovakia.

Differentiated verdicts and the beginning of argumentative style in the contemporary dispute over the legacy of the Prague Spring are unmistakable. In public discourse, the Prague Spring is considered a democratic awakening of the whole society and an original Czech and Slovak contribution to overcoming Soviet rule and the division of Europe.

Bibliography

For a better understanding of the country's history and an analysis of the reform movement, see Golan (1973), Kusín (1972), Skilling (1976), and Hejzlar (1976). Autobiographical contributions by Dubček (1993) and Mlynář (1980) provide the perspective of key figures. For a reconstruction of key events in 1968 and the defeat of the reform movement based on declassified material after the opening of the archives, see Pauer (1995) and Kieran (1997), as well as the edition of primary sources by Navrátil (1998).

Dubček, Alexander, and Jiří Hochman. *Hope Dies Last: The Autobiography of Alexander Dubcek*. New York: Kodansha International, 1993.

Golan, Galia. *Reform Rule in Czechoslovakia*. Cambridge: Cambridge University Press, 1973.

Hejzlar, Zdeněk. *Der Reformkommunismus. Zur Geschichte der Kommunistischen Partei der Tschechoslowakei*. Köln: Europäische Verlagsanstalt, 1976.

Kusin, Vladimir V. *Political Grouping in the Czechoslovak Reform Movement*. New York: Columbia University Press, 1972.

Mlynář, Zdeněk. *Nightfrost in Prague: The End of Humane Socialism*. New York: Karz, 1980.

Navrátil, Jaromir (ed.). *The Prague Spring 1968: A National Security Archive Documents Reader*. New York: Central European University Press, 1998.

Pauer, Jan. *Prag 1968. Der Einmarsch des Warschauer Paktes. Hintergründe, Planung, Durchführung*. Bremen: Temmen, 1995.

Skilling, Gordon H. *Czechoslovakia's Interrupted Revolution*. Princeton, NJ: Princeton University Press, 1976.

Williams, Kieran. *The Prague Spring and Its Aftermath, Czechoslovak Politics, 1968–1970*. Cambridge: Cambridge University Press, 1997.

Notes

1. Karel Kaplan, *The Short March: The Communist Takeover in Czecholovakia, 1945–1948* (London: C. Hurst, 1987).
2. See Zdeněk Mlynář, *Nightfrost: The End of Humane Socialism* (New York: Karz, 1980).
3. Dušan Hamšík, *Writers Against Rulers* (London: Hutchinson, 1971).

4. Alexander Dubček and Jiří Hochman, *Hope Dies Last: The Autobiography of Alexander Dubcek* (New York: Kodansha International, 1993).

5. German extracts in Hanswilhelm Haefs, ed., *Die Ereignisse in der Tschechoslowakei vom 27.6.1967 bis 18.10.1968. Ein dokumentarischer Bericht* (Bonn: Siegler, 1969), 70–78.

6. Zdeněk Hezlar, *Der Reformkommunismus. Zur Geschichte der Kommunistischen Partei der Tschechoslowakei* (Köln: Europäische Verlagsanstalt, 1976), 174.

7. Josef Škvorecký, ed., *Nachrichten aus der USSR. Dokumentation der Wochenzeitung „ Literární listy" des tschechoslowakischen Schriftstellerverbandes. Prag. Februar-August* (Frankfurt: Suhrkamp, 1968), 177.

8. J Jaroslaw Piekalkiewicz, *Public Opinion Polling in Czechoslovakia 1968–69. Results and Analysis of Surveys Conducted During the Dubček Era* (New York: Praeger, 1972), 4.

9. Jiří Lederer, *Jan Palach. Ein biografischer Bericht* (Zürich: Unionsverlag, 1982).

10. Jan Pauer, *Prag 1968. Der Einmarsch des Warschauer Paktes. Hintergründe, Planung, Durchführung* (Bremen: Temmen, 1995), 259.

11. Václav Klaus, *O tvář zítřka* (Prague: Prazska imaginace, 1991), 171.

12. IVVM 93-09 (4.-8.9.1993).

14
Poland

Stefan Garsztecki

The year 1968 was a year of great significance in Polish postwar history and a turning point for the country's breakthrough to democracy in 1989. It saw student protests, an anti-intellectual and anti-Semitic campaign, and power struggles within the ranks of the governing Communist Polish United Workers' Party (PZPR, *Polska Zjednoczona Partia Robotnicza*). It brought the end of revisionism in the Polish Left and bridged the gap between the opposing Left and the Catholic Church—the basis for the success of the independent trade union *Solidarność* at the beginning of the 1980s.

Social and Political Framework of the Country

After 1945, the Soviet model was imposed on Poland by Polish Communists with the help of the Soviet Red Army. The subsequent Stalinist period saw the destruction of national opposition through political trials, discrimination against the Catholic Church, collectivization, and bitter fights within the Communist party. Polish society perceived this process as a form of Soviet occupation and sharply rejected it. In 1956, the end of Stalinism in the Polish October changed this attitude. An end of collectivization, greater freedom for the Catholic Church, and limited liberalization substantially increased approval regarding the political system. The new First Secretary of the Central Committee of the PZPR, Władysław Gomułka, was widely perceived as a national Polish leader, his status only changing in the late 1960s. In spite of this "small stabilization" of the political regime, however, the fights within the PZPR continued.[1]

Dating from the mid-1950s, different factions within the Communist party fought for influence and power. The two opposing factions were the *Puławskis*, named after a street where some members lived, and the *Natolins*, who frequently gathered in a small palace near Warsaw, in Natolin. The Puławskis, some Jewish, were supporters of the Stalinist model and were influential in the first decade of the Peoples Republic of Poland, but after 1956 they favored a liberalization of the system. The Natolins, in contrast, also represented former Stalinists but accepted only minimal changes of the political system after 1956. They personified a more dogmatic, nationalist ferment of the party, whereas the Puławski group was identified with revisionist views. Another group within the party surfaced around Minister of the Interior Mieczysław Moczar. The partisans were composed of former members of the Polish Worker Party (*Polska Partia Robotnicza*), the occupation Communist party, and combatants from either *Gwardia Ludowa* (People's Guard) or *Armia Ludowa* (People's Army), both military organizations of the Communist underground. Some members were from the *Armia Krajowa* (Homeland Army), the underground army of the Polish government in London. Their common denominator was an urge for power propelled by nationalistic and anti-Semitic slogans aimed at their party rivals, especially the Pulawskis. The Natolin fraction increasingly lost its former significance and was partially absorbed by those around Gomułka.[2] Moczar's circle offered younger party members the chance for advancement, integrated the previously divided combatant milieu, and attempted to use student protest as a tool to camouflage their grab for power, but they were ultimately unsuccessful.[3]

Organizational and Social Structure of the Protest Movement

The eruption of student protests in 1968 was rooted in 1956, which saw the end of Polish Stalinism, a personal reshuffle in the PZPR, and the emerging public image of Władysław Gomułka as the representative of a more liberal, more nationalized political system. This hopeful beginning and its subsequent breakdown is the key to understanding the Polish March of 1968. As one Polish activist explains, "In the consciousness of my generation the importance of March lies in the radical destruction of the illusions of the year 1956."[4]

After the Polish October of 1956, young intellectuals like Jacek Kuroń and Karol Modzelewski tried to save some of the already eroding freedoms of this short liberalization period. Kuroń discussed political questions before 1956 as a young boy scout in the *Walterowcy* (dissolved in 1961 by the PZPR). In 1956, he and Modzelewski founded the Union of Revolutionary Youth (*Rewolucyjny Związek Młodzieży*) at the History department of Warsaw University, which was incorporated into the Union of Socialist Youth (*Związek Młodzieży Socjalistycznej*, ZMS) the following year. In spring 1962, 16-year-old Adam Michnik also initiated the Club of Searchers for Contradictions (*Klub Poszukiwaczy Sprzeczności*), a school discussion group in close touch with the Club of the Crooked Circle (*Klub Krzywego Koła*), founded and driven by writers and intellectuals in February 1955 and dissolved by the PZPR in 1962. Other organizations that were part of a broader discussion culture among intellectuals included the Political Discussion Club (*Polityczny Klub Dyskusyjny*), starting in the fall of 1962 at the University of Warsaw with Modzelewski as its chairman and Kuroń and Aleksander Smolar as activists, and the five Clubs of the Catholic Intelligence (*Klub Intelligencji Katolickiej*).[5] With exception of the Catholic clubs, all these initiatives stood for attempts from within the Left, among them many PZPR party members, to save some of the achievements of October 1956, fight for more democracy within the party and in Poland, and fight for the democratic development of Socialism.

Cognitive Orientation of the Movement

Because of the restrictive cultural course of the PZPR, the dissolution of discussion clubs and journals, and the limitation of academic autonomy, tensions grew in the mid-1960s that led Leftist intellectuals to enter a new stage in their confrontation with the oppressive regime. Once again around Kuroń and Modzelewski, a group of young members of ZMS (Union of Socialist Youth) emerged who called themselves *Komandosi*, probably because of their tactic of penetrating party meetings to irritate them with unconventional arguments. After their exclusion from the PZPR in November 1964, Kuroń and Modzelewski formulated an open letter to party members, in which they criticized the party bureaucracy for removing the workers from power.[6] In the spring of 1965, they were sentenced to several years in prison and the *Komandosi* came under close observation by security services.[7]

In March 1964, writers and academics demanded a change of cultural policy, an end to further restrictions, and free and public discussions in a letter to the Prime Minister Józef Cyrankiewicz. Among the thirty-four signers were some of the most famous writers and scholars of the country, who expressed their disappointment with the cultural and political development after 1956 in Poland.[8] The hopes associated with the thaw symbolized by the Polish October were thus almost exhausted by the mid-1960s, not least because of the harsh reactions of party officials to the open critique.

Attitudes Toward the Superpowers and the Cold War

The perception of the events in the Prague Spring, the student unrest in Western capitals, and the escalation of the war in Vietnam also played a significant role in the Polish protest movement. Similar to their colleagues in the West, Polish activists felt the inflexibility and paralysis of the international system. Their Socialistic rhetoric and demand for democratization of Socialism made them opponents of both the bureaucratic Soviet model and the capitalist model embodied by the United States, and natural allies of the reform efforts of the Prague Spring.[9]

Key Events

The starting point of the Polish 1968 was the PZPR's ban on *Forefather's Eve* (Dziady), a play by nineteenth-century poet Adam Mickiewicz, at the Warsaw National Theater for its alleged anti-Russian and anti-Soviet tendencies. As a result, the last performance on January 30, 1968, incited student protest that included members of the *Komandosi*, who demanded "independence without censorship" and marched to the Adam Mickiewicz monument in Warsaw. On February 16, they delivered a petition to the Polish Parliament, the *Sejm*, protesting the ban of the play; the petition was also sent to well-known Leftist writers and scientists.[10] On February 29, a meeting of the Warsaw branch of the Union of Polish Writers (*Związek Literatów Polskich*) adopted a resolution stating the growing interference of the state into cultural affairs and the unclear censorship regulations, and calling for more tolerance and the restaging of the play *Forefather's Eve*. Famous writers and intellectuals, some of them party members like Antoni Słonimski, Jerzy Andrzejewski, Paweł Jasienica, and Stefan Kisielewski, now sharply criticized the policy of the PZPR and its anti-Semitic campaign.[11]

Soon after the Israeli victory in 1967 in the Six-Day War, anti-Semitic campaigns had started in Poland and in other Socialist countries. The faction under Mieczysław Moczar particularly attacked their party rivals, but First Secretary Władysław Gomułka's remarks about a fifth column with respect to the Jewish population in Poland at the Sixth Trade Unions Congress on June 19, 1967, prepared the ground for official propaganda increasingly adopting sharper anti-Semitic tones.[12] Especially after the student protest of January 1968, faked leaflets at the University of Warsaw, likely written in the Ministry of Interior, agitated against "the Zionists" and the *Komandosi* and demanded their expulsion from university. A few days later, on March 4, 1968, students Adam Michnik and Henryk Szlajfer were expelled at the decision of Minister for National Education Henryk Jabłoński. Some *Komandosi*, including Henryk Szlajfer, Jan Lityński, and Seweryn Blumsztajn, were arrested. During a demonstration on March 8 in the university court, students protested against the ban of Mickiewicz' play, demanded the withdrawal of Michnik's and Szlajfer's expulsion, and expressed solidarity with writers and intellectuals under heavy attack in the media. They also defended Poland's democratic and independent traditions, emphasized the values of Socialism, and condemned the contrasting of students' and workers' interests in the official press. The militia and ORMO (*Ochotnicza Rezerwa Milicji Obywatelskiej*, Voluntary Reserve of the Citizens Militia) brutally broke up the meeting.[13]

What followed was student unrest—partly supported by faculty members—throughout Poland's academic centers. Slogans such as "The Press is lying," or "Democracy and Freedom" were common and sometimes also referred to democratization and reforms in Czechoslovakia.[14] The official reaction to these protests was an even stronger propaganda campaign with anti-Semitic overtones. For example, a leaflet at the University of Warsaw entitled "Who are you supporting?" highlighted the Jewish background of some *Komandosi* members.[15] Furthermore, the PZPR mobilized the *aktyw* of workers (a group of activit party members in the factories) against students, although with limited success.[16] In response, a letter from Warsaw University students to First Secretary Gomułka underlined the building of a Socialist Poland and the deepening of Socialist democracy.[17] On March 28, Warsaw University students went further and ratified a Declaration of the Student Movement, which demanded an end to censorship, economic reforms with self-government for workers, independent trade unions and courts, and the establishment of a constitutional court.[18] In doing so, the students had crossed the line between revisionism and revolution.

Scholars and writers were also targets of the propaganda campaign. Even the five Catholic members of parliament, who formed the *Znak* circle that had posed a legal opposition in parliament since 1957 as a remnant of the Polish October, became a target of the official media. On March 11, 1968, they asked the government what it intended to do about militia and ORMO brutality in confronting student demonstrations, and in the parliamentary debate *Znak* circle members Stanisław Stomma and Jerzy Zawieyski vehemently defended the students. Further support came from the Polish Episcopate, which in its pastoral letters of March 21 and May 3, 1968, condemned the attacks on the students and called for a joint dialogue. However, what both were missing was a clear condemnation of the anti-Semitic campaign. Although the second pastoral letter mentioned the anti-Semitic campaign, it only did so in the context of anti-Polish tendencies abroad and did not directly condemn it.[19]

By the end of March 1968, student protest had come to an end as a result of the brutal oppression by the militia and ORMO and the vicious propaganda campaign in the official mass media. Trials and purges all over in the country followed. According to historian Andrzej Friszke, about 2700 people were arrested. Most of them were released after forty-eight hours, but more than 300 remained imprisoned. In a speech to workers in Warsaw on March 19, 1968, Gomułka himself personally attacked Adam Michnik and Jacek Kuroń as organizers of student protest and branded writers and intellectuals, namely Paweł Jasienica, Leszek Kołakowski, Zygmunt Bauman, and others, as instigators. He also condemned Zionism and encouraged Polish Jews to emigrate. In the period up until September 1968, 774 persons were removed from leading governmental and party positions, thirty-three professors and scholars had to leave the university, two thousand army officers were expelled, and various people in the media and publishing lost their jobs. Because of these purges and the officially sanctioned anti-Semitic campaign, about 15,000 people of Jewish origin left the country. Prominent members of the *Komandosi* such as Kuroń, Modzelewski, Lityński, Blumsztajn, and Dajczgewand were sentenced to several years in prison, and even more students were expelled from the university.[20] Gomułka himself could restore his power on the Seventh Plenum of the Central Committee of the PZPR in July 1968.[21]

Forms and Tactics of Protest

Forms of protest changed substantially during the course of events. Initially the opposing Left, writers, and students tried to conduct open political discussions in clubs, the Union of Socialist Youth, and the PZPR. The letter of the thirty-four intellectuals to Prime Minister Cyrankiewicz, Kuroń's and Modzelewski's open letter, and the students' letter to Gomułka followed this principle of openness. The occupation of the University of Warsaw and Warsaw Polytechnic University in March 1968, student strikes, leaflet production, and various demonstrations were developed from this basic principle. As a result of the continuing massive oppression, however, activists turned to more conspiratorial forms. Student movement documents were smuggled to France and published by *Kultura*, a monthly magazine edited by Jerzy Giedroyc in Paris.[22] From 1976 onward, *Samizdat*, meaning independent newspapers, journals, and publishing houses edited by the Polish underground, developed and combined both principles: openness and secrecy.

Transnational Relations

The Polish March did not have many similarities with student protest in France or West Germany and had primarily domestic implications, with the anti-intellectual Gomułka standing in sharp contrast to Dubček in Czechoslovakia. One of the influential intellectuals from the *Komandosi*, Karol Modzelewski, had contacts to French Trotskyites dating from the late

1950s,[23] and the events in Czechoslovakia were closely followed among Polish dissenters. There was an awareness of change taking place in Western societies,[24] and similar to their Western counterparts, left-wing Polish students cultivated their revolutionary mythology.[25] In addition, the Communist propaganda with its reference to the Six-Day War and the anti-Semitic campaign also provoked reflections about international events among Polish students.

Consequences, Narratives, and Politics of Memory

The lingering impression following this general description of the events of spring 1968 is one of defeat. None of the students' demands or the writers' requests were implemented. The Mickiewicz play remained banned, cultural policies were still restrictive, the expulsion of students continued, and the anti-Semitic campaign led to an enormous exodus of intellectuals of Jewish origin. In mid-1968, the democratization of the political system was farther away than it had been before October 1956. Despite some solidarity of workers and ordinary people with the students in Warsaw and other university cities, society remained passive. Conformism and an adaptation to the political system, which was still more liberal than in the Stalinist period, prevented a stronger reaction from the workers. The national legitimatization the system had gained in 1956 would be shattered only in the 1970s.[26]

The events of March 1968 are therefore not a prominent feature of collective memory in Poland. According to a public opinion survey conducted in 1987 and once again in 2003, these events play only a minor role in public memory, in stark contrast to the workers' protests from 1956, 1970, or 1980.[27] Yet for a whole generation of intellectuals, March 1968 was the decisive moment of their political lives.

From a historic perspective, 1968 marks the beginning of the decline of Communism in Poland in four distinct ways. First, it put an end to revisionism and any illusions of an evolution of the system from within the party. Influential intellectuals voluntarily left the party or were expelled. Second, the abyss separating the opposing Left from the Catholic and national milieu was gradually bridged. The support of both for the crushed student youth from both the *Znak* circle in parliament and the Catholic Church paved the way for a rapprochement of these ideologically different milieus in the 1970s and the emergence of a joint opposition against the state. Third, through the anti-Semitic and nationalistic campaign, both the national problem and the religious problem were detected by the dissenting Polish Left. As a result, the Left transcended the borders of socialistic ideology in the following years in favor of preparing the ground for a broader opposition movement. Fourth, the experience of 1968 finally led to the conviction among intellectuals that workers' interests had to be taken into account more actively, and that mere rhetoric of a struggle for democracy and freedom of speech was not enough to convince workers to join their ranks; in other words, opposition had to be less elitist. From August 1980 onward, the Solidarity movement would demonstrate that the Polish Left had learned its lesson from March 1968.

Bibliography

Unfortunately, there is very little literature on Poland in the 1960s available in English. A very good and readable introduction into the topic of dissidents in comparative view is provided by Falk (2003). For the Polish March of 1968, see Eisler (1991, 2006). Probably the best reader on the March events is Kula (1998). For eyewitness perspectives, see especially Kuroń (1990) and Michnik (1977, 1985). A detailed analysis of the development of Polish opposition between 1945 and 1980 is presented by Friszke (1994), who also gives an excellent overview about the Polish Peoples Republic (2003).

Eisler, Jerzy. *Marzec 1968*. Warsaw: Krytyka, 1991.
Eisler, Jerzy. *Polski Rok 1968*. Warsaw: Instytut Pamięci Narodowej, Institute of National Remembrance, 2006.
Falk, Barbara. *The Dilemmas of Dissidence in East–Central Europe*. Budapest: CEU Press, 2003.
Friszke, Andrzej. *Opozycja polityczna w PRL 1945–1980*. London: Aneks, 1994.
Friszke, Andrzej. *Polska. Losy państwa i narodu 1939–1989*. Warsaw: Iskry, 2003.
Kula, Marcin, et al., eds. *Marzec 1968. Trzydzieście lat później. Materiały konferencji*. Vol. I. Referaty, Vol. II. Aneks źródłowy. Warsaw: PWN, 1998.
Kuroń, Jacek. *Wiara i wina. Do i od komunizmu*. Warsaw: NOWA, 1990.
Michnik, Adam. *KościóKościóKołciół, lewica, dialog*. Paris: Instytut Literacki, 1977.
Michnik, Adam. *Polnischer Frieden. Aufsätze zur Konzeption des Widerstands*. Berlin: Rotbuch, 1985.

Notes

1. For an overview of the political development in Poland after 1945, see Andrzej Friszke, *Polska. Losy państwa i narodu 1939–1989* (Warsaw: Iskry, 2003).
2. See Jerzy Eisler, *Marzec 1968* (Warszawa: Krytyka, 1991), 24.
3. See Andrzej Friszke, *Opozycja polityczna w PRL 1945–1980* (London: Aneks, 1994), 113.
4. Quoted from Adam Michnik, *Polnischer Frieden. Aufsätze zur Konzeption des Widerstands* (Berlin: Rotbuch, 1985), 38 (translation by the author).
5. For a detailed analysis of this "club" culture and the events preceding March 1968, see Jerzy Eisler, *Marzec 1968*; idem, *Polski Rok 1968* (Warsaw: Instytut Pamięci

Narodowej, 2006). For the rise of opposition, see Friszke, *Opozycja polityczna*, especially 94. A good overview in English is provided by Barbara Falk, *The Dilemmas of Dissidence in East-Central Europe* (Budapest: CEU, 2003), 13.

6. See the critical reflections on this by Jacek Kuroń, *Wiara i wina. Do i od komunizmu* (Warszawa: NOWA, 1990), 197.
7. See Eisler, *Marzec 1968*, 96.
8. In detail, see Jerzy Eisler, *List 34* (Warszawa: Wyd. Nauk. PWN, 1993).
9. See Dariusz Gawin, "Potłga mitu. O stylu politycznego myłlenia pokolenia Marca 68," in *Marzec 1968. Trzydzieście lat później. Materiały konferencji. Tom I. Referaty*, ed. Marcin Kula et al. (Warszawa: PWN, 1998), 284–313; furthermore, see Friszke, *Opozycja polityczna*, 238.
10. See Eisler, *Marzec 1968*, 146.
11. Ibid., 164.
12. Ibid., 135.
13. Ibid., 193; see also Andrzej Friszke, *Polska. Losy pałstwa i narodu 1939–1989* (Warszawa: Iskry, 2003), 296.
14. In greater detail about the different academic centers see Eisler, *Polski rok*, 305. See also *Marzec 1968. W poszukiwaniu programu odnowy. Satyra Studencka II. NZS PW. Do ułytku wewnłtrznego* (Warszawa, 1981).
15. Eisler, *Marzec 1968*, 224.
16. Ibid., 275.
17. Ibid., 303.
18. Ibid., 316
19. In detail, see Leonid Luks, *Katholizismus und politische Macht im kommunistischen Polen 1945-1989. Die Anatomie einer Befreiung* (Köln: Bołhlau, 1993), 72. See also the assessment of Adam Michnik, *KościóKościóKołciół, lewica, dialog* (Paris: Instytut Literacki, 1977), 67.
20. See Friszke, *Polska*, 299.
21. Eisler, *Polski rok*, 604.
22. See Friszke, *Polska*, 302.
23. See Eisler, *Marzec 1968*, 89.
24. See, for example, a not-very-well-known leaflet from October 1967, published on occasion of the International Day of Solidarity with Vietnam, which explicitly refers to the left in France, West Germany, and other Western countries; Friszke, *Opozycja polityczna*, 238.
25. See Gawin, *Potłga mitu*, passim.
26. See Marcin Zaremba, "Biedni Polacy 68. Społeczełstwo polskie wobec wydarzeł marcowych w łwietle raportów KW i MSW dla kierownictwa PZPR," in Kula, *Marzec 1968*, 144–170.
27. See more detailed Piotr Tadeusy Kwiatkowski, "PRL w Pamięci społeczełstwa polskiego," in Andrzej Szpociłski, ed., *Wobec przeszłołci. Pamiłlprzeszłołci jako element kultury współczesnej* (Warsaw: Instytut im. Adama Mickiewicza, 2005), 74–91.

15
East Germany

Timothy S. Brown

Social and Political Framework of the Country

The German Democratic Republic was founded in October 1949 on the territory corresponding to the Soviet Occupation Zone established following World War II. The Socialist Unity Party (SED), a product of the forced fusion of the Communist and Social Democratic parties in the Soviet Zone in April 1946, became the sole organ of rule in what was effectively a one-party state. East Germany developed a reputation as one of the most stable, successful Soviet satellite states. Its most significant moment of unrest, the workers' uprising of 1953, was limited in scope, coming nowhere close to the size and significance of the Hungarian uprising three years later. The GDR was basically quiescent after 1953, although its failure to meet basic economic and political expectations resulted in a continual exodus of its citizens. Construction of the Berlin Wall in August 1961 helped stabilize the population; by settling the status of a divided Berlin, it led to both a modest improvement in relations between the two Germanys and a period of relative political relaxation in the GDR. This unintended thaw was short-lived, with the Eleventh Plenum of the SED in late 1965 signaling a crackdown on the liberalization in culture and politics. The subsequent period was marked by a succession of freezes and thaws. Erich Honecker's succession to power in 1971 signaled the beginning of a period of liberalization that ultimately proved more superficial than substantial. The period following the mid-1970s was marked by the population's gradual retreat from identification with the regime. Young people, particularly dissidents, increasingly found their way to Protestant Church or into marginal drop-out existences in enclaves like Berlin's Prenzlauer Berg. The perceived loss of state legitimacy contributed heavily to the final breakdown of the GDR in 1989, for which the events of 1968 left an ambiguous legacy.

Organizational and Social Structure of the Protest Movement

It is scarcely possible to speak of a Western-style "protest movement" in the GDR. The SED's totalizing claim on the means and content of public expression profoundly shaped the possibilities of oppositional politics.[1] Scholars have traced a change in the nature of opposition in the GDR from "fundamental" in the late 1940s and 1950s to "reformist" in the 1970s and '80s—in other words, from a total rejection of the system to a belief that the system could be amenable to democratic reform.[2] The physicist Robert Havemann and the singer Wolf Biermann are well-known figures of the reformist tendency. The former, a committed supporter of socialism, was stripped of his post for emphasizing the need for greater democracy in the GDR. The latter, also a loyal critic of the regime, was stripped of his East German citizenship in 1976, an event often cited as a key caesura marking the impossibility of reform in the GDR.[3] Alongside these well-known cases there existed loose networks of affinity, constructed around emancipatory ideas drawn from both sides of the Iron Curtain, linking East German youth both to the older generation of GDR dissidents and to young counterparts abroad. Prominent in these networks were the sons and daughters of regime notables such as the children of Robert Havemann, who were able to take advantage of their comparatively privileged position to develop a certain psychological autonomy relative to the regime. The existence of a young generation charged with ideas of cultural revolution and democratic political rebirth justifies us in speaking of the existence of a "68er generation" in the GDR, even if the political possibilities for the unfolding of a corresponding political movement comparable to those in the West were fatally constrained.

Cognitive Orientation of the Movement

Generational conflict was attenuated in the GDR, both by the experience of state repression and by the structure of education.[4] University students in the GDR were less likely to rebel than their counterparts in the West for the simple reason that higher education was largely closed to young people of nonconformist inclination.[5] At the same time, western New Left rhetoric carried a limited charge in the GDR, as some of its key points—opposition to U.S. imperialism, for example—were standard parts of the rhetorical repertoire of the East German regime. Nevertheless, the GDR 68ers shared important similarities in outlook and worldview with their counterparts in the

West. The memoir literature is rife with examples of the importance they placed on the ideas of the Western student movements, as well as on the democratic socialist renewal in Czechoslovakia. Because the repressive environment prohibited them from forming any sort of protest movement, the GDR 68ers may nevertheless be seen as part of a "discourse community" connecting young people across national and bloc boundaries.[6] This community embraced not just New Left politics but also an accompanying cultural revolution of lifestyle, mores, and sensibility. Already by the mid-1960s beat music became the site around which relatively autonomous youth identities could be constructed.[7] The repression against beat groups and fans following the Eleventh Plenum, including a police assault on a peaceful demonstration of protesting beat fans in Leipzig in 1965, signaled the extent to which the regime saw in the new youth lifestyle an implicit rejection of its aim of bringing up a new "socialist" youth.[8] The subsequent emergence of an East German version of the Western 1960s counterculture was aggressively politicized by the regime.[9] The casual brutality of repressive measures like forced public haircuts for young male beat fans shocked members of the GDR's young dissident intelligentsia, heightening an already strong sense of the contradiction between the state's humanitarian promises and its authoritarian behavior. This contradiction, stemming as much from the indignities and brutalities of everyday life as from any formal political consideration, was a critical factor in a growing disaffection that characterized the East German 1968.

Key Events

The key event of the East German 1968—in both the literal and figurative senses—was the reaction to the crushing of the Prague Spring. More than simply a concrete moment of protest—one, it must be mentioned, that affected not just the 68ers but also the general population, including many workers—it represented the supreme moment of cognitive dissonance in which the contradictions in the state's claims of democracy and humanism were exposed and the pressure to act in the face of injustice, even in the face of considerable personal risk, became great. The implications of the Warsaw Pact invasion went far beyond the disposition of the democratic socialist experiment in Prague—they had to do with the possibility, or impossibility, of reform in the East bloc as a whole. Yet the immediate response to the Warsaw Pact invasion of Czechoslovakia in August 1968 had very much the character of a spontaneous cry of outrage, the extent and force of which has only in recent years begun to be appreciated by historians.[10] Within hours of the invasion, leaflets appeared on the streets of GDR cities, and slogans such as "Russians out of the CSSR" were painted on public buildings.[11]

Spontaneous acts of protest occurred in the following days in factories, schools, and other public institutions in all of East Germany's major cities, and in many smaller ones as well.[12] The state security recorded nearly two thousand acts of protest, mostly involving the distribution of fliers and painting of graffiti, stretching into the early September months.[13] Sabotage and threats against functionaries were recorded,[14] and open public demonstrations, although rare, were not unheard of.[15] Expressions of opposition cut across class and generational lines, involving both young and old, intellectuals and artists, managers and industrial workers.[16]

These protests were ambiguous in their ideological content; far from signaling any particular commitment to "socialism with a human face," they reflected, above all, anger against Soviet domination. Opposition to the Soviet invasion thus must not be conflated with a putative 68er protest movement in the GDR; rather, the crushing of the Prague Spring must be seen as a moment in which the long-building psychological pressures on the GDR's young dissident intelligentsia reached an explosive point, causing some of them to take action against injustice that they could no longer tolerate. The most well-known of those who acted were the group around the Havemann siblings. Of their larger circle—a relatively small group estimated at no more than two hundred young people—only a few acted in response to the invasion, and then only after some deliberation.[17] Their actions included distributing fliers criticizing the invasion, painting "Dubček" on a number of public buildings—including a wall of the Humboldt University—and hanging a Czechoslovakian flag from the balcony of an apartment.[18] Those arrested for these actions and tried in October 1968 included the two sons of Robert Havemann, Frank and Florian, along with five others, including Erika Berthold, Thomas Brasch, and Rosita Hunziger.[19] They received sentences ranging from fifteen to twenty-seven months.[20] Most of the imprisoned were released after a short time and the sentences of the group reduced to probation. Other sanctions such as loss of educational privileges were subsequently enforced.[21] The consequences of the protest illustrated very clearly the lack of space in the GDR in which to pursue democratic initiative from below. The subsequent political activity of members of the group must be read as an attempt to come to grips with this fact.

Forms and Tactics of Protest

For some members of the Havemann group, the aftermath of the Prague protests was marked by an attempt to locate a new, more promising field of political activity. This was accomplished by the founding of a "commune" in East Berlin toward the end of 1968. Here, similarities with Western forms of activism became readily apparent, as did the limitations in the GDR of practices imported from the West. This commune, the "K1/East," as it was informally dubbed by its founders, existed until 1973 with revolving personnel in several different apartments.[22] It was modeled on the infamous *Kommune I* in West Berlin, which created a media sensation around the new lifestyle revolution of drugs, sexual openness, and hippie appearance and played a key role in the radicalization of the West German student movement.[23] Like the founders of the *Kommune I*, the communards in East Berlin saw as their goal the politicization of everyday life. They also aimed to break the grip of the bourgeois family and to overcome repressive psychological programming—in this case, the SED's moralizing around the idea of "socialism." Their attack on bourgeois "socialist" normalcy, carried out with the aid of drugs and music, sexual openness, a critique of traditional gender roles, and group therapy, was accompanied by a intense engagement with texts of Marxism and psychoanalysis, including works on "anti-authoritarian childrearing" smuggled from the West.[24]

The K1/East demonstrates the appeal and relevance of Western models of self-discovery in the GDR circa 1968 and reinforces the extent to which the cultural revolution of the 1960s was able to cross Cold War boundaries. However, the similarities between the East and West Berlin communes must not be overstated. Unlike the *Kommune I*, the K1/East existed in almost complete isolation. Unlike its model in the West, it could not serve as a base for provocative forays into the public sphere, nor could it serve to revolutionize a larger student movement. It was but a tiny bubble of private space—under constant observation by the state security—with little larger influence. Facing this dead end—exacerbated by all the usual problems common to communal living situations—the commune's founder, Frank Havemann, turned toward another solution: working within the ruling party for change, a decision that ultimately led to a split within the group.[25] The attempt at unfolding a New Left sort of politics under the auspices of the regime—for example, marching in a party-organized demonstration with signs reading "We agree with Dutschke"—again illustrated the impossibility of pursuing an independent 68er-type of politics in the face of the SED state's totalizing claims. Young dissidents in the GDR could embrace new ideas of personal and political emancipation from the West, but, unable to form a movement or use public space to dispute the dominant narrative, they were doomed to impotence.

Transnational Relations

The GDR illustrates the key importance of transnational linkages in the protest movements of 1968. From the young beat fans whose devotion to

Western music and clothing styles were criminalized by the regime, to the young dissidents reading the smuggled work of Western intellectuals and haunted by images of Western protests (and scenes of chaos in the streets of Prague) on illegally received West German television, East Germany's 1968 moment was a transnational moment. Smuggled books and music from the West were of key importance, as were transnational media like television and radio. Personal relationships between East and West German 68ers, part of a broader pattern of contact between students on both sides of the Iron Curtain, were not uncommon.[26] Travel played a critical role; in 1967–1968, 2.6 million East Germans visited the CSSR; 1.1 million Czechoslovakians visited the GDR in the same period. The overwhelming majority of East Germans who visited Czechoslovakia in July 1968 were less than thirty-five years of age.[27] GDR 68ers like Frank Havemann were particularly drawn to the political content of the Prague Spring, taking in as much Czech culture as possible, and avidly reading Ludvik Vaculik's manifesto of democratic-socialist rebirth, the "2,000 Words."[28] Belief in the emancipatory potential of the experiment in Czechoslovakia, as much or more than the protest movements in the west, fueled the aspirations of those hoping for a democratization of East German socialism from within.

Consequences, Narratives, and Politics of Memory

Scholars assessing the response in the GDR to the suppression of the Prague Spring, as well as those interested in popular music and youth culture in the GDR, invariably deal with the questions of *whether* or *when* a "1968" took place in East Germany.[29] Alongside this problem, there exists the parallel question of the significance of the events of the year 1968 in the GDR. Thus it is possible to see 1968 in the GDR as the "revolution that did not take place"[30] while simultaneously acknowledging the existence in East Germany of important components of the Western youth revolt.[31] When the narrow lens of "politics" is widened to capture changes in sensibility and lifestyle, the GDR seems to fit better into the pattern of a larger world "1968."[32] This wider perspective renders correspondingly less salient the year 1968, which although key for psychological reasons,[33] was a less important caesura in cultural and political terms than 1965 (the Eleventh Plenum), 1971 (the accession of Honecker), or 1976 (the expulsion of Biermann).[34] The year 1968 in the GDR did, however, play an important role in the politicization of figures who would later be active in the peace and citizens' movements in the GDR, and in this sense the year may be seen as an important marker on the way to the revolution of 1989.[35]

Bibliography

For contextualization in East German history, see Ross (2002) and Eppelmann (2003). For a collection of essays dealing with 1968 in East and West Germany, see *Aus Politik und Zeitgeschichte*, B45/2003. Also see the theme issue "Roundabout '68" in *Berliner Blätter. Ethnographische und ethnologische Beiträge*, Heft 18/1999. On the East German response to the Warsaw Pact invasion of Czechoslovakia, see Wenzke (1995) and Fulbrook (1995). The concept of the 68er Generation in the GDR is treated in Engler (2005). On resistance in the GDR, see the essays in Henke et al (1999). On the counter-cultural component, see Kaiser and Petzold (1997). On youth culture and popular music in the GDR, see Poiger (2000) and Ohse (2003).

Engler, Wolfgang. "Die dritte Generation," in Wolfgang Engler, ed., *Die Ostdeutschen. Kundevon einem verlorenen Land.* Berlin: Aufbau Taschenbuch, 2005, 303–40.

Eppelmann, Rainer et al, ed., *Bilanz und Perspektiven der DDR-Forschung.* Paderborn: Schöningh, 2003.

Fulbrook, Mary. *Anatomy of a Dictatorship: Inside the GDR, 1949–1989.* New York: Oxford, 1995.

Henke, Dietmar et al., eds. *Widerstand und Opposition in der DDR.* Köln: Böhlau Verlag, 1999.

Kaiser, Paul and Claudia Petzold. *Boheme und Diktatur in der DDR: Gruppen, Konflikte, Quartiere, 1970–1989.* Berlin: Fannei & Walz, 1997.

Ohse, Marc-Dietrich. *Jugend nach dem Mauerbau. Anpassung, Protest und Eigensinn (DDR 1961–1974).* Berlin: Ch. Links, 2003.

Poiger, Uta. *Jazz, Rock, and Rebels: Cold War Politics and American Culture in a Divided Germany.* Berkeley: University of California Press, 2000.

Ross, Corey. *The East German Dictatorship: Problems and Perspectives in the Interpretation of the GDR.* London: Edward Arnold, 2002.

Wenzke, Rüdiger. *Die NVA und der Prager Frühling 1968. Die Rolle Ulbrichts und der DDR-Streitkräfte bei der Niederschlagung der tschechoslowakischen Reformbewegung.* Berlin: Ch. Links, 1995.

Notes

1. For a recent summary of these debates, see Corey Ross, *The East German Dictatorship: Problems and Perspectives in the Interpretation of the GDR* (London: Edward Arnold, 2002).
2. See Ranier Eckert, "Dissidenz und Opposition im Schatten der Mauer—die sechziger und siebziger Jahre," in Rainer Eppelmann et al., eds., *Bilanz und Perspektiven der DDR-Forschung* (Paderborn: Ferdinand Schöningh, 2003), 167–72. See also Karl Wilhelm Fricke, "Dimensionen von Opposition und Widerstand in der DDR," in Klaus-Dietmar Henke, Peter Steinbach, and Johannes Tuchel, eds., *Widerstand und Opposition in der DDR* (Köln: Böhlau, 1999), 21–43.

3. Ilko-Sascho Kowalczuk, "'Wer sich nicht in Gefahr begibt. . . . ' Protestaktionen gegen die Intervention in Prag und die Folgen von 1968 für die DDR-Opposition," in Klaus-Dietmar Henke et al., eds., *Widerstand und Opposition in der DDR* (Köln: Böhlau, 1999), 257–274, 268.
4. Engler, Wolfgang, "Die dritte Generation," in Wolfgang Engler ed., *Die Ostdeutschen. Kunde von einem verlorenen Land* (Berlin: Aufbau Taschenbuch, 2005), 308–9.
5. Uta Poiger, *Jazz, Rock, and Rebels. Cold War Politics, and American Culture in a Divided Germany* (Berkeley: University of California Press, 2000), 218.
6. Ute Kätzel, "Kommune 1 Ost," *Freitag* 2002;20:12.
7. See the article by Detlef Siegfried in this handbook.
8. On the Leipzig Beat demonstration, see Dorothee Wierling, "Beat heißt schlagen. Die Leipziger Beatdemonstration in Oktober 1965 und die Jugendpolitik der SED," in Adolf-Grimme-Institut, *Unsere Medien, Unsere Republik 2*: "1965: Warten auf den Frühling," Heft 4, 1993.
9. Paul Kaiser and Claudia Petzold, "Perlen vor die Säue. Eine Boheme im Niemandsland," in *Boheme und Diktatur in der DDR. Gruppen, Konflikte, Quartiere, 1970–1989*, ed. Paul Kaiser and Claudia Petzold (Berlin: Fannei and Walz, 1997), 13–112.
10. Mary Fulbrook, *Anatomy of a Dictatorship: Inside the GDR, 1949–1989* (New York: Oxford, 1995), 193–200; Monika Tantzscher, "Maßnahme Donau und Einsatz Genesung": Die Niederschlagung des Prager Frühlings 1968/69 im *Spiegel der MfS-Akten* (Berlin, 1994).
11. Rüdiger Wenzke, *Die NVA und der Prager Frühling 1968. Die Rolle Ulbrichts und der DDR-Streitkräfte bei der Niederschlagung der tschechoslowakischen Reformbewegung* (Berlin: Ch. Links, 1995), 161–62.
12. Ibid., 167.
13. Ibid. On the various slogans employed in the graffiti see Engler, "Die dritte Generation," 303–40.
14. Fulbrook, *Anatomy of a Dictatorship*, 197.
15. See Wenzke, *Die NVA*, 167.
16. Stefan Wolle, "Die DDR-Bevölkerung und der Prager Frühling," *Aus Politik und Zeitgeschichte. Beilage zur Wochenzeitung Das Parlament* 1992;B36/92:35–45; Fulbrook, *Anatomy of a Dictatorship*, 194–95.
17. Florian Havemann, "68er Ost," *UTOPIE kreativ* 2004;164:544–556; see also Engler, "Die dritte Generation," 312–13.
18. This was the apartment, on the Straußberger Platz, of the younger Havemann son, Florian; see Kaiser, "Kommune 'K1—Ost', Ostberlin," 25.
19. Erika Berthold was the 18-year-old daughter of the *Stellvertretennde Direktors des Instituts für Marxismus-Leninismus beim ZK der SED*. Thomas Brasch was the 23-year-old son of the *Stellvertretende Kulturminister*. Rosita Hunziger was the daughter of the sculptress Ingeborg Hunziger. Also arrested were Sandra Weigel, Nichte von Helene Weigel, and Hans-Jürgen Uzkoreit; Kätzel, "Kommune 1 Ost." These were seven of some 313 arrests made between August and December 1968; see Wenzke, *Die NVA*, 171.

20. Kowalczuk, "'Wer sich nicht in Gefahr begibt. . . . ' 266.
21. See Franziska Groszer, "Aufbruch und andere Brüche. Die Kommune 1 Ost," in *Wie weit flog die Tomate?* (Berlin: Heinrich-Böll-Stiftung und Feministisches Institut, 1999).
22. Paul Kaiser, "Kommune 'K1—Ost', Ostberlin," unpublished radio broadcast manuscript for Deutschlandfunk-Radio, copy in possession of the author, p. 21. The commune was also known as the "Havemann Commune" because of the participation of three of the dissident physicist's children, Frank and Florian Havemann and Franziska Großer; other members were Gert Großer, Klaus Labsch, Erika Berthold, Rosita Hunziger, Thomas Bratsch, and Sandra Weigel; see Kaiser and Petzold, *Perlen vor die Säue*, 33; on the commune, see also Groszer, "Aufbruch und andere Brüche; Ute Kätzel, "Kommune 1 Ost"; on Ute Kätzel, see also "Erika Berthold und die Kommune 1/Ost," in Ute Kätzel, ed., *Die 68erinnen. Porträt einer rebellischen Frauengeneration* (Berlin: Rohwolt, 2002), 220–37.
23. See the article by Martin Klimke in this handbook.
24. Kätzel, "Kommune 1 Ost," see also Groszer, "Aufbruch und andere Brüche."
25. Kaiser and Petzold, "Perlen vor die Säue, 33.
26. See Havemann "68er Ost," 546; see also Frank Havemann in Land and Possekel, *Fremde Welten*, 220; Kaiser, "Kommune 'K1—Ost', Ostberlin," 28; Enzensberger, *Die Jahre der Kommune I* (Köln, 2004), 233; Dieter Kunzelmann, *Leisten Sie keinen Widerstand! Bilder aus meinem Leben* (Berlin: Transit, 1998), 91; Kleinert in Engler, "Die dritte Generation," 311.
27. Marc-Dietrich Ohse, *Jugend nach dem Mauerbau. Anpassung, Protest und Eigensinn (DDR 1961–1974)* (Berlin: Ch. Links, 2003), 190.
28. Ibid., 194.
29. See Ohse, *Jugend nach dem Mauerbau*, 218; Dietrich Mühlberg, "Wann war 68 im Osten? Oder: Wer waren die 68er im Osten?" in *Berliner Blätter. Ethnographische und ethnologische Beiträge* (Berlin: Institut für Europäische Ethnologie der Humboldt-Universität zu Berlin, Heft 18, 1999), 44–58; See Kätzel, "Kommune 1 Ost."
30. Fulbrook, *Anatomy of a Dictatorship*, 193.
31. Ohse, *Jugend nach dem Mauerbau*, 219.
32. See Michael Rauhut, "Am Fenster: Rockmusik und Jugendkultur in der DDR," in *Rock! Jugend und Musik in Deutschland.* (Berlin: Die Deutsche Bibliothek, 1995), 70–77.
33. On the psychological effect see Jonathan Grix, *The Role of the Masses in the Collapse of the GDR* (Basingstoke: Macmillan, 2000), 16.
34. See Robert Grünbaum, "Die Biermann Ausbürgerung und ihre Folgen," in Eppelmann et al, *Bilanz und Perspektiven der DDR-Forschung*; see also Eckert, "Dissidenz und Opposition."
35. Ute Kätzel and Annette Simon have emphasized the importance of the 1968 generation in the GDR for the citizens' movement of 1989; see Kätzel, "Kommune 1 Ost"; Annette Simon and Jan Faktor, *Fremd in eigenem Land?* (Gießen: Psycho-Sozial, 2000). For a skeptical treatment of the role of GDR intellectuals and artists in the revolution of 1989, see Grix, *The Role of the Masses*, 16. Mary Fulbrook makes a similar point regarding 1968; see Fulbrook, *Anatomy of a Dictatorship*, 200.

16
Romania

Corina Petrescu and Serban Pavelescu

Within the larger context of 1968, Romania stands out through the quasi-total lack of consonance with the events unfolding on the international stage. Open opposition to the regime came about only almost a decade later. The rationales behind this state of affairs were manifold and had both internal and international ramifications. This chapter outlines the reasons behind Romania's position and argues in favor of considering the events leading to Ceaușescu's demise in 1989 not only as an instance similar to the evolution of other East European states at the time but also as the heritage of 1968.

Social and Political Framework of the Country

By the mid-1960s, Romania was still preponderantly a developing agrarian country. The main components of the country's economic policy were sustained industrialization with an emphasis on the heavy and mechanical industries and the collectivization of agriculture.[1] The combination of these tendencies led to accelerated migration of workers from the agricultural to the industrial sector and from rural to urban spaces. These migratory fluxes affected Romanian society overall, profoundly affecting its systemic coherence and cohesion.[2]

Romania's political regime and power structures were similar to those of other Eastern European Communist states. The Communist party (RCP) dominated society institutionally, politically, and ideologically. By the mid-1960s, however, the party underwent serious changes that affected state structures equally. Statutes were revisited to increase the number of members, allowing those of "bourgeois" origin to join. Slowly, professional qualification rather than ideological indoctrination became the criterion for advancement within party structures. The key to these formal changes lay in events that marked the evolution of the Romanian party and its relations to Moscow during the decade preceding 1968.

In Romanian history, Khrushchev's years leading the Soviet Union are associated with the withdrawal of Red Army troops in 1958. Negotiations began in the summer of 1955, but it was only support of the Soviet Union in solving the Hungarian crisis of 1956 that worked in favor of the Romanians. In rewarding Romania in this manner, Khrushchev demonstrated that his assurance of recalling Soviet troops from Eastern Europe was not an empty promise. The withdrawal attempted to remedy the Soviet Union's badly damaged image soon after its violent intervention in Hungary. As anti-Russian sentiments had a long tradition in Romania, this achievement was cheered as a great success.

Although Romanian leader Gheorghe Gheorghiu-Dej[3] did not agree with Khrushchev, he was skilled enough to escape being purged after the latter's condemnation of Stalinism in 1956. After the withdrawal, the Dej regime concentrated on obtaining economic advantages such as ties with Western countries and non-integration into the supranational planning scheme (Valev Plan) supported by the Soviets. Beginning in the 1960s, the Soviet Union tried to prescribe specific economic functions for each of its members, reducing less-developed countries to mere sources of raw materials for more advanced ones. Romania's consistent refusal to accept its role as Eastern Europe's granary halted this initiative. The country focused on a fast industrialization track destined to ensure the country's detachment from the Soviet Union, while involvement in the supranational planning scheme would have reversed the country's goal by increasing its dependency on the Soviet Union.[4] However, this did not entail separation from the principles of hardcore Stalinism, which remained a dominant feature of the regime. On the contrary, one can easily claim that it was precisely the refusal to restructure its fora that led the Romanian leadership farther away from its Soviet counterpart.[5]

Attitudes toward the Superpowers and the Cold War

Unlike other parties in Eastern Europe, the RCP kept an equal distance from both China and the Soviet Union during the inceptive years of their conflict. Political pragmatism determined Dej's neutrality: wanting economic and political autonomy for his country, Dej viewed China's ascension as an important political player as a guarantee for achieving his goals. In this tense context, Romanian authorities took one more step in ensuring the country's international position before the April 1964 release of the statement that cemented Dej's power and symbolized Romania's declaration of independence from the Soviet Union. During the Cuban missile crisis, they informed the United

States that they had not been consulted by the Soviet partners and that should the Cold War become hot, Romania would remain neutral.[6]

In April 1964, the Political Bureau of the party met to discuss the Sino–Soviet conflict. To adopt a position, the bureau analyzed the history of Romanian–Soviet relations. A text was released under the title, "Declaration of the Romanian Workers' Party Concerning Problems of the International Communist and Working Class Movement." The document was daring because it was the first time when a "small" party expressed its views with respect to issues concerning the Communist bloc.

The declaration raised the RCP's popularity among Romanians, just as the 1958 withdrawal had done. At a cultural level, the document marked the end of a phase in which Russian language and Soviet culture had been the dominating foreign influences, resulting in a blow to the symbolic Soviet presence.[7] At a social level, living conditions improved because of an increase in consumer goods. There was also a liberalization of the political regime, which included pardoning political prisoners. Thus, the declaration represented not only the departure point in an open move to extract Romania from Moscow's tutelage but also the début of fervent searches by the Romanian Communists for an alternative principle to validate their ideological and political hegemonic claims over society. The choice of nationalism as a legitimizing resource and the *mésalliance* between the two ideologies—Communism and nationalism—in the official party line offer one explanation for the events of 1968 in Romania and for the country's later development. Bucharest's independence from Moscow and the lack of direct Soviet intervention in Romania can primarily be explained by the stability of the Romanian regime. Neither Dej, during his later years, nor Ceauşescu presented a threat to the Socialist *Weltanschauung*. Both mimicked liberalization to reinforce the Stalinist model.

After his assent to power, Nicolae Ceauşescu[8] took over and amplified Dej's political line. In 1965, the RCP's Ninth Congress celebrated not only the succession to power but also the beginning of the process of rewriting party and state history in a nationalist tenor.[9] Prefacing what was to become one of the most extravagant cults of personality,[10] the party launched a campaign to mythologize the historical past and to rewrite it in a revolutionary tone. Ultimately, Ceauşescu's goal was to destroy Dej's emblematic status as a challenger of the Soviet Union and to represent himself as the country's first legitimate Communist leader.

Internationally, the discourse of the Romanian leadership toward the Soviet Union materialized in increasingly critical tones. In accordance with the Declaration of 1964, Bucharest attempted to assume the role of mediator in the Sino–Soviet conflict and pursued economic and political ties with the

Western world. This course of action resulted from a combination of opportunity and necessity. In the context of the open dispute between the two
states and parties,[11] the Romanian leadership launched a normalization of
its ties to the West. The year 1968 represented the success of this course, val-
idated by General Charles de Gaulle's visit to the country in May and his
encouragement of the Romanian line of action.[12]

Key Events

Ceauşescu saw his opportunity for action in the armed intervention of the
Warsaw Pact in the Prague Spring. Romania had acted contrary to the Soviet
Union before; in March 1968, at a meeting concerning the Test Ban Treaty,
Romania clearly detached itself from other Warsaw Pact members and
became "unreliable." One immediate consequence was the isolation of the
country.[13] Romania was not summoned to further military exercises, including the march in Czechoslovakia.

Given this history, a statement condemning the Soviet-led intervention
was not surprising. Even so, the vehemence of Ceauşescu's speech on August
21, 1968, was impressive.[14] He proclaimed a Socialist country's internal
affairs the concern of their own leadership, and not of other states. He
declared intervention as incongruous with true Marxist-Leninist principles
and demanded its discontinuation. Lest Romania be taken by surprise by an
invasion, Ceauşescu instituted armed Patriotic Guards made of workers,
peasants, and intellectuals to defend the country's independence. He reiter-
ated the indisputable unity of Romania's population regardless of nationality and emphasized that the leadership's highest responsibility was toward
this unified people and the working class.

Ceauşescu's main arguments involved legitimacy. This is unsurprising
given that legitimacy was his main concern regarding his own power position. He condemned the invasion because he saw it as unlawful even from
the point of view of the Warsaw Pact. The key words in his address were
"independence" and "sovereignty." He tailored this appeal to Romanian
anti-Soviet sentiments, which allowed him to stand before his people as
their resolute defender and thus validate his regime's claims to legitimacy
and power. His bravado was a matter of *Realpolitik*. Only ninety-six hours
after this intervention, the tone had mellowed and official discourses underlined the friendly relations between Romania and the Soviet Union despite
their differences with respect to "a number of problems including the
Czechoslovak one."[15] As long as Ceauşescu did not question or attempt to
redefine the core of Socialist ideology, Brezhnev did not view him as a
real threat. He tolerated Ceauşescu's behavior and did not envision a

Czechoslovak solution for Romania. Ceauşescu fully embraced his role as Eastern Europe's *enfant terrible*, yet he never conceived of breaking with Socialism or Stalinism.

Forms and Tactics of Protest

In 1968, Romania was a country focused on political legitimization. Authorities followed an intensely nationalistic course while also celebrating an increasingly open and highly popular anti-Soviet discourse. The society was strongly heterogeneous as a result of migratory fluxes caused by forced industrialization and collectivization. Thus, the coherence of social classes in urban areas and communities in rural areas was shaken.[16] A real tradition of labor unions and professional solidarity did not exist among workers and was in the process of disintegrating among peasants. In addition, the intelligentsia was traditionally dependent on the power structure.[17] As a consequence, Romanian society lacked any element favorable to the emergence of protest or dissidence movements. Yet another inhibiting element was the Orthodox Church, which preferred formal obedience and occult actions to open resistance.[18] In this context, August 1968 offered the Romanian leadership the ideal stage to enact a powerful performance in support of its efforts to legitimize itself, which it attempted to do as a means of preempting a coalescence of social protest against the regime. Ceauşescu's speech on August 21, 1968, along with nationalist and anti-Soviet propaganda, formed the foundation of the regime's self-legitimizing discourse for at least a decade. The effect on Romanian society was profound.

The lack of revisionist or dissent movements that would include Romania in the general European context of the year 1968 constitutes an atypical occurrence not only for that time but also with respect to Romanian history in the aftermath of World War II. During the Soviet occupation following the summer of 1944, Romanian society engaged in strong opposition to the installation and consolidation of the Communist regime. This confrontation continued in some form—active or passive resistance to the collectivization process, armed resistance, or incessant adherence to the forbidden Greek-Catholic religious cult—until the early 1960s.[19] Yet, with few noteworthy exceptions, Romania did not know the development of dissident currents amid the intelligentsia with resonance in the masses, as was the case with Hungary and Czechoslovakia. It also lacked labor union movements and collaboration between workers and intellectuals, as in the case of Poland's *Solidarity*. Nor did the Romanian Orthodox Church (or the Catholic or Protestant churches, for that matter) play a role similar to that of the Protestant Church in East Germany or the Catholic Church in Poland.

Consequences

The Communist leadership did not disregard these facts nor its lack of legitimacy when it reconsidered both its national discourse and its international course during the mock liberalization of the late 1960s. Although under Ceauşescu's regime the synthesis between national values and Communist ideology produced a political culture that almost equaled the integration level of the Soviet Union,[20] the two decades separating August 1968 from December 1989 (Romania's anti-Communist revolution) attest to a gradual degradation of the party's position in society.

The 1977 miners' strike in the Jiu Valley was the largest protest of the time. A spontaneous move, the strike came about and evolved within the specific conditions of the profession. Having itemized social and economical objectives, it did not evolve in an active contestation of the regime. Socio-professional specifics and the particular urban ecology of the Jiu Valley region favored the repression mounted by the authorities immediately after the end of the strike.[21]

The other component of the opposition to the regime gaining shape in the second half of the 1970s was the dissidence of cultural figures, among them most notably Paul Goma, Mihail Botez, Dorin Tudoran, Radu Filipescu, Gabriel Andreescu, Doina Cornea, Mircea Dinescu, Liviu Cangeopol, and Dan Petrescu.[22] Their criticism of Romanian society can be seen in relation to the Final Act from Helsinki, the Czechoslovak Charta 77 movement, and the organizational début of the trade union in Poland. Yet the manner in which this dissidence was structured and the resources it mobilized in formulating its discourse allow for a better understanding of the reasons behind the lack of such a movement during the previous decade.[23]

Dissidence in Romania was an intellectual and solitary venture *par excellence*.[24] The seeds coagulating and structuring a coordinated action that could create the necessary space for a subversive discourse were practically absent. The repressive apparatus was omnipresent and highly effective, and the rapport between intellectuals and other social classes was weak and did not allow for the development of strong communication channels. This incapacity to coherently pose resistance to social and cultural pressure from a position of solidarity persisted until the end of the 1980s.[25] The dissidents' message became public only if they could get it across Romanian borders and have it broadcast by one of the Romanian-language radio stations in the West. The beginnings of an organized effort to unify these voices and to transform private dissent into collective opposition coalesced only at the end of the Socialist era.[26]

August 1968 was a time of great dynamic in Romania. Ceauşescu's energetic condemnation of the Soviet Union allowed him to hijack popular enthusiasm to serve his political goals. Few considered contesting his authority, as this would have painted the individual as a supporter of the Soviet Union. The population gathered around the party, its leader, and the state, convinced of their true concern for the nation's well-being. At no other point in time did either Ceauşescu or the party enjoy such popularity. The enemy was at the Eastern frontier, but the decisiveness of the party's young leader prevented it from treating Romania as it had Czechoslovakia. He kept it at arms distance, but at a distance nonetheless.

Bibliography

Research on the Romanian dimension of 1968 and its national and international consequences is scarce. The only comprehensive study on Romania in relation to the Prague Spring that also reproduces documents of the time is Retegan (2000). An overview of the events leading to Romania's unique position in 1968 is provided by Deletant (1998), Tismăneanu (2003), and Cioroianu (2005). For a selection of documents on Romania's relations to the Warsaw Pact, see Deletant, Ionescu, and Buţă (2004). For studies about Ceauşescu's cult of personality see Fischer (1989), du Bois (2004), and Cioroianu (2004). An introduction to concepts of dissidence is offered by Arato (2000), Cangeopol and Petrescu (2000), and Zub/Cioflîncă (2005).

Arato, Andrew. *Civil Society, Constitution, and Legitimacy.* Lanham, MD: Rowman and Littlefield Publishers, 2000.

du Bois, Pierre. *Ceausescu au pouvoir: Enquête sur une ascension.* Genève: Georg Editteur, 2004.

Cangeopol, Liviu, Dan Petrescu. *Ce-ar mai fi de spus: Convorbiri libere într-o ţară ocupată,* ediţia a II-a. Bucureşti: Nemira, 2000.

Cioroianu, Adrian. *Ce Ceausescu qui hante les Roumains: Le mythe, les représentations et le culte du Dirigeant dans la Roumanie communiste.* Bucharest: Curtea Veche et L'Agence Universitaire de la Francophonie, 2004.

Pe umerii lui Marx: O introducere în istoria comunismului românesc. Bucureşti: Curtea Veche, 2005.

Deletant, Denis. *Romania under Communist Rule.* Bucharest: Civic Academic Foundation, 1998.

Deletant, Denis, Mihail E. Ionescu, and Viorel Buţă. *Romania and the Warsaw Pact, 1955–1989: Selected Documents.* Bucharest: Politeia-SNSPA, 2004.

Delsol, Chantal, Michel Maslowski, and Joanna Novak, eds. *Dissidences.* Paris: Presses Universitaires de France, 2005.

Fischer, Mary Ellen. *Nicolae Ceauşescu: A Study in Political Leadership.* Boulder, CO: Lynne Rienner, 1989.

Retegan, Mihai. *In the Shadow of the Prague Spring: Romanian Foreign Policy and the Crisis in Czechoslovakia, 1968.* Iaşi: Center for Romanian Studies, 2000.

Tismăneanu, Vladimir. *Stalinism for all Seasons: A Political History of Romanian Communism.* Berkeley: University of California Press, 2003.

Zub, Alexandru and Adrian Cioflîncă, eds. *Cultură politică şi politici culturale în România modern.* Iaşi: Editura Universităţii "Alexandru Ioan Cuza," 2005.

Notes

1. Trond Gilberg, *Modernization in Romania since World War II* (New York: Praeger, 1975), 142f.
2. Bernard Paqueteau, "La société contre elle-même: Choses vues en Roumanie," *Commentaire* 59 (1992): 621–28; Steven Sampson, "Muddling through in Romania (or why the mămăligă doesn't explode)," paper presented at the Second International Congress of Romanian Studies, Avignon, France, 1984.
3. Gheorghe Gheorghiu-Dej (1901–1965) was a railway worker who gained prominence during the 1933 strikes. He was imprisoned in the Târgu-Jiu concentration camp but escaped in 1944. He was a member of the Communist Party since 1935 and during the war became the leader of the "Centre of Prison" (Communists who spent the war in Romania). As such, he took control of the Communist Party together with the Pauker-Luca group (Communists delegated by Moscow to ideologise Romania). He was elected General Secretary of the Party in October 1945. Until his natural death in 1965, he was First Secretary of the Central Committee and President of the State Council.
4. Ibid., 33.
5. An excellent analysis of the mechanism governing such evolutions can be found in Vladimir Tismăneanu, *Stalinism for all Seasons. A Political History of Romanian Communism* (Berkeley: University of California Press, 2003), 168–87.
6. Ibid., 38.
7. See Pavel Ţugui, *Istoria şi limba română în vremea lui Gheorghiu-Dej. Memoriile unui fost şef de secţie a CC al PMR* (Bucureşti, Ion Cristoiu, 1999); Bogdan Barbu, *in americanii! Prezenţa simbolică a Statelor Unite în România Războiului Rece* (Bucureşti: Humanitas, 2006), 152–166.
8. Nicolae Ceauşescu (1918–1989) was a militant for the Communist Youth Organisation (UTC) before the war. In the 1940s, he was sentenced and imprisoned in various places for his underground activity. After 1944, he returned to the UTC and held important offices in the army and agriculture. Benefiting from the elimination of the Pauker-Luca group, he became member of the Politburo after 1953–1954. He was also Central Committee Secretary responsible for cadre policy. Between 1965 and 1989 he was leader of the Party, and after 1967 he was also head of state. Together with his wife, he favored the personalization of power within the party and the state.
9. Tismăneanu, *Stalinism*, 190–92.
10. From among the numerous studies about Ceauşescu's regime and his cult of personality, we rely on Mary Ellen Fischer, *Nicolae Ceauşescu. A Study in Political Leadership* (Boulder, CO: Lynne Rienner, 1989), 160–90.
11. John Michael Montias, "Background and Origins of the Romanian Dispute with COMECONÇ" *Soviet Studies* 16, no. 2 (1964): 125–51; Vladimir Tismăneanu,

"Gheorghiu Dej and the Romanian Worker's Party: From De-Sovietization to the Emergence of National Communism," Woodrow Wilson International Center for Scholars, Working Paper No. 37, Cold War International History Project, Washington DC, 2002.

12. Şerban Pavelescu, "Entre mefiance et confiance. Les relations franco-roumaines dans les premieres decennies de la guerre froide," *Revue Historique des Armes* 244 (2006): 98–107.

13. Retegan, 93.

14. "Cuvîntarea tovarăşului Nicolae Ceauşescu în faţa adunării populaţiei din capitală," *România liberă*, August 22, 1968: 1.

15. Nicolae Ceauşescu cited in Retegan, 224.

16. See Daniel C. Nelson, "Workers and Political Alienation," in *Elite–Mass Relations in Communist Systems*, ed. Daniel C. Nelson (New York: St. Martin's, 1988), 146f; Daniel C. Nelson, "Vertical Integration and Political Control in Eastern Europe: The Polish and Romanian Cases," in *Slavic Review* 40 no. 2 (1981): 210–27.

17. Antoine Roger, *Les fondements du nationalisme roumain. 1791–1921* (Genève: Librairie DROZ, 2003), 50–62.

18. Olivier Gillet, "Nationalisme et ethnicité dans l'ecclésiologie de l'Eglise orthodoxe roumaine au XXe siècle," *L'Autre Europe*, no. 36/37 (1998): 140–62.

19. Doru Radoslav, "Rezistenţa anticomunistă armată din România între istorie şi memorie," in *Comunism şi represiune în România. Istoria tematică a unui fratricid naţional*, ed. Ruxandra Cesereanu (Iaşi: Polirom, 2006), 82–99; Dorin Dobrincu, "Colectivizarea agriculturii şi represiunea împotriva ţără nimii din România (1949–1962)," in *Cesereanu* 108–26; Cristian Vasile, "Comunismul şi Biserica: represiune, compromitere," in *Cesereanu* 170–90.

20. Cristina Petrescu, "Seven Faces of Dissent. A Micro Perspective on the Study of Political (Sub)Cultures under Communism," in *Cultură politică şi politici culturale în România modernă*, ed. Alexandru Zub and Adrian Cioflîncă (Iaşi: Editura Universităţii "Alexandru Ioan Cuza," 2005), 307.

21. Ion Bogdan Vasi, "The First of the Working Class: The Social Movements of Jiu Valley Miners in Post-Socialist Romania," *East European Politics and Societies* 18, no. 1 (2004): 139f.

22. Petrescu, 309–33.

23. For an outstanding study on the situation of Romanian writers under the Communist regime, see Irina Culic, "The Strategies of Intellectuals: Romania under Communist Rule in Comparative Perspective," in *Intellectuals and Politics in Central Europe*, ed. Andras Bozoki (Budapest: Central European University Press, 1999), 43–71.

24. Petrescu, 306ff.

25. See Traian Ungureanu, *Despre Securitate. România, ţara "ca şi cum"* (Bucureşti, Humanitas, 2006), especially 17–31.

26. See Mircea Dinescu, *Moartea citeşte ziarul* (Bucureşti: Cartea Românească, 1990), 71–108; and Liviu Cangeopol and Dan Petrescu, *Ce-ar mai fi de spus. Convorbiri libere într-o ţară ocupată*, ediţia a II-a, (Bucureşti, Nemira 2000), 319–23.

17
Hungary
Máté Szabó

Social and Political Framework of the Country

In Hungary, as in other countries of the Eastern Bloc, a totalitarian Stalinist regime was established in the late 1940s under decisive Soviet influence. The change away from such a regime began earlier in Hungary than in other Eastern Bloc states. By 1953, hardliners and moderates within the Communist elite were already clashing irreconcilably. This inner battle between opposing wings of the party also created opportunities for the articulation of critical or otherwise nonconformist political movements by actors outside of the Party leadership.

Following the Soviet military defeat of the 1956 revolutionary uprising, a wave of repression that continued through 1958 succeeded in suppressing acute resistance against the regime. However, this repression was not able to stifle critical, anti-totalitarian thought permanently. New conflicts emerged within the Party leadership that ultimately resulted in increased tolerance for the articulation of dissidence. Nevertheless, some prominent critics of the system were forced out of government, such as Prime Minister András Hegedűs.

The Kádár regime lasted from 1956 to 1989; it bore the name of its Communist leader, János Kádár, and defined its political strategy as a "struggle on two fronts." It directed its efforts against both the Revisionism represented by revolutionary leader Imre Nagy and the Stalinism symbolized by former Communist leader Mátyás Rákosi, exiled to the Soviet Union until his death in 1968. The government chose not to secure power through repression but, rather, aimed at "legitimacy through consumption"; as a result, the population's material hopes received increased attention in the form of economic and social policy that incorporated market orientation into the centralized, planned economy. This strategy resulted in the period of New Economic Mechanism (1968–1973). The approach to nonconformist thought was adjusted to "soft" methods, such as censorship; show trials and prison sentences against dissidents were ended.

Organizational and Social Structure of the Protest Movement

Hungary in the 1960s featured a heterogeneous spectrum of critical intellectuals ranging from reform-oriented economists to artistic avant-gardists, who predominantly adhered to ideas of democratic socialism and were able to express these ideas in various literary and artistic forms. Although the party thus did allow a variety of opinions, it did, however, claim the exclusive power to make final decisions. There were almost no public protests in the period investigated—a time characterized by repression—but the economic reforms brought the Hungarian population considerable social improvements and a distinct increase in personal freedoms.

In Hungary, 1968 was a year of drastic changes that would strongly influence the later development of dissidence and opposition. The reform wing within the Party leadership succeeded in implementing relatively extensive economic reforms through the New Economic Mechanism. The state-planned sector of the centralized economy was limited considerably in favor of supporting a "second economy" to be regulated by market mechanisms. At the same time, the defeat of the Prague Spring and Hungarian military participation in the Soviet intervention led many critical intellectuals to lose faith in the Kádár regime's call for democratization and sparked public dissent. The turning point was a call by members of the "Budapest School" for solidarity with the Czechoslovakian democracy movement.[1] This marked the first occasion of public protest by Hungarian intellectuals since the uprising of 1956.[2] Some Budapest School members participated in an international summer school of Left-oriented philosophers and social scientists on the island of Korcula in Yugoslavia. From there, they issued a declaration against the Soviet intervention in Prague. This event is often viewed as the beginning of Hungarian dissent. Following their experience on Korcula, these Hungarian philosophers returned to Budapest and formed a core of dissent. As Hungary was increasingly pushed into following the anti-reformist course espoused by the Soviet leader, Brezhnew, some of these philosophers were forced to emigrate in 1974.

Cognitive Orientation of the Movement

Communism was established as the dominant social and political ideology in Hungary through state terrorism following 1947; however, competing philosophies developed under the "repressive tolerance" of the Kádár regime. Although conflicts continued among orthodox Leninists, Kádárists, and economically liberal Reform Communists within the Party leadership, a new opposition movement took shape following the invasion of Czechoslovakia.

First, after 1968, a current of liberal-democratic orientation emerged from the milieu of the Reform Communists. It existed primarily among Budapest intellectuals who turned to liberal and communitarian ideas after the Prague Spring. Among its most prominent representatives were the several students of Marxist philosopher György Lukács, namely, Ágnes Heller, János Kis, and György Bence, as well as writers György Dalos and Miklós Haraszti.[3] From this cohort, also known as the "Urbanists," came the Hungarian samizdat in the 1970s and, later, in 1988, the Alliance of Free Democrats (*Szabad Demokraták Szövetsége*, or SZDSZ).

A second source of dissidence was formed by nationally oriented Populism, which has influenced Hungarian literature and art up to today and which developed in its own direction within the dissent following 1968. The Populist opposition, among whose most important representatives were writers Sándor Csoóri and István Csurka and historians József Antall, Csaba Kiss, György Szabad, and Lajos Für (all prominent politicians of the post-Communist era), led to the 1988 founding of the Hungarian Democratic Forum (*Magyar Demokrata Fórum*, or MDF), which won the first free elections in 1990.

Although there were latent differences between liberal-democratic and national-conservative oppositional currents in other countries, the rivalry between Populists and Urbanists was of singular intensity in Hungary and formed a trademark of the Hungarian opposition. The roots of this rivalry can be traced to the Hungarian national movement against the Habsburg monarchy in the early nineteenth century. The Populists (*népies*) advocated the idea of a national path between East and West, an "organic" alternative beyond Western modernism. Their central terms were nation, identity, and community. A parallel current emerged among the neo-Marxists of the Budapest school who, confronted with the regime's repression, felt themselves increasingly indebted to liberal, universalist values and the Western European Enlightenment orientation toward progress. This particular current left Marxism behind, along with Western conceptions of market economics and parliamentary government. The split between Urbanists and Populists from the 1960s onward formed the dominant principle structuring the later development of Hungarian opposition. The Communist party leadership likewise differentiated its political strategy, regarding the opposition as two distinct currents.[4]

Attitudes toward the Superpowers and the Cold War

The dominant foreign policy in Hungary was compulsory anti-Americanism and pro-Soviet orientation. In Hungarian youth subcultures, the influences of Castro, Guevara, and Mao as strategic revolutionary thinkers, along with worldwide protest against the Vietnam War, played an equally important role. Events in Vietnam, the assassination of Martin Luther King, Jr., and the death of Che Guevara also provided opportunities for official Marxist-Leninist ideology and foreign policy to deepen its support among young people. Western popular culture, U.S. protest songs, and the provocative style of hard rock and free jazz music were further outlets of protest against U.S. dominance. At the same time, there existed mass admiration for the technological development of Western consumer society and mass culture. As a result, 1968 saw the start of Coca-Cola production and distribution in Hungary, despite the drink's status as a symbol of rejected Western consumer society.

The critical currents of Western and non-European Marxism condemned and criticized the Soviet Union for its bureaucratic despotism and betrayal of "real" Marxism. However, until the invasion of Czechoslovakia, many Hungarians viewed the Soviet Union as the lesser evil when compared with the United States. The participation of Hungarian troops in the military invasion of Prague triggered protest as well as disillusionment and passive resistance toward Communism, Marxism, and the Soviet Union. Some dedicated Communists committed suicide, and a group of activists took the initiative to protest publicly against the Soviet intervention. Another typical way Hungarians protested against the Soviet Union or displayed support for Czechoslovakian activities was through support of Hungarian economic and social reforms. The reforms continued until Brezhnev demanded more loyalty to the roots of the Socialism; reforms were halted by János Kádár in 1973.

Key Events

The main events for Hungary in 1968 were the inception of the New Economic Mechanism and Hungarian participation in the Warsaw Pact invasion of Czechoslovakia. Both of these moments had the effect of calming political protest in Hungary. The general intellectual and cultural mood was expectant of economic and social reform, and only few people understood the intervention's long-term effect as a roadblock to all reformist efforts.

In Hungary, the Reform Communist moderates triumphed over the anti-reform hardliners, who were against internal transformation and committed to following Soviet foreign policy. Among the protests, the key event was the declaration of Hungarian philosophers condemning Soviet intervention in

Czechoslovakia. The Communist leadership reacted relatively smoothly to this protest action; the protesters continued teaching, researching, and publishing within Hungary until the breakdown of reforms in 1973. György Lukács, leader of the Budapest School, joined protesters and made statements on the issue of Czechoslovakia, offering a compromise between acceptance of the intervention and demand for democratic Socialism.

The conflicts in Vietnam, the United States, and Western Europe, or the geographically more relevant military coup in Greece, also encouraged the emergence of revolutionary New Left student groups in Budapest. Some Greek Communist emigrants were also involved in this rather tiny informal network, which maintained contact with Chinese and Albanian embassies in Budapest. The network produced documents and leaflets and organized gatherings at the Greek embassy and other public spaces on the anniversaries of Hungarian and international Communist upheavals.

A potentially more dangerous challenge to the regime was the apolitical but broad diffusion of new countercultural elements among young people. Rock music merged with spontaneity, new forms of communication, and new sexual norms. The phenomenon of youth subculture was the object of harsh criticism by Communist dogmatism, but the official position was a commercial institutionalization of an apolitical new "youth style," which was co-opted through official recordings, competitions, and festivals to produce a "Socialist" rock and youth culture. This institutionalization brought formal controls, such as issuing permits to musical activities, individual songs, and events. In addition, state security was able to exert strict control over musicians, fans, and concerts by using a wide range of informants. These new mechanisms of control over dissent came to force when an informal circle of hippies in Budapest was sentenced because they sang fascist marching songs, their public trial equally condemning the lifestyle and symbolism of the hippies living in Budapest as such.

Forms and Tactics of Protest

When evaluating forms and tactics of protest in Hungary, constant government repression and the curious mixture between reformist and repressive orientations within the ruling Communist elite play a decisive rule. Intra-elite conflicts were relatively persistent in the Hungarian regime after 1956, and in 1968 tension reached a boiling point. János Kádár's strength was that he could handle these tensions by constantly assuming the role of mediator between the two conflicting lines while also ensuring the support of the Soviet leadership. In fact, he received Soviet support until 1988 because he accepted the role of the primary pro-Soviet agent within Hungary after 1956.

Violent protest forms were absent in Hungary in 1968. The repression after the 1956 revolution blocked this avenue of strategy among Hungarian dissidents and reformers. Protest actions that disturbed public order, such as marches or blockades, were avoided or only used by marginal, radical groups. The main bulk of the protest was of a symbolic, cultural, discursive, and communicative character. Dissident intellectuals produced critical essays, poems, and analyses, which were then censored and publicly criticized by partisans of the regime.

Protest in its broadest definition could be observed in the lifestyle changes and cultural orientation toward Western youth subculture, and the search for jobs, which would provide maximum uncontrolled leisure opportunities in youth culture. The introduction of Coca-Cola was symbolic for this "hedonism," as was the market entrance of the first legal contraceptive, Bisecurin, which appeared in pharmacy shops in 1968 and expanded on options for sexual freedom.

Only a minority of students, young intellectuals, and artists went further in acclaiming free and autonomous spaces and relations beyond existing Communist conformism, searching for autonomy and creativity in culture and everyday life. Some of these initiatives crystallized around alternative theater and ballet, such as Péter Halász and the Orpheo group, or around other decorative art, construction, or design personalities like Miklós Erdélyi or Galántai Gyorgy. Underground music groups such as Syrius and Kex were also influential. These Western-type groups received public attention in youth centers and festivals; however, they were constantly subject to political control and occasionally even sanctions. There was some overlapping between the alternative Marxism of the Budapest school and the Western-style artistic experiments, but this was not institutionalized as a social movement. Eventually, many artists were forced to leave the country as a result of repression; some examples are Péter Halász, Miklós Erdélyi, and Baksa Soós. Other artists chose to remain embedded within the alternative subculture. In general, the Westernized, "urbanist" tradition of the Hungarian protest culture developed further toward philosophical, political, and artistic radicalism, whereas the populist thread was not visible in the protest scene but turned out to be an intellectual protest potential for future developments.

Transnational Relations

In the context of Warsaw Pact countries, Hungary was relatively open to outside influences. Although it did not reach the contemporary openness of Yugoslavia, Czechoslovakia, or Poland, it was not as closed as Bulgaria, Romania, or the German Democratic Republic. Western consumer culture was not excluded or condemned as such but was imported in a controlled manner. Similar to other Eastern regimes, Hungary accepted the economic facet of Western Marxism as a criticism of capitalism, U.S. imperialism, and consumer society; however, it blocked and rejected it as radicalism within the context of democratization and autonomy. The Hungarian regime condemned Mao`s China, the Marxism of Marcuse—who was translated in Hungarian only for high party leaders but not for the public—and New Left student radicalism, but supported the cults of Castro and Guevara. Relations to Western Marxism and student movements existed but were restricted to small groups of dissenting intellectuals, who enjoyed some freedom of travelling abroad. The experiment in Czechoslovakia and dissenting policy in Romania and Yugoslavia were widely known, partly because of the millions of ethnic Hungarians who lived in these countries and communicated with those living in Hungary. Those living in Czechoslovakia, Romania, and Yugoslavia enjoyed considerable cultural autonomy during the reform era, which resulted in a huge amount of newspapers, book editions, and broadcasts in Hungarian that found their way to Hungary as well. Traveling to and from these countries was less restricted than travel to Western countries. Even China reached radical student groups in Hungary following their launch of Hungarian broadcasting and printed Hungarian propaganda material through Albania. There were broadcasts like Radio Free Europe, the BBC, or the Voice of America in Hungarian that covered dissent and protest if it contained an anti-Communist character.

All in all, people in Hungary could reach a wide range of official and unofficial sources of information. Active connections with radical movements were restricted to some elite dissenting intellectuals and artists who adopted sympathy with the New Left or with young Western artistic radicalism. However, the Hungarian participation in the occupation of Czechoslovakia, as well as the international press coverage of the intervention, made it also an experience of the general Hungarian public. Discussions and tensions within Communism following the intervention were presented in the official media from a Moscow-friendly point of view. Hungary was thus more influenced by conflict within the Eastern Bloc in 1968 than by student protest or ethnic riots.

Consequences, Narratives, and Politics of Memory

The experience in Hungary was very different from both Western upheavals and Eastern mobilizations and elite changes. Hungarian intellectuals and artists, particularly those who were younger and more Western oriented, were following the conflicts abroad, and later some of their experiences were recollected in their creative or reflective works such as the films of Miklós Jancsó; the novels of Tibor Déry, György Dalos, György Konrád; the philosophy of György Lukács, Mihály Vajda, or Ágnes Heller; the scholarship of Hungarian sociologists András Hegedűs or Iván Szelényi; or within the creative Hungarian rock music.

The lack of dramatic collective experiences meant that 1968 did not become the type of common focal point of collective memory that 1956 remained, despite the toughest Hungarian cultural censorship. There was no strong, official criticism or propaganda regarding the Czechoslovak experiment. Its failure was an important point of internal and external legitimacy of the Kádár regime. One may look on 1968 in Hungary as a victory of the Kádár regime over its former anti-revolutionary, dogmatic image and over the revisionism of the Czech Party before the intervention. Kádár and his performance in reforming the Hungarian economy received both Western and internal social and political support, not to mention a sense of legitimacy for accomplishing changes within the framework of the Eastern Bloc.

This honeymoon period lasted until 1973, when under Soviet pressure and internal opposition to reform, the New Economic Mechanism experiment was abolished. Supportive politicians lost their positions, and a stricter, more defensive policy toward intellectual dissent was implemented. Thus, the period between 1968 and 1973 became an important legitimating legacy of the reformist character of the Kádár regime. Using this legacy, the government tried to establish new cooperation with the West and to open the regime for economic and cultural opportunities during the 1980s. This period then marked a time of more tolerance toward dissent that formed an important base for the system transition in 1989, when in Hungary, as in most of the countries of the Eastern Bloc, the Soviet Empire failed to exercise further control and transformations toward the rule of law, democracy, and market economy occurred.

In this way, and in contrast to Czechoslovakia, 1968 never played a prominent role in the creation of Hungarian historical consciousness. In Hungary, 1968 stands for the victory of Kádár and of "Kádárism," which was characterized by the dissent as the "dictatorship over the needs" or by Western publicists as "Goulash Communism," with the regime gaining legitimacy by fulfilling material needs and allowing consumerism. The regime itself regarded 1968 as a silent victory that resulted in a strong, long-lasting power structure that allowed few dissenting voices.

After 1989, the anti-Stalinist revolution against the Soviet Union in 1956 became the new source of legitimacy and republicanism in Hungary. In many ways, 1956 acted as a genuine Hungarian contribution to the history of anti-Socialist efforts and overshadowed 1968 in both domestic and international discussions on twentieth-century postwar history in Hungary. It is an irony of history that although 1968 serves as a symbol for radicalism and revolution in the Western hemisphere, and to a certain extent also in the Eastern Bloc, for Hungary, 1968 is associated with the sacrifice of autonomy in foreign policy in exchange for temporary internal social and economic autonomy; in other words, a moment of reformism and clever opportunism in Hungarian history. In this way, it is not surprising that 1968 does not stand out as an extraordinary point of reference in contemporary historical research in Hungary.

Bibliography

For overviews of the Kádár regime, see Shawcross (1974) and Tökés (1996). For new Hungarian research see Huszár-Szabó (1999), Romsics (2000), and Huszár (2001/2003). An historical study of the 1960s in Hungary compared to other Eastern Bloc countries is presented in Fischer-Galati (1963), and economic reforms in Hare et al. (1981. For the history of protest movements in Hungary, Csizmadia (1996) offers a three-volume edition. For interviews, insider reports, and documents see Dalos (1985, 1986), Kis (1989), Heller (1999), and Eichwede (2000).

Csizmadia, Ervin. *A magyar demokratikus ellenzék.* vol. 1–3. Budapest: T-Twins, 1995.

Dalos, György. *Kurzer Lehrgang-Langer Marsch.* Berlin: Rotbuch, 1985.

Dalos, György. *Archipel Gulasch.* Bremen: Temmen, 1986.

Eichwede, Wolfgang ed. *Samizdat Alternative Kultur in Zentral und Osteuropa: Die 60er bis 80er Jahre.* Bremen: Temmen, 2000.

Fischer-Galati, Stephen ed. *Eastern Europe in the Sixties.* New York: Praeger, 1963.

Hare, Paul, Hugo Radice, and Nigel Swain, eds. *Hungary: A Decade of Economic Reform.* London: George Allen and Unwin, 1981.

Heller, Ágnes. *Biciklíző majom.* Budapest: Múlt és Jövő, 1999.

Huszár, Tibor. *Kádár János politikai életrajza,* vol. 1 and 2. Budapest: Kossuth, 2001 and 2003.

Huszár, Tibor and János Szabó eds. *Restauráció vagy kiigazítás: A kádári represszió intézményesülése.* Budapest: Zrínyi, 1999.

Kis, János. *Politics in Hungary: For a Democratic Alternative.* (Highland Lakes, NJ: Atlantic Research and Publications, 1989.

Paetzke, Hans Henning. *Andersdenkende in Ungarn.* Frankfurt am Main: Suhrkamp, 1986.

Rainer M., János eds. *"Hatvanas évek" Magyarországon.* Budapest: 1956-os Intézet, 2004.

Révész, Sándor ed. *Beszélő évek 1957–1968.* Budapest: Stencil, 2000.

Romsics, Ignác *Magyarország története a XX. Században.* Budapest: Osiris, 2000.

Shawcross, William. *Crime and Compromise: Janos Kadar and the Politics of Hungary Since Revolution.* New York: E.P. Dutton, 1974.

Tökés, Rudolf. *Hungary's Negotiated Revolution. 1957-1990*. Cambridge, MA: Cambridge University Press, 1996.

Notes

1. The "Budapest School" consisted of the Hungarian students of György (Georg) Lukács, an internationally known philosopher living in Budapest following his emigration from Moscow.
2. György Dalos, *Archipel Gulasch* (Bremen: Temmen, 1986), 19.
3. Dalos, 17–36.
4. Csizmadia, 2001, 71.

18
Yugoslavia

Boris Kanzleiter

The protesting Yugoslav students in 1968 believed that they were part of a global youth generation in revolt. They used political symbols and cultural codes similar to those employed by their comrades in age and belief elsewhere, but the protest in the *Socialist Federal Republic of Yugoslavia* (SRFY) showed two characteristics that made it exceptional. First, unlike protest in most other European countries, Yugoslav protest was not directed against the fundamental values and ideologies of the ruling political system. In essence, the Yugoslav students protested in the name of the principles of the communist system against its hypocritical and frustrating reality. The second particular characteristic was the astonishing integration of differing ideas of the student movements both from the capitalist and socialist countries. Thus, 1968 in Yugoslavia was genuinely a protest between East and West. It was a hybrid that bridged the Iron Curtain of the Cold War.

Social and Political Framework of the Country

The unique characteristics of the student movement in Yugoslavia refer to a particular political context. The League of Communists of Yugoslavia (LCY) was probably the only ruling party worldwide that interpreted the global student revolt as a confirmation of its own political agenda. In May 1968, the influential LCY leader Veljko Vlahović stated that the protests around the world should be "evaluated positively." The slogans for "self-management" on the demonstrations in France and elsewhere were showing that Yugoslavia was following the right path.[1] However, sympathy was not limited to the protest movements in the West. Special attention was given to the developments in Czechoslovakia. The LCY leadership openly stated support for the reform experiment of Alexander Dubček and strongly condemned the Soviet-led intervention of August 1968.

The position of the LCY can only be understood against the background of Yugoslavia's postwar history. The Communists took power in 1945 after a four-year antifascist partisan struggle. Although initially following the Soviet model, they eventually resisted subordination to Moscow on the basis of their own strength. An irreversible split with the Soviet Union in 1948 led to ideological re-conceptualization within the Yugoslav party. Central to its new vision was the commitment to "workers self-management"; this entailed the introduction of mechanisms of direct workers control in key industries that aimed to prevent the "bureaucratization" of the state and the party and created a new groundwork for the legitimization of the proclaimed "own way to socialism." The LCY also introduced a new idea on the international scene. After the split with Moscow, LCY leader and state president Josip Broz Tito accepted material help from the West and started to cooperate with the United States. However, the LCY did not wish to become subordinate to Washington either. In the late 1950s, to balance between the blocs of the Cold War, the Yugoslav leaders moved toward the founding of the Non-Alignment Movement, which tried to stimulate political and economic cooperation between Yugoslavia—as its only European member—and a number of important postcolonial countries like India, Mexico, and Egypt.

In the period of the Cold War, the Yugoslav model of a "third way" attracted a lot of sympathy around the world. However, inside Yugoslavia, the picture looked less friendly. The proclamation of "workers self-management" was widely perceived as pure demagogy because real democratization never took place. The rapid economic growth triggered an exceptionally fast process of urbanization and industrialization, but although the living standards of the growing urban population improved, the gap between traditionally poor regions in the South and the prosperous regions in the North grew. Social imbalances increased particularly after the introduction of market mechanisms in 1965. The reforms were designed to overcome economic stagnation but led to massive unemployment, especially among young people.

The structural problems provoked open conflicts inside the LCY. During the summer of 1966 the widely feared chief of the Secret Service, Aleksandar Ranković, was removed from office. With his dismissal, a liberal wing in the LCY saw its chance to realize their program of faster modernization through the introduction of a "socialist market economy" and world market integration. These politics were accompanied by the intention to democratize the party and growing openness in the fields of media and culture. Taboo topics like the imprisonment of thousands of real or imagined "state enemies" in the late '40s and '50s entered discussions, and former partisan commander and later dissident Milovan Djilas were released from prison. It was this atmosphere of intensifying public debate, but also deepening social contradictions and institutional crisis that formed the context for the student movement.

Organizational and Social Structure of the Protest Movement

Given the monolithic structure of the political system, students in Yugoslavia could not simply set up independent organizations. By the middle of the 1960s, however, they found other channels to express their feelings. Editors of the official student press wrote increasingly bitter articles about the structural problems of the university system, which had expanded rapidly after the war but lacked funding and quality.[2] As the political climate opened up, the range of topics became more expansive. In the beginning of 1968, the magazine *Susret* published a series of reports about the unemployment of youth, migration of young people as *"Gastarbeiter"* (migrant workers) to Germany, and the miserable housing condition of Gypsies in the forgotten slums of Belgrade. The papers became genuine critical voices that articulated the grievances of young people. With interest and sympathy, they also reported about growing student unrest around the globe.

The opening of the student press reflected developments in the official Student League of Yugoslavia (SSJ), which was the publisher of most youth magazines. Starting at their conference in March 1966, SSJ leaders took an increasingly critical position regarding social problems and authoritarian political structures. To overcome the widespread apathy of students, they demanded better material conditions at the universities and more student participation in and the democratization of university institutions. This position was seen to be in line with the official reform discourse, but it also provided an opening for small groups of young activists, who called for more radical action to end shortcomings.

In June 1968, their wishes became reality and protest exploded. The weeklong strike at the Belgrade University and the subsequent spreading of revolt over the whole country spontaneously led to the establishment of *akcioni odbori* (action committees) and *zborovi* (conventions). During the strike, they interacted with branches of the SSJ and some university committees of the LCY that supported the protest. The emergence of independent forms of organization was of utmost importance because it challenged not only the ideological conceptions of the LCY but also its mechanisms of control. The LCY leadership reacted with repression. The struggle for the organizational autonomy remained at the core of the protest movement until its final repression in 1974.

Cognitive Orientation of the Movement

The student movement in Yugoslavia shared the struggle for freedom, justice, and self-determination, which can be defined as the underlying moral and political principles of the global protests of 1968.[3] A particular characteristic of the Yugoslav movement was that students articulated their demands on the groundwork of the official ideology. A statement of striking students and professors at the philosophical faculty in Belgrade on June 4, 1968, said: "We do not have our own program. Our program is the program of the most progressive forces of our society—the program of the LCY and the constitution. We demand that it should be put consequently into practice."[4]

The development of the cognitive orientation of the protest movement and its identity reflected the high degree of political and cultural freedom achieved in Yugoslavia in the late 1960s and early 1970s. Students were well-informed about the international development of protests and ideological debates of the New Left in the West. The influential works of Herbert Marcuse, for example, were published in Serbo-Croatian from 1965 onward.[5] In the magazine *Praxis*, which was edited by university professors in Belgrade and Zagreb, conceptions of a "Marxist Humanism" were discussed.[6] In theaters, young people could see the musical "Hair" and modern experimental plays. Influenced by avant-garde film in Western Europe, a *crni talas* (black wave) developed that promoted stylistic experimentation touching on contemporary problems of human alienation ranging form social exclusion to sexual liberation.[7]

Student activists in Yugoslavia identified with the youth revolts in both East *and* West. As the political system was neither entirely Stalinist nor completely capitalist, students in Yugoslavia were protesting explicitly against both. Although the strikers in June 1968 called for "Democratization" and "Freedom of Demonstration,"[8] they also protested against "capitalist restoration" through the disputed Reform program of the "Liberals" in the LCY.[9] This ambiguous orientation was summarized in the popular slogan: "Down with the red bourgeoisie!"

Attitudes toward the Superpowers and the Cold War

As in the rest of the world, the Vietnam War and the invasion of the Soviet-led Warsaw pact in Czechoslovakia had a decisive effect on the student movement. Already in December 1966, students in Belgrade took to the streets against the U.S. intervention in Vietnam. They demolished the American Culture Center in the inner city and tried to attack the U.S. Embassy before they were assaulted by riot police. The moral protest against the shocking brutality of the war, which was visualized by the mass media, was at the core of both this and the following demonstrations against the Vietnam War. However, there were at least two more elements. First, the "imperialist aggression" of the United States in Vietnam was perceived as a direct threat to the uncertain independence of Yugoslavia. Second, many Yugoslavs identified with the Vietnamese people because of their own experiences in World War II, when Germany and its local allies massacred hundreds of thousands of civilians. Student activists therefore denounced the U.S. intervention in Vietnam as "fascist."[10]

The attitude toward the Soviet Union was similarly hostile. Dating from the split with Stalin, the LCY denounced the hegemonic ambitions of the Soviets. The intervention of the Soviets and their allies in Czechoslovakia in August 1968 shocked the public. Fears that an intervention could also occur in Yugoslavia were widespread and led to the mobilization of the army. For the student activists, the situation was a double disaster. They lost a potential ally in Czechoslovakia, and the Yugoslav party also used the fear of foreign intervention to promote a feeling of national unity. This limited the possibilities open to the student movement for attacking internal contradictions and problems.

Key Events

The protest cycle of the Yugoslav student movement lasted a full decade and contained three phases.[11] The first open sign for the development of an independent student movement was the demonstration against the Vietnam War in 1966. Although the LCY in principle supported the protest, it spiraled out of control. Slogans were also shouted against the party leadership, who the protesters criticized for not acting seriously enough against the Americans. An important result of the protest was the constitution of informal networks of activists that involved key figures like Vladimir Mijanović and Alija Hodžić, who would play a leading role in future protests.

A second phase of the movement started with the protests of June 1968 and lasted until autumn 1971. The occupation of Belgrade University, the spreading of protests to other university centers, and the widespread sympathy the students received from important segments of cultural life and groups of workers had shocked the party leadership. Although Tito himself had agreed in a speech on the June 9 that students had good reasons to protest, the LCY started a lasting campaign against the student movement and its supporters immediately after the strike ended. In July 1968, the entire party organization at the Philosophical Faculty in Belgrade was expelled from the LCY. The activities, however, went on and led to two more strikes—in

Belgrade in October 1970 and Ljubljana in May 1971. At the same time, small, underground groups were formed.

The third phase started with the suppression of the "Croatian Spring" at the end of 1971.[12] Although the student activists of the New Left were outspoken critics of this nationalist movement, the massive purge that followed it at the end of 1971 affected them equally. In 1972 and 1973, a series of key protagonists of the student movement were brought to trial and sentenced to prison.[13] At the same time, the "liberal" party leadership in Serbia was forced to resign. In the following years, student activists tried to regain the initiative, but the political climate had fundamentally changed. In 1974 a long-debated new Constitution was passed that gave in to nationalist demands. The reform phase ended in "Decentralization without Democratization."[14] At the same time, the LCY leadership started the final campaign to silence the editors of *Praxis*, who had always been sympathetic to the critical students. In February 1975, eight *Praxis* professors and academics were expelled from Belgrade University, which triggered a final moment of open student protest.[15]

Forms and Tactics of Protest

The forms and tactics of the protest movement developed in the context of changing political opportunity structures. In the first two phases of the movement between 1966 and 1971, open protest tactics like public meetings, demonstrations, and strikes were employed. Some of the protest tactics were imported from outside. For example, in April 1968 the first sit-in activity against the war in Vietnam was organized in the commercial centre of Belgrade.[16] During the night between May 10 and 11, 1968, several hundred students blockaded the German Embassy throughout the night until the early morning hours to show solidarity with the protest against the Emergency Laws (*Notstandsgesetze*) in Germany.[17] After 1971, public protest became increasingly limited. As repression grew stronger, student activists tended to develop forms of dissident activities such as closed discussion circles in private flats.

Transnational Relations

Although the Yugoslav student movement developed in a unique national context, international topics and the global protest movement played an important role in its shaping. References to the international protests were widespread. Belgrade students in June 1968 baptized their occupied university *Crveni univerzitet Karl Marks* (Red University Karl Marx), just as the

German students in Frankfurt am Main had done a few days earlier, and the key programmatic document of the strike in June 1968 was called *Akciono-politički program* (Political Action Program). Although different in content, the title refered to the groundbreaking "Action Program" the Czechoslovak Communists had adoped three months before.

Transnational relations were not only symbolic. Yugoslav student activists were able to develop limited direct contact with activists elsewhere. Functionaries of the SSJ were present at conferences and meetings of student organizations around the world, and activists of foreign student organizations were also coming to Yugoslavia.[18] Contacts also developed at unofficial levels; for example, influential leftist intellectuals like Herbert Marcuse, Erich Fromm, Leszek Kolakowski, Ágnes Heller, and Ernest Mandel were guests at a "summer school" on the Croatian island of Korčula, which was organized by university professors from Zagreb and Belgrade who were members of the *Praxis* group. The symposium, which was held every year between 1964 and 1974, developed into a unique meeting point for intellectual debate across the barriers of the Iron Curtain. The non-dogmatic reinterpretation of Marxism served as common ground for these intellectuals. Hundreds of Yugoslav students had a chance to exchange ideas with the international guests and with the students who came from abroad to participate.[19]

Consequences, Narratives, and Politics of Memory

The student movement of 1968 undoubtedly marked a significant rupture in the political development of the SFRY. It was the first open large-scale revolt after the consolidation of power by the Communist Party. The Philosopher Miladin Životić writes that the year 1968 was the beginning of the delegitimization of the political system and the "demystification" of political power in the state that collapsed in Civil War in 1991. The historical results of the uprising were the creation of "a new sensibility, a new social climate and a new intellectual situation." It "created a generation, which began to think differently and which opened itself critically towards the world."[20]

Given the importance of the student movement, it is astonishing that the scientific investigation of the protests in Yugoslavia is still in its very beginnings. The reasons for the lack of investigation seem to be various. First and foremost, the topic was taboo in socialist Yugoslavia. The interest that developed in the opening phase after Tito's death in 1980 was of only short duration. During the wars of the 1990s, in all former republics of Yugoslavia, the "national question" dominated not only the political agenda but also intellectual life. The outspoken pro-Yugoslav student movement in this context was not a topic that could deliver material for new narratives of the "national" histories, which reject the multinational Yugoslavia as an "artificial" state that was created and maintained by pure force. The movement is however present in its lasting effect on cultural production in film and literature. The lack of attention given to the analysis of the topic in the former Yugoslavia is likely related to the almost complete absence of the Yugoslav student movement in publications dealing with the global 1968 movement.

Bibliography

The most detailed and differentiated study was completed back in 1978 by sociologist and former *Praxis* member Nebojša Popov. Publication of the study, however, was banned until 1990.[21] Since then, Popov has continued to publish on the topic. His last publication is an edited conversation of former *Praxis* intellectuals that also deals with the student movement.[22] Apart from Popov's work, Ralph Pervan's study from 1978 is the only significant scientific work on the student movement.[23] In 1984, Mirko Arsić and Dragan Marković published a rather journalistic account of the protest movement.[24] All works, however, contain shortcomings because they are based only on published sources and do not discuss the Yugoslav 1968 in the context of the global student revolt.

Arsić, Mirko and Dragan R. Marković. *'68. Studentski bunt i društvo.* 2nd ed. Beograd: Istraživačko centar SSO Srbije, 1988.
Ćirić, Darko and Lidija Petrović Ćirić, eds. *Beograd šesdesetih godina XX veka.* Belgrad: Musej grada Beograda, 2003.
Fink, Carol, Phillip Gassert, and Detlef Junker. *1968: A World Transformed.* Washington DC: The German Historical Institute/Cambridge University Press, 1998.
Pervan, Ralph. *Tito and the Students. The University and the University Student in Self-Managing Yugoslavia.* Nedlands: University of Western Australia Press, 1978.
Popov, Nebojša. *Sukobi. Društveni sukobi - izazov sociologiji.* 2nd ed. Beograd: Centar za Managing Yugoslavia. Nedlands: University of Western Australia Press, 1978.
Sekelj, Laslo. *Yugoslavia: The Process of Desintegration.* New York: Atlantic Research and Publications, 1993
Sher, Gerson S. *Praxis—Marxist Criticism and Dissent in Socialist Yugoslavia.* Bloomington: Indiana University Press, 1978.

Notes

1. *Borba*, 23 May 1968.
2. For a good account of the structural problems at the universities see Ralph Pervan, *Tito and the Students: The University and the University Student in Self-Managing Yugoslavia* (Nedlands: University of Western Australia Press, 1978).

3. Carol Fink, Phillip Gassert, and Detlef Junker, "Introduction," in Carol Fink, Phillip Gassert, and Detlef Junker, eds. *1968—A World Transformed* (Washington, DC: The German Historical Institute and Cambridge University Press, 1998) 3.

4. "Drugovi radnici, građani i omladinci," in *jun—lipanj 1968. Dokumenti*, ed. Editorial board Praxis (Zagreb: Praxis, 1971), 83.

5. His main work, "The one dimensional man," a bitter critique of the social relations in the industrialized countries in West and East, was published in Yugoslavia in 1968. Herbert Marcuse, *Čovek jedne dimenzije. Rasprave o ideologiji razvijenog industrijskog društva* (Sarajevo: Veselin Masleša, 1968).

6. The magazine *Praxis* was started in 1964 and quickly achieved a considerable international reputation. Gerson S. Sher, *Praxis—Marxist Criticism and Dissent in Socialist Yugoslavia* (Bloomington: Indiana University Press, 1978).

7. Some films of the *crni talas* produced considerable international attention. Želimir Žilniks drama "Rani radovi" (Early works), which takes up the theme of the student protest, won the Berlinale film award in 1969. One of the most significant works of this period is Dušan Makavejev's, WR: Misterije organizma" (WR: Mysteries of the Organism) (1971), which takes up Wihelm Reich's psychoanalytic theories of sexual liberation as a foil to repressive power. D. J. Goulding, *Liberated cinema. The Yugoslav experience*, 2nd ed. (Bloomington: Indiana University Press, 2002).

8. Rezolucija studentskih demonstracija, in: Editorial board Praxis, ed., *Dokumenti*, 61–63.

9. The resolution of the students of the Faculty of Philosophy in Belgrade states, for example: "We are in favor of social ownership and against intentions to form joint-stock holding capitalist enterprises." In respect to the migration of "Gastarbeiter," it says: "It hurts us that thousands of our people have to go and serve and work for world capital." "Drugovi radnici, graćani i omladinci," in *jun— lipanj 1968. Dokumenti*, ed. Editorial board Praxis (Zagreb: Praxis, 1971), 83.

10. In demonstrations against the Vietnam War, posters with a swastika over the stars and stripes banner of the United States were shown. Darko Ćirić and Lidija Petrović Ćirić, eds., *Beograd šesdesetih godina XX veka* (Belgrad: Musej grada Beograda, 2003) 63.

11. For the most complete accounts to date of the protest cycle between 1966 and 1974, see Nebojša Popov, *Sukobi. Društveni sukobi—izazov sociologiji*, 2nd ed. (Beograd: Centar za filozofiju i društvenu teoriju, 1990).

12. The "Croatian Spring" was initiated by a group of leading Croatian LCY figures in 1970. They demanded more rights for the Croatian Republic. With the radicalization of the movement in November 1971, a student strike at Zagreb University broke out. The nationalist platform of protesters was, however, opposed to the student movement of the New Left. Beginning in December 1971, the LCY leadership conducted a massive purge of the activists of the "Croatian Spring" Dušan Bilandžić, *Hrvatska moderna povijest*, (Zagreb: Golden Marketing, 1999), 655.

13. Amongst them were figures who had maintained constant activity since 1968 or even before, such as Milan Nikolić, Pavluško Imširović, Jelka Kljajić, Božidar Jakšić, Lazar Stojanović, Kosta Ćavoški, Ljiljana Mijanović-Jovičić, Danilo

Udovički, and Vladimir Mijanović. Srđa Popović, ed., *Poslednja instanca*, vol. 2 (Belgrade: Helsinški odbor za ljudska prava u Srbiji,2003), 443ff.

14. Laslo Sekelj, *Yugoslavia: The Process of Desintegration* (New York: Atlantic Research and Publications, 1993), 6.

15. On the case of the *Praxis* professors, see Nebojša Popov, *Contra Fatum. Slučaj Grupe Profesora Filozofskog Fakulteta u Beogradu 1968–1988* (Beograd: Mladost, 1989).

16. *Susret*, April 17, 1968.

17. *Večernje novosti*, May 11, 1968.

18. On April 6, 1968, for example, delegates from a series of countries participated in a meeting of the SSJ on the international student protests in Belgrade. The delegates from the Berlin branch of the *Socialist German Students Union* (SDS) spoke about the international Vietnam Congress in February 1968 in Berlin. *Student*, April 9, 1968.

19. Božidar Jakšić , "Praxis i Korčulanska ljetnja škola. Kritike, osporavanja, napadi," in *Sloboda i nasilje. Razgovor o časopisu Praxis i Korčulanskoj letnjoj školi*, ed. Nebojša Popov (Beograd: Res Publica, 2003), 167–232.

20. Slobodan Divjak, "Studentske demonstracije 1968. i 1991—Sličnosti i razlike," *Treći program* 23, no. 1–2 (1991):50.

21. Popov, *Sukobi*.

22. Popov ed, *Sloboda i nasilje*.

23. Pervan, *Tito and the students*.

24. Mirko Arsić and Dragan R. Marković, *'68. Studentski bunt i društvo*, 2nd edn (Beograd: Istraživačko centar SSO Srbije).

19
Switzerland[1]

Nicole Peter

Although the phenomenon of 1968 has met with considerable scientific interest in neighboring countries, it has so far been almost completely ignored by Swiss scholars. Compared to the dimensions of the French May of 1968 or the effect of the extra-parliamentary opposition of the German APO, events and developments in Switzerland in the summer of 1968 were rather modest in scale, particularly since the public manifestation of protest was largely confined to Zurich.

However, in recent years vivid interest in the subject has developed, particularly within the humanities, using the practice of research previously established across Europe as the main frame of reference. Within this framework, two competing points of view should be highlighted. The first concerns the period wherein "1968" does not appear as a singular event, limited to one or two years, but, rather, as the culminating point of an era spanning from the late 1950s to the mid-1970s. During this era, Western societies were fundamentally transformed into consumer societies. The second perspective does not present "1968" as a revolution not having taken place but, rather, as a transnational communicative event. Although the Swiss interpretation includes neither subversive riots nor revolting students, results of an analysis of Swiss events are nevertheless comparable to other findings.

Social and Political Framework of the Country

Although Switzerland differed from its neighbors in that it remained virtually untouched by the atrocities of World War II, it transformed into a consumer society from the mid-fifties onward, with similar social and economic developments as other Western societies. Crucial decisions concerning modern postwar Swiss society had already been taken during the thirties and forties.

During the war, a system of social compromise was established that would persevere for several decades, reconciling progressive economic liberalism with cultural and ideological conservativism. The ideals of armed neutrality and mental national defense were melded in the myth of Swiss exceptionalism, which served as an ideological barrier against National Socialism and was effortlessly transformed after the war into anti-communism.[2] During the Cold War, the characteristics of this myth were political concordance and formal neutrality or, rather, unilateralism with a stabilizing effect on governmental institutions. This allowed for substantial economic growth from the onset of the new boom. Thanks to an intact infrastructure untouched by the war, the Swiss economy took off from a very advantageous starting point. Until the late sixties, Switzerland prospered in ways previously unknown, and with considerable effect on all social strata. This prosperity led to the emergence of a new type of consumer society that radically differed from prewar industrial society. The overall improvement of the standard of living suggested a certain leveling, where class differences seemingly vanished. For the first time, consumer goods were accessible to the masses.

Insofar as governmental control and social cushioning protected the national community from the risks of transformation, the economic dynamism was welcome. Because the main domestic debates made use of the semantics of the conflict between East and West, the myth of the mental national defense (now understood as anti-communism) could easily be used as an effective weapon against any and all attempts to opposition; the critique of social conditions was seen by the conservative elements in society as part of a conspiracy instigated by the communist East, no matter what the position of the critic.

Organizational and Social Structure of the Protest Movement

In France and the Federal Republic of Germany, universities were the starting points and strongholds of social protest. However, although protest in Switzerland did germinate in universities—particularly those in the Western areas—student protest was neither applied to society as a whole nor did it become visible in the streets. Rather, recent research reveals that Swiss protest was the result of many groups and networks from Left, with nonconformist and artistic milieus coming together in various types of action and participating in organizing demonstrations. Nevertheless, the demonstrations of the summer of 1968 that were held mainly in Zurich and seen as a climax of the Swiss protest movement were portrayed as student protest and therefore were understood as analogous to French and German events of the same time. Thus, the interpretation by the media that dominated public discourse viewed the struggle for an urban center for the young as the Swiss version of what had previously happened in other parts of Europe.

Actually, the movement was rather polymorphic; its formation and the linking of the various groups can be traced back to the early sixties. At that time, structural and social difficulties resulting from the boom had become virulent, and the gap between social change and intellectual conservativism was almost unbridgeable. The rhetoric of mental national defense and of anti-communism steadily lost its influence. Although overall, blue-collar workers were integrated into the new lifestyle, there was considerable potential for protest among the middle classes. While bourgeois or left-wing intellectuals were publicly questioning Swiss reality, hooligans and rockers had withdrawn from civil society. Across the country, in the crowded universities, students called for democratic reform of the antiquated structures while artists broke from the cultural establishment and a young, new Left sought to distance itself from the old Left parties. These groups joined forces in their protest against nuclear armament and subsequently united in the anti-Vietnam movement.

The *Fortschrittliche Arbeiter-, Schüler- und Studentenschaft* (FASS)[3] was in charge of organizing the demonstrations of the summer of 1968 in Zurich and reflected the social disparity of people involved. Students and pupils were represented only by a few radicalized minority groups, and the majority of members consisted of a young opposition of workers beyond the political and cultural establishment. As it appeared in the streets, the Swiss protest movement of 1968 was quintessentially a youth movement.

Cognitive Orientation of the Movement

The theoretical and methodological foundation of the Swiss activists consisted of a blend of various ideological concepts. The emergence of this foundation was accelerated by debates on the Vietnam War. While protests were initially dominated by pacifists and were strongly humanitarian in attitude, over time, within nonconformist discourse, "Vietnam" evolved into a keyword for general criticism of Swiss society, which ultimately followed the social criticism of the European New Left. While the traditional Left had lost some of its potential for social transformation, the New Left moved on to name the deficits of their societies. In Switzerland, one main reason for dissent was the overall conservative mentality. The politically and culturally stagnant society appeared atavistic in spite of the rapid economic change. First and foremost, protesters demanded participation and democratization.[4] Contrary to the narrative of Swiss exceptionalism, activists increasingly saw the problems of Swiss society in their geopolitical context. Following the movements in other European countries, they analyzed theories that linked Marxism to existentialism, or Marxism to psychoanalysis, and stressed the aspect of alienation. The works of Jean-Paul Sartre, Herbert Marcuse, Frantz

Fanon, and Mao Tse Tung, among others, formed the literary canon of the movement. In the course of Left engagement against the Vietnam War, ideas from these theories were assembled to form an international, anti-imperialistic interpretation.

The mesh of social and cultural criticism, of the striving for individual and collective emancipation, and of the opposition against the Vietnam War constituted the specific cognitive identity of the Swiss movement of 1968.

Attitudes toward the Superpowers and the Cold War

Despite the fact that mainstream Swiss society was markedly conservative, anti-Communist, Western, and consumer centered, the attitude of protesters in Switzerland was ambivalent vis-à-vis both superpowers. As in other Western European countries, criticism of traditional values was initiated or accompanied by the youth culture imported from the United States. Incidentally, this youth culture included criticism of the established American way of life. The image of the United States—which had previously been untainted—was now painted in shadowy hues, amalgamating fundamental rejection of Western consumer society and fierce anti-imperialism. Although the establishment interpreted the colonial wars in the Third World along the lines of anti-Communist ideas, anti-imperialism allowed for a very different understanding by seeing the line of demarcation between relatively weak states and the powerful, extortionist imperialists. The view on Switzerland was ambivalent. On the one hand, protesters saw it as an ideological and economic accessory to the United States; on the other hand, they viewed Switzerland through an anti-imperialistic lens as a victim of the American quest for hegemony.

While this anti-imperialistic terminology was applied to the United States, for the time being the Soviet Union remained the positive point of reference for revolutionary transformation. In the early 1960s, there existed a climate of rigid anti-communism, within which intercessions for—and solidarity with—the Soviet Union as voiced by the young Left were seen as subversive. This changed radically when Soviet-led Warsaw Pact troops Warsaw Pact invaded Prague in the late summer of 1968, concluding the Swiss New Left's dissociation from the Soviet Union. Thereafter, the Soviet Union was seen as nothing more than "America painted red."

Key Events

After the mid-1960s, Switzerland witnessed an increase in politically mobilizing events, a development that stretched into the 1970s. Demonstrations against Vietnam became more frequent; in the early stages, participants appealed to authorities for stronger engagement in foreign politics. At the same time, opposition against antiquated structures emerged in universities and demanded democratization of the academic system. Although criticism of university policies in western Switzerland was initially linked to an analysis of general societal problems, this was not duplicated in the German fashion until the late 1960s. The end of June 1968 marked the first climax of protest activities in Switzerland—considerably later and less pronounced than events in other parts of Europe.

Protests escalated violently in the summer of 1968, but only in Zurich. The key issue in the mid-June demonstrations was the demand for an independent youth center. Shortly before, police forces had clashed with a concert audience; there were widespread fights between youngsters and the police following a performance by Jimi Hendrix.[5] Although most people in the audience had not participated in previous protest marches, the combination of police brutality with political agitation by FASS in the form of a sensational flyer calling for "rebellion" and demanding "satisfaction" offered motive for identification and solidarity with the activists. This likely contributed to many young spectators joining protesters a few weeks later. What had happened in between was a gradual escalation of tension with protesters, police, city government, and the media in key roles. Criticism of police violence was linked to the demand for a youth center. After a demonstration, protesters occupied a building that provisionally housed the Globus department store. The troubles surrounding efforts to use the building as a youth center finally led to what made local history as the "Globus Riots." Forces clashed in ways previously unknown; in the cellars of the provisional center, police officers assaulted arrested demonstrators. This violence led to the end of the "Movement of 68," at least for the moment. City government issued a prohibition against demonstrations that was enforced between the second and fifteenth of July 1968. Peace and order were restored.

This episode resounded throughout the country. The controversy surrounding the youth center may not have constituted a revolution, but it did represent a rare occasions when the establishment was challenged. Impressed by protest movements across Europe as portrayed by the influential mass media, the population at large saw its way of life at risk. Alternately, activists viewed local events in an international context of repression, extortion and revolution.

Forms and Tactics of Protest

From the early 1960s on, modes of articulation in the Swiss left underwent changes, with its exponents tending away from the left establishment toward the New Left. They anticipated alternative forms of expression and political action that would expand the repertoire of manifestations of the "Movement of 68." With their visionary topics, the anti-nuclear and peace movements set the tone for civil opposition that challenged the political concordance and led to new protest movements. Leaving behind institutions and patterns for forming political opinions, activists copied the American civil rights movement with its range of "-ins."

Initially, protest expressed itself as appeal. The first teach-in on Vietnam was organized by *Fortschrittliche Studentenschaft Zürich* (FSZ)[6] and took place in 1965 at the Federal Institute of Technology; several more teach-ins followed, in addition to sit-ins, go-ins, paint-ins, and love-ins. Furthermore, the movement activists organized touring exhibitions, street theatres and demonstrations that no longer followed the pattern of labor movement demonstrations and served the intended purpose of scandalizing bystanders with confrontational slogans and banners. Provocative actions were used to establish a kind of counter-publicity, particularly in connection with the Vietnam War. By the late 1960s, demonstrations increasingly focused directly on governmental institutions and powerful companies. One such action was directed at the influential liberal daily paper *Neue Zürcher Zeitung*, and was met with great indignation. Protesters decorated *Neue Zürcher Zeitung*'s headquarters with a Vietcong flag in March 1968 as a means of protesting the manner of reporting on the Vietnam War. In retrospect, this event shows the ambivalence of Swiss activists toward mass media. Appellative action and direct attacks sought publicity through the reporting of mass media. This was both a motivation and a means for identification; activists followed the resulting publicity closely. At the same time, as the attack on the *Neue Zürcher Zeitung* indicates, they were very skeptical about the media, and criticism of "manufacturing consent" was omnipresent in their actions.

Transnational Relations

The reflection of events in the media combined with international personal relationships shows how the international Left was both a point of reference for and enmeshed with the Swiss movement. However, the closeness of these contacts varied from region to region because of linguistic barriers. Nevertheless, the ostentatious cultivation of relationships with members of the European Left markedly contradicted the established myth of Swiss unilateralism. Although the media portrayed European movements as one collective, Swiss activists put great effort into publicizing and fortifying their trans-European relationships. Beginning in the early 1960s, a specific form of internationalism manifested itself through nonconformist media, some newly established and vividly reflecting Western European discourse. Magazines such as *Neutralität, Zeitdienst*, the *Tessin Quaderni*, or the *Voix universitaire* appeared in Lausanne and stressed their international orientation.

Media networking was just one aspect of bilateral relationships; another facet was visible at the personal level. Whereas developments throughout Europe were noted in the regions, personal relations mainly developed with like-minded groups and individuals of neighboring countries speaking the same language. Thus, young intellectuals and students in western Switzerland concentrated on connections with the French Left, leading to the formation of the *Mouvement démocratique des étudiants* (MDE) in the early 1960s. This group went beyond student interests and closely cooperated with the French Left on issues of anti-colonialism and anti-imperialism. Italian-speaking Swiss activists sought to link mainly with Italian proponents. The *Movimento giovanile progressista* (MGP) that was founded in 1967 was a pillar of the Tessin movement of 1968[7]; it shaped itself according to Italian ouvrierism, organizing panel discussions with Giangiaccomo Feltrinelli and Enrico Filippini, and later participating in conventions in Florence and Bologna. Of course, the Left in the German-speaking part of Switzerland linked with representatives in Western Germany, establishing contact during conventions on the Vietnam War in Frankfurt and Berlin. These connections led to the extension of an invitation to Rudi Dutschke in the spring of 1968.

Consequences, Narratives, and Politics of Memory

After the violent confrontation between police forces and demonstrators in the summer of 1968, protests diminished. Swiss proponents of the protest movement turned away from issues of global politics and focused on internal problems. The main issues were xenophobia, conscientious objection, ecological problems, and equal rights for women. As in neighboring countries, the movement of 1968 in Switzerland underwent a transformation that eventually led to its splitting into a labor-oriented and an anti-authoritarian wing. At the same time, the *Frauenbefreiungsbewegung* (FBB)[8] emerged, initially considering itself part of the Movement of 68, but eventually breaking away.

New protests broke out in the early 1970s, finding widespread support within society. More recent studies suggest that the Swiss movement actually did not culminate until this time, when women, adolescents, and students succeeded in mobilizing people on a larger scale. The so-called *Bunker Movement* reactivated demand for an independent youth center, whereas the Home Campaign sought to liberate inmates of orphanages and educational establishments. Furthermore, protests now reached universities in German-speaking areas of Switzerland. Students increasingly linked questions of academic policies to social issues; several working groups were founded, and some organized an "anti-capitalistic and anti-fascist information week" at Zurich University in the summer of 1971. In response, the dean shut down the university for a week.

In retrospect, the protest movement can be seen as a seismograph of social change. Politically, it aimed to challenge the system of concordance and to force Switzerland to adopt a new view on foreign politics in a global context. The issues addressed sensitized Swiss society for the flip side of socio-economic change and paved the way for new social movements. On the organizational level, networks and parties that had emerged from the 1968 movement stirred things up. Although among radical activist groups only the *Progressive Organisationen der Schweiz* (POCH) were somewhat politically successful in their own right, all of these groups forced the Left establishment to reform.

However, 1968 has left very few traces in Swiss social memory. The youth movement of the early 1980s clearly sought to distance itself from what 1968 represented. Though it showed little of the revolutionary fire of its predecessors, one of its primary goals was still an independent youth center. The riots of the 1980s far exceeded those of 1968 in both intensity and duration and are regarded as the most extensive protest movement in Swiss post-war history. Apart from that, 1968 remained in public memory as the symbol for anti-authoritarian or cultural revolt, whereas both individual events and individual activists have been forgotten.

Bibliography

An overview of the social and political framework of the country is provided by König et al. (1998) and Kriesi (1981). Studies on the organizational and social structure of the movement can be found in Fernandez (1990), Lachenmeier (2002), Lerch (2001), Schär (2006), and Spirig (2005). For the constitution of the cognitive orientation of the movement, see, for example, Peter (2006) but also Tanner (1998). Studies of the splitting of the movement of 1968 in Switzerland into labor oriented and an anti-authoritarian wing is provided by Stahel (2006), Schär (2006), and Bittner (2006). Finally, for studies on the new women's liberations movement, a field that also is still very at the beginning, turn to Bucher/Schmucki (1995) and Kunz (2006).

Bittner, Stefan. *Höhenflüge im Underground. Die Bärglütli und ihre Sommer-Camps 1971–1973. Ein Schweizer Hippie-Dropout-Phänomen als Ausdrucksform des "romantischen Komplexes"*. Unpublished Liz., Bern, 2006.
Bucher, Judith and Barbara Schmucki. *FBB: Fotogeschichte der Frauenbefreiungsbewegung Zürich*. Zürich: Limmat, 1995.

Fernandez, Jimena. *Mai 68 dans les universités de Suisse romande. Développement des mouvements et impact du facteur international.* Unpublished Liz., Fribourg, 1990.

König, Mario et al. *Dynamisierung und Umbau. Die Schweiz in den 60er und 70er Jahren.* Zürich: Chronos, 1998.

Kriesi, Hanspeter, René Lévy, et al. *Politische Aktivierung in der Schweiz 1945–1978.* Diessenhofen: Rüegger, 1981.

Kunz, Barbara. *Von der Rebellion zur Emanzipation. Zürcher 68erinnen erinnern sich: Soziale und kulturelle Praxis 1965–1974.* Unpublished Liz., Zürich, 2006.

Lachenmeier, Dominik. *Die Arena—eine Gruppierung der Basler '68er-Bewegung' zwischen 'etablierter' und 'alternativer' öffentlichkeit.* Unpublished Liz., Basel, 2002.

Lerch, Fredi. *Muellers Weg ins Paradies. Nonkonformismus im Bern der Sechziger Jahre.* Zürich: Rotpunkt, 2001.

Peter, Nicole. *Die Dritte Welt der schweizerischen Linken: Genese eines heterotopischen Ortes 1964–1968.* Unpublished Liz., Zürich, 2006.

Schär, Renate. *"Erziehungsanstalten unter Beschuss." Heimkampagne und Heimkritik in der Schweiz in den 1970er Jahren.* Unpublished Liz, Bern, 2006;

Spirig, Christine. *Zwischen Jugendbewegung und Hochschulreform. Die Zürcher Studenten 1967–1969.* Unpublished Liz., Zürich, 2005.

Stahel, Thomas. *Wo-wo-wonige! Stadt- und Wohnpolitische Bewegungen in Zürich nach 68.* Zürich: Paranoia City, 2006.

Tanner, Jakob. *"'The Times They Are A-Changin'—Zur subkulturellen Dynamik der 68er Bewegung,"* in Ingrid Gilcher-Holtey, *1968—Vom Ereignis zum Gegenstand der Geschichtswissenschaft.* Göttingen: Vandenhoeck & Ruprecht, 1998, 207–23.

Notes

1. Translation: Erica Burgauer
2. The main idea of the mental national defense was the creation of a national community within Switzerland and the creation of a Swiss identity beyond class differences.
3. Progressive Workers, Pupils, and Students.
4. See Olivier Pavillon, "La Nouvelle Gauche en Suisse romande, des années 60 au milieu des années 80: un essai de mise en perspective," *Cahiers d'histoire du mouvement ouvrier,* 21(2005): 7-30; Pierre Jeanneret, "Le Mouvement démocratique des étudiants," *Cahiers d'histoire du mouvement ouvrier,* 21 (2005): 43-84.
5. The youngsters' mood was stirred up when the police disbanded forcefully a spontaneous gathering of the concert audience members. So far, the motives of the riots are still uncertain.
6. Progressive Students Zurich.
7. In the southern part of Switzerland, the MGP, which consisted of different cultural and ideological trends, was one of the important parts of the movement. See Dominique Wisler, *Drei Gruppen der Neuen Linken auf der Suche nach der Revolution,* Zürich: Seismo, 1996, 20–23.
8. Women's liberation movement.

20
Scandinavia

Thomas Ekman Jørgensen

Social and Political Framework of Scandinavia

The three Scandinavian countries, Denmark, Norway, and Sweden, are often and for good reasons seen as a homogeneous entity. All three countries have a long history of social democratic political hegemony that has managed to spread its norms and ideas to larger parts of society. This is very much the case in Sweden, where virtually uninterrupted social democratic government since the 1930s has left its clear mark on the Swedish elites. In Denmark and Norway there has been a more balanced competition between the liberal and conservative parties and the social democrats. For the events around 1968, this social democratic hegemony is particularly important since the movements in Scandinavia are intimately connected to the hegemonic narrative of social democratic modernity.

In crude terms, this narrative consists of the workers' movement as the main agent of history that leads the country from the ineffective and unjust rule of the upper classes to a *folkhem* (or "home for the people"). This ideal represents an egalitarian society in which poverty and need are abolished and welfare for all is guaranteed by a state that redistributes the returns of economic growth. This entails an explicit class compromise in which the social democratic state provides the stability and structural requirements of the capitalist economy, which in turn provides the economic basis for the welfare state.[1] The consequences of this master narrative for Scandinavian politics are at the center of the movements of 1968 and provide one common aspect. Another important common factor is the extensive political and cultural consensus in the Scandinavian societies; despite the social democratic hegemony, they were all marked by a political culture of broad compromises and integration of diverse groups into the decision-making process.

Although the countries share political and cultural values, their geography is strikingly diverse. First and foremost, it is a question of size. Sweden is the fourth largest country in Western Europe, more in the league of France and Spain than with tiny Denmark. In addition, its oblong shape makes the distances from north to south extremely long, creating isolated economic and political centers. Sweden shares this feature with neighboring Norway. For this reason, the concept of center and periphery is crucial in the two countries, and is important to the critique connected to 1968. Denmark, in contrast, is very small and quite centralized around Copenhagen. Although geographically Norway and Sweden are alike, geopolitically Denmark and Norway share NATO membership, whereas Sweden has a strong, neutral position.

Organizational and Social Structure of the Protest Movement

The movements that are usually connected to 1968 in Scandinavia all have their roots in the preceding decade. In Denmark and Norway, political parties became the focus of the New Left, whereas in Sweden the protest movements were closely linked to the reform of the communist party during the 1960s. In Denmark, the communist party split on the issue of the invasion of Hungary and de-Stalinization in the late 1950s. The reformist wing was excluded, and its members went on to found the Socialist People's Party (*Socialistisk Folkeparti*, SF), which was increasingly successful in making considerable electoral gains during the first half of the 1960s. Having thus proved that explicit socialism without affiliation to Moscow had considerable appeal among the electorate, the Left in the neighbor countries followed suit. The left wing of the Norwegian social democrats formed their own SF in 1961 as a protest against the NATO-friendly party leadership, whereas the Swedish communists, facing electoral defeat, attempted to weaken their ties to the Soviet Union and orthodox communism to present a more palatable version of socialism.[2]

These parties were all characterized by eclectic ideology with strong national agendas in order to distance themselves from orthodox, "fifth column" communism. They challenged the social democratic class compromise through a combination of improvement on welfare and vague promises of a democratic socialism. Importantly, they were traditional parties marked by the political pragmatism necessary for parliamentary democracy. This also applied to the CND, which was particularly strong in Denmark (less so in Norway and very weak in Sweden); despite its "movement" image, it was to a large extent a traditional political pressure group that used unorthodox methods to convey the message to the acknowledged decision-makers in parliament.[3]

This changed in the middle of the decade, partially because of reactions to the Vietnam War. In particular, the younger generations stood up against the opportunism of the established leaders and called for more stringent, Marxist policies instead of party-political pragmatism.

In Denmark, SF split on the issue, and the left wing of the party formed the VS (*Venstresocialisterne*, Left Socialists), which for a short period became the political home of all sorts of left-wing protest, from Maoism over radical unionists to countercultural currents.[4] Predictably, many of these groups left the party to found new, revolutionary groups and parties, creating an undergrowth of *groupuscules* through the 1970s. VS, however, continued as an important forum for political discussion and remained the most important party on the revolutionary Left. However, the real novelty came with the student revolt in 1968, when an unusually successful student movement managed not only to set off a radical reform of the universities but also to mobilize a large number of students, making the universities the most important recruitment pool for the Left.[5] In this way, the student movement became the most important organization on the Left, dominating the political discussions and often also the VS, which at times resembled a student debate club. The influence of the students was also apparent in the dominating intellectual milieu around the magazine *Politisk Revy* (Political Revue), by far the most important forum for Leftist debate through the 1960s and 1970s, as student activists entered the editing board and produced much of the content.

In Norway, radicalism came relatively later and was in many ways connected to the movement against membership of the European Economic Community (EEC) in the early 1970s. Similar to its Danish counterpart, the Norwegian SF was a stern opponent of the EEC and allied itself with the communists and independent socialists to form a successful socialist bloc (*Sosialistisk Valgforbund*) in the 1973 elections. Apart from friction with the communists, who soon left the coalition, the electoral alliance united the forces in Socialist Left (*Sosialistisk Venstreparti*). In the extra-parliamentary arena, the Popular Movement Against EEC Membership (*Folkebevegelsen mot norsk medlemskap i fellesmarkedet*) was the organizational focus of the Left (see following), together with the Maoist, so-called ML (Marxist-Leninist), movement and its front organizations such as the Vietnam Movement and the music movement. Students and other activist groups often focused on those groups or on the issues they presented as the framework for their activities.

In Sweden, the challenge to the pragmatism of the communist leadership came from the Maoist opposition within the party. The communist party had avoided splits during the first part of the 1960s by allowing considerable ideological space for its members. For this reason, it consisted of several competing groups, from crypto-social democrats to Maoists.[6] At the zenith of the reform wave at the party congress in 1967, when the party openly distanced itself from Leninism, adopted the new name Left Party Communists (VPK, *Venstrepartiet Kommunisterna*) and leaned toward the New Left (labeled "modernism"), the Maoists left to form their own Communist League of Marxists-Leninists (KFML, *Kommunistiska Förbundet Marxist-Leninisterna*, later to take over the Comintern-style name SKP, or Swedish Communist Party). This group first and foremost thrived on the Vietnam issue. As the abortive student revolt in Sweden ended in a shift to the right for the majority of the students, the Vietnam Movement became the main player on the extreme Left.[7] Its radical organization, DFFG (*De Förenade FNL-Grupperna*, The United FNL Groups) served as a front organization for the KFML/SKP and to some extent played the same role for the recruitment of activists that the student movement played in Denmark. In the 1970s, the popular culture movement, also connected to the Maoist circles, became very important. Centered on the magazine *Folket i Bild/Kulturfront* (Images of the People/Culture Front), it promoted a noncommercial culture rooted in the Swedish popular tradition.

Cognitive Orientation of the Movement

There is a marked difference among the countries in the success of Maoism in Norway and Sweden and its rather isolated status in Denmark. Where all three countries had considerably similar ideological traits in the early 1960s, the latter half of the decade saw some distinct departures. The ideological hallmark of the SF parties and the Swedish modernists had been eclecticism mixed with moral judgment, both elements of distancing themselves from Stalinist dogmatism and the instrumentalism of Bolshevist conspiracy. They took a moral stand against the arms race, colonialism, and consumer society while offering a humanist brand of socialism with space for discussion and the acceptance of democracy.

In Denmark, the student movement took off on a similar basis. The universities were in need of democratic reform both in terms of student participation in daily affairs and through open discussion of the curricula and scientific traditions of the different institutes. These debates were often fuelled by Habermasian ideas of free discussions and Marcuse's thoughts on providing alternatives to one-dimensional positivism. However, this soon developed into more radical ideas about providing scientific ammunition for the class struggle as well as constructing the correct analysis of Danish capitalism to lay out the strategy for its abolishment. Hence, the Danish Left developed a marked preference for abstract analyses and an exegetic view of the classical texts.

This was quite different from the Maoism found in Norway and Sweden. Here, the New Left eclectic and pacifist ideology of the early 1960s was seriously challenged by Maoist organizations, which emphasized ideological orthodoxy and full solidarity with the armed struggle of the liberation movements. During the 1970s, these ideas were enlarged by a particular focus on popular issues in the Germanic *Volk/Folk* sense of the word. The culture and traditions of the broad masses were cultivated as an explicit alternative to capitalist and commercial culture. The Maoists reached back to the history of the popular movements of the nineteenth century (workers', farmers', and religious movements) and hailed the image of the authentic peasant unspoiled by capitalism. Simplicity and authenticity were the main components of this invented tradition of a popular counterculture. Hence, while the political analysis of the movement often remained on a very basic level of Maoist phrases, its practical and aesthetic program was quite well developed.[8] This was consciously connected to the ongoing conflict between center and periphery in the two countries. While the industrial and administrative centers in the south and east of Sweden were seen as decadent fortresses of soulless planning and heartless capitalism, northern and western Sweden in particular were seen as the seat of true Swedish culture. This dichotomy corresponded to government initiatives to centralize labor and thus depopulate the unproductive periphery.

One tempting cultural explanation of the difference between Denmark and Norway/Sweden could be the historical role of Puritanism on the Scandinavian Peninsula and its marginal role in Denmark.[9] Maoism, with its emphasis on orthodoxy and discipline, was undoubtedly attractive to the underlying Puritan values of Norway and Sweden, whereas those values were much less prominent in Denmark. Another short-term explanation is the strength of the Danish student movement, which valued new, daring, and complex interpretations of Marxism over the one-liners of the Little Red Book. No less orthodox, the student leaders preferred to style themselves as independent-thinking intellectual guides rather than as custodians of the thoughts of a far-away chairman. One important common trait, however, was the challenge to the modernist vision presented in particular by the social democrats. The movements pointed to the weaknesses of the class compromise, the limits of central planning, and the shortcomings of the welfare state.[10] Instead, they proposed more "humane" visions of a society that was not dependent on high productivity and did not reduce man to a wheel in the big machine of welfare capitalism.

Attitudes toward the Superpowers and the Cold War

Through the 1960s, the immediate relevance of the Cold War decreased markedly in Scandinavia. Although Norway was directly involved in the U2 affair and Greenland was an important part of the American early warning system, the conflict between the superpowers became ever more distant after the Cuban missile crisis. During the wars in Algeria and Vietnam, the indirect involvement through the alliance was a recurrent theme on the Left in Denmark and Norway in the early and mid-1960s. By 1968, however, focus shifted to more immediate events at home. In Denmark, the developments at the universities and the creation of a student movement took some of the attention away from geopolitical issues. This tendency prevailed generally through the following years as U.S. involvement in Third World conflicts became less direct than it was in the 1960s.

Particularly in Denmark, anti-Americanism was moderated by the significant influence of American countercultural products and practices. American comics, music, and especially drugs had a large effect on the Left as a whole. Even in intellectual circles, there was a marked difference between criticism of the official United States and the other America of like-minded activists.

In Sweden, the stern neutrality of the social democratic government made it difficult to mobilize on any anti-American agenda before the Vietnam War. However, as the war became the major theme of the Swedish Left, anti-Americanism flourished.[11] The United States as both the oppressor of the Third World and the home of commercial culture came to represent everything that the Left despised. Tellingly, American counterculture was generally viewed with skepticism or even contempt by the Swedish Left.

Where Scandinavia had been geographically on the fringes of the Cold War, the Maoists in Norway and Sweden suddenly placed their countries on the front line as the Chinese leadership declared that the Soviet Union presented a greater danger than the United States. Swedish Maoists turned to the anti-Russian traditions of the past century to evoke the image of a threatening, imperialist power on their doorstep. They even went so far as to advise members to join the army to secure a reliable defense against a Russian attack. In Norway, similar ideas were fuelled by the massive Soviet military presence on the Kola Peninsula as well as Soviet activities in Norwegian- administered Svalbard and naval exercises being held practically in their backyard.

Key Events

Of all three countries, Denmark presents the most eventful history. Not only was there a sustained student revolt, but this was preceded by a strong CND, the Vietnam Movement, and the countercultural "youth revolt." Here, 1968 presents a high point in a series of events that shaped a very independent and self-confident movement. Clashes with the police were relatively frequent, culminating in 1970 at the meeting of the World Bank in Copenhagen that developed into actual street fighting between the police and the activists. Despite the surrounding moderate political culture, there was a continuous strain of activism and confrontation seeking at the fringes of the Danish Left, which continued through the 1980s and 1990s.[12] This created spectacular events, which were much less frequent in Norway and Sweden.

The student revolt consisted of a period of confrontation that stretched from 1968 well into 1971. The initial demonstrations and occupations at the University of Copenhagen were very successful in starting a general reform of the universities. However, as the reform took shape, the students became ever more radical in their demands and grew to be more experienced activists. This resulted in an increasing wave of confrontations in 1970–1971 over the path of the reforms. Different from the original engagements of 1968, these were largely unsuccessful but resulted in the creation of a well-organized, national student movement with a large potential for mobilization.

In Sweden, attempts were made to copy the continental student revolts. In 1968, the students at Stockholm University occupied the student house for three days—an act that did not seriously disturb research or teaching. This act failed to create a large student movement; on the contrary, many students were pushed rightwards by the activism. Most of the students did not approve of radicalism and preferred the more serious right wing. The main event lay outside the student circles, in the far north. In the winter 1969–1970, the miners in arctic town of Kiruna went on strike against the state-owned mining company. Apart from the immediate attraction of sturdy miners displaying working-class radicalism in the dark, arctic night, the strike also pointed to the limits of the social democratic class compromise. The mining company was state owned and thus more or less directly controlled by the social democrats who were supposed to serve the workers' interests. This of course boosted the confidence of the radical Left that a revolution from below was possible and in many ways provided a foundation for the populist agenda of the 1970s.

In Norway, the most important single event came later, namely, the referendum for Norwegian EEC membership in 1972. This event, interpreted as an onslaught of the continental, capitalist community on the Norwegian working class, became a common cause for the Left. As the social democrats officially argued for a "yes" vote, the groups left of the hegemonic workers' party used this opening to mobilize on an issue that easily could be interpreted as another sacrifice of the workers' interests on the altar of the class compromise. The issue also connected to the tension between center and periphery and played out as a conflict between official Norway and the "Norway of the people"[13]—both themes dear to the Left. The parties on the Left, mainly SF and the communists (although only for a short period), as well as a number of independent Leftists, joined forces against the EEC and former SV (*Sosialistisk Venstreparti*, Socialist Left Party), which gained considerable electoral support in the 1973 election. Apart from this, the Popular Movement against EEC Membership and the Maoist anti-EEC front organization AKMED (*Arbeiderkomiteen mot EEC og dyrtid*, Workers' Committee Against the EEC and Inflation) mobilized the Left in the extra-parliamentary work against Norwegian membership. Increasingly, the heated debate transformed the arguments of class struggle into nationalist rhetoric regarding Norwegian independence. The result of the referendum was a rejection of membership, but the year-long mobilization continued to play an important part in the Leftist and grass-root milieus.

Forms and Tactics of Protest

Denmark also stands out in terms of movement tactics. Whereas the events in Sweden and Norway were mostly of a rather peaceful sort, with only a few minor confrontations, the Danish movement contained a confrontational, semi-anarchist element of a more continental character. The early student movement had strong anarchist traits such as collective decision-making and, importantly, explicit use of confrontation as a means of mobilization and consciousness creation. Hence, the Danish movement used deliberate physical provocation, occupations, and happenings—often with confrontation as the explicit aim—as a part of their tactics, especially between 1968 and 1970. In the 1970s, though, the more theoretical wing got the upper hand within the movement, which became more introverted and aimed for "theoretical clarity" while mobilizing through study circles rather than spontaneous activism. In the early 1980s, however, the squatter movement would put full confrontation back on the agenda. This movement also dates back to the time around 1968 when the weapon of occupation was used not only in the universities but also to create new communities in abandoned buildings, most spectacularly in Christiania, where squatters took over a large army barrack and formed their own, still existing, free city.

In Norway and Sweden, the movements were more traditionally organized in terms of goals and means. In Sweden, the Bolshevik party model still had an important place within a Left that was split between a reformed communist party and traditionalist Maoism. The student revolt itself was soon appropriated by outside forces that wanted to manipulate the currents in the direction of their own movement. Thus, important student leaders were often affiliated with political parties. The same goes for the Vietnam Movement, whose moderate wing was an official cross-party cooperation, whereas the radical movement, the DFFG, was the front organization of the KFML/SKP. Mobilization, a key criterion of success, took place through these front organizations. The KFML/SKP would use the general public attention to the war in Vietnam to play on American atrocities and the struggle of the Vietnamese people to make people take the first step on what was supposed to be the road of political consciousness.[14] The means were flyers, selling left-wing magazines on the streets, or mostly peaceful demonstrations. The few incidents of clashes or copying of "continental" methods of protest such as occupations were at best half-hearted.

In Norway, the bottom-up approach of the popular movement tradition had large appeal. Again, the lack of a significant revolt-like situation restrained the development of nontraditional methods of protest. Indeed, Norway stands out through its lack of open contestation in comparison with most Western European countries. Anarchist ideas existed, although without the confrontational elements, but in general the Norwegian Left worked through rather traditional political movements like the anti-EEC initiatives or, in the case of the Maoists, through the classic model of avant-garde party and broad front organizations. The latter could draw on the long traditions of popular, anti-establishment movements from the historically influential Christian Revivalism to the early workers' movement. Indeed, the victory in the EEC referendum was seen as the victory of the people over the establishment. The forms of this victory, however, remained largely within the established framework of political action.

Transnational Relations

The international character of 1968 certainly applies to Scandinavia, although in various ways. In Denmark, with one foot on the continent and one in the North, the transfer of ideas and practices is rather easily traceable. Berlin, and to some extent Italy, was an important direct model for the Danish student revolt (the events in Paris and at Columbia took place when the Danish revolt was already well under way). Prominent student leaders had spent time in Berlin and returned with a range of ideas for the Copenhagen revolt, such as the establishment of a critical university, a concept which was explicitly taken from Germany. Indeed, the big southern neighbor continued to play the most important role, though the favorite destination soon became Frankfurt rather than Berlin. Another important factor was the American connection in the counterculture (briefly overshadowed by the Dutch Provos in 1966–1967). Although the countercultural scene in itself imploded around 1970, the aesthetic effect of American music and comic books left clear marks on the Left. The comic book scene remained especially vivid both in terms of translations of first American (Robert Crumb, "Freak Brothers") and later French series (Jean Giraud/Moebius), as well as home-grown comics like the brilliantly freewheeling Claus Deleuran, who was printed in the otherwise high-brow *Politisk Revy*.

Paradoxically, although Sweden was known as a haven for American draft evaders, it had far less American influence, probably because of the weak role of the countercultural movement. Sweden had a very short-lived Dutch-inspired Provo movement whose most memorable action was its own funeral and dissolution in January 1967,[15] whereas the abortive student revolt was clearly inspired by Paris events. Otherwise, the greatest outside influence came from the Third World. Since the 1950s, Swedish authors had habitually travelled the southern continents and returned with tales of oppression as well as a certain fascination for the fighting peoples of the south. In the 1960s, China was a favorite destination for—to use Paul Hollander's expression—"political pilgrims"[16] far beyond the Maoist die-hards. Certainly, these contacts were qualitatively different than the European ones, where the culture and language barrier was smaller, and as such the inspiration from the Third World was often articulated as a mirror of Swedish problems or values. One example was the puritan interpretation of the idealist Chinese Cultural Revolution as a counter-image to the super-ficial Swedish consumer society. As the populist element of the movement attained hegemony in the 1970s, the outside influences lost their position to the domestic agenda.

Norway was even more parochial in its outlook, not least as a result of fact that the EEC referendum was the radical high point of the movement. However, the Norwegian scientific community was very international in its outlook in the 1960s and enjoyed widespread respect abroad; for example Stein Rokkan, a pioneer in the comparative study of state formation, whose scientific standing was hardly matched by anyone else in Scandinavia. Around 1968, the radical students profited considerably from the close con-nections between Norwegian philosopher Hans Skjervheim and Jürgen Habermas. In contrast to Germany, where he was in conflict with the stu-dent movement, the critique of positivism made Jürgen Habermas a favorite reference in the radical students' attacks against established scientific tradi-tions. This was also the case in Denmark, where the students tellingly had to study the Norwegian translations.

Consequences, Narratives, and Politics of Memory

The consequences of 1968 in Scandinavia as a whole have been a remarkable dismantling of traditional hierarchies, and in many ways a thorough cultural revolution. Most visible, perhaps, is the abandonment of formalities such as the formal singular pronoun and other linguistic signs of hierarchy. To this day, even prime ministers (though not the royal families) will be addressed informally by journalists, just as students address professors by their first names. The already present egalitarian ideas were given a considerable boost, even more than in other Western countries, in the universities as well as in private industry. Indeed, one may argue that 1968 in Scandinavia has played a large part in shaping today's high-tech flexible and innovative Scandinavian economy.

On the more political level, the New Left of the early 1960s has left its mark on the parliamentary scene through the existence of a Leftist opposition to social democracy in parliament: in Denmark and Norway early on through the non-communist Left, and in Sweden through the integration of New Left ideas into the communist party, which made it possible for the VPK to simply cancel the communist part of its name after 1990 and continue as VP (*Vänsterpartiet*, Party of the Left). Also, the Leftist wave of the 1960s and 1970s created a situation of hegemony in which intellectual became synonymous with Leftist.

However, this should not overshadow the important integration of the Leftist challenge by the social democracies themselves. Especially in Sweden, the attacks on the insufficient and alienating welfare state were taken quite seriously and led to reforms of the trade unions, with more decisions being taken locally as well as rearticulating social policy along the lines of the critique from the Left.[17] On the whole, the reactions of the establishment remained integrative and open.

The politics of memory have reflected this: 1968 has been integrated into the grand narrative of Scandinavian progressivism, despite its explicit critique of this narrative. The student revolt and the Leftist movements of the 1960s and 1970s were colorful examples of the particular Scandinavian mixture of individual freedom and social responsibility. In Sweden and Norway, the support for Mao's China and the dogmatism of the Maoist movements have been downplayed[18] or presented as youthful idealism; "also remember the good sides" seems to be a widespread motto of those that remember those decades. This was also the case in Denmark until the 1990s, where a group of journalists began an almost decade-long crusade against the old activists. Although the Danish Left as a whole was less totalitarian than the Norwegians and Swedish, the debate about the moral problems of having supported communist dictatorships raged fiercely in Danish newspapers. Hence, the country is still largely split on how to evaluate those years, as a progressive chapter of the national history or as dark years in which fundamental democratic values were discarded for the communist dictatorships.[19]

Bibliography

The development of literature on 1968 in Scandinavia is quite well underway in Sweden, and Denmark and Norway are currently catching up. For those not proficient in Scandinavian languages, however, there is little available.

The most influential Swedish book remains Salomon (1996) on the Vietnam Movement, covering important aspects of the Swedish experience. Josefsson (1996) describes the Swedish student revolt thoroughly, and öst-berg (2002) has written a short overview of the years around 1968. For those not reading Swedish, Etzemüller (2005) gives good insight to the Swedish events in his comparison between Germany and Sweden.

In Denmark, Nielsen (1991) compares Denmark and Germany and focuses on the integrative elements of the Danish reactions to 1968 stretching well into the 1970s. Apart from that, Andersen and Olsen (2004) offer an anthology that gives an idea about the different interpretations of 1968, though not much actual history of the period. Other accounts consist of a coedited issue of the journal *Den jyske historiker* about the 1960s, *Opbrud i 1960erne* (no. 101, 2003), Jensen and Jorgensen (2007) on the student revolt and its aftermath, and my dissertation on the concept of nation on the Left in Denmark and Sweden, *Transformations and Crises* (2004).

In Norway, the newly published Førland and Korsvik (2006) anthology fills a gap in the research. Otherwise the books are few: Sjöll (2005) has published a book on the Maoist movement and the anti-EEC movement is described in Bjørklund (1982). The Norwegian students are described in the anthology by Hjeltnes (1998).[20]

Andersen, Morten and Niklas Olsen, eds. *1968—Dengang og nu*. Copenhagen: Museum Tusculanum, 2004.

Etzemüller, Thomas. *1968—Ein Riss in der Geschichte? Gesellschaftlicher Umbruch und 68er- Bewegungen in Westdeutschland und Schweden*. Konstanz: UVK, 2005.

Førland, Tor and Trine Korsvik, eds., *1968—opprør og motkultur på norsk* (Oslo: Pax, 2006)

Heinemann, Tom. *Uro—25 års gadekamp*. Copenhagen: Tiderne skifter, 1995.

Hjeltnes, Guri, ed. *Universitetet og studentene. Opprør og identitet*. Oslo: Forum for universitetshistorie, 1998.

Jensen, Steven and Thomas Jørgensen. *1968—og det der fulgte*. Copenhagen: Gyldendal, forthcoming.

Josefsson, Sven. *året var 1968*. Gothenburg: Historiska institutionen i Göteborg, 1996.
Jørgensen, Thomas. *Transformations and Crises. The Left and the Nation in Denmark and Sweden 1956–1980*. New York: Berghahn Books, forthcoming.
Madsen, Peer and Jens Madsen, *Fra sandkasse til kadreparti? VS's dannelse og udvikling 1967–73*. Copenhagen: VS Forlaget, 1980.
Nordentoft, Johannes and Søren Rasmussen. *Kampagnen mod Atomvåben og Vietnambevægelsen 1960–1972*. Odense: Odense University Press, 1991.
Nielsen, Henrik. *Demokrati i bevægelse*. århus: århus Universitetsforlag, 1991.
östberg, Kjell. *1968 när allting var i rörelse*. Stockholm: Prisma, 2002.
Salomon, Kim. *Rebeller i takt med tiden. FNL- rörelsen och 60- talets politiska ritualer*. Stockholm: Rabén Prisma, 1996.
Sjøli, Hans. *Mao min Mao. Historien om AKPs vekst og fall*. Oslo: Cappelen, 2005.
Wiklund, Martin. *I det modernas landskap. Historisk orientering och kritiska berättelser om det moderna Sverige mellan 1960 och 1990*. Stockholm: Symposion, 2006.

Notes

1. See Martin Wiklund, *I det modernas landskap. Historisk orientering och kritiska berättelser om det moderna Sverige mellan 1960 och 1990* (Stockholm: Symposion, 2006).
2. Thomas Jørgensen, "Split or Reform? The Danish and Swedish CP's Facing the Post- Stalin Era", in*West European Communism after Stalinism. Comparative Approaches*, ed. Thomas Jørgensen and Maud Bracke (Fiesole: EUI Working Paper, HEC 2002/4, 2002), 45–75.
3. Johannes Nordentoft and Søren Rasmussen, *Kampagnen mod Atomvåben og Vietnambevægelsen 1960–1972* (Odense: Odense University Press, 1991).
4. Peer Madsen and Jens Madsen, *Fra sandkasse til kadreparti? VS's dannelse og udvikling 1967–73* (Copenhagen: VS Forlaget, 1980).
5. Steven Jensen and Thomas Jørgensen, *1968—og det der fulgte* (Copenhagen: Gyldendal, forthcoming).
6. Kent Lindkvist, *Program och parti* (Lund: Arkiv för studier i arbetarrörelsens historia, 1982), 62–73.
7. Even though this was mainly caused by right-wing mobilization of nonpolitical students, Sven Josefsson, *året var 1968* (Gothenburg: Historiska institutionen i Göteborg, 1996), 108.
8. Thomas Jørgensen, *Transformations and Crises. The Left and the Nation in Denmark and Sweden 1956–1980* (Oxford: Berghahn Books, forthcoming).
9. Sidsel Eriksen, "Vækkelse og afholdsbevægelse," *Scandia* 1988;2:251–95.
10. Jenny Andersson, *Mellan tillväxt och trygghet. Idéer om socialpolitik i socialdemokratisk socialpolitisk ideologi under efterkrigstiden* (Uppsala: Uppsala Universitet, 2003), 42–62.
11. Eva Block, *Amerikabilden i svensk dagspress 1948–1968* (Lund: Bibliotheca historica lundensis, 1976) gives clear indications of growing anti- Americanism from the mid-1960s in Sweden as a whole.
12. Tom Heinemann, *Uro—25 års gadekamp* (Copenhagen: Tiderne skifter, 1995).

13. See Tor Bjørklund, *Mot strømmen. Kampen mot EF 1961–1972* (Oslo: Universitetsforlaget, 1982), 162–207.

14. Kim Salomon, *Rebeller i takt med tiden. FNL- rörelsen och 60- talets politiska ritualer* (Stockholm: Rabén Prisma, 1996), 147–167.

15. Thomas Etzemüller, *1968—Ein Riss in der Geschichte? Gesellschaftlicher Umbruch und 68er- Bewegungen in Westdeutschland und Schweden* (Konstanz: UVK, 2005), 118–19.

16. Paul Hollander, *Political Pilgrims: Western Intellectuals in Search of the Good Society* (New Brunswick, NJ: Transaction, 1998).

17. Bo Stråth, *Mellan medbestämmande och medarbetare* (Stockholm: Svenska metallindustriarbetareförbundet, 2000), 135.

18. A clear example is Tor Førland and Trine Korsvik, eds., *1968—opprør og motkultur på norsk* (Oslo: Pax, 2006).

19. Mikkel Thorup, "Den politiske højrefløj og 1968," in: *1968—Dengang og nu*, ed. M. B. Andersen and N. Olsen (Copenhagen: Museum Tusculanum, 2004): 87–110.

20. Guri Hjeltnes, ed., *Universitetet og studentene. Opprør og identitet* (Oslo: Forum for universitetshistorie, 1998).

21

Spain and Greece

Kostis Kornetis

Social and Political Framework of the Countries

By the time some junior officers under the leadership of Colonel Papadopoulos staged their April 1967 coup to prevent an alleged Communist takeover in Greece, Spain had already weathered an anti-Communist crusade following the end of the Spanish Civil War (1936–1939). In fact, it was experiencing a second, more complex phase, as the Communist threat of the 1930s seemed to be safely distant and new elites played an important role in Spanish society. In structural terms, it is possible to identify a variety of common features between the two countries' economic and social development. Both Spain and Greece consisted of a dominant peasantry, a large petty bourgeoisie, and comprador oligarchy. At the same time, they each had similar small-scale commodity-type production coupled with delayed industrialization under the aegis of foreign capital.[1] Despite U.S. capital investments, the marked scarcity of employment opportunities in both Spain and Greece in the late 1950s led to sustained labor power emigration, primarily to West Germany and Belgium. Compared to other European countries, both nations experienced the effects of the postwar economic boom fairly late; consumerist trends toward such products as televisions, washing machines, refrigerators, and automobiles were unknown before the mid-1960s.[2] In Greece, consumerism reached a mass level only after the Colonels' seizure of power and was favored by a booming economy and the dictators' inclination toward a series of populist measures including agricultural debt cancellation and various other benefits for hitherto unprivileged sectors of Greek society (primarily rural people, but also such diverse professions as farmers, building contractors, and taxi drivers). Tourism also began to exert a considerable social effect, as both Spain and Greece attracted a large number of travelers in the early 1960s.

Although Greece and Spain exhibit parallels during this time period, the specific social and political conditions of each country are significant. For example, the *Falange* party was a major factor in the evolution of Franco's regime in Spain. Over time, several important ex-Falangists stated that the regime had gradually betrayed its own goals, and this dissension triggered internal unrest and some early critiques of Franco's politics. The second key factor was the role of religious institutions. Organizations such as *Opus Dei* wielded significant influence in Spanish society and played a more significant role than the Orthodox Church or other religious organizations in Greece. A third factor of difference lay in the emergence of a strong trade union movement during the 1960s and 1970s; whereas Greek trade unionism was strictly corporative, Spanish workers' strikes became more frequent expressions of social discontent. Finally, a major factor specific to Spain were the various dynamics of repressed local nationalisms.

In terms of higher education, the universities in both countries were traditionally made up of a male-dominated, socially elite student body. Although they were conditioned by the outcome of the civil wars and became propagators of official ideology, some signs of unrest emerged at the beginning of the 1950s. In 1951, Greek students mobilized for unification with the British colony of Cyprus; during the same decade, clashes erupted at the University of Madrid in February 1956 as the next generation of civil war victors demanded a more balanced, less ideologically charged education. The mobilizations sparked the first harsh reprisals from the authorities in both countries, which in turn acted as a catalyst for the further politicization of the student body. José Maravall has argued that the Spanish university conflicts of 1956 took place partly because this particular group of students represented the first university cohort born during the Civil War.[3] This same pattern is evident in Greece some years later. Also, the unprecedented urbanization experienced by Greece and Spain in the 1950s was accompanied by a rising concentration of youth in big cities, which enhanced the perception of young people as a separate social category.

Organizational and Social Structure of the Protest Movements

The 1960s signaled a change in the composition and numbers of the student body. In Spain, economic improvement had a dramatic effect on increasing access to higher education,[4] and anti-regime activity was correspondingly boosted by the increase in student power. During the late 1950s and early 1960s, student movements were defined by a prevailingly cautious approach and inefficient recruitment processes, resulting in small nuclei of clandestine action and practically non-existent movement visibility.

The growing student numbers and the new political opportunities offered by the *tardofranquismo* (late Francoism) increased movement visibility and sparked radicalization. By the mid-1960s, the situation in Spanish universities was already explosive and was enhanced by the fact that none of these students were deterred from action by the traumatic effect of the direct experience of the armed conflict of the late 1930s. There was also an inherent sense of envy regarding the activism of university students abroad. The movement acquired momentum by an attack on the lack of democracy within the state-controlled Falangist student union SEU (*Sindicato Español Universitario*) and by the demand for the creation of an independent representative union. This battle culminated in the spring of 1965, when the regime decided to dissolve the union and promulgate a new education law that introduced radical changes in the university system. The SEU was the only Francoist institution ever brought down by a social movement.[5]

The Spanish student movement is often viewed as having two phases, the first lasting from 1960 to 1965 and the second from 1965 to 1969.[6] The outlawed Communist Party (PCE) played an important role in the first phase: It was quick to organize people under the umbrella organization FUDE (*Federación Universitaria Democrática Española*). The People's Liberation Front (FLP), originating in the late 1950s, was another major student group. Its ideology shifted from radical Catholic, to Trotskyite, then finally Castro-Guevarist. Despite its Marxist core, the FLP collaborated with left-wing Catholics, as did the PCE.

Barcelona served as a second locus of activist energy. The presence of Latin American intellectuals such as Colombian writer Gabriel Garcia Márquez, the city's proximity to France, and the general prestige of the "gauche divine," a widespread progressive movement among Catalan intellectuals, contributed to an atmosphere that endorsed disobedience. In March 1966, five hundred students demanding greater democratization of the university closed themselves in the monastery of Sarriá. They were joined by thirty professors and the resident monks and remained barricaded within the monastery for three days before police evacuated them. The role of the supportive, equally rebellious young professorship, the *Profesores No Numerarios* (PNN), was also important to the student revolt.[7] The event became known as the "Caputxinada" and was later labeled a precursor to 1968.[8] Soon the students' primary demand was for free student elections. In particular, the Spanish Young Communist League repeatedly argued in early 1967 that "elections are the milestone of the socio-political organization of the students."[9]

The pragmatic thinking recognizable in the students' organized discourse is common to both Spanish and Greek Communists.[10] In Greece, as in Spain, the trebling of student numbers in the early 1960s had political consequences. For the first time, left-wing, working-class, and lower-middle-class youth were able to enroll in university, which led to a shift in activist focus away from strictly educational issues. One example was the Democratic Youth Movement Grigoris Lambrakis, or *Lambrakides*, an avant-garde organization created in May 1963 in the aftermath of the assassination of left-wing deputy Grigoris Lambrakis in Salonica.[11] This movement was characterized by street activism and is best known for its involvement with the "July Events" (a series of protests against the arbitrary sacking of liberal Prime Minister George Papandreou by King Constantine in the summer of 1965). The protests led to the complete paralysis of the country and, similar to the Caputxinada, were characterized as an "early 1968."[12] The left-wing activist Sotiris Petroulas, killed during the demonstrations, was the first student to become a generational symbol in Greece.

Greek students faced a stalemate on the imposition of the Colonels' coup in April 1967. Army officers took over university administration, and students who had already attracted police attention were imprisoned. By 1968, the primary student leaders of the pre-dictatorship period were either imprisoned or exiled, and by 1970, 140 students had been tried by martial courts and expelled from university.[13] As protest within universities was impossible, a small number of young radicals joined the ranks of various resistance organizations in nonsystematic acts of violence, including planting bombs. Although this represented a dramatic departure from the *Lambrakides'* peaceful protests, this generation was influenced by *tiersmondisme* and by the conceptualization of anti-dictatorial activities as liberation struggles. The resistance groups attempted to operate secretly but were frequently unsuccessful, and most of them were soon detected and dispersed.

Cognitive Orientation of the Movements

While the Colonels were abolishing democracy in Greece in April 1967, Spain was experiencing an attempt to liberalize the system from within. The *apertura* (opening) took place under the dynamic Minister of Tourism and Information Manuel Fraga Iribarne, who favored a series of anti-authoritarian measures. Growing disturbances, including workers' strikes in 1962 and the university turmoil in Madrid and Barcelona in 1965, contributed to the primacy of the *aperturistas*, those officials prepared to contemplate reform, as opposed to the intransigent conservatives (*inmovilistas*). The regime's reluctant orientation toward limited reform offered new political opportunities for anti-regime forces and proved extremely significant in terms of social mobilization.[14]

From this point on, censorship would no longer precede but would follow publication, leaving publishers, newspaper editors, and journalists "to guess what they could get away with."[15] Soon, the literary world conflicted with the regime in a direct political way with the emergence of a politicized publishing sector. This surprised the Francoist authorities, as it included "previously unthinkable works of social comment, history, politics, even translations of Karl Marx which caught the regime's censors on the hop, by showing up their cosmetic attempts at *apertura . . .* as window dressing."[16] Through the offerings of a series of new publishing houses, Spanish students encountered international intellectual streams along with long-demonized Marxist thinking. In addition, although newspapers were often viciously prosecuted and cinema and theater indiscriminately censored, "censorship was counterproductive in that it produced a hyper-politicization of culture, with censors, artists, and public keen to read the political into everything."[17]

Similarly, the suspension of preventive censorship in Greece in 1970 also favored the creation of about 150 new publishing houses specializing in political works. Two thousand new titles were printed, including a series of translations of classic political texts, ranging from Plato to Machiavelli. For the first time, a large series of non-orthodox, left-wing literature (Guevara, Debray, Debord) was printed in Greece, which served as a spark for new radicalism. Despite some incoherence, the liberalization of Spain and Greece favored greater dissemination of information and enhanced cultural alertness; these elements were crucial in reinforcing the sophistication of the anti-regime audiences, and ultimately of the protest movements. In addition, the influence of foreign and home-grown counterculture, facilitated by the opening of the two regimes, led to greater political and personal emancipation. Changes were not only aesthetically and intellectually apparent but were also recognizable in social behavior.

Forms and Tactics of Protest

Following the dissolution of the SEU in 1965, Spanish students became increasingly radicalized. From 1967 to 1968 onward, clashes moved beyond university campuses and internal student disputes. Confrontations with the police became a common phenomenon and could be sparked by routine issues such as failure to obtain permission for an assembly. These confrontations often developed into violent clashes that further radicalized the students. At the same time, the students expanded their action repertoire to include smashing the cafeteria, blocking traffic around the campus, and throwing stones at policemen.[18] In response, campuses often remained closed for extended periods, which in turn caused student strikes. These mobilizations were removed from the rigidity and hierarchical nature of the clandestine cells on which the old Left depended and to which the Francoist police were accustomed. What is more, occupations and expressive action were often more effective as a means of exerting pressure than strikes.[19]

In contrast to the period of clandestine action, when public space was devoid of any exchange, public areas now became the objects of open contestation. Because indoor assemblies were prohibited, public spaces became a limitless territory of open confrontation. The student repertoire switched to collective action expressed in large demonstrations and open confrontations with police forces both in Greece and Spain. Greek anti-regime students of the early 1970s began to favor mass protest and acquired greater following, higher visibility, and occasionally open support. Liberalization allowed students the creation of mobilizing structures beyond the semi-clandestine "democratic committees of struggle," such as the Hellenic European Youth Movement and, later, the regional societies. Young people also emphasized the use of all possible legal avenues for securing civil rights. The turning point was the initiation of a legal battle with the authorities on the issue of the right of students to elect their own committees; this marked the first direct clash with the regime.

Attitudes toward the Superpowers and the Cold War

Before May 1968, the Vietnam War had already been an important topic in Spain. According to a leaflet circulated by the Young Communist League, "the Spanish student movement, just like the movement of all countries, reveals a great sensibility in the solidarity for the Vietnamese people. . . . This is about mobilizing the broadest sectors in solidarity with Vietnam and against the Americans."[20] For left-wing students, American setbacks in Vietnam were an indication that imperialism was a "paper tiger." These students perceived two Americas: one that produced counterculture and another that employed imperialist strategy. Greek students even viewed themselves as similar to young Americans. Movies such as *Woodstock, Easy Rider, The Strawberry Statement* and Stuart Hagmann's film on the 1968 uprising of Columbia University students gave rise to mini-demonstrations. This was a strikingly direct way of reenacting or mimicking the foreign movements. As Dimitris Papanikolaou pointed out, "the Greek youth were effectively dis-placing . . . their opposition to the dictatorship by adopting the countercultural energy of *Woodstock*. . . . They were thus *locating* their struggle in (the context of) the 60s and *dis-locating* the abusive topos of the Greek dictatorship."[21] Similarly, a British report on the students of Santiago de Compostela who staged a sit-in at the rectorate in early 1968 stressed that they passed the whole night singing "a Galician's version of 'We shall overcome,'" thus directly linking this movement with its American counterparts.[22]

By 1973, Greek students were also inspired by two other models: the student uprising against the dictatorial regime in Thailand and the shock generated by Pinochet's September 1973 coup in Chile. While Chile's authoritarian turn reinforced Western leftists' lack of trust in the capacity of a democratic state to make socialist reforms without suffering a *coup d'état*, in Greece it was seen as proof that American interests were ruthlessly pursued in the same manner all over the world and always at the expense of people's democratic rights. One leaflet stated, "The assassins of the Chilean people and the Greek Junta have been trained in the same centers of international subversion in the USA."[23] This tendency of identifying with international incidents demonstrated the students' belief that they were part of a global struggle with international points of reference and a common enemy: American imperialism.

In Spain, students saw the United States as a factor behind Franco's survival and were influenced by neocolonial theories regarding the existence of U.S. military bases in Spain and the American ability to use Spanish airspace. These theories were similar to Greek polemics concerning the U.S. Air Force and the use of the Sixth Fleet in the Eastern Mediterranean during the Arab–Israeli wars of 1967 and 1973. After all, Greek leftists believed that the Colonels' coup was engineered by the United States; thus, in key moments of the student movement, the cry, "Americans out!" was dominant. In later years in Spain, anti-American discourse was also coupled with militant nationalism concerning national sovereignty issues.[24]

The Soviet Union served as another point of reference. A defining moment was the dramatic rift within the exiled Greek Communist Party in the winter of 1968, which produced two rival factions: the one expressing a neo-Stalinist and the other a mildly Eurocommunist tendency. *Rigas*, the New Left student organization, believed in "the possibility of the creation of viable models of socialism that, instead of conforming to the emerging Stalinist straitjacket, would be flexible enough to fit indigenous conditions and needs."[25] Despite their Communist indoctrination, these so-called "reformists" were equally appalled by American atrocities in Vietnam as by Soviet aggression and the crushing of the Prague Spring. On the contrary, the youth organizations of the orthodox Communist Party (KNE and Anti-EFEE) remained staunchly pro-Soviet in their ideological tenets and dogmatically Stalinist in their practices, reflecting the attitude of the party officials. In contrast to the Spanish Communist Party, which often remained separate from Soviet imperatives, "orthodox" Greek Communists criticized May 1968 in Paris as a sheer opportunistic circus. Instead, they endorsed the Soviet defeat of the Prague Spring, which was considered to be a dangerous deviation from the "right path" to socialism.

Key Events

The situation on Spanish campuses intensified in the spring of 1968, when the autonomy of the university was violated by the police. On March 29, during a very violent clash with the police in the University of Madrid, several professors protected students as they exited the university. The entire faculty of Madrid University resigned en bloc after the dean was struck to the ground and other professors were beaten. The university was temporarily shut down, giving rise to a solidarity strike by technical college students. In both Spain (1968) and Greece (1973), the government regarded the disturbances as issues of public order and attempted to deal with them as such.[26] Both Franco and Papadopoulos believed in conspiracy theories concerning the origins of the student movements; Franco was convinced that the movements could be ascribed to foreign agitators,[27] whereas Papadopoulos attempted to find connections to with older generations and exiled Communists.

While unrest was accelerating in France, Valencian singer Raimon's recital on May 18, 1968, in the Faculty of Political Science, Economics and Commerce of the Complutense University of Madrid turned into an unofficial assembly and gave rise to a demonstration, which was dispersed by the police. Compared to their Greek counterparts, a bolder attitude in sloganeering characterized the Spanish students, six thousand of whom attempted to walk to the city centers that day carrying banners declaring "Workers and Students against oligarchy!," "Popular Democracy," and "Socialist Spain." Violent clashes with the police followed.[28]

Both Spain and Greece were different from other Western European societies in turmoil because they were still ruled by authoritarian regimes ready to employ violence to silence protest. As a British diplomat noted, "With the evident intention of reminding students that Spain was different from France, the Supreme Court had earlier issued a statement drawing attention to decrees of 1938 and 1939 which outlawed Communism and imposed heavy prison sentences on those who indulged in Communist activities."[29] Nevertheless, emulation of foreign movements increased from the fall of 1968 onward, with anti-regime students boycotting exams, proclaiming communes, paying homage to Che Guevara, occupying the dean's office, and smashing Franco's portraits on university premises. The return to classes after the closure was a traumatic moment, as it signaled the permanent presence of policemen on campus. A state of emergency was proclaimed and the rights of *habeas corpus* were suspended in 1969. The combination of student revolts, workers' strikes, and the Basque autonomist ETA's (Basque Homeland and Freedom) advances precipitated the last signs of intransigence of the Francoist regime; a series of executions in the early 1970s, along with Franco's death in 1975, set the process of democratic transition in motion.

For the Greek movement, a "late 1968" came in 1973. By that time the tenor of student politics had changed, as anti-regime students acquired a greater following and higher visibility. In February 1973, several thousand students barricaded themselves for two days inside the law school building in downtown Athens. They demanded the release of male students who were violently conscripted into the army for being involved in student unrest. The fact that the law school, situated in the very heart of Athens, was occupied by thousands of students marked the first serious encounter between the movement and the government. The regime did not retaliate, however, until a second occupation occurred in March 1973, during which police stormed the building, beat the students savagely, and made numerous arrests.

The Greek Junta's attempt to introduce controlled liberalization in the summer of 1973 proved to be a turning point. The Colonels hoped to win public support for the regime, silence criticism abroad, and ensure authoritarianism with a democratic façade. The experiment aimed to remove martial law, soften censorship, allow for more social interaction, and eventually grant a general amnesty to political prisoners.[30] By early November 1973, almost all corporate student demands were satisfied by Spyros Markezinis' administration, which had been appointed by Papadopoulos, including the restoration of the deferral of military service for activists. However, the thorny question of free student elections remained. With this pretext, the Polytechnic School of Athens was occupied on November 14, when students who found themselves in its premises decided to boycott classes and occupy the building. The takeover was not organized like the law school occupations but was rather spontaneous.[31] Apart from a strong and influential pirate radio station that was run by the students from within the Polytechnic, patrols, a first-aid department, a cafeteria, and a unit for the writing and distribution of leaflets operated inside the building. All these functions were supervised by the Central Coordination Committee.

Almost five thousand people remained barricaded inside for three consecutive days, transmitting anti-Junta messages from the pirate station, the most famous being the all-encompassing "Bread, education, freedom." Surprisingly, the police did not intervene during these three days, and the Polytechnic became a liberated niche outside of which thousands of people gathered. However, in the early hours of the fourth day, November 17, snipers and policemen started shooting at the crowd outside the school. Soon thereafter, a tank crashed through the Polytechnic gate. This incident left behind a number of dead and wounded, and martial law was once more imposed on the country.[32] A week later, Papadopoulos was ousted by the head of the Secret Police, Brigadier Dimitrios Ioannidis, who became a shadow dictator for the next eight months. His representative, the one to appear in public, was his trusted General Faidon Ghizikis, self-proclaimed

President of the Republic. Ioannidis fell from power himself after the Turkish invasion of Cyprus in August 1974, which signaled the handover of government to the politicians and the definite end of seven years of dictatorial rule.

Transnational Relations

The student culture that developed was marked not only by Greek and Spanish internal politics but also by a strong current of radical youth culture coming from abroad. With 1968, a mimetic tendency spread among the students in an attempt to reenact the international protest movements. The general wave of 1968 infiltrated Greece and Spain and was modified according to the existing domestic standards, conditions, and needs. Students appropriated the international paradigm in terms of their own realities. The political conscience and distinct characteristics of these movements were determined by a broader influx of information and semantic codes, including dress, music, and literature, and the awareness that there were parallel student movements operating abroad.

Cross-national diffusion of protest, aided by a network of Greek and Spanish students abroad, thus led to the adoption of similar strategies concerning organization, action forms, and ideological frames.[33] This resulted in the development and diffusion of a "student left master frame,"[34] evoking Gilcher Holtey's comment that "it was the mimesis of all possible revolutions that united the students who were in revolt."[35]

Consequences, Narratives, and Politics of Memory

It is not a given that the student movements took place because of the dictatorships or that without them the students would not have been radicalized as in the rest of the world. However, both in Spain and Greece, the responses of the respective regimes deepened the crises and reinforced the students' initiatives. The first concessions led to demands for even greater levels of freedom of information, political pluralism, and democratization. Therefore, the student movements managed to play a key role in discrediting the regimes' respective attempts to liberalize from within, alongside playing a crucial role as new actors in societal transformation.

Finally, this generation of students acted as a national *avant-garde*, both in terms of its self-perception and action repertoire. New collective identities emerged, driven by local necessities but also bearing the strong imprint of the 1960s protest movements. Whereas the Spanish case is more straightforward vis-à-vis its real or imaginary contact with the international protest movement, Greece is a different story because the military coup of 1967 rendered student mobility impossible for quite a long time. Despite this difference, the

Greek experience of 1973 drew on the previous European models and can thus be placed within the broader protest cycle of 1968.

As in Greece, the Spanish university revolt had a significant communicative effect, whereas its subversive potential was overexposed by the mass media, particularly the anti-regime press. In later years, neither public perception nor Spanish historiography has interpreted the Spanish student movement as crucially important to the period known as "Second Francoism." Therefore, there has been no such explosion of testimonies and media coverage as has happened in Greece with regard to the iconic moment of the Athens Polytechnic in 1973, which "functioned as a symbol of democracy, promoted by mass media and politicians," "attributing authority and power to a portion of the post-dictatorship Greek student youth," and ultimately becoming a national celebration.[36] The memorialization of the Polytechnic was the major legitimizing incident of the democratization process (*Metapolitefsi*) in Greece, which is illustrated by the fact that the first post-Junta elections were scheduled for November 17, 1974, thus appropriating and transforming the specific date into a national symbol.

The Greek and Spanish student movements possessed common trajectories despite their chrono-topical divergence. The opening up of the regimes had a similar impact as elsewhere in Europe: it provided a space for action and allowed for the import of intellectual stimuli similar to that in France, Italy, and Germany. However, the emulation of the European and American models, a new revolutionary consciousness, or university issues are not sufficient to account for student mobilization. The rigidity of the authoritarian regimes and their value systems, their brief periods of liberalization, and their subsequent intolerance were defining factors in the radicalization of students, who regarded themselves as bearers of modernization. By linking, partially, the local with the international, culture with politics, and political radicalism with everyday practices, anti-regime students accelerated the modernization processes that took place at breakneck speed in Greece and Spain in the years following the respective transitions to democracy.

Bibliography

For a contextualization in post–Civil War Spanish history, see Carr (1982), Gracia (2002), and Preston (1976). For a comprehensive analysis of the legal apparatus of the Greek dictatorship, see Alivizatos (1983). Bermeo (1995) offers an insightful classification of the Greek case compared to the Latin American dictatorships. A general overview of the most crucial socio-political aspects of the Colonels' regime is provided by Athanasatou (1999).

For a specific study of the social conflicts that emerged in the 1960s in Spain, see Fusi (1986) and Álvarez-Junco (1995); for Greece, see Sain Martain

(1984). Dafermos (1999) is the most thorough analysis to date of the anti-dictatorship student movement of 1972–1973 in Greece. Its equivalent for the Spanish case are Maravall (1978), Giner (1976), and a recently published collected volume by Hernández Sandoica, Baldó Lacomba, and Ruiz Carnicer (2007). Graham (1995) gives a rich background on the basic cultural tenets that permeated Spanish society ever since the end of the conflict. For a thorough analysis of Greece's main exponents of popular culture in the 1960s and 1970s, see Papanikolaou (2007) and Van Dyck (1998). For the societal dynamics and the role of new elites involved in the transitional processes of the two countries to democracy, see Diamandouros (1983) and O'Donnel (1986).

Alivizatos, Nikos. *Oi politikoi thesmoi se krisi. Opseis tis ellinikis empeirias.* Athens: Themelio, 1983.

Álvarez-Junco, José. "Movimientos Sociales en España: Del modelo tradicional a la modernidad post-Franquista," in *Working Paper H2-I/95.* Madrid: Fundación José Ortega y Gasset, 1995.

Athanasatou, Gianna, et al., eds. *I Diktatoria 1967–74. Politikes praktikes, ideologikos logos, antistasi.* Athens: Kastaniotis, 1999.

Bermeo, Nancy. "Classification and Consolidation: Some Lessons from the Greek Dictatorship," in *Political Science Quarterly* 110, no. 3 (1995): 435–52.

Carr, Raymond, and Juan Pable Fusi Aizpurua. *Spain: Dictatorship to Democracy.* London: Allen & Unwin, 1982.

Dafermos, Olympios. *Foitites kai diktatoria. To antidiktatoriko foititiko kinima 1972–1973.* Athens: Gavriilidis, 1999.

Diamandouros, Nikiforos. "1974. I metavasi apo to aytarchiko sto dimokratiko kathestos stin Ellada: Proeleysi kai ermineia mesa apo mia notio-eyropaiki prooptiki,'" in *Epitheorisi Koinonikon Erevnon* 49 (1983):52–87 [translated from the original in Julian Santamaria, ed. *Transición a la democracia en el sur de Europa y America Latina.* Madrid: Centro de Investigaciones Sociologicas, 1982, 199-241].

Fusi, Juan Pablo. "La reaparición de la conflictualidad en la España de los Sesenta," in Josep Fontana, ed., *España bajo el franquismo.* Barcelona: Editorial Crítica, 1986, 160–69.

Gracia, García Jordi and Miguel Ángel Ruiz Carnicer. *La España de Franco (1939–1975). Cultura y vida cotidiana.* Madrid: Síntesis, 2002.

Graham, Helen and Jo Labanyi, eds. *Spanish Cultural Studies.* Oxford: Oxford University Press, 1995.

Hernández Sandoica, Elena, Marc Baldó Lacomba, and Miguel ángel Ruiz Carnicer, eds. Estudiantes contra Franco (1939-1975). Oposición política y movilización juvenil. Madrid: La esfera de los libros, 2007.

Maravall, José. *Dictatorship and Political Dissent. Workers and Students in Franco's Spain.* Cambridge: Cambridge University Press, 1978.

O'Donnel, Guillermo, et al. *Transitions from Authoritarian Rule: Tentative Conclusions About Uncertain Democracies.* Baltimore, MD: Johns Hopkins University Press, 1986.

Papanikolaou, Dimitris. *Singing Poets Literature and Popular Music in France and Greece.* Oxford: Legenda, 2007.

Preston, Paul, ed. *Spain in Crisis. The Evolution and Decline of the Franco Régime.* Sussex: Harvester, 1976.

Sain Martain, Katerina. *Labrakides. History of a Generation.* Athens: Katarti, 1984.

Van Dyck, Karen. *Kassandra and the Censors. Greek Poetry Since 1967.* Ithaca, NY: Cornell University Press, 1998.

Notes

1. Nicos Poulantzas, *The Crisis of the Dictatorships. Portugal, Greece, Spain* (London: Humanities Press, 1976).
2. Jordi Gracia García, Miguel ángel Ruiz Carnicer, *La España de Franco (1939–1975). Cultura y vida cotidiana* (Madrid: Editorial Síntesis, 2002), 272.
3. José Maravall, *Dictatorship and Political Dissent: Workers and Students in Franco's Spain* (Cambridge: Cambridge University Press, 1978), 164.
4. Antonio Nadal Sánchez, "El movimiento universitario y la represión," in *La Universidad española bajo el regimen de Franco (1939–1975)*, ed. J. J. Carreras Ares and M. A. Ruiz Carnicer (Zaragoza: Institución Fernando el Católico, 1991), 459.
5. Raymond Carr and Juan Pablo Fusi Aizpurua, *Spain: Dictatorship to Democracy* (London: Allen & Unwin, 1982), 149.
6. Maravall, 110.
7. For a comprehensive analysis of the PNN controversy see Salvador Giner, "Power, Freedom and Social Change in the Spanish University, 1939–75," in *Spain in Crisis. The Evolution and Decline of the Franco Régime*, ed. Paul Preston (Sussex: Harvester, 1976), 183–233.
8. Antoni Batista and Josep Playá Maset, "Un mayo del 68 en marzo del 66. La Caputxinada fue uno de los primeros éxitos del antifranquismo," *La Vanguardia* February 27, 1996.
9. PCE leaflet, 31-1-67. PCE Archive.
10. Ibid.
11. Katerina Sain Martain, *Lambrakides. Istoria mias Genias* (Athens: Katarti, 1984).
12. See, for example, Christos Vernardakis and Giannis Mavris, *Kommata kai politikes symmachies stin pro-diktatoriki Ellada. Oi proypotheseis tis Metapolitefsis* (Athens: Exantas, 1991), 240–67.
13. Minas Papazoglou, *Foititiko Kinima kai Diktatoria* (Athens: Epikairotita, 1983), 14–16.
14. José Álvarez Junco, "Movimientos Sociales en España: Del modelo tradicional a la modernidad post-Franquista," in Working Paper H2-I/95 (Madrid: Fundación José Ortega y Gasset, 1995).
15. Preston, *Franco a Biography* (London: Harper Collins, 1993), 727.
16. I. De Riquer, B. Permaner, "Adapting to Social Change," in *Spanish Cultural Studies: An Introduction*, ed. Helen Graham and Jo Labanyi (Oxford: Oxford University Press, 1995), 265.
17. Jo Labanyi, "Censorship or the Fear of Mass Culture" in Graham and Labanyi, *Spanish Cultural Studies*, 207–14, here 214.
18. PRO, FCO9/526, Confidential, British Embassy Madrid to Foreign Office, A. L. S. Coltman to A. E. Palmer, "Spanish Student Developments," annex "Political groups in Madrid University," 31/5/1968.

19. Ibid.
20. Organización universitaria del PCE, "Comité universitario estatal—informes," 1968–69, Archivo Histórico del PCE, box 123, folder 1/1.
21. Dimitris Papanikolaou, *Singing Poets. Literature and Popular Culture in France and Greece. (Oxford: Legenda, 2007)*
22. PRO, FCO9/526A, Restricted, British Embassy Madrid to Foreign Office, L. S. Coltman to G. Fitzherbert, "Student Agitation," 27/3/1968.
23. 'Κάτω η χούντα του Πινοσέτ! Ζήτω η αντίσταση του χιλιανού λαού! Απόφαση του Κ.Σ. του «Ρήγα Φεραίου»' (1 October 1973) ["Down with the Junta of Pinochet! Long Live the Resistance of the Chilean people! Decision of the C.C. of 'Rigas Feraios"], *Thourios* 1973;New Period, 2:63
24. A leaflet circulated by the Young Communist League in 1970 stated "Solidarity to the Arab, Palestinian and Indochinese people! Yankee bases out of our Land. NIXON OUT OF SPAIN!" Organización universitaria del PCE en Madrid, Comité Universitario, Informes, Archivo del PCE, box 123, file 2/1.2, "Contra la llegada de Nixon," 1970.
25. Thanasis D. Sfikas, "Review of *New Voices in the Nation: Women and the Greek Resistance, 1941–1964*," *Journal of Modern Greek Studies* 1998 16 (2):378–81.
26. Juan Pablo Fusi, "La reaparición de la conflictualidad en la España de los Sesenta," in Josep Fontana, ed., *España bajo el franquismo* (Barcelona: Editorial Crítica, 1986), 160–69, here 164.
27. Preston, *Franco*, 735.
28. *Ibérica*, 25/5/1968, cited by *Horizonte Español* 1972;1:119.
29. PRO, FCO9/526, Confidential, British Embassy Madrid to Foreign Office, A. L. S. Coltman to A. E. Palmer, "Spanish Student Developments," 31/5/1968.
30. See Nikos Alivizatos, *Oi politikoi thesmoi se krisi. Opseis tis ellinikis empeirias* (Athens: Themelio, 1983), 282.
31. Olympios Dafermos, *Foities kai diktatoria. To antidiktatoriko foititiko kinima* (Athens: Gavriilidis, 1999), 154.
32. The exact number of people who were killed during the night of November 16 to 17, 1973, has never been ascertained. According to the official statement of the time, the number of fatalities was twenty. Later evidence, however, estimated the number of victims to be sixty.
33. Donatella Della Porta, "1968. Zwischennationale Diffusion und Transnationale Strukturen," in Ingrid Gilcher-Holtey, ed., *1968-Vom Ereignis zum Gegenstand der Geschichtswissenschaft* (Goettingen: Vandenhoeck & Ruprecht, 1998), 136–37.
34. Doug McAdam, "Culture and Social Movements," in *New Social Movements. From Ideology to Identity*, ed. Enrique Laragna, Hank Johnston, and Joseph R. Gusfeld (Philadelphia: Temple University Press, 1994), 42.
35. Ingrid Gilcher-Holtey, *"Die Phantasie an die Macht." Mai 68 in Frankreich* (Frankfurt: Suhrkamp, 1995), 49.
36. Ioanna Lambiri-Dimaki (ed.), Introduction to the collective volume *I Koinoniologia stin Ellada simera. I oloklirosi tis Trilogias (1959-2000)* (Athens: Papazisis, 2002), 21–106, here 46.

Part 3

Transnational Networks and Narratives after 1968

22
Terrorism

Dorothea Hauser

Although the political mobilization of students and workers throughout (Western) Europe in the late 1960s comprised violent forms of protest in some countries, the practical pursuit of concepts of armed struggle meant to trigger a revolutionary response by the masses proved to be—with the notable exception of West Germany and Italy—a brief and peripheral episode.

Coinciding with the decline of the protest movements, the birth of guerilla groups like the Angry Brigade in Great Britain and the Red Youth in the Netherlands was but the somewhat desperate endeavor of a very small number of militants anxious to perpetuate the dwindling dynamics of "1968." Because their activity met with little sympathy, let alone support from former activists, their political impact was almost negligible. Even the anti-imperialist Dutch Red Youth, who had initially chosen the German Red Army Faction (RAF) as their role model and had received military training in a camp of the Popular Front for the Liberation of Palestine (PFLP) in South Yemen, did not achieve much more than local significance, as a couple of bomb attacks they carried out in 1971–1972 against police targets and a mayor's home remained essentially confined to the city of Eindhoven. Furthermore, their assaults caused only property damage—something that also holds true for their British counterpart. The libertarian Angry Brigade, already virtually extinct in 1971 but assumed to be responsible for about twenty-five bombings aimed at banks and the homes of Tory politicians between 1970 and 1972, in fact explicitly declared "we attack property not people."[1]

In France, by contrast, the *Gauche Prolétarienne* (GP) was a relatively large organization that temporarily contemplated urban guerilla tactics. Indeed, this Maoist group, which amalgamated the most radicals after May 1968, possessed a strong foothold both with intellectuals and in factories. Deliberately referring to the French anti-Nazi resistance of the 1940s, the GP set up the *Nouvelle Résistance Populaire* (NRP) as its armed wing as early as summer 1969 to combat an alleged *fascisation* in France. Yet, the NRP's manifold activities, eighty-two actions between July and October 1969 alone, fell somewhat short of outright armed struggle and often comprised symbolic acts like the short detention of politicians and entrepreneurs for questioning. After the GP had been officially forbidden in 1970, and with some of its leading members taking to more civil projects like the creation of the newspaper *Liberation*, it dissolved and renounced armed struggle altogether in 1973; one of its members, Pierre Overney, had been killed by a security guard while distributing pamphlets the year before.

The emergence of indigenous terrorist factions in France—*Action Direct* (AD)—and, more sporadically, in Belgium—*Cellules Communistes Combattantes* (CCC) and *Front Révolutionnaire d'Action Prolétarienne*—did not take place until the early 1980s.

Among the AD's less than a dozen steady affiliates there was only one, Jean Asselmeyer, who had already been politically active in 1967–1968[2]; these were rather isolated organizations that were neither perceived as being related to the 1968 movement by the terrorists nor by the country's former activists.[3] In fact, the AD was largely dominated by militants of Spanish origin who had before been engaged in anti-Franco campaigns on French soil and beyond.[4] Nevertheless, the AD later cooperated with the third generation of the German RAF and Italian terrorist splinter groups. The miniscule Belgian CCC, in turn, which refused to join the "European anti-imperialist front" called for by the RAF and AD in 1985, originated in 1983 from RAF support groups and was ideologically controlled by the Spanish-born Frenchman Frédéric Oriach.

Terrorist Armed Struggle

West Germany and Italy, then, were the only European countries experiencing significant revolutionary terrorism in the wake of "1968."[5] It induced serious political repercussions in their democratic systems that reached their dramatic climax in 1977 and 1978, respectively. Thereafter, left-wing terrorism largely lost its environmental setting and, hence, its political effect in both countries. Still, the phenomenon proved to be persistent—in the German case lasting for almost thirty years.

Exceptional as the terrorist aftermath of protest may have been, the various clandestine factions that first sprung up around 1970 in West Germany and Italy were initially ideologically and personally connected to the foregoing revolt. They played on the ambivalent sentiments of a broad radical leftist milieu that did not necessarily embrace terrorist acts as a means to further the revolutionary cause, but in its fundamental opposition to a democratic system despised as "fascist" still felt obliged to a certain solidarity which ranged from—often critical—sympathy to practical support. In this context, the legacy of Germany's Nazi past and Italy's Fascist history, albeit in a somewhat intricate and often purely instrumental manner, played a decisive role as both point of reference and political weapon. The specific digestion of this reference, however, differed considerably, not the least because in Italy the memory of the anti-Fascist partisan *Resistenza* between 1943 and 1945 offered positive identification. As a further difference, the Italian case was marked, as "a history of long duration,"[6] by a second wave of protest in 1977. Most notably, from 1969 onward, Italy witnessed massive neofascist terrorism that, as part and parcel of a conspiratory anti-Communist "strategy of tension,"[7] was to some extent facilitated by the Italian secret service, the U.S. Central Intelligence Agency, and parts of the army. Right-wing terrorist acts preceded, and for many years by far exceeded, left-wing ones. Moreover, against the backdrop of frequent assaults by neofascist thugs, the arming of leftist groups in Italy initially took place for predominantly defensive purposes.

In Germany, by contrast, the notion of an urban guerilla came from the center of the protest movement and had a much more willful character, with internal debates to that effect dating back to 1966.[8] In the end, only a small number of West Germany's mainly intellectual activists, beyond to some degree sympathizing with the idea and its protagonists, actually got involved in armed struggle. Yet, the clandestine factions that eventually emerged were clearly the product of the anti-authoritarian wing of the German student rebellion and its fusion with leftist subcultures thriving in walled West Berlin in the late 1960s and, to a lesser extent, in Frankfurt.

Organizational and Social Structure

The West German protest movement spun off of four distinct guerilla groups: the Tupamaros, the RAF, the 2nd June movement, and the Revolutionary Cells (RZ). The RZ, a network of anonymous, semi-clandestine cells, originated in 1973 in Frankfurt, before one of its branches decidedly turned to international, even mercenary-style terrorism and became infamous with the Carlos Connection. The other three armed factions were all launched in divided Berlin's Western half and, with the exception of the RAF, remained essentially limited to West Berlin.

The Tupamaros, though short-lived, were the very first to seek military training in an El Fatah camp in Jordania in October 1969 and the first to become a clandestine militant group on return. Like their counterpart in Southern Germany, the Tupamaros Munich, the group's approximately fifteen core members were communards of mainly middle-class origin with a history of activism in the SDS and the militant wing of the Berlin Blues. Organized as a network of autonomous conspiratorial cells, the Tupamaros were, nonetheless, clearly dominated by two leading figures, Georg von Rauch and Dieter Kunzelmann, who before had been a principal provocateur of the *Kommune I*. The realization of their terrorist plans, however, was often seriously hampered by a lack of discipline brought about by the Tumpamaros' frequent drug abuse. After Kunzelmann's arrest in 1970 and von Rauch's death in a shootout with the police in December 1971, the group ceased to exist. Some members subsequently folded into the RAF, but mainly they joined the somewhat anarchic 2nd June movement. The latter, initiated in January 1972, considered itself to be the RAF's proletarian counterpart, although the social background of its members barely met this claim. Still, RAF and 2nd June arranged a policy of reciprocal information regarding imminent attacks in summer 1977 and finally joined forces in 1980.

The Red Army Faction, publicly also referred to as Baader-Meinhof Gang, became the most prominent, tenacious terrorist group in West Germany, declaring its breakup as late as April 1998. Launched in May 1970, the RAF set out to be a tautly organized and ambitious revolutionary undertaking with a meticulous sense for the logistics of clandestinity and armed combat. Its members mostly had a bourgeois background and were, apart from the gifted dropout Andreas Baader, highly educated university students and professionals. Baader and his girlfriend Gudrun Ensslin, a clergyman's daughter, had already gained some fame through an arson attack on two department stores in April 1968. The other cofounders were Horst Mahler, a well-established leftist lawyer, and Ulrike Meinhof, West Germany's most renowned left-wing journalist of the late 1960s. As in other German guerilla groups, there was a relatively high proportion (34 percent) of female members. Although the number of core affiliates never exceeded forty, the RAF initially found significant backing among the protest generation. Polls revealed in 1971 that a fourth of West Germans under age thirty sympathized with the RAF and a sizable 14 percent of the total population were ready to help or shelter RAF members. After the arrest of all key figures in summer 1972, the Baader-Ensslin twin leadership was able to mobilize and widely control a second RAF generation from within prison walls, surrounded by a ramified network of support groups, including lawyers, that provided communications, assistance, and future recruits.

In contrast to West Germany, ultra-left armed factions in Italy were, like the preceding protest movement itself, much more socially enrooted. They were, just like parties and governments, also extremely numerous and fragmented. Almost five hundred different left-wing groups, many of them ephemeral, claimed responsibility for terrorist attacks between 1969 and 1980. About three thousand participants were directly involved in these assaults, and the number of accomplices was even higher. In the late 1970s, left-wing terrorist groups could resort to an estimated potential of ten thousand people for logistics and support among the youthful autonomist movement alone. In contrast, Italian terrorism remained confined to Northern Italy and Rome. Except for the much higher proportion of women involved in ultra-left armed groups (25 percent), the social composition of terrorist factions of the Left[9] and the Right was largely similar, with both drawing from a wide range of the social stratum.

The plethora of terrorist groups in Italy was, for the most part, linked to the 1977 *autonomi* revolt rather than the 1968 protest movement. This does not apply, however, to clandestine organizations like the *Gruppi di Azione Partigiana* (GAP), the *Nuclei Armati Proletari* (NAP), and the Red Brigades (BR). The GAP, led by the millionaire publisher Giangiacomo Feltrinelli after having received military training in Jordania, had a somewhat exemplary function. Founded in spring 1970, it disintegrated just two years later after Feltrinelli died, reportedly blowing himself up in a premature blast. The NAP spontaneously emerged in 1974 from the ranks of *Lotta Continua*, after this most important extra-parliamentary opposition group since 1969 shied away from matching its violent rhetoric with adequate action. Partly because of its somewhat impulsive beginnings, the NAP, organized in loosely knit cells, exposed a high degree of dilettantism and a somewhat existential streak in its glorification of violence as a cathartic act. Multiple arrests brought about its abrupt end in 1977.

The BR rose to become the most notorious, long-lasting Italian armed group. With a judicially estimated total of 426 members, they were also the largest. The BR emerged in October 1970 from local workers' and students' committees in Northern Italy to perpetuate the 1969 labor conflicts within the large factories of Milan and Turin. The social background of its founders somewhat resembled the make-up of 1968 in Italy: Renato Curcio and his girlfriend Mara Cagol came from the Catholic left-wing student stronghold Trento, Alberto Franceschini represented staunch Communist tradition as well as genuine *Resistanza* links, and Mario Moretti constituted the factory element. Other than the RAF, BR members were neither bent on full illegality nor on the build-up of a nationwide revolutionary army. Instead, the BR was strictly organized into regional columns and local cells. Over time expanding into Rome, Genoa, and Venice, these cells were increasingly seen as making up a combatant Communist party. From 1974 on, when the core BR decided for clandestinity, the organization was further centralized through the establishment of a so-called strategic command. With Cagol killed in a shootout in 1975 and most key members arrested until 1976, Mario Moretti headed the BR in its most bloody phase, although the decision for an escalation of violence into lethal terrorism had been already taken before. In 1977, then, the BR was virtually overwhelmed from an inflow of violence-prone youth, thereby linking extremists of the successive protest movements. Splitting up into concurrent factions in the early 1980s, the BR finally disbanded in 1988.

Cognitive Orientations

Neither Italian nor German left-wing terrorist factions had an idea about the society they were fighting for in their armed struggle. Their motivations, however, are sufficiently clear, as is the framework of their ideological justifications and references. This holds true for the 2nd June movement, which took little effort in theoretical substantiation. Its naming in January 1972 alluded to a defining date of the German protest movement: the killing of a student demonstrator by a policeman in 1967. Although the event had taken place five years before, this was meant to prove an attitude of self-defense, and thus conveys the extent to which a threat justifying terrorist action had to be manufactured. In contrast, the RAF's elaborate manifests, largely authored by Ulrike Meinhof, were certainly important for the group's public outreach to sympathizers. Within the RAF they were almost meaningless, as Meinhof's academic Marxist determinism was out of place with the RAF's triumphal voluntarism that focused on liberation and revolutionary identity, not class struggle.

Overall, German terrorist organizations were decidedly anti-imperialist, anti-American, and anti-Zionist, if not anti-Semitic. Radically re-localizing its declared internationalism, the RAF showed a clear nationalist sentiment that was sometimes voiced with surprising pathos. In this context, the traditional national side of Meinhof's GDR-style Communist anti-fascism indeed rejoined with the Baader-Ensslin existentialist trait. The latter, under the peculiar conditions of an imprisoned but acting RAF command, quickly developed into a subjectivist ideology that celebrated Andreas Baader as the epitome of an adamant guerilla representing the new revolutionary avant-garde. In addition, and contrary to popular belief, the RAF's fixation on Germany's Nazi past had nothing to do with an attack "against the Auschwitz generation."[10] In reality, the RAF cultivated a mere cynical reference to the Holocaust. On the one hand, it frivolously, but effectively, exploited it for self-description, and hence mobilization, in its campaigns against its alleged torture in prison. On the other hand, as was true for most West German guerillas, the Holocaust served as the somewhat paradoxical rationale for the RAF's militant anti-Zionism.

Besides their critical fixation on the Communist party PCI, the *Resistenza* undoubtedly was the main reference for Italian terrorist factions, as they already signaled with their naming. Internationalism, by contrast, had relatively little significance in their cognitive framework. Dating from 1973, however, the armed groups' symbolic and legitimatory appropriation of the memory of a "red resistance" was increasingly endangered by the PCI's historiographic reappraisal that preceded its "Historic Compromise" with the Christian Democrats. In 1975, therefore, when the traditional identificatory links with the PCI had been shattered and, simultaneously, the blatant drop in neofascist violence weakened the urgency of militant anti-Fascism, the BR abruptly reoriented on an "attack against the heart of the state" and toward an anti-imperialist ideology. Nevertheless, the terrorism of the Red Brigades still retained an overwhelmingly national focus, the abduction of NATO general Dozier in 1981 taking place only in the final phase of the BR's multiple splits and downfall.

Attitudes toward the Superpowers and the Cold War

For German guerillas, the United States definitely was "the archenemy of mankind."[11] In an odd historical vein, they characterized not only West Germany but also Nazi Germany as client states of the United States. In fact, the RAF claimed that Allied bombing of Germany had been the main reason for the lack of resistance "against the Hitler clique" and that even the Nazi aggression against the Soviet Union in 1940 had been nothing but "the Anti-Communist extermination maneuver of US-imperialist strategists."[12] To no one's surprise, then, Ulrike Meinhof publicly complained in 1972 that "the Americans have not been charged by us after the war."[13]

The RAF's attitude to the Eastern Bloc, by comparison, was less clear-cut. As anti-imperialists, they were critics of Soviet-style orthodox Communism, and rather looked for inspiration in Mao and Third World liberation movements. In contrast, as the principal antagonist of the detested United States, the Soviets were never subjected to more than academic critique and the liberating aspirations behind the Iron Curtain to less than indifference. Instead, all West German armed factions welcomed the low-key support they regularly received from Communist East Germany with regard to transit possibilities and the like. There is also evidence that, in 1971, the RAF was willing to seek support from North Korea, by all measures even at the time one of the most rigidly orthodox Communist states in the world.

Somewhat paradoxically for a state that was seen as being on the Cold War frontline by the architects of the "strategy of tension," leftist extremists in Italy showed little interest in the superpowers' global quarrels. This was not only because of the inherent localism of Italy's radical left. Important, too, was the strength of the Italian Communist party as well as the fact that, thanks to the *Resistenza*, postwar Italy had been far less dominated by the Allies than West Germany. Hence, in Italy, anti-Americanism was much more muted, whereas legal Communism was already fully catered to at home.

Key Events

The forty-four days of the so-called "German autumn" of 1977—the successive bloody kidnapping of the head of the German Federal Employers' Association, Hanns-Martin Schleyer, by the RAF and a plane with German tourists by Palestinian terrorists, to liberate imprisoned RAF members—and the fifty-five days of the bloody kidnapping of the Italian Christian Democrats' leader Aldo Moro in spring 1978 by the BR equally aimed at the liberation of imprisoned affiliates, must be singled out as the two most important and dramatic events in the history of 1970s European left-wing terrorism. In both countries, these highly symbolic showdowns between terrorists and the state were felt to be the so far most serious legitimation crises in postwar history and resulted in an almost complete political standstill that due to the governments' unaccommodating reaction prompted fears of a democracy on the verge of collapse. The result, however, was quite to the contrary. Instead of an authoritarian turn, these cathartic events, ending with the killing of Schleyer and Moro as well as the collective suicide of the imprisoned RAF leadership, brought about the strategic defeat of left-wing terrorism and eventually led former 1968 activists to reconcile with a democratic system they had hitherto fundamentally rejected.

Forms and Tactics

From the beginning, German guerilla groups showed a greater readiness for lethal attacks than Italian groups. Indeed, given the traditionally high level of political violence in Italy[14] and the neofascist menace, left-wing militants demonstrated a remarkable restraint from deadly attacks. Although in Milan a major portion of the radical left was already equipped with arms in 1972, they did not use them until 1974. Also, unlike German extremists, they avoided clashes with the police. Apart from bloodless kidnappings, the seventy actions carried out by the BR until 1974 consisted mainly of small-scale attacks on industrial targets or personnel. The practice of kneecapping, however, had by then already become a typical feature of the Brigades. Although acts of violence of neofascist origin were ten times higher than those of leftist extremists between 1969 and 1974, this ratio reversed completely in the second half of the 1970s.

The RAF's bombing campaign of May 1972, which targeted the Springer press and American forces, deliberately took up topics that had been the focus of criticism in 1968. The second RAF generation's assaults, by comparison, lacked propagandistic direction, as its attacks and kidnappings were all carried out solely for the sake of liberating imprisoned affiliates. Yet, it must be noted that the first act of left-wing terrorism in West Germany was the Tupamaros' failed bomb attack on West Berlin's Jewish community center on November 9, 1969, the anniversary of the 1938 Nazi *Kristallnacht*, and that its last act with human victims was the RAF's 1991 attack on a bus with Russian-Jewish émigrés in Hungary.

Transnational Relations

In spite of its declared internationalism, the transnational relations of the first generation of the RAF and the 2nd June movement remained rudimentary and somewhat aloof. Although the border between latent and manifest cooperation, especially with Palestinian terrorist factions, was often blurred, until 1977 it remained essentially limited to military training and arms supplies, with Arab countries like Yemen and Iraq not offering much more than retreat. However, in 1974, for instance, a joint RAF–Palestinian scheme to highjack an Israeli passenger plane to liberate imprisoned terrorists was apparently foiled. The German RZ's international wing, in contrast, naturally had quite strong transnational links and took part in actions like the 1973 attack on OPEC in Vienna or the 1976 hijacking of an Air France plane that bloodily ended in Entebbe. On a propagandistic level, too, the activity of RAF support groups in neighboring countries and the Europe-wide solidarity of intellectuals with the RAF's torture campaigns was quite a successful transnational project, as was, for example, demonstrated when the French philosopher Jean-Paul Sartre visited Andreas Baader in prison in 1974.[15]

Analogous to its cognitive orientations, Italian terrorism lacked substantial transnational links, even if the future GAP founder Feltrinelli had supplied German student leaders with explosives back in 1968. In fact, there was a short contact between the BR and Palestinian terrorist factions only in summer 1978, the initiative coming from the Palestinians. Different from West Germany, anti-Zionism never was a basic leftist ideologem in Italy, where the army had tried to save Jews from German persecution during World War II.

Consequences, Narratives, and Politics of Memory

The terrorist aftermath of 1968 has been engraved in public memory in West Germany and Italy under the term "leaden times" (*Bleierne Zeit*) and "Years of lead" (*anni di piombo*). Even today, it has strong repercussions on the perception of the protest movements in both countries. In particular, the precise nature of the relations between the revolt and the emergence of clandestine violence remains a refractory issue. This is all the more so because today's globalized terrorist menace at the same time morally highlights and factually belittles the terrorism of the 1970s.[16] On the one hand, terrorism has undoubtedly been instrumental to attempts to unjustly vilify the generation of 1968 as a whole. On the other hand, terrorism has, at least with respect to West Germany, been aptly called the "crucial Achilles' heel"[17] of any monumentalistic interpretation of 1968; that is, an interpretation that squares the movements' anti-democratic stance with its alleged civilizing and democratizing effects.

Bibliography

For the Angry Brigade in Britain, see Vague (1997); for *Action Directe* in France, see Dartnell (1995). For Italy, see Della Porta (1995) for an overview, Moss (1989) for a thorough, and Cantazaro (1991) for a multifaceted account. Essential for all aspects of German leftist terrorism is Kraushaar (2006) and Weinhauer (2006), unfortunately not available in English, whereas ID-Verlag (1997) presents the RAF's extensive texts. Aust (1987) chronicles the actions and characters of the RAF in detail but lacks context and analysis, as does Baumann's (1977) personal account of the 2nd June movement. For a comparative approach including state response see Katzenstein's (1998) synthesis and Varon (2004).

Aust, Stefan. *The Baader-Meinhof Group: The Inside Story of a Phenomenon.* London: The Bodley Head, 1987.

Baumann, Bommi. *How It All Began: A Personal Account of a West German Urban Guerilla.* Vancouver: Pulp, 1977.

Catanzaro, Raimondo, ed. *The Red Brigades and Left-wing Terrorism in Italy.* London: Printer, 1991.

Dartnell, Michael. *Action Directe: Ultra-Left Terrorism in France, 1979–1987.* London: Frank Cass, 1995.

Della Porta, Donatella. "Left-Wing Terrorism in Italy." In *Terrorism in Context,* edited by Martha Crenshaw, 105–59. University Park: Pennsylvania State University Press, 1995.

Id-Verlag, ed. *Rote Armee Fraktion. Texte und Materialien zur Geschichte der RAF.* Berlin: ID, 1997.

Katzenstein, Peter. *Left-Wing Violence and State Response: United States, Germany, Italy and Japan, 1960s–1990s.* Institute for European Studies Working Paper 98.1. Ithaca, NY: Cornell University, 1998.

Kraushaar, Wolfgang ed. *Die RAF und der linke Terrorismus.* 2 vols. Hamburg: Hamburger Edition, 2006.

Moss, David. *The Politics of Left Wing Violence in Italy, 1969–1985.* London: Palgrave Macmillan, 1989.

Vague, Tom. *Anarchy in the UK. The Angry Brigade.* London: AK, 1997.

Varon, Jeremy. *Bringing the War Home. The Weather Underground, the Red Army Faction, and Revolutionary Violence in the Sixties and Seventies.* Berkeley: University of California Press, 2004.

Weinhauer, Klaus et al., eds. *Terrorismus in der Bundesrepublik. Medien, Staat und Subkulturen in den 1970er Jahren.* Frankfurt: Campus, 2006.

Notes

1. Tom Vague, *Anarchy in the UK. The Angry Brigade.* (London: AK, 1997), 40.
2. The others were born between 1952 and 1959.
3. Even when alluding to the death of Pierre Overney, the AD and its predecessor NAPAP tried to court the nascent autonomous youth movement rather than the former GP spectrum. In 1977 NAPAP assassinated the Renault guard who had killed Overney, and an AD commando "Pierre Overney" executed Georges Besse, the general manager of Renault, in 1986.
4. Mainly in the Southern France based *Groupes d'actions révolutionnaires internationalistes* (GARI).
5. Interestingly, the only other state where "1968" had a serious terrorist sequel was Japan, thus, in a wider context, limiting the phenomenon to the countries that had made up the axis powers of World War II. See Dorothea Hauser, "Deutschland, Italien, Japan: Die ehemaligen Achsenmächte und der Terrorismus der siebziger Jahre," in *Die RAF und der linke Terrorismus*, ed. Wolfgang Kraushaar (Hamburg: Hamburger Edition, 2006), 1272–1298.
6. Luisa Passerini, "Das Jahr 1968 in Italien. Eine Geschichte der 'langen Dauer,'" in Etienne François, et al., eds., *1968—ein europäisches Jahr?* (Leipzig: Leipziger Universitätsverlag, 1997), 79–88.
7. Besides a mass of speculative literature, there is yet no solid work on the subject. For some aspects, see Daniele Ganser, *Nato's secret Armies: Operation Gladio and Terrorism in Western Europe* (London: Frank Cass, 2005).
8. See the chapter by Martin Klimke in this volume.
9. For details, see Donatella della Porta, *Il terrorismo di sinistra* (Bologna: Il Mulino, 1990).
10. Lutz Taufer, "Gegen die Auschwitz-Generation," *Jungle World* 45 (1997).
11. ID-Verlag, ed., *Rote Armee Fraktion. Texte und Materialien zur Geschichte der RAF* (Berlin: ID, 1997), 258.
12. Ibid, 202.
13. Otto Schily and Hans-Christian Ströbele, *Plädoyers einer politischen Verteidigung. Reden und Mitschriften aus dem Mahler-Prozeß* (Berlin: Merve, 1973), 141.
14. Between 1946 and 1971, almost 150 people were killed during demonstrations alone, 14 of them policemen, and by 1977 there were another 96 deaths during protest marches.
15. France, where Italian and German terrorism was often enough sympathetically watched by former activists who at the same time were strictly opposed to armed struggle as an option for their own country, also became a safe haven for Italian militants (and in 1985 even guaranteed them immunity from extradition).

16. Left-wing terrorism resulted in more than sixty fatalities, including terrorists, in West Germany and in about two hundred in Italy, with many more, often seriously, wounded.

17. Edgar Wolfrum, "'1968' in der gegenwärtigen deutschen Geschichtspolitik," *Aus Politik und Zeitgeschichte*, B 22–23 (2001), 28–36, here 35.

23

The Women's Movement

Kristina Schulz

In modern societies, social inequality has produced hierarchical structures that are grounded not only on classifications of class and race but also on biological sex. A social movement known variously as the "women's movement," the "women's liberation movement," or the "feminist movement" made personal relationships between men and women a central political issue. These movement names are often used interchangeably; however, they have differing meanings in different linguistic contexts. Among the social movements in the late nineteenth and early twentieth centuries, and the second wave of feminism of the 1960s–1970s, the term "feminist movement" or "mouvement féministe" was commonly used in English- and French-speaking areas, whereas the adjective "feminist" in German implied a connotation of radicalism generally only attributed to the new feminist movement.[1] In most countries, the formation of the new women's movement was strongly influenced by leftist discourses; second-wave feminists classified their movement as "radical" to distance themselves from first-wave "feminism," which was seen as a bourgeois idea. In France, West Germany, Switzerland, or Great Britain, radical feminists regarded the traditional women's organizations with skepticism until at least the second half of the 1970s.

Trying to define the women's movement is therefore complicated by the choice between dealing with one social movement, including both the first and second wave, or with two related yet clearly distinct social movements, each having its own mobilization dynamics.[2] This chapter is based on the assumption that the 1970s feminism in Western European countries and the United States was one specific and historically determined form of feminism, defined as a process in which women became political subjects.[3] In many countries, though the feminism of the 1960s and 1970s was related to the first wave of feminism by unfilled requirements and concerns, in these later decades it explicitly developed into a social movement.

According to Dieter Rucht, a social movement consists of two key components. First, there is a network of groups who are prepared to organize protests aimed at social change. Second, a "social movement" needs a number of individuals who will attend protests and demonstrations or contribute resources.[4] Thus, the word "movement" suggests two ideas simultaneously: that of a distinct group with identifiable members, and that of a larger social movement supported by a mass of unidentified women.

Roots of the Movement

During the past thirty years, historians have documented various manifestations of female resistance, including both individual action and collective protest. The structural transformation of women's resistance in the modern era corresponded to the emergence of a new bourgeois ideal of womanhood since the late eighteenth century. This ideal affected not only middle-class women but also women of the emerging working class. The idealization of the private sphere occupied by mothers and housewives reduced women's activities to the household, whereas wage-earning, conceived as part of a public sphere and executed mostly by men, became increasingly important. Therefore, women's resistance in the nineteenth century in the social environment of the middle class shifted from collective protest in public (hunger riots, carnival-like rituals, and public mockery) to private forms of protest such as individual denying of norms, excessive reading, illness, sexual refusal, homoerotic friendships, and religiosity.[5]

Nevertheless, women in many countries began building women's associations from the mid-1850s on. The "first wave" of the women's movement refers to the period from 1890 until World War I. After the war, though women's organizations in most countries were not able to regain prewar levels of mobilization, many continued protest activities until World War II, which, in most countries, put an end to feminist activities. Some women's organizations survived the war years or were reestablished in the postwar period, but we know little about feminist activities immediately following the war. Even though the "women's question" was raised periodically during the two decades after World War II, it was only after the events of 1968 that feminist activities intensified and led to the emergence of a new social movement carried out by women.

Cognitive Orientation and Aims

When women began to collectively analyze their situation, they concluded that to understand their growing dissatisfaction and subaltern positions in both family and working life, they had to take into account what they all had in common: they were women. Thus, gender became a central category of the women's movement's self-conception, drawing significantly from theories on femininity circulating in Europe in the 1960s and 1970s. Three paradigms contributed to the analysis of specific conditions of women's subordination in politics, economy, and culture.

The first of these paradigms was radical feminism. The women's movements in Europe were preceded by the U.S. women's liberation movement, which appeared at the end of the 1960s. Though sometimes reinterpreted in a different way, key concepts of American radical feminism informed European thinking about the possibilities of women's emancipation. As in other countries, traditional U.S. women's organizations disappeared from the political landscape after World War II. The first sign of a renewed feminist engagement was the foundation of the National Organization of Women (NOW) in 1966. Among the initiators was Betty Friedan, sociologist, psychologist, journalist and author of *The Feminine Mystique*. In addition to NOW, many autonomous women's groups appeared in 1967 and afterward. Whereas NOW affirmed a moderate, reformist strategy tied to classical feminist grievances, the activists of those new groups—coming partly from the community organizing projects of the New Left and the civil rights movement—propagated a new, radical feminism. Intellectuals such as Shulamit Firestone and Kate Millet emphasized that they were aiming for social revolution independent from a socialist revolution. Whereas revolution in Left terms was linked to class struggle, the feminist revolution was an overarching women's project, spanning social origins. Radical feminists also proclaimed that the struggle for liberation could not be delegated to other social groups but should be the result of an active process by the oppressed. In this sense, the feminists joined the theoretical position of the New Left. In opposition to the Old Left, the New Left abandoned the idea that revolutionary action relied on one single principal agent, the proletariat. Both assumptions were adopted by European feminists.

Simone de Beauvoir's *The Second Sex*, published in 1949, provided a second paradigm for the new women's movement. De Beauvoir argued that there was no direct link from biological differences between men and women to social discrimination against women For de Beauvoir, the oppression of women was historically, not naturally founded. *The Second Sex* therefore attempted to comprehend this historical process and to show mechanisms and institutions contributing to a continuing unjust situation. According to de Beauvoir's existentialist point of view, each individual realized his or her own existence. Over centuries, philosophy, religion, literature, and science linked biology and nature with gender relations and thus legitimized gender-specific inequalities.

Women defined themselves as insignificant in relation to male significance. De Beauvoir suggested three procedures to liberate women. She proposed uncovering the myth of eternal womanhood, exercising a creative, professional work, and fostering socialist revolution as the starting point of a complete transformation of society. After viewing the actual development of women's situation in socialist societies in the 1950s and 1960s, Simone de Beauvoir lost her faith in the feminist potential of a socialist revolution; beginning in the early 1970s, she established the priority of feminist struggle over class struggle and actively supported the collective actions of the French Women's Liberation Movement. The cognitive orientation of the women's movement was influenced by the author's philosophical assumption that "THE woman" was not determined by her anatomical, biological sex, but by society, and that therefore the struggle for liberation must begin with challenging social order. Simone de Beauvoir was considered the mother of feminism by many within the new women's movement, and *The Second Sex* was their Bible.

Finally, a new reading of psychoanalysis and the sexual revolution was also paradigmatic for the new women's movement. Psychoanalysis had been renewed and reinterpreted in the 1950s and 1960s, both through a post-structuralist interpretation linked to Jacques Lacan and through New Left interest in psychoanalysis and therapy embedded in a new conception of social order embraced by European and North American intellectuals following the late 1950s.

During the 1950s and 1960s, French heterodox psychoanalyst Jacques Lacan (1901–1991) fundamentally revisited psychoanalytical thought. He paved the way for a new understanding of psychoanalysis within the context of philosophy, linguistics, and structural anthropology. His reinterpretation affected the cognitive orientation of the women's movement because it enabled the imagining of transformative strategies for gender relations. Lacan indicated the direction of a new interpretation of feminine sexuality and feminine submission by connecting the oppression of women to repressive structures in the symbolic order. Furthermore, he referred to linguistic structures and stressed their subversive potential. Based on Lacan's assumptions, feminist activists interpreted language as the starting point of social change. Lacan also accentuated and revaluated the early mother–child relationship. By giving weight to early childhood, during which the father was typically absent, Lacan prepared a theory of women's liberation based on feminine specificity and feminine autonomy.

Lacan and his disciples contributed to the expansion of psychoanalysis, particularly in France. Many intellectuals believed this paradigm—its therapeutic praxis as well as popularized forms such as simply talking about sexuality—to be the starting point not only to deal with forms of individual mental disorder but also to solve social problems. Supporters of Lacan's interpretation of psychoanalysis developed a feminist praxis that stressed the therapeutic effect of small-group discussions. Furthermore, they discovered the emancipative and revolutionary potential of a specific feminine use of language—*écriture feminine*.

Classical psychoanalysis was also the object of New Left criticism. The term "New Left" covers an intellectual movement formed in the late 1950s in many European countries and the United States; it also refers to leftist social movements from the 1960s onward. New Left thought and activism was a reaction to contemporary developments in countries ruled by socialism, such as the Soviet intervention in Hungary in 1956, or the increasing degree of concern about Stalinist terror. The New Left embraced organizational autonomy from traditional leftist groups and disagreed with key aspects of classical Left doctrine. The New Left's intellectual leaders conceptualized a theory of social transformation by including ideas of the early Frankfurt School, the surrealists, the Situationists, and the writings of Wilhelm Reich. They developed a cognitive orientation that combined psychoanalysis and revolution to accentuate power relations in the sphere of reproduction. The women's movement integrated central elements of the New Left's cognitive orientation into a feminist self-conception, particularly the definition of a new revolutionary subject and transformation strategy.

Classical Left thought was oriented toward the proletariat as the main subject of revolution. Based on critical thinkers such as Charles Wright Mills (1916–1962) and Herbert Marcuse (1891–1979), the New Left broke in a radical way with this absolute term of socialist analysis of capitalist societies. Searching for a new historical subject, the New Left concentrated on individuals and groups who were excluded from the system of social appeasement and comfort because of their skin color, social origin, or education. This opened an intellectual space in which women could recognize themselves as subjects of social change. Furthermore, the reproductive sphere was particularly important for the New Left. Whereas classical socialist thought put the accent on the realm of production, the New Left considered mechanisms of social reproduction to be the starting point for change of social structure. Thus, New Left theory emphasized the revolutionary potential of women by focusing on oppression and alienation in that area.

The cognitive orientation of the women's movement also integrated New Left transformation strategy. The New Left developed a new conception of collective action from a belief in the clarifying effect of provocation. They used provocative and symbolic forms of action to enable activists as well as spectators to realize the overwhelming power of public authorities, bureaucracy, and members of the political and economic elite. Also, New Left transformation strategy put the emphasis on self-organization in counter-institutions such as free universities and urban communes as free space in which people should anticipate a revolution of everyday life. Finally, anti-authoritarian thinking was particularly important for the New Left in West Germany. Intellectuals studied the works of Theodor W. Adorno on "The Authoritarian Personality" and from it deduced the importance of children's education for social transformation. These reflections led to a reevaluation of the social role of mothers in society and became an often-discussed subject within the new women's movement.

In summary, we can systematically profile five elements of the cognitive orientation of the new women's movements. First, new feminism rejected a Marxist perspective that reduced discrimination to the problem of class struggle. Instead, new feminist theory tried to link a socialist analysis of capitalism with extensive criticism of patriarchy. Second, new feminism went beyond classical feminist issues. Whereas first-wave feminism in Europe and the United States sought legal equality between men and women, particularly the right to vote, second-wave feminism aimed to overcome the separation of private and public spheres and to do away with gender-based hierarchies in all areas of society. Third, new feminism developed a strategy of transformation that attempted to uncover and scandalize mechanisms of power execution. Political and educational institutions along with cultural elements like language and literature were suspected of reproducing masculine domination. One of the central goals of the new feminists was therefore to raise consciousness among women. In contrast to the majority of the first wave's feminists, new feminists defined the women's movement as a revolutionary movement. While preceding generations of activists were convinced that legal and political achievements would naturally contribute to gender equality, new feminists thought that the structures of a male-dominated society had to be overthrown in an active liberation process. Fourth, the new feminist movement's organizational structure was based on the concept of the small group. Explicitly dissociating themselves from conventional women's associations and political parties, new feminists emphasized the informal structures of their movement and the high degree of autonomy of largely decentralized groups. Finally, new feminism defined a new subject of social and historical change. The movement was conceived as a "women's only" movement, temporarily willing to agree to alliances with other revolutionary movements but principally fixed on the idea of the women's movement's complete autonomy.

Organizational Structure

From a conceptual point of view, a social movement is not an organization. When we refer to the term "organization," we therefore have to differentiate between informal coordinating networks structuring the mobilization process of social movements (*social movement organization*, SMO), and the organizational infrastructure of a movement. In spite of the organizational resources and critical mass of supporters first-wave women's associations utilized, they played only a marginal role in the formation of the second-wave movement. During its formative stage, the new movement's organizational infrastructure relied on spontaneously built, informal groups at the local level, such as those involved in the campaign for free abortion. In France this was the *Mouvement pour la liberation des femmes* (MLF), in Germany the *Aktion 218*, in Switzerland the *Frauenbefreiungsbewegung* (FBB) and the MLF, and in the Netherlands the *Dolle Minnas*. The individual protest culture of each country determined the role played by these supporting groups. For instance, in West Germany, regional action committees were built during the course of the abortion struggle. They were loosely coordinated by *Aktion 218*, who brought together delegates from women's groups throughout the country. The mission of this informal group was purely operational and consisted of organizing regular meetings to inform delegates from regional groups about recent developments and to plan protest activities. The regional groups then widened the scope of their concerns from abortion to manifold aspects of women's emancipation. In contrast, the French Women's Liberation Movement was already constituted when the abortion campaign started. MLF Activists viewed the abortion issue as a subject able to mobilize countrywide support for women's rights and to forge alliances with such powerful partners as the unions and left-wing parties.

During the second half of the 1970s, women's centers (*Frauenzentren, Centres de femmes, centri culturale*) became locations of feminist agitation. One question constantly under discussion was whether women's centers and other women's projects such as houses for battered women or women's emergency telephones should receive public support, and correspondingly how far would they accept public interventions in the decision-making process of the institution. These debates resulted in diverse organizational models with varying degrees of independence. Some groups attempted to achieve gender equality by pointing out gender discrimination within and by order of public institutions. Other groups concentrated on the realization of relatively autonomous women's projects, such as women's health centers, which sought recognition by health insurance agencies. Yet other organizations focused on founding counter-institutions that refused all forms of public intervention and support. Although the overall organizational structure of the women's movement varies from country to country, it is still possible to summarize some general characteristics. Many of the groups were built around a decentralized structure reliant on local networks, exhibited weak bureaucracy accompanied by a collective decision-making structure, and employed a broad, informal definition of membership, embedded in a low degree of formality.

Feminist activists also attempted to establish international contacts to advance their goals. Moments of successful cooperation were numerous; one example took place in Brussels in 1976 when European feminists organized an international tribunal denouncing violence against women. International women's congresses and summer universities helped to develop international networks as well. As a social movement, feminism is deeply inscribed in the political culture of Western democracies. Beginning in the 1980s, women in Eastern European countries also began to develop and demonstrate a sensibility toward gender discrimination and were supported by Western movements. They began to criticize the failure of the Soviet system in this area; one strategy they employed was distributing forbidden texts such as Western feminist literature or clandestine periodicals.[6]

Relation to the 1968 Protest Movement

The relation to the 1968 protest movement was difficult but constitutive. Early women's groups appeared in the course of the students' movement and benefited from the context of mobilization. The 1968 protest movements' activities had a positive effect on women's willingness to participate in a "revolutionary" project. Women who had an academic background made friends and built relationships with other women during movement activities such as community life, Free Universities, *Kritische Universität*, and demonstrations. Those contacts were crucial for the creation of autonomous women's groups within the 1968 movement.

In many countries, women moved away from their leftist comrades, and in most cases tensions resulted in an explicit break. Women rebelled against male adherents of the 1968 protest movement in France, the United States, and the German Federal Republic. They accused the male activists of reproducing mechanisms of discrimination against women within daily movement practices. When student and filmmaker Helke Sander appealed in vain in September 1968 to delegates of the German *Sozialistischer Deutscher Studentenbund* (Socialist German Students League, SDS) to take into consideration the "women's question," one woman from the *Aktionsrat zur Befreiung der Frauen* (Women's Liberation Action Council) threw tomatoes at the podium, marking a definite break between the "male movement" and women's activists from the *Aktionsrat*. In France, the slogan "Le steak d'un révolutionnaire est aussi longtemps à cuire que celui d'un bourgeois" ("A revolutionary's steak takes as long to be done as a bourgeois' steak") expressed women's vehement opposition to male chauvinism within the

1968 protest movement. However, their chosen forms of action—symbolically charged actions, cartoons, plays on words—by which they expressed their distinctiveness vis-à-vis the male movement were still inspired by that very movement. Even today, the 1968 protest movement is a subject of controversy among former women's movement activists.

It is important to note that in many countries such as France, the German Federal Republic, and Italy the women's movement did not derive directly from the 1968 protest movement. The women's groups that were founded within the 1968 movements disintegrated, as did the movements they stemmed from. However, later women's groups could rely on the organizational resources such as preexisting networks, potential allies, means of communication, and recruitment potentials that grew from the movements of 1968. Social movement theory has given weight to the idea that "a history of prior activism increases the likelihood of future activism."[7] Many examples show that the significance of 1968 for the women's movement can hardly be overestimated.

Key Activities

Social movement theory distinguishes between an expressive logic of action that is identity-orientated and an instrumental logic of action that is centered on changes in the political arena. With regard to the cultural dimension of feminism and movement practices that enhanced internal mobilization and movement solidarity (music, consciousness-raising groups, women's literature, specific use of language, symbolically charged actions, etc.), it has been noted that the women's movement followed a mainly expressive logic of action.[8] However, the women's movement was originally not a purely identity-orientated movement but, rather, has from its beginning challenged the political order and addressed the state as a key target. The struggle for free abortion is emblematic in this respect. Women's movements played with the rules of the political field by using the designated channels for articulating interests in democratic societies, but also by consciously compassing them. To systematize the diversity of feminist activities, it seems to be helpful to distinguish between expressions and activities of symbolic and social feminism. According to this distinction, symbolic feminism aimed at a perceptual change that included a shift of attitude and behavior, whereas social feminism sought to directly influence the political decision-making process. Symbolic feminism considered women "qua women" and developed specific means of individual and collective "liberation," such as a specific feminine use of language (*écriture feminine*), consciousness-raising by therapy or encounter groups, or creative activities.

Representatives of social feminism centered on social institutions and aimed at social rather than at individual mental change. They concentrated on campaigns against sexual violence or pornography and on the installation of women's centers and houses for battered women. Social feminists desired equal opportunities for men and women in all areas of society, especially in employment.

The variety of themes and growing internal differentiation of feminism led to a multiplication of activities and forms of collective action. Demonstrative-appellative, sometimes direct action was particularly important for the women's movement. Activists threw wet nappies in political assemblies to put pressure on political decision-makers, demonstrators burned bras in public and distributed cartoons of the pope and other personalities defending the interdiction of abortion. As a reaction to the decision of the communal authorities in Geneva to shut down the autonomous women's center, militant feminists laid bricks in order to close the town hall in a symbolically charged action. Countless demonstrations on the local, national, and sometimes even international level took place. The women's movements also made use of institutions of meaning-making by initiating mass petitions and collecting signatures against women's deprivation of the right to control their own bodies, and by getting the attention of mass media. In Switzerland, pro-abortion associations such as the FBB launched a referendum in favor of liberalization of the abortion law in 1977.

Consequences and Narratives

The women's movement of the 1970s was characterized by the competition between different groups struggling with the definition of the direction, strategies, and goals of feminism. These conflicts were reflected in narratives about the movement's founding myth. Even today, women's movement activists disagree about the birth of the women's movement; they are polarized by the question of how far "1968" was influential in the formation of the new women's movement. Radical feminists described it as a mainly male-dominated movement. To most feminists, the 1968 claim for free sexuality aggravated women's sexual exploitation, so that the "sexual revolution" was the center of criticism. Nevertheless, some groups stressed the effect of "1968" as a trigger for change, an awakening, and the beginning of a new era. Others clearly stated that change did not happen until the women's movement occurred, and that the women's movement developed not from but against the spirit of 1968.

Strictly speaking, the movement's date of birth was not the only point of contention. Conflicts surrounding the relative importance of 1968 were symptomatic of other ideological differences. By accepting or refusing continuity with the events of 1968, different currents within the women's movement negotiated the forms and content of feminist engagement such as the modes of mobilization (mass or elite), instruments of the struggle (consciousness-raising by psychoanalysis or by provocative actions) and its direction (symbolic level, *écriture féminine* or material/legal level). The significance of 1968 was in this context symbolic rather than historical.

Internal conflicts contribute to the decomposition of social movements. However, in the case of the women's movements, these conflicts had some positive effects as well. They led to a broad diversification of grievances and ensured that women's concerns were put on the agenda in such different domains as public health, the academy, and labor.

When social movement researchers measure movement success, they face complications because movements compete with other forms of social transformation, and thus social change can hardly be attributed to one single social actor. Therefore, analysis of social movement's effects has to balance factors. In view of the problem of imputation, we can only give a rough draft of the consequences of the women's movements, taking into account four areas. First, public women's politics have been reformed in many countries since the mid-1970s and reached new heights in the 1980s. Whereas officials formerly posed the "women's question" as a problem of family and population politics up to the 1970s and centered on the protection of women as potential mothers, women's politics in the 1980s added the aspect of women's promotion in the public sphere to that of women's protection. Secondly, there were shifts in the organization of work. The women's movement radically challenged a mode of social organization based on separation between family (married women and mothers) and work (unmarried women and men). Feminists asked for equal rights and equal pay; this eventually led to measures promoting equality in employment. Third, feminist scholars made advances in the realms of knowledge and learning; they struggled for the institutionalization and recognition of women and gender studies in academia. In the early 1980s, gender-specific study and research programs began to be integrated in official curricula. Though initially poorly financed, women's studies were eventually successful in convincing authorities that these matters deserved financial support. The women's movement also promoted teaching and research activities outside the university. Progressive nonprofit organizations like adult education centers, libraries, and archives began to offer courses on women's employment, women's rights, adult education for women, and aspects of mental and physical health. Finally, there occurred a marked change in gender stereotypes, attitudes, and opinions. The women's movement questioned the perceived biological grounds for

male domination over females. Feminists denounced mechanisms that contributed to a definition of women as the "weaker sex" and showed how biological arguments were used to legitimize a social order based on women's
subordination. Instead, they argued for the importance of social attributions
in the distribution of power between men and women. Understanding the
social mechanisms of oppression not only allowed women to develop new
perspectives on how to escape traditional feminine role expectations but
also upset the traditional stereotypes of masculinity.

The fact that women run for office to reach the highest positions in government in several countries may be a hint to such a change. But the fact
that women in European academia represent only a tenth of all professor-
ships may also show that, when it comes to change, each sector of society
has its own rhythm.

Bibliography

Usually researchers on the women's movement treat either the first or the
second wave movement. The *classic overview* is provided by Morgan (1984).
Literature on the early women's movement is exhaustive; for an *international
dimension* see Rupp (1997); for a national overview on the *French case* see
Riot-Sarcey (2002), for *Germany* Gerhard (1990) and Wischermann (2003).

Some works focus on the *old and on the new movement*, as Ryan (1992), or on
the *in-between*, as Chaperon (2000). Gubin et al. (2004) provide an excellent
reader on *transversal issues* of feminism. The new women's movement is still a
new field of historical analysis, though sociologists and anthropologists
started earlier; see, for instance, Picq (1993). For a first overview of *the international dimension*, turn to Dahlerup (1986) and Smith (2000). From a *comparative point of view*, see Apostolidou (1995), Rucht (1994), and Schulz (2002).

Apostolidou, Natascha. *Die neue Frauenbewegung in der BRD und Griechenland.* Frankfurt:
    Helmer, 1995.
Chaperon, Sylvie. *Les années Beauvoir: 1945–1970.* Paris: Fayard, 2000.
Dahlerup, Drude, ed. *The New Women's Movement: Feminism and Political Power in
    Europe and the USA.* London: Sage, 1986.
Gerhard, Ute. *Unerhört: Die Geschichte der deutschen Frauenbewegung.* Reinbek/Hamburg:
    Rowohlt, 1990.
Gubin, Eliane et al., ed. *Le siècle des feminisms.* Paris: Les éditions de l'atelier, 2004.
Morgan, Robin, ed. *Sisterhood is Global: The International Women's Movement Anthology.*
    New York: Anchor Books, 1984.
Riot-Sarcey, Michèle. *Histoire du feminism.* Paris: La Découverte, 2002.
Rucht, Dieter. *Modernisierung und neue soziale Bewegungen. Deutschland, Frankreich und
    USA im Vergleich.* Frankfurt: Campus, 1994.

Rupp, Leila. *Worlds of Women: The Making of an International Women's Movement.* Princeton, NJ: University Press, 1997.

Ryan, Barbara. *Feminism and the Women's Movement: Dynamics of Change in Social Movement Ideology and Activism.* New York: Routledge, 1992.

Schulz, Kristina. *Der lange Atem der Provokation: Die Frauenbewegung in der Bundesrepublik und in Frankreich 1968–1976.* Frankfurt: Campus, 2002.

Smith, Bonnie G., ed. *Global Feminisms Since 1945.* London: Routledge, 2000.

Wischermann, Ursula. *Frauenbewegung und öffentlichkeiten um 1900: Netzwerke. Gegenöffentlichkeiten. Protestinszenierungen.* Frankfurt: Helmer, 2003.

Notes

1. See Ute Gerhard, "Concepts et controverses," *Le siècle des féminismes*, Eliane Gubin et al. eds. (Paris: Les Editions de l'Atelier, 2004), 47–63.
2. See Ute Gerhard, "Die langen Wellen der Frauenbewegung—Traditionslinien und unerledigte Anliegen," in *Atempause. Feminismus als demokratisches Projekt*, ed. Ute Gerhard (Francfurt: Fischer 1999), 12–38.
3. Joan W. Scott, "Lire autrement l'histoire du féminisme" in *La citoyenne paradoxale. Les féministes françaises et les droits de l'homme* (Paris: Albin Michel, 1998), 35.
4. Dieter Rucht, "The Impact of National Contexts on Social Movement Structures: A Cross-Movement and Cross-National Comparison" in *Comparative Perspectives On Social Movements: Political Opportunities, Mobilizing Structures, and Cultural Framings*, ed. Doug McAdam, John D. Mc Carthy, and Mayer N. Zald (Cambridge: Cambridge University Press, 1996), 186.
5. Claudia Honegger and Bettina Heintz, eds., *Listen der Ohnmacht. Zur Sozialgeschichte weiblicher Widerstandsformen* (Frankfort: EVA, 1981); Gisela Bock, *Frauen in der europäischen Geschichte. Vom Mittelalter bis zur Gegenwart* (München: Beck, 2000), 87.
6. Linda Racioppi, Katherine O'Sullivan See, "Organizing women before and after the fall: women's politics in the Soviet Union and post-Soviet Russia" in *Global Feminism since 1945*, ed. Bonnie G. Smith (London: Routledge, 2000), 205–34.
7. Doug McAdam, John McCarthy, and Mayer N. Zald, "Social Movements" in *Handbook of Sociology*, ed. Neil J. Smelser (Newbury Park, CA: Sage Publications, 1988), 708.
8. See Dieter Rucht, "The Strategies and Action Repertoires of New Movements" in *Challenging the Political Order. New Social and Political Movements in Western Democracies*, ed. Russell J. Dalton and Manfred Kuecheler (Cambridge: Oxford University Press, 1990), 156–75.

24
The Environmental Movement

Christopher Rootes

Roots of the Movement

There is a popular version of recent history that portrays every instance of protest and every social movement as a part or a consequence of the participatory surge of the late 1960s. But, particularly in the case of the environmental movement, that is to misunderstand and misrepresent the course of events.

Environmental movements have their origins in the conservation and public health campaigns and organizations of the nineteenth century. Interest in natural history was stimulated both by the Enlightenment, which encouraged scientific inquiry, and by the great age of European exploration, which brought knowledge of exotic species and, in some cases, their rapid extinction. Natural history societies abounded and, although amateur nature study groups and professionalized science began to part company during the nineteenth century, specialized conservation societies proliferated. These early organizations were not simply concerned with the preservation of wilderness for its own sake, or the conservation of natural resources for future use. A number were also concerned with human well-being and with the built and natural environment. Thus, in England, the first prominent national environmental conservation society, the Commons Preservation Society, was established in 1865 to protect public access to open land, principally so that an increasingly urbanized population might find recreation in ready access to nature.

The fortunes of early environmental organizations ebbed and flowed during the twentieth century. Their growth was stimulated by periods of affluence in which the pressures of economic development coexisted with new opportunities for leisure and increased mobility, and in which human impact upon the natural environment was especially visible. Although concern about the environment never disappeared or failed to sustain groups, it remained principally the province of elite groups and professionals, and organizations rarely extended beyond the boundaries of the states within which they originated. As Europe recovered from the destruction of World War II, new and reorganized environmental protection organizations emerged, usually with broader social bases of support.

The rise of environmental concern was already advanced in the 1960s, but this was still primarily an elite concern. Nevertheless, the World Wide Fund for Nature (WWF) was launched in Britain in 1961 by an appeal through the pages of a mass-market tabloid newspaper, and it rapidly collected large sums by public subscription.

Although critiques of industrialized agriculture had already been published in Europe, it was the 1962 publication of Rachel Carson's *Silent Spring* in the United States that marked a change in the development of environmental consciousness, not because its warnings about the effects of indiscriminate use of pesticides were new but because they were published in a popular magazine and created a media sensation. The time was ripe, and *Silent Spring* was translated and republished in Europe where its impact was arguably greater than in the United States.[1] The rise of mass popular concern about the effects of ill-considered human manipulation of the natural environment was underway. The conditions for the emergence of environmental consciousness had been laid by the development of a rapidly growing, increasingly affluent and educated citizenry, and the parallel development of systematic mapping and scientific understanding both of the natural world itself and of the effects of human activity upon it. Nevertheless, mass environmental movements only emerged in the wake of the ferment associated with the student movements that attracted nearly global attention in 1968.

The 1968 Movement and the Environment

Environmental concerns were rarely prominent among the grievances that animated the student protesters of the 1960s. Most student activists of the 1968 generation were preoccupied with politics and history, the U.S. war in Vietnam and the unresponsiveness of established politicians and state authority. But as the protest movement developed an increasingly radical critique of the shortcomings of capitalism and liberal democracy, it often gave at least a small place to criticism of the environmental degradation entailed by rampant economic development guided principally by the pursuit of profit, wasteful consumption, and the "society of the spectacle." However, this embryonic environmental critique was generally a minor strand. As the student and anti-war movements progressed rapidly from civil libertarianism and anti-militarism to Marxism, the celebration of the proletariat was widely accompanied by a materialist version of Marxism that had little time for the niceties of aesthetics, let alone the interests of nonhuman species.

There was, however, another dimension to the ferment of the late 1960s. The counterculture that accompanied the rise of the New Left in the United States developed, especially after the New Left's turn to increasingly violent confrontation in 1969, a "diffuse environmental sentiment."[2] This had parallels in the "alternative" scenes of European cities, including Amsterdam and Copenhagen. Even U.S. rural communes had European parallels, notably in Scandinavia and in France.

In general, environmental movements might best be seen as legatees of the late 1960s ferment rather than as part of it, although their relationship varied from one European country to another.

France

One of the more evocative slogans of May 1968 in Paris was "*sous les pavés, la plage*" ("beneath the cobblestones, the beach"), but the environment itself was not a salient theme of the protests. However, since the French May is widely credited with having unblocked what the journalist Olivier Todd memorably called "a formidably constipated society," it is scarcely surprising that *les événements* should have reverberated in nature conservation circles. In 1968, the French Federation of Nature Protection Societies (FFSPN) was formed in an attempt to bring together a score of local and regional conservation organizations to make serious claims on the attention of a government that had hitherto dismissed them as "defenders of little birds."[3] The precise timing was mere coincidence since the rise of nature protection organizations was already under way before 1968. They had developed in response to the same general stirrings in French society that produced a new middle class and a demand for participation of which 1968 was the symbolic marker rather than the instigator, the unstopping of a bottle in which pressure had been building for decades.[4] A more direct product of the ferment of 1968 was a group founded in 1970 by scientists critical of the French scientific establishment. This group, *Survivre et Vivre* (Survive and Live), was focused upon the social uses of science and the emerging environmental issues rather than on nature conservation.

There were, nevertheless, direct connections between the student movement of 1968 and the emergence of the modern environmental movement. The most direct was in the person of Brice Lalonde. A leader of the French National Union of Students at the Sorbonne in 1968 and a prominent figure in the student revolt, in 1970, Lalonde was among the founders of *Les Amis de la Terre*, the French branch of Friends of the Earth. He went on to organize the campaign of the agronomist René Dumont, when in 1974, Dumont became the first ecologist to contest the French Presidency. He later became environment minister (1991–1992) in Socialist governments before founding *Génération Ecologie*, the short-lived rival to the French Greens party. Another, rather more complicated, biographical connection is provided by Daniel Cohn-Bendit. The key figure in the protests at the Nanterre campus that sparked the May revolt, he became an environmental activist in Germany, deputy mayor of Frankfurt, and later a Greens Member of the European Parliament, alternating his allegiances between the German and French Greens.

The anti-nuclear movement was the key link between the 1968 events and the broad environmental movement. Activists from *Les Amis de la Terre* participated alongside local protesters in the first anti-nuclear demonstrations in Alsace in 1971. This marked the beginning of a decade-long mobilization. Just as the principal grievance of the 1968 protesters had been the centralization of power in the French state, so its policies of expanding the activities of a nuclear energy industry, monopolized by the state, shrouded in secrecy, dismissive of local concerns, and effectively publicly unaccountable, were taken as evidence that nothing had changed. Political ecologists opposed nuclear power out of opposition to "authoritarian, centralized, technicist conceptions of society, the extreme expression of which would be the 'nuclear society.'"[5] Developing themes from the May movement, their critique was political and social rather than simply technical or scientific; it was a critique of both the increasingly centralized, incessantly growth-oriented, consumerist market economy and the state. Thus the political ecology activists of the 1970s were "first and foremost the children of May 68."[6]

The decade after 1968 was a period of rapid proliferation of regional nature protection associations, but in 1977, the anti-nuclear mobilization reached a crescendo in the violent confrontations at the site of the proposed fast breeder reactor at Creys-Malville. Combined with the re-election of the conservative majority in 1978, this was taken as proof of the obduracy and inaccessibility of the centralized state. It exacerbated the localism and decentralization that had long characterized the French environmental movement. Although local associations oriented toward practical conservation flourished, national organizations withered; even *Les Amis de la Terre* disappeared for a time, and only at the end of the century did Greenpeace regain significant support.

Germany

In Germany, the ferment of the 1960s contributed directly and indirectly to the development of the environmental movement. The formation in 1966 of a grand coalition, when the SPD for the first time entered government in partnership with the conservative CDU, created a vacuum of effective parliamentary opposition. The liberal FDP, the only remaining opposition in the Bundestag, was concerned that German democracy was too passive for its own good and encouraged the formation of local citizens' groups as means of injecting substance into the forms of democracy.

Such *Bürgerinitiativen* (citizens' initiatives) emerged earlier to highlight local political issues, and although they criticized the unresponsiveness of governments and bureaucracies and advocated greater citizen participation, most were politically nonpartisan.[7] Nevertheless, they were genuinely grassroots initiatives, and in their embodiment of participatory democracy they laid a bridge to the critique of representative democracy raised by the Left and the student movement. Thus, they were a foundation of the Green political movement that emerged later.[8] They gained momentum from the political situation, and were encouraged by the actions of the Brand SPD government (elected 1969) in highlighting environmental issues and supporting enhanced citizen participation. During the 1970s, the citizens' initiatives were increasingly networked by the BBU (Federal Alliance of Citizens' Initiatives for Environmental Protection) and focused upon the nuclear issue.

This was their point of contact with the other main legacy of the late 1960s: the extra-parliamentary opposition.[9] The uneasy alliance of citizens' initiatives with these latter groups, especially in and around university towns, and in the struggle against the nuclear state, was the foundation of the strong, politically-engaged environmental movement of the 1980s.[10]

Italy

In Italy, an anthropocentric political ecology movement emerged from the student and workers' protests of 1968–1969. Focused mainly upon issues of health and the urban environment, it raised the critique of the distribution of power.[11] Only later did it embrace the nature protection issues highlighted by older, science-based organizations, which themselves "remained small and separate worlds."[12] Although all strands of environmental sentiment were mobilized in opposition to nuclear energy, their perspectives differed sharply and cooperation was limited.[13] It took the 1987 anti-nuclear referendum to bring the several organizations to a common realization that a systematic approach was required.[14]

Britain

In Britain, the events of 1968 were less dramatic and the links with, and impact upon the environmental movement were less direct. Even in the

1960s, Britain had an institutionalized and influential network of environmental protection organizations. Precisely because it was so influential and comfortable in its relationships with governments, the network was viewed with suspicion and disdain by the Left, who tended to dismiss it as a special interest lobby defensive of privileged interests. While prominent student activists responded in 1970 to David Brower's call to set up a UK branch of Friends of the Earth (FoE), those activists had previously failed to interest the National Union of Students in environmental issues.[15] Friends of the Earth was an immediate success, but despite its employment of media stunts to dramatize its concerns with pollution and waste, it was quickly accorded insider status and employed mainly conventional tactics. One example occurred when it played a leading role in the public inquiry into the nuclear reprocessing facility at Windscale. It was not until the formation of Greenpeace UK in 1977 that more demonstrative environmental politics acquired an organizational identity in Britain.

Other Countries

In the Nordic countries, the impact of the spirit of 1968 on environmentalism was especially immediate. In Sweden, students were the chief protesters against hydro-electric schemes and transport infrastructure projects in the late 1960s.[16] In Denmark, which even before 1968 had a well-developed New Left and counter-culture, a group of students staged a spectacular demonstration in 1969 at the annual meeting of a venerable and conservative natural history society to launch an environmental movement, and formed NOAH. What is most remarkable about this latter development is that it was science students, influenced by but not part of the New Left student revolt and reacting against the quiescence of the conservative nature conservation establishment, who took the initiative, placed issues of ecology firmly in the arena of public debate, and became a grassroots movement concerned with the democratization of scientific knowledge.[17]

In the Netherlands, too, intimations of the new environmentalism anticipated 1968, most notably in the activities of the anarchist Provo movement from 1965 and a variety of other unorganized environmental action groups. However, it was only after the eruption of student protest in 1969, and through convergence with the Amsterdam counterculture and rising public concern about pollution, that an environmental movement developed.[18]

The Nuclear Nexus

The anti-nuclear mobilizations of the 1970s were crucial in transmitting the legacy of 1968 to the broad environmental movement, especially in

Germany and France. Proposals to introduce or rapidly expand nuclear power stations were mostly made in response to anxieties about energy security exacerbated by the oil crisis of 1973. But they were made in societies where politics had been enlivened by the 1960s movements, and where the very idea of the strong state had been radically challenged. Energy policies that depended upon large capital investments, controversial advanced technology, and high security, and were tainted by associations with nuclear weapons, were bound to collide with aspirations to "participation" that were both recent and substantially unrealized. When it was originally introduced, nuclear energy encountered negligible public opposition, but its expansion was proposed at a time when generalized concerns were increasing about the impacts of industrialization, pollution, and indiscriminate use of chemicals in agriculture upon human health and the natural environment, and so the conjunction between anti-state and environmental concerns was readily made.

The nuclear issue provided a singularly effective rallying point for the political tendencies stimulated by or emerging from the 1968 movement, but it was more ambiguous in its relationship to the environmental movement. Whereas nature protection associations had long histories, were institutionalized and embedded in relationships with official conservation agencies, and were involved a wide range of constructive and reformist practical activities that only rarely spilled over into direct political confrontation and mass mobilization, anti-nuclear movements were more novel and their concerns more urgent. Because they were usually organized around attempts to prevent construction of new nuclear installations, the timescale for possible success was relatively short. Thus, intense but short-lived mass mobilizations were necessary. Moreover, because anti-nuclear movements were usually conceived as single-issue campaigns, they were typically organized as broad coalitions of preexisting groups, very often including small left-wing parties whose members were attracted not merely by the opportunity to proselytize, but by the fact that the anti-nuclear issue entailed considerations of international relations and critique of the forms of the state.

The way the anti-nuclear issue combined environmental concern with issues of concern to other political groupings ensured the likelihood that anti-nuclear movements would be broad coalitions of environmentalists, ecologists, and political radicals—particularly representing the radical Left. Under the right conditions, the contacts forged in such movements might evolve into Green parties, as they did in Germany. In this manner, Green parties may reasonably be seen as one of the more potent and enduring legacies of the ferment of the 1960s rather than as party political translations of less directly political environmental social movements. One reason is that political ecology—the political philosophy that guides many Green parties—is a more radical and inclusive worldview than environmentalism. Where

Green parties have grown directly out of social movements, it is more often out of specifically anti-nuclear movements than broader environmental movements.

The notable exception was Britain, where an abundance of coal and increasing production of North Sea oil and gas meant that government did not commit to rapid expansion of nuclear energy capacity. Muted protests, and tactful policing of those that did occur, impeded the development of an anti-nuclear protest movement comparable to those of France or Germany, and so deprived Britain of the impetus that contributed to the radicalization of environmentalism in those countries.

The advent in the 1970s of more radical environmental organizations with more human-centered agendas, confrontational repertoires of action and radically democratic aspirations challenged the older nature protection organizations even as they contributed to the heightened awareness of environmental issues and sense of political efficacy that enabled those organizations to enter a period of rapid growth. Even where the traditional nature protection organizations kept their distance from the new ecological radicals, they were influenced by them in the modification of their agenda—to embrace opposition to nuclear energy, and to take greater account of the human contexts of nature protection—and in their tactics. They did not generally take up the baton of street protest, but became less cautious about cooperating with those who did, and about challenging governments and corporations on matters of policy. By the 1990s, environmental movements were broad networks of organizations with diverse constitutional structures, agendas, repertoires of action, and local, national, and transnational affiliations.

It is fair to say that the broad-ranging critique of political, economic, and social institutions that the protest movements of the 1960s embodied was responsible for triggering the shift in environmentalist circles from seeing environmental ills as a series of unwanted and unintended side effects of industrialism to a more fundamental critique that regards environmental degradation as a consequence of growth itself.[19] However, this remains a matter of contention and a step too far for many environmental protection associations. It is certainly true, however, that the student protests of the late 1960s inspired young environmentalists to establish new, more activist organizations, thus beginning a process of organizational and tactical innovation that has continued. The radical "disorganizations" that spread during the 1990s, such as Earth First! and Reclaim the Streets, were the work of younger activists dismayed by what they saw as the timidity of the likes of FoE and Greenpeace. In their radical commitment to participatory democracy and nonviolent direct action, they are authentic inheritors of the spirit of 1968.

Transnational Environmentalism

Internationalism did not begin in 1968, as the existence of WWF and, before it, the International Union for the Conservation of Nature (IUCN), attests. The aspiration to a global environmental movement probably owes something to the views of the blue planet transmitted in the 1960s from NASA satellites, and it was undoubtedly encouraged by recognition of the transboundary impacts of pollution. Nevertheless, the media attention to a student revolt that appeared to be transnational both in its mobilization and its issues colored the new environmental organizations of the 1970s. Characteristically, both the iconic organizations of that decade—FoE and Greenpeace—began in North America. In their concern to innovate, both clearly reflected the spirit of the times, yet both were moved more by the urgency of ecological issues than by the prevailing passion for participatory democracy, perhaps because both were the initiatives of activists of a somewhat older generation. In their subsequent development the two have diverged; FoE emphasizes decentralization and internal democracy even at the expense of effectiveness, especially in the development of Friends of the Earth International,[20] and Greenpeace maintains a strict hierarchical organizational discipline in the pursuit of campaign effectiveness.

The development of other transnational environmental networks in Europe owes more to the assumption of environmental competence by the European Commission than to any direct impact of 1968. It is only in the loosest sense that one can speak of a singular European environmental movement; the shadows of highly particular national cultures, histories, and political structures lie across even this most global of concerns, so that environmental movements are still mainly national, regional, or local rather than transnational.[21]

Conclusion

The experience of 1968 defined a political generation, which then began its long march through the institutions of the liberal democratic states of the global north, innovating and transforming organizations and institutions as it went. But, more than that, it was also a profound influence upon everything it touched, the established nature protection organizations among them. In recent years, the numbers of supporters of the new campaigning and tactically innovative environmental organizations of the 1970s (FoE and Greenpeace) have tended to stagnate or decline, even as those of more cautious nature protection organizations have continued to grow. Yet for all their preoccupations with the management of nature reserves and practical conservation projects, the latter are not the politely lobbying organizations of the 1960s. Many are now willing to join campaigns in alliance with the likes of FoE and Greenpeace against climate change and the global social injustices it brings. The generation of 1968 may have uncorked the bottle, but the fluid of aspiration for a better, more just world continues to lubricate the wheels of an ever more extensive environmental movement.

Bibliography

Jamison et al. (1990) offer an exemplary analysis of the early development of the modern environmental movement in Sweden, Denmark, and the Netherlands, but there is, unfortunately, no comparable work in English on other European countries. Flam (1994) presents analyses of anti-nuclear movements in the major western European states. Richardson and Rootes (1995) describe and analyze the development of Green parties. Rootes (2004) presents an overview of the social scientific literature on environmental movements. Although van Koppen and Markham (2007) is focused upon nature protection organizations, it offers up-to-date accounts of most of the major players in environmental movements in eight European states and the United States. Rootes (2007) brings together analyses of reported environmental protests in seven states in the years from 1988.

Flam, Helena, ed. *States and Anti-nuclear Movements*. Edinburgh: Edinburgh University Press, 1994.

Jamison, Andrew, et al. *The Making of the New Environmental Consciousness: A Comparative Study of the Environmental Movements in Sweden, Denmark and the Netherlands*. Edinburgh: Edinburgh University Press, 1990.

Richardson, Dick, and Chris Rootes, eds. *The Green Challenge: The Development of Green Parties in Europe*. London: Routledge, 1995.

Rootes, Christopher, ed. "Environmental Movements." in *The Blackwell Companion to Social Movements*, edited by David Snow, et al., 608–40. Oxford: Blackwell, 2004.

Rootes, Christopher. *Environmental Protest in Western Europe*. Oxford: Oxford University Press, 2007.

van Koppen, C. S. A., and William Markham, eds. *Protecting Nature Organizations and Networks in Europe and the USA*. Cheltenham: Edward Elgar, 2007.

Notes

1. Andrew Jamison, et al., *The Making of the New Environmental Consciousness: A Comparative Study of the Environmental Movements in Sweden, Denmark and the Netherlands* (Edinburgh: Edinburgh University Press, 1990), 20.

2. Robert Gottlieb, *Forcing the Spring: The Transformation of the American Environmental Movement* (Washington, DC: Island, 1993), 93–105.

3. Cécilia Claeys-Mekdade and Marie Jacqué, "Nature Protection Associations in France," in *Protecting Nature Organizations and Networks in Europe and the USA*, ed. C. S. A. van Koppen and William Markham (Cheltenham: Edward Elgar, 2007), 72.

4. See Alain Touraine, *The May Movement* (New York: Random House, 1971); Michel Crozier, *The Stalled Society* (New York: Viking, 1973).

5. Alain Touraine, et al., *Anti-Nuclear Protest: The Opposition to Nuclear Energy in France* (Cambridge: Cambridge University Press, 1983), 21.

6. Ibid., 16.

7. William Markham, "Networking Local Environmental Groups in Germany: The Rise and Fall of the Federal Alliance of Citizens' Initiatives for Environmental Protection (BBU)," *Environmental Politics* 14, no. 5 (2005): 670.

8. Andrei Markovits and Philip Gorski, *The German Left: Red, Green and Beyond* (Cambridge: Polity, 1993), 100f.

9. See the article by Martin Klimke in this volume.

10. William Markham, "Nature Protection in Germany: Persistence and Change in a Turbulent Century," in van Koppen/Markham, *Protecting Nature*, 96f.

11. Mario Diani, *Green Networks: A Structural Analysis of the Italian Environmental Movement* (Edinburgh: Edinburgh University Press, 1995), 23–26.

12. Giorgio Osti, "Nature Protection Organizations in Italy," in van Koppen/Markham, *Protecting Nature*, 124.

13. Diani, *Green Networks*, 29–33.

14. Osti, *Nature Protection*, 125.

15. Robert Lamb, *Promising the Earth* (London: Routledge, 1996), 35–38.

16. Jamison et al., *New Environmental Consciousness*, 27.

17. Ibid., 66–90.

18. Ibid., 132–39.

19. Ibid., 21.

20. Brian Doherty, "Friends of the Earth International: Negotiating a Transnational Identity," *Environmental Politics* 15, no. 5 (2006): 860–80.

21. Christopher Rootes, "Is There a European Environmental Movement?" in *Europe, Globalization, Sustainable Development*, ed. John Barry, et al. (London: Routledge, 2004), 47–72.

25

Narratives of Democratization
1968 in Postwar Europe

Philipp Gassert

In retrospect, 1968, the year of global revolt halfway between the end of World War II and the end of the Cold War, looked like a failed revolution. None of the protests that erupted from Berkeley to Berlin, from Bangkok to Buenos Aires, and from Prague to Tokyo led to the overthrow of existing orders. While the protagonists struggled in the belief of a common cause, opposing the domestic and international status quo in the name of participatory democracy, political freedom, and personal self determination,[1] they also found themselves united in their failure to gain what they aspired to. Like its more famous European precursor, the 1848-1849 bourgeois revolutions, the 1968-1969 uprisings seemed to have been doomed from the beginning; likewise, they ended in crushing defeat.[2] Democracy may have been in the streets in the late 1960s, but it did not make it to halls of power.

At first this ultimate outcome of the setbacks of 1968 was hidden to West European radicals. In France, Charles de Gaulle succeeded in upstaging the Paris May by calling an early election, which produced a political landslide in favor of the right. Activists were not discouraged, however: They continued to envision themselves on the road to revolution. Artists portrayed 1968 as the beginning of a long struggle ("début de une lutte prolongée"). Michel Rocard, who headed the radical Socialist Party (PSU) and who would later become prime minister during President Francois Mitterrand's long reign, declared on the day after the first round of de Gaulle's snap elections that "revolution was possible."[3] Endorsing French sociologist Alain Touraine's analysis, the British historian Eric Hobsbawm whole-heartedly agreed in 1969 that the May movement had started "a new period in social history.[4]

In a parallel development, West Germany's Sozialistischer Deutscher Studentenbund (Socialist German Student Association, or SDS) hit a wall in May 1968. The established political forces had finally pushed through the so-called emergency laws; opposition against these laws had galvanized the revolt and served as an umbilical cord among various groups and organizations. It had even spawned cooperation between labor unions, student opposition, and New Left intellectuals.[5] Without this common cause, coordination among these various groups disintegrated. Despite these and other conspicuous failures, Herbert Marcuse, who counted among the most prominent intellectual mentors of the transatlantic New Left, thought that the events of 1968 had shown that revolutionary change was in the wings. After all, the Paris May had taught the lesson that revolution could be started outside its traditional locus—the politically apathetic (old) labor class. Against this backdrop, the growing decentralization of the student movement was even among its particular strengths.[6] With the possible exception of Italy, where labor input was greater, where the mobilization continued well into the 1970s, and where the established order was almost brought to its heels during the "lead years,"[7] this story repeated itself all over Western Europe time and again. Representative democracy braved the specter of revolution in 1968. Established politics remained surprisingly untouched by the theatrical scenes that played themselves out in the boulevards and lecture halls of Western Europe.

Calls for freedom, self-determination, and democracy were heard throughout East Central Europe as well. In Poland and Czechoslovakia—though to a much lesser degree in other Warsaw Pact countries—a renewed wave of post-Stalinist protest activity erupted during 1967–1968, only ten years after the debacle of the Polish October and the Hungarian Uprising of 1956. As in Western Europe, revolts were quickly defeated. Other than in the West, where unrest continued well into the 1970s, the end was drastically more sudden during the summer of 1968. Soviet tanks made sure that the vision of a "third way" between communism and capitalism would enjoy a very short "Prague Spring." After the Czechoslovak challenge had been vanquished, the idea of "socialism with a human face" continued to enjoy much attraction. However, its chances for realization were much diminished. As Hobsbawm observed in retrospect, "the writing appeared on the wall."[8] Prague 1968 had been a testing ground for a new order. In its failure it prefigured the great transformation of 1989–1990. Many of the critical intellectuals who had been among the leading voices in 1968 would become central figures in the opposition movements of the 1970s and 1980s.[9]

In East Central Europe, the end was quick. In Western Europe, however, the protests dragged on. Protagonists continued to harbor illusions well into the 1970s. It was only against the backdrop of terrorism and the economic crisis of the second half of that decade that a thorough evaluation of the 1968 movements' failures and achievements took place. Early critics had blamed the movements of 1968 for their uncritical romanticism,[10] claiming that their "pathos of liberation" undermined essential freedoms.[11] Others settled for a different interpretation, which has grown in influence and continues to shape much of the post-1968 memory debate, including many mainstream publications. They believed that although unsuccessful in the narrow political-revolutionary sense, the protest movements were prime movers and shakers in the transformation and modernization of European societies. Thanks to 1968, the West had become more democratic.[12] The protest movements were reinterpreted as catalysts for the 1960s' "cultural revolution."[13] Influential voices spoke of 1968 as the germinating crisis of postindustrial society.[14]

It is against the backdrop of this emerging post-1968 narrative of a fundamental democratization of political cultures and all-encompassing liberalization of Western societies that I examine the events of the late 1960s. The problem needs to be studied on three distinct, but interrelated, levels. First, we must examine 1968 in the context of the democratization of Western societies in its most basic ("Tocquevillian") sense: a secular modernization process, making human beings more equal by leveling distinctions of class, gender, ethnicity, race, region, and religion. How are the 1968 movements embedded in these larger social transformations? Second, what did contemporary Western European protagonists of 1968 mean when they demanded democratization in the context of global revolution? How was the term "democracy" then being understood? Finally, in a third step I turn my eyes east and discuss East Central European visions of democracy of the late 1960s. I conclude with a few remarks about the significance of 1968 in the context of emerging civil society and democracy in postwar European memory and history.

Democratization and Postwar Prosperity

Although political democracy was restored in 1945 in most Western European countries (with the exceptions of Fascist Spain and authoritarian Portugal), the social fabric of Western Europe was not yet democratic in the broader meaning of the term, especially compared with the contemporary yardstick of the United States, where white, middle-class democracy had been growing since the nineteenth century.[15] Class privileges persisted throughout Western Europe (especially in Britain); family and gender relationships were modeled along patriarchal, authoritarian lines. Morality was still being regulated by traditional authority, namely, through church dogma in Catholic Southern Europe and through illiberal civil and criminal codes in Republican France and Protestant Northern Europe. Culture was elitist and fiercely guarded against the masses, while access to higher education was selective and mostly limited to young male members of the elite. People neither enjoyed nor sought social or geographical mobility.[16]

In the late 1940s, swaths of Western and Northern Europe were still locked in traditional agrarian ways. The exceptions were the industrial core areas of Britain and Central and Western Europe, which had already been transformed by nineteenth-century industrialization. Hundreds and thousands of villages in central and southern France and Italy, as well as Scandinavia, were barely connected to the outside world.[17] By the second half of the 1970s, however, this old Europe had practically vanished. People were now linked to the realms of national and international culture by new means of communication, especially television, which had caught on during the 1960s. They also were more closely connected to each other across national borders, thanks to the increasing trade and exchange among capitalist economies of the European Economic Community. Whereas in the late 1940s the United States seemed to be ahead in the race toward consumer society by almost a decade, these differences had leveled out by the time of the oil price shock in 1973–1974.

The postwar economic boom was the prime catalyst for dramatic social change.[18] By the 1970s, Western European societies were much more democratic. As Western Europeans were reaping the fruits of prosperity, their life expectations changed. To some extent, the lifestyle revolutions can be explained with the help of a generational paradigm. An important agent was the unusually large population bulge of the baby boom generation, which made both Eastern and Western Europe younger than ever before in history. Because these young people came of age during an equally unprecedented economic boom, they commanded substantial economic resources, which further fuelled an expanding consumer society. With decreasing working hours, elongating school enrollments, and more free time, young people had the time and money available to enjoy the promises of consumer society. Although consumption could be used to set up new distinctions, its inherent democratizing tendencies were obvious.[19]

A good example of the democratization of Western societies is the much maligned sexual revolution, which became such a prominent feature of the years around 1968.[20] As we now know, sexual liberation primarily served to broaden the consensus about how sexuality could be addressed in public; sexual practices did not change that much. Whereas nudity or even open depictions of sexual acts had long been part of the Western artistic heritage, access had been perceived as limited to a select few. As the 1959 British *Lady Chatterley* case made abundantly clear, sexual liberation was as much about class barriers as it was about sex. On balance, sexual liberation concerned "free speech for all," that is, public debates about and/or representations of sex, with the public now stretching well beyond the narrow confines of the elite. As social scientific data suggest, sexual habits remained stable, with most people living in long-term monogamous relationships. In fact, expectations of fidelity increased and were now applied to both partners. Earlier this was not often the case, as men were allowed more license than women. Furthermore, sex was democratized in the sense that both sides could now expect pleasure. Finally, marriage was no longer a socially mandated precondition to sexual intercourse.

Because these societal and cultural transformations followed similar paths throughout Western Europe, contemporary observers—including many critics of the emerging consumer ("mass") society—discovered strong connections between various countries. Often these changes were debated in reference to American influences, harking back to the old nineteenth-century Tocquevillian paradigm. Western European observers were influenced by key American sociological treatises such Dwight MacDonald's cultural pessimistic critique of consumer society or the more affirmative texts such as John Kenneth Galbraith's *The Affluent Society* and Daniel Bell's *The End of Ideology*. It was the fear of American influences and cultural Americanization that provided the backdrop for a pan-European debate, against which the New Leftist terminology of democratization would slowly evolve.[21]

As decades of research have shown, the movements of 1968 did not emerge from nowhere but, rather, were part of these long-term transformations. The preceding decades of social change were a necessary precondition for the movements of 1968, which could not have happened if societies had not already loosened up. They also came on the top of an ongoing, extra-parliamentarian political mobilization that had started in the 1950s. Social scientific data demonstrate that from the early 1960s, people (especially young people) had become more interested in politics. Political interest reached an all-time high in the late 1960s and early 1970s.[22]

Specific movements paved the way throughout the Western world. In Britain, the Netherlands, Scandinavia, and West Germany, the Campaign for Nuclear Disarmament (CND) was an important precursor. It helped discredit the establishment and set the tone by providing successful examples of civil disobedience and helping with the establishment of networks on which the more spectacular 1968 wave of protests would build.[23] In France, the anticolonial struggle in Algeria served a similar catalyst function,[24] whereas in the United States, it was the Civil Rights Movement and the Vietnam War. Thus, social change and a growing societal mobilization set the stage for what was to come during the second half of the 1960s.

The Western New Left and Participatory Democracy

Against this backdrop of overall societal democratization and political mobilization, a New Left critique of established democracy emerged. In part, this new branch of Marxism was a reaction to disillusionment over Stalinism after the Hungarian uprising of 1956; to a larger extent, it was an intellectual reaction to postwar prosperity and the changing nature of Western societies and economies, which by 1968 were rooted much less in industrial production than twenty years before. In the late 1960s, the outlines of the new postindustrial service economy became visible. A group of French industrial sociologists, many of whom were teaching at "new universities" such as Nanterre, tried to understand these developments by focusing their inquiries on the technicians, midlevel managers, engineers, and other well-educated members of what they called "the new working class" (*nouvelle class ouvrière*).[25]

Thus, the subject of social change was redefined. It no longer resided with the working class but with the intelligentsia and skilled, white-collar groups. Being better educated and better fed than their nineteenth-century predecessors, the "new working classes" showed an interest in topics beyond workplace democracy (*Mitbestimmung, autogestion*). As the French sociologist André Gorz stated, they were more inclined to focus on larger social and cultural concerns: "The cultural battle for a new conception of man, of life, education, work, and civilization, is the precondition for the success of all other battles for socialism because it establishes their meaning."[26] This highly influential view of 1968 as being grounded in new white-collar groups, whose importance had grown because of the postwar boom, seemed to be vindicated by the Paris May in particular. This new working-class thesis and the student protest provided a template for later reinterpretations of 1968 as cultural revolution.

Within New Left theory, the cultural sphere took precedence, although political revolution was still seen as a necessary and obtainable reality. Movements, not parties, were meant to heighten the awareness of the general public by "direct action" and provocation. Focusing on the early writings of Marx and more recent theoretical approaches such as psychoanalysis or existentialism, the New Left stressed alienation rather than exploitation.[27] Herbert Marcuse explained the difficulties in precipitating change in real existing Western democracy with its almost unlimited capacity to tolerate dissent. He stressed a built-in and deeply ingrained "repressive tolerance," which deprived people of their subjectivity and made them unconscious regarding their real situation.[28]

Similar debates can be observed throughout Western Europe and North America.[29] American voices had been deeply shaped by the Leftist German emigration of the 1930s, and specifically members of the Frankfurt School. They competed with British, French, and Italian ideas by authors such as Raymond Williams, Jean-Paul Sartre, and Antonio Gramsci. European (particularly West German) intellectuals and students discovered the heritage of the anti-Nazi emigration of the 1930s.[30] Groups like the Situationist International became interested in the writings of the socialist émigrés. The spread of the unorthodox socialist heritage of the 1920s was clearly magnified through transatlantic channels of communication, which had been established within the framework of youth exchange during the Cold War.[31]

Inspired by the ideas of non-orthodox Leftist thinkers and by critical sociological evaluations of the impact of postwar social change on agents of revolution, the question of democracy and democratization was being recalibrated. Personal fulfillment and self-determination were moving higher on the agenda. Quality-of-life questions and cultural concerns became more prominent. How was personal fulfillment possible in the context of an overbearing consumer society? The latter was perceived not as liberating—as the pop artists of the early and mid-1960s had argued—but as shaped by a highly manipulative "culture industry."[32] Many activists agreed with Marcuse's analysis that the working class had been integrated into the mainstream of society through the means of Cold War anti-Communism, growing productivity, and the lure of consumer society.[33]

Comparative analysis of key texts and demands shows that protest movements all across Western Europe and across the Atlantic demanded democracy in this all-encompassing, "cultural" sense. The question of democracy became more pressing, as it was no longer seen merely as a way to govern, as conservative defenders of parliamentary democracy and the status quo interpreted it. Rather, democracy was a social system in which human beings enjoyed more personal autonomy and better chances of participating in decision-making processes. Terms such as "participatory democracy," "*autogestion*," "*autogestione*," and "*Mitbestimmung*" expressed these demands.[34] In a somewhat contradictory fashion, they combined ideas of personal autonomy and fulfillment with an all-encompassing approach to democracy that made the "private political." In addition, New Leftist critiques of the manipulative tendencies of "real existing democracy" often overlapped with center-left liberal thinkers such as German intellectuals Ralph Dahrendorf and Jürgen Habermas, who had long been demanding a more thorough democratization of society.[35] In West Germany, this question was often tied to coping with the Nazi past; democratization carried the burden of facing German guilt.[36]

Among the Western European protest movements, the term "democracy" thus acquired a very specific meaning that was strikingly different from liberal and conservative usage. It also was markedly dissimilar from the understanding of democracy among the Western European old Left and the Communist parties of the European East (and their Western European fellow travelers). First, as has already become clear, democracy was not limited to the proper functioning of parliamentary institutions. As Johannes Agnoli argued in one of the key critiques of West German democracy, citizens were often excluded from decisions by so-called democratic institutions: "The state had become the legal instrument, to keep the masses from political decisions. It has made political rule into a preserve of more or less closed power elites."[37] Second, it was through a change of society that democracy would be achieved, in its real, all-encompassing and participatory sense. In this sense, the political was not a semi-autonomous sphere of societal action; it was less crucial than social reform. Any organizations, even old Left labor institutions, were seen as impediments to the goals of democratic liberalization. As Gabriel and Daniel Cohn-Bendit demanded during the Paris May, all organizations should be dissolved in a constant revolutionary movement.[38]

Obviously, these demands for an anti-institutional participatory democracy (or "basis democracy" in 1970s terminology) did not lead to an outright transformation of Western European political systems. They were also greeted with a distinct lack of enthusiasm by the leaders of the late Stalinist European East. Still, the question has been asked (and continues to be debated) to what extent the movements of 1968 made democracy a more acceptable proposition for society at large. In hindsight, defenders of "1968" have often argued that during the late 1960s and early 1970s, a Hegelian "list of reasons" was at work.[39] As the argument goes, protagonists of the 1968 protest movements were highly critical of parliamentary democracy. However, in the long run, their demands made Western European societies safe for democracy. In fact, as social scientific data show, democracy became more accepted, especially in the post-fascist democratic governments of continental Europe.[40]

Here, we are faced with a paradox. The radical left (albeit not the majority of those who had taken the streets in 1968) moved away from democratic models into highly authoritarian Maoist, Trotskyite, and Leninist splinter groups, while at the same time conservative critics of the movements of 1968 overcame their uneasiness about Western-style democracy. Faced with the specter of revolution, conservatives now seemed to make their peace with democracy.[41] Did the democratization of Western societies thus happen as a result of the New Leftist anti-authoritarianism of 1968? Did change come from larger social transformations? Or was it in part a reaction to the perceived totalitarianism of the student movement? These questions are still open for historical debate.

The strong anti-institutional, basic democratic impulse of the New Left therefore merits closer inspection. In hindsight, it seems to be linked to the arrival of a new social formation: postmodern society. The anti-authoritarian movements of 1968 were not just opposed to the state; they were suspicious of *any* organizations. The rebels of the French May demanded the dissolution of (left-wing) political parties in a continuous revolutionary movement. In West Germany, the *Subversive Aktion* saw itself as an avant-garde, which by setting mass processes in motion, would make itself superfluous in the end.[42] With their distrust of organized politics, organized interest groups, and organized labor, the nonconformist, civil-libertarian approach of the New Left was well-adapted to a postmodern social formation in which people were less willing to define their personal identity, social contacts, and political loyalties through the filter of all-encompassing, "modern" societal organizations such as churches, parties, or unions.[43]

Given the keen sense for gaining attendance and notoriety through the media, the movements of 1968 also contributed to different styles of political communication. With its general tendency toward self-dramatization and medial staging of protests, 1968 is increasingly being perceived as a catalyst for a different relationship between politics and the media. In fact, in postmodern Western "media democracies," politicians are much more dependent on electronic means of communication. They can no longer rely on individual group loyalty to move political agendas forward. While 1968 did not pave the way into media democracy, it certainly experimented with new forms of communication, which would later be adopted by mainstream politics.[44]

Finally, the postmodern political style that slowly emerged during the wake of 1968 received another important impulse from the left-libertarian, anti-authoritarian democratic movements of the late 1960s. Although they failed in realizing the goal of all-out revolution (which had not been shared by all, yet probably by a majority, of the protesters), Western Europe and North America saw the emergence of a whole range of social movements and civic groups that focused on grass-roots politics. Centered on quality-of-life issues such as product and food safety, health, environmental care, and peace, the movements of 1968 directly fed into the myriad new social (and often single-issue) movements that sprang up all over Western societies during the late 1960s and 1970s.

In Western Europe, 1968 was thus the product of long-term social and cultural transformation, which for a brief historic moment seemed to blaze the path toward a new revolution. Building on postwar economic miracles, the 1968 cultural and political revolutionaries made good on the promises of consumer society and have therefore rightly been dubbed the "children of Marx and Coca-Cola."[45] Yet in the political sense, they challenged an order that was rapidly waning. The rebels of 1968 stormed barricades that had been abandoned by their former defenders. They precipitated a political backlash in many Western democracies. Indeed, judged against their intentions and in a narrow political sense, the revolutionary impulse of 1968 might even have been counterproductive. Yet in the cultural realm, its radical tendencies spilled over into mainstream societies and helped to further democratize the West in the larger societal sense of the term. In questions of style and in the peculiar terms of how politics are being carried out, 1968 had a more lasting impact. New ways to communicate were opened up, and politics moved out of the old organizational framework of parties and unions. The private and the political became more aligned, and even conservatives would now occasionally take democracy to the streets.

East Central European Workers' Democracy

Western European protesters were highly conscious of the simultaneous East Central European freedom struggles of 1968. Before a court in Paris, the young Franco-German exchange student Daniel Cohn-Bendit, the student leader of Nanterre, identified himself as Kuroń-Modzelewski, using the names of two leading Polish dissidents. Kuroń's and Modzelewski's 1965 "Open Letter to the Party" became one of the most widely circulated texts among the students of the Sorbonne in May 1968.[46] Rudi Dutschke, West Germany's most famous revolutionary, who was himself a former refugee from the GDR, traveled to Prague in late 1968 to attend a Christian peace conference that attracted youth from both Eastern and Western Europe. In a lecture at Charles University, Dutschke reminded the Czech audience that he rejected representative government as well as Stalinism because both led to the depoliticization of the masses. According to Dutschke, the Prague Spring had kindled the hope of creating a "producers' democracy" leading to a true "democratic self organization of the masses."[47]

Western observers of 1968 sympathized with the East Central European freedom struggles because they perceived them as being of a similar kind. As the preface to the English edition of the "Open Letter to the Party" suggested, "the worldwide wave of protests, rallies, marches, sit-ins, and battles with the police have brought consternation to the capitalist establishment of the West and the bureaucratic establishment of the deformed workers' states of the East, they have brought hope and inspiration to truly revolutionary socialist forces everywhere."[48] Likewise, the French introduction stressed that Kuroń and Modzelewski were revolutionary Marxists who had complete confidence in the working class, condemned any move to the ideological right, and were most of all concerned with an anti-bureaucratic proletarian revolution. In keeping in line with the general infatuation with Trotskyism and non-orthodox Marxism/Leninism, Western interpreters saw the Eastern European uprisings as following the tradition of anti-Stalinist socialist thought of the 1930s.[49]

Indeed, Kuroń and Modzelewski adamantly opposed "parliamentary regimes." They favored the liberation "of a large group of countries from capitalist domination." Yet they argued for a "workers' democracy" that granted autonomy at the local and factory level, allowed unions independent of the state, and channeled more resources from heavy industry into consumption—a conventional goal that had been on the agenda of many of regimes since the mid-1960s. In addition, they demanded an end to the political police, a standing army, censorship, and one-party rule.[50] In a similar fashion, the resolution that was passed at the Fourth Czechoslovak Writers' Congress in the summer of 1967 was in line with Alexander Dubček's "Third Way." It did not argue for sweeping "counterrevolution," as Soviet leader Leonid Brezhnev alleged.

Therefore, East Central European critical intellectuals such as the Czech writer Vaclav Havel and his Polish counterpart Adam Michnik had by no means been original adherents of Western-style democracy.[51] This would happen only later, during the 1980s. Concepts like "freedom" and "democracy" could still be perceived outside the post-1989 triumphalist Western notion of these terms; they were still imbued with a thorough socialist meaning. In fact, it was precisely because Dubček tried to square the circle by envisioning a less centralized, open, and liberal form of socialism that the Prague Spring turned out to be so contagious throughout the Eastern bloc, including in the GDR.[52]

Thus, it is only in hindsight that crushing the Prague Spring in August of 1968 rendered the idea of a "third way" of a democratic "socialism with a human face" obsolete. Eastern European opposition figures like Alexander Solzhenitsyn continued to serve as an inspiration to Western observers for many years to come.[53] Whereas some members of the Polish and Czechoslovak revolutionary generation of 1968 no longer saw an alternative to "going West," either in the literal sense of the term if they were being expelled by Communist regimes or in the figurative meaning of the phrase, most remained committed socialists almost all the way to the end. Havel and others continued to draw a clear distinction between Socialism and Communism. Havel's Socialism was "a temperament, a nonconformist state of the spirit, an anti-establishment orientation, and aversion to philistines, and an interest in the wretched and humiliated." Much of his critique would have applied to aspects of Western society and culture as well. Originally Havel did not aspire to bring neoliberalism and capitalism to the East; in this sense he is similar to Lech Walesa in the 1980s.[54]

Whereas Communist regimes managed to suppress civic unrest for almost two more decades, their critics lost faith in communism's ability to reform itself.[55] Working through the established Communist Parties was no longer an option after Prague 1968. Though Alexander Dubček received a hero's welcome on Wenceslas Square during the Czech "Velvet Revolution" of 1989, it was obvious that he, the failed leader of the Prague Spring and the proponent of "Socialism with a human face," would not lead his country into the post-Communist era. Rather, that role would go to the most prominent speaker of the 1970s dissidents, Vaclav Havel. Although the democratic impulse of 1968 had not led to an immediate overthrow of the existing order, its long-term consequences were nonetheless remarkable. During the 1980s, the dissidents of the Polish March and the Prague Spring would emerge as the voices that kept the democratic dream alive. In 1989 Havel, Kuroń, Michnik, and other intellectual protagonists of 1968 would become the driving forces behind the peaceful revolutions in East Central Europe.

Conclusion

In retrospect, 1968 has often been linked to the overall democratization of Western societies. In addition, in West Germany, the 1969 "change of power"—when the twenty-year reign of conservative Christian Democrats ended and centrist-Social Democrat Willy Brandt became chancellor—was often seen as being linked to 1968.[56] Yet here, as in France, where de Gaulle would step down in 1969, the changing of the guard was engineered entirely within the realm of traditional party politics. With the notable exception of West Germany, where the change of parliamentary majority was long overdue, the moderate, democratic right either strengthened its grip on power or returned to office. This was the case especially in the United States and Britain, where the conservative, neoliberal impulse became dominant with the 1979 "Thatcher Revolution."[57] In the long run, and combined with larger social and economic shifts such as those engendered by the 1973 oil price shock, the democratic critique of 1968 contributed to the intellectual undermining of New Deal liberalism and the social democratic Keynesian welfare state that had become such a prominent feature of Western politics since 1945.

Rather than precipitating a shift of established politics to the left, 1968 contributed to a conservative backlash. By the late 1970s, the social-democratic impulse of the 1950s and 1960s had been nearly exhausted, although it remained influential well into the 1980s and 1990s. Furthermore, in hindsight it is clear that the right was not unaffected by the changes of the Sixties. The patriarchal, authoritarian "Grandpa conservatism" of Western European postwar leaders such as Adenauer, Spinelli, and de Gaulle was dead; conservatives became more liberal, modern, and democratic in the broader sense. New conservative leaders such as Germany's Helmut Kohl or

Britain's Margaret Thatcher initially pretended to turn the clocks back to the 1950s. In fact, they had learned from their adversaries and employed many of the techniques that the movements of 1968 had pioneered, including a more direct, "democratic" approach to the media. In Germany, the conservative Christian Democratic Union experienced a thorough democratization of its decision-making bodies.[58] Similarly, Britain's Conservative Party abolished many privileges class conveyed. Thus, the leftist challenge of 1968 seems to have changed the Right as well.[59]

Furthermore, it must be stressed that although 1968 was about democracy, neither East Central nor Western European movements came out in support of centrist liberal, Western-style, representative democracy. To the contrary, by challenging the respective orders, the protagonists hoped to introduce a more wholesome, all-encompassing idea of democracy—worker's democracy in the case of the East, participatory and basic democracy in the West. Therefore, the democratic idea of 1968 was opposed to the real, existing, parliamentary, representative democracy of the West. The movements of 1968 had no place for representative democracy, which many leading protagonists despised and did not accept as "true" democracy at all. Because of its anti-institutionalism, 1968 was opposed to democracy as it existed in Western society. Quite a few of the protagonists came dangerously close to earlier totalitarian impulses, going back to Rousseau or the late Marx.

The 1968 democratization narrative thus rings hollow if we narrowly focus on the original intentions of the protagonists. From their point of view, "pluralism" was a thinly disguised ideological veil that kept capitalist exploitation in place. For the same reason, their basic democratic model was opposed to liberal representative democracy. Yet, at least in the post-fascist Western core of the old "Carolingian" Western Europe, where liberal democracy was still on historically shaky grounds in the 1960s, the challenge to parliamentary democracy strengthened the much despised "system" and proved that parliamentary democracy could reform itself. In one of the most poignant ironies of 1968, it was the continental conservatives, many of whom (or whose older predecessors) had been skeptical or outright critical of modern mass democracy, who finally came on board. Faced with the challenge of 1968, liberal parliamentary democracy became safe from both right- and left-wing radicalism.[60]

It was only during the 1980s and 1990s that outspoken critics of 1968 came around to accept, albeit grudgingly, "real existing" forms of democracy. This was in part due to the triumph of the Eastern European democratic revolutions of 1989–1990, which strengthened liberal democracy all over Europe. By this time, many of the Western protagonists of 1968 had also learned that gaining access to parliaments enabled them to press their progressive agendas.

This shift was prominently represented by the rise of Green Parties in France, Germany, and Italy, which had a huge impact on the political agendas in the Western world. Over time, the generations of 1968 showed a remarkable pragmatism and capacity for change (or opportunism, as those who remained true to the cause thought indeed). Although the movements of 1968 did not immediately democratize existing institutions, by calling for cultural self-determination, by criticizing authoritarian structures, and by strengthening counter-hegemonic values, in the long run they contributed to strengthening the democratic impulse all over Europe.

Notes

1. Ronald Fraser, *1968: A Student Generation in Revolt* (New York: Pantheon Books, 1987); Carole Fink, Philipp Gassert, and Detlef Junker (eds.), *1968: The World Transformed* (Cambridge: Cambridge University Press, 1998); Ingrid Gilcher-Holtey, ed., *1968: Vom Ereignis zum Gegenstand der Geschichtswissenschaft* (Göttingen: Vandenhoeck and Ruprecht, 1998).
2. For comparisons with 1848–1849, see Charles Tilly, *European Revolutions, 1492–1992* (Oxford: Blackwell, 1993); Sidney Tarrow, *Power in Movement: Social Movements, Collective Action, and Politics* (New York: Cambridge University Press, 1994).
3. Michael Seidmann, *The Imaginary Revolution: Parisian Students and Workers in 1968* (New York: Berghahn Books, 2004), 272.
4. Eric Hobsbawm, *Revolutionaries* (1973) (New York: New Press, 2001), 291.
5. Michael Schneider, *Demokratie in Gefahr? Der Konflikt um die Notstandsgesetze: Sozialdemokratie, Gewerkschaften und intellektueller Protest (1958-1968)* (Bonn: Verlag Neue Gesellschaft, 1986).
6. Herbert Marcuse, "Welche Chancen hat die Revolution?" Interview with *Pardon*, December 1, 1968, reprinted in Wolfgang Kraushaar, ed., *Frankfurter Schule und Studentenbewegung: Von der Flaschenpost zum Molotowcocktail 1946 bis 1995*, vol. 2: Dokumente (Frankfurt/Main: Rogner & Bernhard bei Zweitausendeins), 489; and ibid., "Zur Situation der Neuen Linken," December 4, 1968, 498.
7. Robert Lumley, *States of Emergency: Cultures of Revolt in Italy from 1968 to 1978* (London: Verso, 1990); even in Italy the established order prevailed, with the Communist Party accepting the "Historic Compromise"; see Paul Ginsborg, *A History of Contemporary Italy: Society and Politics, 1943–1988* (New York: Palgrave Macmillan, 2003).
8. Eric Hobsbawm, "1968: A Retrospect," *Marxism Today* (May 1978): 130–36.
9. For Poland, see Andrzey Paczkowski, *The Spring Will Be Ours: Poland and the Poles from Occupation to Freedom* (University Park, PA: Pennsylvania State University Press, 2003), 380–86; for the CSSR, see Tony Judt, *Postwar: A History of Europe Since 1945* (London: Penguin Books, 2005), 436–447.

10. Richard Löwenthal, *Der romantische Rückfall: Wege und Irrwege einer rückwärtsgewandten Revolte* (Stuttgart: Kohlhammer, 1970); Erwin K. Scheuch, ed., *Die Widertäufer der Wohlstandsgesellschaft: Eine kritische Untersuchung der "Neuen Linken" und ihrer Dogmen* (Köln: Markus, 1968).

11. Wilhelm Hennis, *Verfassung und Verfassungswirklichkeit: Eine deutsches Problem* (Tübingen: Mohr, 1968), 35–36.

12. This interpretation went back to Jürgen Habermas, "Die tatsächlichen Erfolge," in *Protestbewegung und Hochschulreform* (Frankfurt/Main: Suhrkamp, 1969), 28ff.; a summary of contemporary and later voices in Ingeborg Villinger, "'Stelle sich jemand vor, wir hätten gesiegt': Das Symbolische der 68er Bewegung und die Folgen," in Gilcher-Holtey, *1968: Vom Ereignis zum Gegenstand*, 246–47.

13. Gilcher-Holtey, "France," 275–276; Robert Inglehart, *The Silent Revolution: Changing Values and Political Styles Among Western Publics* (Princeton, NJ: Princeton University Press, 1977); for a critical evaluation that challenges the idea that the cultural revolution was closely linked to postwar transformation, see Ginsborg, *Italy*, 343.

14. Claus Leggewie, "1968: A Laboratory of Post-Industrial Society: Reasessing the 1960s in Germany," in Fink et al., *1968: The World Transformed*, 277–294.

15. The rise of middle-class democracy is, of course, the theme of Alexis de Tocqueville, *Democracy in America* (Paris, 1835/1840), whose definition of democracy remains in use; see Manfred G. Schmidt, *Demokratietheorien: Eine Einführung*, 3rd rev. ed. (Opladen: Leske + Budrich, 2000), 130–147.

16. For an excellent evaluation of the state of Europe circa 1945, see Eric Hobsbawm, *The Age of Extremes: A History of the World, 1914–1991* (New York: Pantheon, 1994).

17. For an example of rural transformation post- and pre-1960s, see the classic by Lawrence Wylie, *Village in the Vaucluse*, 3rd ed. (Cambridge, MA: Harvard University Press, 1974).

18. On growth, see Barry Eichengreen, "Economy," in Mary Fulbrook, ed., *Europe Since 1945* (Oxford: Oxford University Press, 2001), 95–145.

19. Detlef Siegfried, "Understanding 1968: Youth Rebellion, Generational Change, and Postindustrial Society," in Axel Schildt and Detlef Siegfried, eds., *Between Marx and Coca-Cola: Youth Cultures in Changing European Societies, 1960–1980* (New York: Berghahn Books, 2006), 63.

20. This is one of the big themes masterly explored in great detail by Arthur Marwick, *The Sixties: Cultural Revolution in Britain, France, Italy, and the United States, c. 1958–c.1974* (Oxford: Oxford University Press, 1998).

21. Volker Berghahn, "America and Social Change in Germany," in Detlef Junker et al., eds., *The United States and Germany in the Era of the Cold War: A Handbook*, vol. 1: *1945–1968* (Cambridge: Cambridge University Press, 2001), 495–507.

22. Axel Schildt and Detlef Siegfried, "Introduction: Youth, Consumption, and Politics in the Age of Radical Change," in Schildt/Siegfried, *Marx and Coca-Cola*, 9–10.

23. Lawrence Wittner, "The Nuclear Threat Ignored: How and Why the Campaign Against the Bomb Disintegrated in the Late 1960s," in Fink et al., *1968: The World Transformed*, 439–440.

24. A. Belden Fields, *Student Politics in France: A Study of the Union Nationale des Etudiants des France* (New York: Basic Books, 1970); Ingrid Gilcher-Holtey, *"Die Phantasie an die Macht": Mai 68 in Frankreich* (Frankfurt, Main: Suhrkamp, 1995), 100–104.

25. Serge Mallet, *La nouvelle classe ouvrière* (Paris: Editions du Soil, 1963); André Gorz, *Stratégie ouvrière et néocapitalisme* (Paris: Editions du Soil, 1964); for a summary, see Gerd-Rainer Horn, "The Changing Nature of the European Working Class: The Rise and Fall of the 'New Working Class' (France, Italy, Spain, Czechoslovakia)," in Fink et al., *1968*, 351–71

26. Gorz, *Strategy for Labor* (Boston: Beacon, 1967), 132.

27. Ingrid Gilcher-Holtey, "Kritische Theorie und Neue Linke," in Gilcher-Holtey, *1968: Vom Ereignis zum Gegenstand*, 168–187.

28. Herbert Marcuse, "Repressive Tolerance," in Robert Paul Wolff, Barrington Moore, Jr., and Herbert Marcuse, *A Critique of Pure Tolerance* (Boston: Beacon Press, 1969), pp. 95–137; *One-Dimensional Man* (Boston: Beacon Press, 1964), 7.

29. Maurice Issermann, *If I Had a Hammer: The Death of the Old Left and the Birth of the New Left* (New York: Basic Books, 1987).

30. Claus-Dieter Krohn, "Die Entdeckung des 'anderen Deutschland' in der intellektuellen Protestbewegung der 1960er Jahre in der Bundesrepublik und den Vereinigten Staaten," *Exilforschung* 13 (1995):16–52.

31. Philipp Gassert, "Atlantic Alliances: Cross-Cultural Communication and the 1960s Student Revolution," in Jessica Gienow-Hecht and Frank Schumacher, eds., *Culture and International Relations* (New York: Berghahn Books, 2003): 134–156; Martin Klimke, *The "Other" Alliance: Global Protest and Student Unrest in West Germany and the U.S., 1962–1972* (Princeton, NJ: Princeton University Press, forthcoming 2008).

32. Theodor Adorno and Max Horkheimer, *The Dialectic of Enlightenment* [1944] (London: Verso, 1997), 120–67.

33. Herbert Marcuse, "Vietnam: Analyse eines Exempels," *Neue Kritik* 36/37 (1966): 30–38.

34. Ingrid Gilcher-Holtey, *Die 68er Bewegung: Deutschland, Westeuropa, USA* (Munich: Beck, 2001), 113; the locus classicus for the concept of participatory democracy of course is "The Port Huron Statement" [1962], reprinted in Judith Clavier Albert and Stewart Edward Albert, eds., *The Sixties Papers: Documents of a Rebellious Decade* (New York: Praeger, 1984), 176–96.

35. Paul Nolte, *Die Ordnung der deutschen Gesellschaft: Selbstentwurf und Selbstbeschreibung im 20. Jahrhundert* (Munich: Beck, 2000); Christina von Hodenberg, *Konsens und Krise: Eine Geschichte der westdeutschen Medienöffentlichkeit, 1945–1973* (Göttingen: Wallstein, 2006).

36. Philipp Gassert and Alan Steinweis (eds.), *Coping with the Nazi Past: West German Debates on Nazism and Generational Conflict, 1955–1973* (New York: Berghahn Books, 2006).

37. Johannes Agnoli, "Die Transformation der Demokratie," in Johannes Agnoli and Peter Brückner, eds., *Die Transformation der Demokratie* (Frankfurt: Europäische Verlags-Anstalt, 1968), 7–87.

38. Gabriel and Daniel Cohn-Bendit, *Linksradikalismus—Gewaltkur gegen die Alterskrankheit des Kommunismus* (Reinbek bei Hamburg: Rowohlt, 1968), 270.

39. Konrad H. Jarausch, "Epilogue: 1968 and 1989," Fink, *1968*, 465; Lother Baier et al., eds., *Die Früchte der Revolte: über die Veränderung der politischen Kultur durch die Studentenbewegung* (Berlin: Wagenbach, 1988).

40. Compare Gabriel A. Almond and Sidney Verba, *The Civic Culture: Political Attitudes in Five Nations* (Princeton, NJ: Princeton University Press, 1963) with *The Civic Culture Revisited: An Analytic Study* (Boston: Little, Brown, 1980); Detlef Siegfried, *Time is On My Side: Konsum und Politik in der westdeutschen Jugendkultur der 60er Jahre* (Göttingen: Wallstein, 2006), 443–44.

41. Moritz Scheibe, "Auf der Suche nach der demokratischen Gesellschaft," in *Wandlungsprozess in Westdeutschland: Belastung, Integration, Liberalisierung 1945–1980*, ed. Ulrich Herbert (Göttingen: Wallstein, 2002), 270–75.

42. Wolfang Kraushaar, *1968 als Mythos, Chiffre und Zäsur* (Hamburg: Hamburger Edition, 2000), 232.

43. The term, originally emerging as philosophical critique, goes back to Jean-François Lyotard, *La condition postmoderne: rapport sur le savoir* (Paris: Minuit, 1979), and is now being widely used to describe the emergence of a new social formation.

44. Michael A. Schmidtke, "'1968' und die Massenmedien—Momente europäischer öffentlichkeit," in: Jörg Requate and Martin Schulze Wessel, eds., *Europäische öffentlichkeit: Transnationale Kommunikation seit dem 18. Jahrhundert* (Frankfurt: Campus, 2002), 273–94; Martin Klimke and Joachim Scharloth, eds., *Handbuch 1968 zur Kultur- und Mediengeschichte der Studentenbewegung* (Stuttgart: Metzler, 2007).

45. Schildt/Siegfried, *Between Marx and Coca-Cola*, 1.

46. Jerzy Eisler, "March 1968 in Poland," in Fink et al., *1968: The World Transformed*, 243.

47. Ulrich Chaussy, *Die drei Leben des Rudi Dutschke; Eine Biographie* (Berlin: Christoph Links, 1993), 224–228.

48. *Revolutionary Marxist Students In Poland Speak Out (1964-1968)*, ed. George Lavan Weissman (New York: Merit Publishers, 1968), 2.

49. Ibid., 9–10.

50. Ibid., 74, 77, 83.

51. Paul Berman, *A Tale of Two Utopias: The Political Journey of the Generation of 1968* (New York: Norton, 1996), 224–30; Roger Garaudy, *Le Grand Tournant du Socialisme* (Paris, 1969).

52. Mary Fulbrook, *Anatomy of a Dictatorship: Inside the GDR, 1949–1989* (Oxford: Oxford University Press, 1995), 193; Mark Kramer, "The Czechoslovak Crisis and the Brezhnev Doctrine," in Fink et al., *1968: The World Transformed*, 141–45.

53. Charles Schüddekopf, interview with Heinrich Böll, in Axel Eggebrecht (ed.) *Die zornigen alten Männer: Gedanken über Deutschland seit 1945* (Reinbek: Rowohlt, 1979), 134.

54. Havel quoted in Berman, *Tale*, 224.
55. Armin Mitter and Stefan Wolle, *Untergang auf Raten: Unbekannte Kapitel der DDR-Geschichte* (Munich: Bertelsmann, 1993), 367–70.
56. Arnulf Baring, *Machtwechsel: Die ära Brandt-Scheel* (Stuttgart: DVA, 1982); Manfred Görtemaker, *Geschichte der Bundesrepublik Deutschland: Von der Gründung bis zur Gegenwart* (Munich: Beck, 1999).
57. David Farber, *The Age of Great Dreams: America in the 1960s* (New York: Hill and Wang, 1994); Jonathan Hollowell, ed., *Britain Since 1945* (Malden: Blackwell Publishers, 2003), 48.
58. Frank Bösch, *Macht und Machtverlust: Die Geschichte der CDU* (Munich: DVA, 2001).
59. Judt, *Postwar*, 541–42.
60. Axel Schildt, "'Die Kräfte der Gegenreform sind auf breiter Front angetreten': Zur konservativen Tendenzwende in den Siebzigerjahren," *Archiv für Sozialgeschichte* 44 (2004): 449–78.

Afterword
The Future of 1968's "Restless Youth"

Tom Hayden

On September 4, 1968, CIA director Richard Helms sent President Lyndon Johnson a 233-page report entitled "Restless Youth," only for the eyes of the president and his adviser Walt Rostow, who had requested the analysis. Helms warned the president of "the peculiar sensitivity which attaches to the fact that CIA has prepared a report on student activities both here and abroad." Under American law, the agency was permitted to surveil movements abroad but strictly forbidden to spy on American youth. The director therefore recommended that Johnson authorize the FBI to utilize "more advanced techniques" to investigate young radicals than laws at the time allowed.

The CIA report included France, Germany, Italy, the Netherlands, Poland, and several Arab, African, and Asian countries; it neglected Latin America, except for Argentina. Helms wrote of being "disappointed, as perhaps you will be, by our inability to be more *precise* about the motivation and direction of this worldwide movement," blaming some of the ambiguity on the "somewhat unfocussed nature of the movement itself." He hinted that more investigative techniques or technology might extract "that precision of information which would make a more positive report possible." He did understand, far better than the president, something "new" was in the air. Declassified transcripts show that Johnson was convinced that an international communist conspiracy lay behind the protests, and ordered the CIA to investigate. The most politically important finding of the CIA report was, however, that "There is no convincing evidence of control, manipulation, sponsorship, or significant financial support of student dissidents by any international Communist authority [. . .] the dissidents are contemptuous of the Neanderthal leaderships entrenched in most national communist parties, including the CP/USA."

I was 27 years old as the year 1968 unfolded. When the decade began, I was the first in my family to attend a university, and my non-conformist instincts led me to the campus paper and the sociology department at the

University of Michigan. While pursuing an institutional career, I was a follower of Jack Kerouac as well, whose *On The Road* was published in my senior year, 1957. During that same year, black high school students integrated a high school in Bill Clinton's Little Rock, Arkansas, amidst beatings, insults and federal military protection. Two years later, after I directly encountered black students risking their lives in the South, I became a committed activist.

Like most of my friends, I was feeling that our future was already prepared, and would be only a recycling of the past. I drafted the 1962 manifesto of Students for a Democratic Society, whose opening passage was studied carefully for clues by the CIA: "We are people of this generation, bred in at least modest comfort, housed now in universities, looking uncomfortably to the world we inherit." This was hardly the Communist Manifesto, but a careful statement of middle class anxiety over the world we were inheriting, especially the immediate crisis of racism and, in the near background, the nuclear arms race. While a few of the SDS founders came from Marxist traditions and families, most members of the founding generation were home-grown radicals in the American populist tradition. Our prophets were John Dewey, C. Wright Mills, and J.D. Salinger. Experience was our teacher. Organizing and dialoging with "ordinary people" was our technique. Participatory democracy was the name of the process. As we could not vote, direct action and expression were the avenues.

Most of the early SDS believed that movements from "below" would catalyze a liberalism which had been neutered by Cold War anti-communism, that the civil rights and student movements would energize the mainstream to tackle poverty and structural unemployment, that the military budget could be diverted to much-needed peacetime investments at home and abroad. Instead, we were betrayed by the party of our elders, the Democrats, who promised "no wider war" in 1964, only to draft hundreds of thousands of us by 1965. The Vietnam War, an extension of Cold War thinking, became the dominant feature of our lives in the second half of the Sixties. Civil rights reforms devolved into hundreds of black ghetto uprisings. Dr. King was rebuked by the *New York Times* for daring to criticize the war. Chicanos finally achieved recognition for rural farmworkers but were treated brutally when they opposed the war. Flower power and free speech evolved into resistance against police guarding military induction centers. Radical consciousness was spurred not only by Vietnam and racism, but by the stunning fate of reformers I had known: John F. Kennedy, Martin Luther King, Robert Kennedy, and many lesser-known figures. The killings seeming to escalate and concentrate in 1968.

Now I was some sort of revolutionary, improvising in the vortex. I began 1968 at a tri-continental Congress in Havana, shortly after the killing of Che Guevara in Bolivia. The Tet Offensive erupted that month. I gave up community organizing in Newark in the face of the war's escalation. Suddenly I found myself leading a building occupation at Columbia University. Then, with King and Kennedy dead, I went through five days of street confrontations, two beatings and two arrests at the Chicago Democratic Party convention, and found myself sitting in someone's living room watching civil rights marchers in Northern Ireland. They were singing "We Shall Overcome," and it was a revelation. The anthem of our movement was universalized, and yet I knew so little about these young Irish radicals. My Irish heritage – beginning with the Famine generation – had been effectively sanitized from my memory behind the lace curtains of assimilation.

I began paying more personal attention to the global dimension of the Sixties. I understood and broadly identified the revolutions in Cuba and Vietnam, but who were these people like myself all across Europe? My contacts with European movements were indirect at best. I had interviewed U.S. and Vietnamese parties to the Paris peace talks in summer 1968, which exposed me to the student-led revolution then occurring in France. I also spent some time in Czechoslovakia in late 1967 at meetings with the Vietnamese, which led me to ties with a hopeful student underground before the Soviet invasion of August 1968, just before the events of Chicago. All that was clear was that a "generation of '68" was everywhere, across all boundaries and curtains, from the lace curtain variety to the iron kind. One could not help but feel that an inevitable historical force was playing out, that no Machiavellians seemed able to stop it.

Then, as it reached its peak of frenzy, about 1969-70, one could feel the tide begin to turn. The movements themselves were convulsed by division. The Marxist sectarians were not dead at all, merely hatching in the garbage we left unattended. After factions ripped its body apart, SDS was closed down as "too bourgeois." No one could transcend the inevitability of the women's movement as it shredded the male hierarchies. The counterculture was shocked by Altamont[1] and Manson.[2] Drug euphoria devolved into the dark trips of paranoia, depression, and schizophrenia. Thousands of veterans came home with bad papers and strung out. Richard Nixon – wasn't he the man we thought we dumped in 1960, the year it all began? – soon became president of the United States.

And yet there was a double paradox. First, as the Sixties organizations were disintegrated under factionalism and COINTELPRO[3], the *spontaneous* Sixties movements were exploding as never before. In the five years after 1968, these rapid changes unfolded like domestic dominoes:

- The Vietnam War began to end in 1969 and imploded in the years 1973-75.
- Nixon and his vice president, Spiro Agnew, were driven from office.
- The compulsory military draft was ended.

- The War Powers Act was passed as a curb on the imperial presidency.
- The Democratic Party and national election rules were radically reformed.
- Earth Day arose apparently from nowhere, historical environmental laws were passed, and the planet Earth was seen in a photo for the very first time.
- After 25 years of failing passage, the 18-year-old vote became law.
- Black studies, Latino studies, women's studies, and environmental studies were integrated into the curriculum of high schools and universities.
- Everyone was humming The Yellow Submarine and quoting Allen Ginsberg.
- Several national blue-ribbon commissions (the Kerner report on the ghettos, the Scranton report on the campuses, the Walker report on Chicago) seemed to vindicate the New Left analysis of causes and solutions.

It is important to remember these reforms in the blurred and contentious struggles to recall the Sixties. To say they were merely superficial cooptation is to miss the significance of the sacrifices made and the empowerment gained for millions of people. If they were only superficial reforms, why did the state oppose them so ferociously for so long? Furthermore, to say the Sixties were about only a "cultural" shift rather than a political one is to ignore the lasting legal, regulatory and institutional significance of these reforms. But one cannot read the list without wondering where it all has gone. Are we still restless, or pacified, or in between? This is the second paradox: the Sixties largely ended when our most popular demands succeeded. When order was reformed, order was restored.

From all this experience, I understood a model of social change, which I think of as a persistent struggle between social movements and Machiavellians. Before the beginning, there are hidden memories, legacies of social movements beneath the icy silence of conforming apathy. Then the shoots of present and future movements unexpectedly disturb the peace: the 1955 Montgomery bus boycott, or the Hungarian Revolution of 1956. Gaining momentum, the movements appear suddenly at the margins, among the structurally disenfranchised. The Machiavellians are surprised, react first with repression but also with probes promising cooptation and gradual and, at first, token reform. The movements touch chords of memory in the mainstream, continue to grow through transformative moments (for example, the shooting of an innocent person), and face their own divisions between the radicalized and the pragmatic. As their core ideas reach the mainstream and are accepted by majority opinion, the Machiavellians splinter over whether to grant reforms once thought beyond the possible. As the reforms are achieved, the mass base of the movement subsides, leaving the radical elements stranded and quarreling. The counter-revolution becomes intense as the moderate Machiavellians are perceived to betray the cause of whatever supremacy is at stake (white over black and brown, men over women, colonists over natives, and so on). The once-radical reforms become the new status quo, the counter-movement is contained, the pragmatists become a new elite, the Machiavellian order is renewed, and the conflict continues on the battlefield of memory. In this model, reform is another term for the moment of synthesis in dialectics.

This is a multi-class model, not a Manichean single-class one. It incorporates the natural world as a revision of both capitalist and social models of political economy. It allows for the possibilities of revolution and counter-revolution but only as extreme and temporary cases. This model emphasizes social movements as more important forces of history rather than personalities, parties or social movement organizations. On the organizational level, the most important actors are catalytic groups more than bureaucratic ones. Social movements arise at the margins but successful ones always eventually penetrate the institutions, making inside-outside strategies more useful than simply oppositional ones (this, I believe, is perhaps what Rudi Dutschke was implying with his concept of the "long march through the institutions").[4]

In my view, the Sixties may be fading, but are far from over. Even Bill Clinton thinks that the basic dividing line in American politics is between those with a generally favorable view of the Sixties phenomenon (who tend to be Democrats) and those who are still attempting to erase the achievements of the Sixties altogether (the neo-conservatives, for example). To quote Clinton is not to define him as a Sixties radical, but as a Sixties pragmatist and opportunist, who began as a war resister and ended by bombing the Balkans. Nevertheless, his affections lie with the Sixties, and the right wing has demonized him as an example of all that went wrong with our generation. More precisely, his is an example of what happens when the individual will to power competes with and precedes the desire to change values and priorities. As of this writing, he and his wife Hillary, who was an observer in Chicago in 1968 and wrote her senior thesis on radical community organizing (within the system), may be the last members of our generation to win and hold these high offices. What then will be the Sixties legacy?

I think it is crucial to realize that starting in 2010, at the fiftieth anniversary of everything that happened in the Sixties, the turning point will lay in the battle over memory. The current attention to the fortieth-anniversaries of events – the books, films, and media attention to 1968 for example – will then pale before the relentless re-examination of all the events – local, national, global – that occurred in that incredible decade. Only then will the Sixties, like the Thirties before, be ready for the graveyard both literally and historically. The cultural discourse over the meaning of the fiftieth anniversary will lie between three broad views:

- those who want to restore and revitalize the Sixties heritage to propel future social movements;
- those who want to bury the Sixties to make the world safe for their various supremacist ideologies;
- those who want to manage the stories of the Sixties to prove that the institutions always reform themselves and prevail.

The question is, what side will we be on?

I strongly embrace the first narrative, not to dwell in the past glories of social movements but as a sustaining thread between past, present and future. I regret that I entered the Sixties movements shorn of any consciousness of previous social movements. I am reassured by the persistence of Sixties consciousness into the 21st century. For example, a recent study of the American movement against the Iraq War found that anti-war protesters are concentrated among the young (18 to 27) and the old (46 to 67).[5] This means to me that the anti-Vietnam spirit never died completely but went underground in American culture, surfacing once again during Iraq in full support of a new generation of radicals and activists, many of whom have cultural or family roots in the Sixties but original visions of their own.

In Europe there may be a similar pattern of resistance to Iraq, American imperialism and especially corporate neo-liberalism, not only among the young, but among the generations who battled against empire and for socialism, labor rights, health insurance and other democratic reforms of the market aimed at insuring human dignity. In Latin America, the generation that supported Che – now joined this year in global commemoration of his martyrdom – has defeated dictatorship and seen a succeeding generation come to political power, propelled by radical social movements, to resist the destruction of democratically chosen social safeguards in the name of US-led corporate free trade.

All across the world, the drama, contradictions and dangers of the Cold War are being recycled in a Manichean notion of the War on Terrorism with unlimited budgets, unlimited boundaries, and unlimited secrecy brothers. The European people, with their historical experience, may be best suited to devise serious alternatives to the doomed future prophesied by Machiavellians with vested interests in their so-called "long war." Sooner of later, the new generations will question and resist the programmed future of counter-terrorism, economic privatization, environmental chaos, and sordid alliances justified in the name of this War.

Above all, Europeans may help us chart the most peaceful transition away from imperialism and empire. By all measures, the Europeans – along with the Canadians and Japanese – are models for America that show there can be an improved quality of life after Empire. We are living in a time of epochal transition from the uni-polar model of empire (whether the empire of Capital or that of the United States) to a more realistic, pluralistic model of a multi-polar world, influenced in turn by a third model that derives from the Sixties, a model of democratic social movements capable of both influencing their nation states for the better while creating new cultural norms – on human rights and global warming, for example – that can hold both nation state and multinational corporation accountable. This third model, or participatory democracy from below, needs to gain force and go much deeper, towards an enforceable living wage standard and corporate accountability, for example. But we are seeing a growing global struggle between expanding the rights gained in the Sixties (and the Thirties before) and the contraction of those rights in the name of market, militaristic, and theological fundamentalisms.

The future of the Sixties therefore lies ahead, somewhere between survival and oblivion.

Notes

1. Altamont was the San Francisco Bay Area site of a 1969 Rolling Stones concert where the Hells' Angels beat a black man to death in front of the stage while the Stones were singing "Sympathy with the Devil." The Stones were heroes of the counter-culture, and many fantasized that the Angels were potential revolutionaries.
2. Charles Manson and his communal "family" brutally murdered the actress Sharon Tate at her Los Angeles home for inexplicable reasons. Jerry Rubin and Bernadine Dohrn, among others, had made statements fancifully identifying with the Manson "tribe" at various times.
3. COINTELPRO was the FBI's counter-intelligence program unleashed against anti-war, black, Latino and radical groups, including leaders like Rev. Martin Luther King. COINTEL consisted of deploying undercover agents and paid informants to spread false and inflammatory rumors, incite militant rhetoric and action, and generally disrupt or discredit groups the FBI considered threats to the status quo. Among others, I was targeted to be "neutralized" in a May 1968 FBI memo.
4. See the chapter by Martin Klimke in this book.
5. Michael T. Heaney and Fabio Rojas, "Partisans, Nonpartisans, and the Anti-war movement in the United States," American Politics Research, Sage Publications (http://apr.sagepub.com/cgi/content/abstract/35/4/431).

About the Authors

Timothy S. Brown teaches history at Northeastern University in Boston, Massachusetts. He is the author of *Bolsheviks, Beefsteaks and Brownshirts: A Cultural History of the Radical Extremes in the Weimar Republic* (forthcoming). He is currently at work on a book entitled *1968: West Germany in the World*.

Madeleine Davis is lecturer in politics at Queen Mary, University of London. Relevant publications include "The Marxism of the British New Left" (Journal of Political Ideologies 2006;11[3]) and "Labourism and the New Left" (John Callaghan, Steve Fielding, and Steve Ludlam, eds., *Interpreting the Labour Party: Approaches to Labour Politics and History*. Manchester: Manchester University Press, 2003). She is currently writing a book on the British New Left.

Michael J. Frey is a Ph.D. student at the Ruhr-Universität Bochum. His thesis focuses on the transnational relations of student movements in the early 1960s in the United States and Germany.

Stefan Garsztecki was born in Bergheim, Germany. He studied political science, history, and geography in Bonn (MA), Trier (PhD), and Poznań. He currently works at the Department for East and Central European Studies at the University of Bremen. His main research topics are political culture and the transformation processes in Poland and other countries in the region.

Philipp Gassert is DAAD Visiting Associate Professor of History at the University of Pennsylvania in Philadelphia. He is the author of numerous books and articles on postwar German and European history as well as American and International history, including *Amerika im Dritten Reich: Ideologie, Propaganda und Volksmeinung 1933–1945* and *1968: The World Transformed* (edited with Carole Fink and Detlef Junker).

Ingrid Gilcher–Holtey is professor of contemporary history at the University of Bielefeld, associated member of the Centre de sociologie européenne (CSE/MSH–Paris), and visiting professor at St. Antony's College, Oxford. Her research focuses on the history of social movements, intellectual history, and the history and sociology of the European literary field. Her main publications include *1968—Vom Ereignis zum Gegenstand der Geschichtswissenschaft* (ed., 1998), *"Die Phantasie an die Macht." Mai 68 in Frankreich* (1995, 2001), *Die 68er Bewegung Deutschland, Westeuropa, USA* (2003, 2005), and *Zwischen den Fronten. Positionskämpfe europäischer Intellektueller im 20. Jahrhundert* (2006).

Agata Grzenia was born in Poland. She has studied German and Slavic philology at the Ruhr University of Bochum and at the University of Cracow since 2001. In 2004, she obtained a Bachelor of Arts. She also works as a translator and is involved in German and Polish cross-cultural work and dialogue of reconciliation.

Dorothea Hauser was born in Heidelberg, Germany. She is a historian and author based until recently in Paris, now in Berlin. Publications on terrorism in West Germany and Western Europe include *Baader und Herold. Beschreibung eines Kampfes* (1997, 1998, 2007) and "Deutschland, Italien, Japan: Die ehemaligen Achsenmächte und der Terrorismus der siebziger Jahre" (in Wolfgang Kraushaar, ed., *Die RAF und der linke Terrorismus*, Hamburg, 2006).

Thomas Hecken, PhD, is assistant professor for German philology at Ruhr-Universität Bochum. His publications include *Theorien der Populärkultur* (Bielefeld, 2007), *Avantgarde und Terrorismus* (Bielefeld, 2006), *Gegenkultur und Avantgarde 1950–1960* (Tübingen, 2006), and *Populäre Kultur* (Bochum, 2006).

Thomas Ekman Jørgensen was born in Copenhagen, Denmark. He studied history in Copenhagen, Berlin, and Florence, where he finished his PhD on the Danish and Swedish Left in 2004. He has published extensively on the 1968, the New Left, the communist parties in Scandinavia, and youth movements during the First World War.

Boris Kanzleiter was born in Stuttgart, Germany. He is an historian and a publicist. He is currently working on a PhD on 1968 in Yugoslavia and lives in Belgrade and Berlin.

Martin Klimke is a research fellow at the Heidelberg Center for American Studies at the University of Heidelberg and currently a postdoctoral fellow at the German Historical Institute in Washington, DC. He is the coeditor of a handbook on the cultural and media history of the West German student movement of the 1960s and is coordinator of the international Marie Curie research network *European Protest Movements Since 1945*, supported by the European Commission. His most recent book is *The "Other" Alliance: Global Protest and Student Unrest in West Germany and the U.S., 1962–1972* (Princeton University Press, forthcoming).

Kostis Kornetis was born in Salonica, Greece. He studied History and Political Science in Munich, War Studies in London, and Film Studies in New York. He earned his PhD from the European University Institute, Florence, with a thesis on the Greek and Spanish student movements of the 1960s and 1970s. He is currently an Assistant Professor of History at Brown University.

Jan Kurz was born in 1969 in Würzburg, Germany. He studied history and Jewish studies in Freiburg, Heidelberg, Bielefeld, and Fiesole, where he wrote his PhD thesis on the student movement in Italy. His thesis was published in 2001 (Cologne: SH-Verlag). His research concentrates on the Italian Student Movement of 1968 as well as on youth movements during the Second World War. He lives and works as publisher in Hamburg.

Holger Nehring is a lecturer in Contemporary European History at the University of Sheffield. He has published widely on the transnational history of protest movements in post–World War II Europe and is currently working on two monographs: *The Politics of Security: The British and West German Protests against Nuclear Weapons and the Social History of the Cold War, 1957–1964* and *The Last Battle of the Cold War: Peace Movements and German Politics during the 1980s*.

Niall ó Dochartaigh is a college lecturer in Political Science and Sociology at the National University of Ireland, Galway. He is the author of *From Civil Rights to Armalites: Derry and the Birth of the Irish Troubles* (Cork University Press, 1997; Palgrave, 2005)

Niek Pas has been an assistant professor at the Institute for Media Studies, University of Amsterdam, since 2005. In 2003 he completed a PhD thesis on protest movements in the Netherlands in the 1960s, entitled *Imaazje! De verbeelding van Provo (1965–1967)* (Amsterdam, Wereldbibliotheek, 2003), which was an inquiry into the international dimension of Provo by focusing on its relationship with the mass media. Niek Pas studied Political History and French Literature at Utrecht University and at the Institut d'études Politiques, Paris. Other major publications, forthcoming, include a handbook of French History and a monograph about the perception of the Algerian War in the Netherlands (1954–1962).

Jan Pauer was born in Prague and is a historian and research fellow at the Research Center for East European Studies at the University of Bremen, Germany. From 1990 to 1993, he was a member of the historians commission chartered by the Czechoslovakian government to analyze the events of 1967–1971 in Czechoslovakia. His research concentrates on political culture in both the Czech and Slovakian Republic, cultures of law, transformation processes after 1989, German–Czech relations, opposition movements in Eastern Europe, and politics of memory. He is the author of *Prag 1968—Der Einmarsch des Warschauer Paktes. Hintergründe, Planung, Durchführung* (Bremen, 1995; Temmen, Praha, 2004; Argo).

Şerban Liviu Pavelescu is a senior researcher at the Institute for Political Studies of Defense and Military History of the Romanian Ministry of Defense. He is also a PhD candidate in political science at the Institute d'Etudes Politiques de Paris.

Nicole Peter studied history in Zurich and Hamburg. She holds a master's degree in History from the University of Zurich. The main subjects of her researches are the Swiss left-wing movement and collective identities.

Corina L. Petrescu holds a PhD in German Studies from the University of Wisconsin–Madison. Her first book entitled *Subversive Spaces in National Socialist Germany* is forthcoming with Peter Lang.

Christopher Rootes is a professor of Environmental Politics and Political Sociology and the director of the Centre for the Study of Social and Political Movements at the University of Kent at Canterbury. Joint editor of the journal *Environmental Politics*, he edited *The Green Challenge: The Development of Green Parties in Europe* (with D. Richardson; Routledge 1995), *Environmental Movements: Local, National and Global* (Cass, 1999), *Environmental Protest in Western Europe* (Oxford, 2003, 2007), and *Acting Locally: Local Environmental Mobilizations and Campaigns* (Routledge, 2008).

Joachim Scharloth is an assistant professor at the department of German at the University of Zurich, Switzerland, and visiting professor at the University of Freiburg, Germany. He is the coeditor of a handbook on the cultural and media history of the West German student movement of the 1960s and coedited a volume and a collection of primary sources on the Zurich summer of 1968. His most recent book is a study on the influence of the 1968 movement on the culture of daily life in West Germany (forthcoming). Furthermore, he is scientist-in-charge of the international Marie Curie research network *European Protest Movements Since 1945* supported by the European Commission.

Kristina Schulz is an historian. She did her PhD on women's movements in the 1960s and 1970s in France and Germany and published several pieces on women's movements and the "sexual revolution." Working at the department of Sociology at the University of Geneva, she also completed postdoctoral research on the material and symbolic effects of German society's transformation since 1990, resulting in a publication inspired by Pierre Bourdieu's study "The Weight of the World." She is currently a member of the department of Social and Economic History at the University of Lausanne and is conducting research on "Switzerland as an intersection point of intellectual transfer (1939–45)."

Detlef Siegfried is an associate professor of Modern German History and Cultural History at the University of Copenhagen. His major publications include *Dynamische Zeiten. Die 60er Jahre in den beiden deutschen Gesellschaften* (coeditor, 2000), *Between Marx and Coca–Cola. Youth Cultures in Changing European Societies, 1960–1980 (coeditor, 2006)*, and *Time Is on My Side. Konsum und Politik in der westdeutschen Jugendkultur der 60er Jahre* (2006).

Máté Szabó was born in Budapest and is a professor of Political Science with the focus on social movements and political protest at the Eötvös Loránd University Budapest. He has been a fellow and visiting professor in Berlin, Hamburg, Bremen, Mainz, and Frankfurt/Oder. His research and publications focus on civil society and political and cultural discourses in Hungary. He is also a member of the international research project *The Alternative Eastern Europe: Dissent in Politics and Society and Alternative Culture in Comparative Perspective 1968–1989*.

Jakob Tanner is a professor at the History Institute and the Research Institute for Social and Economic History at Zurich University; a main focus of his research is the history of science and popular forms of knowledge. He is a permanent fellow of the Collegium Helveticum (Swiss Federal Institute of Technology/UZH) and a founding member of the Centre for the History of Knowledge (SFIT/UZH). His homepage can be found at www.fsw.unizh.ch

Marica Tolomelli was born in Bologna, Italy. She studied history in Bologna, Toulouse, and Bielefeld, where she obtained her PhD on the Italian and West German student movement of 1968 (*"Repressiv getrennt"—"orga-nisch verbündet." Studenten und Arbeiter 1968 in der Bundesrepublik Deutsch-land und in Italien*, Opladen, 2001). She currently works at the History Department of the Bologna University. Her major research fields and publications concentrate on European social history since 1945 as well as comparative Italian and German history (*Terrorismo e società*, Bologna, 2006).

Louis Vos is a professor of Modern History at the Catholic University of Leuven (Belgium). His field of research includes the history of nationalism, student movements, and youth movements. With Lieve Gevers, he wrote the chapters on student movements in the nineteenth and twentieth centuries for Walter Ruegg's (ed.) *A History of the University in Europe*.

Index

Action Direct (AD), 270, 279
action group "K–231," 169
Adenauer, Konrad, 97–98, 318
Adorno, Theodor W., 104, 286, 322
Agnoli, Johannes, 314, 323
Aktion, 218 287
Aktionsrat zur Befreiung der Frauen (Women's Liberation Action Council), 288
Ali, Tariq, 1, 8, 54, 94, 96, 134
Althusser, Louis, 129
American Committee for Non-Violent Action (CNVA), 37, 40, 42, 44
American Fellowship of Reconciliation, 38
American Friends Service Committee, 40
Anderson, Perry, 48, 52, 55, 133, 136
Andreescu, Gabriel, 206
Andrzejewski, Jerzy, 182
Angry Brigade, 132, 136, 269, 278–79
Animals, the, 75
Antall, József, 211
Antonioni, Michelangelo, 71–72, 78
Apprentice Boys, 148
Arbeiderkomiteen mot EEC og dyrtid, Workers' Committee Against the EEC and Inflation (AKMED), 246
Arendt, Hannah, 7, 9
Armia Krajowa (Homeland Army), 180
Armia Ludowa (People's Army), 180
Asselmeyer, Jean, 270
Ausserparlamentarische Opposition (APO), 99, 229

Baader, Andreas, 79–80, 105, 272, 274, 277–78
Baader-Meinhof Gang (Red Army Faction), 272
Bachmann, Josef, 104
Baez, Joan, 66
Bakunin, 114
Barratt-Brown, Michael, 53
Bauman, Zygmunt, 184
BBC, 1–2, 215
Beatles, 66–68, 75, 172
Beatniks, 19, 30
Beatrix, Princess of the Netherlands, 17
Bell, Daniel, 8, 311
Bence, György, 211
Beneš, Edvard, 164

Benjamin, Walter, 66, 77
Benn, Tony, 53
Bensaïd, Daniel, 120
Berke, Joseph, 28, 31–32
Berlin Blues, 272
Bernstein, Michèle, 26
Berthold, Erika, 192, 196–97
Bewegung, 2. Juni (Movement June 2), 99, 271–72, 274, 277, 286
Biermann, Wolf, 190, 194, 197
Bilak, Vasil, 171
Black Panther Party, 106, 110, 145
Black Power Movement, 127, 132
Blackburn, Robin, 54
Boato, Marco, 85, 94, 96
Bolshevik Party, 246
Botez, Mihail, 204
Brandt, Willy, 299, 318, 324
Brasch, Thomas, 192, 196
Brecht, Bertolt, 67
Brežnev, Leonid, 168, 173, 202, 210, 212, 317, 323
Brigate rosse (BR), Red Brigades, 76, 91, 273, 275–76, 278
British Conservative party, 137, 319
British Council for Peace in Vietnam (BCPV), 126
British Direct Action Committee, 37, 39
Brower, David, 300
Buikhuisen, Wouter, 13
Bunker Movement, 235
Busch, Ernst, 67

Cagol, Mara, 91, 273
Calkins, Ken, 36, 44
Campaign Against Racial Discrimination (CARD), 127
Campaign for Democracy in Ulster (CDU), 145, 147
Campaign for Nuclear Disarmament (CND), 38–39, 41–42, 47, 50–51, 53, 126, 132, 240, 244, 311
Campaign for Social Justice (CSJ), 139, 143, 145, 147
Cangeopol, Liviu, 204–5, 207
Capanna, Mario, 91, 94, 96
Carmichael, Stokely, 127
Carson, Rachel, 296

Carter, April, 38
Castoriadis, Cornelius, 48, 122
Castro, Fidel, 27, 115, 212, 215, 255
Catholic Movement for the Reformation of
  the Synod, 170
Ceauşescu, Nicolae, 199–207
Cellules Communistes Combattantes (CCC),
  270
Chelsea Cain, 74, 80
Christian Democratic Party (CDU), 98, 299,
  318–19, 324
Christian People's Party, 170
Christian Social Union (CSU), 98
Chruščev, Nikita, 3, 45–46, 127, 165, 200
Clan na Gael, 144
Clapton, Eric, 67
Classe Operaia, 86
Claussen, Detlev, 77, 80
Clementis, Vladimír, 166
Club of Committed Non–Party Members
  (KAN), 170
CoBrA (painters from Copenhagen, Brüssel,
  Amsterdam), 24
Cohn-Bendit, Daniel, 1, 8, 18–19, 29, 118,
  123, 298, 314, 316, 323
Cohn-Bendit, Gabriel, 123
Collettivo Politico Metropolitano, 91
Columbia Broadcasting System (CBS), 62, 67
Comités Viétnam de Base (CVB), 115
Comités Viétnam Nationaux (CVN), 115
Commons Preservation Society, 295
Communist Party, 3, 27, 168, 314, 318, 320,
  325
  Belgian Communist Party, 157
  British Communist Party (CPGB), 46, 53,
    126, 128, 130, 134
  Communist Party, Denmark, 240
  Communist Party East Germany, 189, 275
  Communist Party, Hungary, 211
  Communist Party of France (PCF), 114
  Communist Party of Spain (PCE), 255, 259
  Communist Party of the Soviet Union,
    25–26, 114, 127
  Communist Party, West Germany, 98
  Czech Communist Party (KPC), 164–65,
    167, 169–75, 216
  Greek Communist Party, 255, 259
  Kommunistischer Bund Westdeutschlands
    (KBW), Communist League West
    Germany, 103
  League of Communists of Yugoslavia
    (LCY), 219–25, 227
  Partito Comunista Italiano (PCI), Italian
    Communist Party, 84, 86–87, 168,
    273, 275–76

Polish Communists, 179, 180
Romanian Communist Party (RCP),
  199–201, 206
Slovak Communist Party, 166, 171
Spanish Young Communist League, 255,
  258, 266
Swedish Communist Party (SKP), 240–42,
  247, 249
Venstrepartiet Kommunisterna (VPK), Left
  Party Communists, Sweden, 242, 249
Confédération française et démocratique du
  travail (CFDT), 118, 123
Confederation generale du travail (CGT),
  General Workers Union, 118–19
Connolly Association, 144
conscientious objectors (COs), 34
Conseil pour le maintien des occupations, 27
Controllo Operaio, 86
Cornea, Doina, 204
Crosland, Tony, 49, 56
Crumb, Robert, 248
Csoóri, Sándor, 211
Csurka, István, 211
Curcio, Renato, 85, 91, 273
Currie, Austin, 147
Cyrankiewicz, Józef, 181, 184

Dadaists, 28
Dahrendorf, Ralph, 313
Dajczgewand, Józef, 184
Dalos, György, 211, 216–18
de Beauvoir, Simone, 283–84, 292
de Certeau, Michel, 119, 123
De Förenade FNL-Grupperna (DFFG), The
  United FNL Groups, 242, 247
de Freitas, Michael, 127
de Gaulle, Charles, 202, 307, 318
Debord, Guy, 23–26, 30–31, 120, 257
Debray, Régis, 115, 121, 123–24, 129, 257
Degenhardt, Franz Josef, 63, 67
Deleuran, Claus, 248
Democratic Party of Slovakia, 166
Democratic Youth Movement Grigoris
  Lambrakis (Lambrakides), 256
Democrazia Cristiana (DC), Christian
  Democrats, 84, 87, 95, 275–76
Derry Citizens Action Committee (DCAC),
  140–41, 147–48
Derry Housing Action Committee (DHAC),
  140, 147
Déry, Tibor, 216
Devenney, Sammy, 148
Devlin, Bernadette, 145, 147–48, 150
Dinescu, Mircea, 204, 207
Djilas, Milovan, 221

Dolle Mina, 14, 287
Doors, the, 67
Dozier, James (NATO General), 275
Dubček, Alexander, 150, 163, 166, 170–73, 175–77, 184, 192, 220, 317–18
Dumont, René, 298
Dutch Red Youth, 269
Dutschke, Rudi, 19, 91, 99–101, 103–4, 106, 109, 120, 172, 193, 235, 316, 323, 329
Dylan, Bob, 58, 66, 77

Earth First!, 302
Edgar Broughton Band, 64
Eisler, Hanns, 67
El Fatah, 271
Engels, Friedrich, 48
Enragés, 28, 31, 112, 123
Ensslin, Gudrun, 105, 272, 274
Enzensberger, Hans Magnus, 109, 120
Enzensberger, Ulrich, 99, 110
Erdélyi, Miklós, 214
ETA (Basque Homeland and Freedom), 260
European Economic Community (EEC), 241, 245–48, 250
European Federation Against Nuclear Arms, 37
Evans, Mike, 66

Falange Party, 254
Fanon, Frantz, 101, 128, 232
Federación Universitaria Democrática Española (FUDE), 255
Federal Alliance of Citizens' Initiatives for Environmental Protection (BBU), 299, 305
Feltrinelli, Giangiacomo, 91, 95–96, 235, 273, 277
Filipescu, Radu, 204
Filippini, Enrico, 235
Firestone, Shulamit, 283
Fitt, Gerry, 145
Floh de Cologne, 64
Folkebevegelsen mot norsk medlemskap i fellesmarkedet (Popular Movement against EEC Membership), 241, 246
Fortschrittliche Arbeiter-, Schüler- und Studentenschaft (FASS), 231, 233
Fortschrittliche Studentenschaft Zürich (FSZ), 234
Fourier, Charles, 114
Fraga Iribarne, Manuel, 256
Franceschini, Alberto, 91, 273
Franco, Francisco, 4, 154, 259–60, 264–66, 270

Frauenbefreiungsbewegung (FBB), 235–36, 287, 290
Free Democratic Party (FDP), 98, 299
Freetown Christiania, 65
Frémion, Yves, 19–21
French Federation of Nature Protection Societies (FFSPN), 297
French National Union of Students, 297
French Trotskyites, 184
Friedan, Betty, 283
Friedman, Ken, 19, 21
Friends of the Earth (FoE)/Friends of the Earth International, 298, 300, 303, 305
Fromm, Erich, 225
Front Révolutionnaire d'Action Prolétarienne, 270
Fugs, the, 63–64
Für, Lajos, 211

Galbraith, John Kenneth, 311
Gandhi, 34, 38, 40–41
Garcia, Jerry, 78
Gauche Prolétarienne (GP), 269–70, 279
Geismar, Alain, 1, 8, 123
Génération Ecologie, 298
German Federal Employers' Association, 276
Gestion Ouvrière, 86
Gheorghiu-Dej, Gheorghe, 200–201, 206–7
Ghizikis, Phaidon, 261
Giedroyc, Jerzy, 184
Giraud, Jean, 248
Goebbels, Joseph, 175
Goma, Paul, 204
Gomulka, Wladyslaw, 173–74, 179–80, 182–84
Gorz, André, 312, 322
Gramsci, Antonio, 49, 55, 165, 313
Granada Television, 18
Grateful Dead, the, 75, 78
Greek Junta, 259, 261
Green Party
  France, 298
  West Germany, 107–8
Greenpeace, 298, 300, 302–4
Greenwald, Robert, 72
Gruppi di Azione Partigiana (GAP), 273, 277
Guevara, Ernesto Che, 6, 101, 104, 115, 157, 212, 215, 257, 260, 326
Gwardia Ludowa (People's Guard), 180
Gyorgy, Galántai, 214

Habermas, Jürgen, 103–4, 110, 142, 148, 313, 321
Hagmann, Stuart, 258
Halász, Péter, 214

Hall, Stuart, 20–21, 47, 49, 51–52, 129
Hamon, Hervé, 121–22
Haraszti, Miklós, 211
Havel, Václav, 170, 317–18, 324
Havemann, Florian, 192, 196–97
Havemann, Frank, 192–94, 197
Havemann, Robert, 190, 192
Hegedus, András, 209, 216
Hellenic European Youth Movement, 258
Heller, Ágnes, 211, 216–17, 225
Hendrix, Jimi, 6, 63–64, 76, 233
Hitler, Adolf, 109, 175, 275
Ho Chi Minh, 6, 104
Hobsbawm, Eric, 8, 94, 307–8, 320–21
Hodžic, Alija, 223
Hoffman, Abbie, 66, 72
Hoggart, Richard, 52
Hollander, Paul, 248, 252
Holtom, Gerald, 39
Honecker, Erich, 189, 194
Hoyland, John, 68
Hughes, John, 53
Huizinga, Johan, 14
Hume, John, 143
Humphrey, Hubert, 102
Hungarian samizdat, 211
Hunziger, Rosita, 192, 196–97
Husák, Gustav, 163, 166, 171, 173, 175

Industrial Workers of the World, 34
International Confederation for
    Disarmament and Peace (ICDP), 37
International Conference of Students (ICS),
    159
Internationale Antimilitaristische
    Vereinigung (International Anti-
    Militarist Union), 34
International Fellowship of Reconciliation,
    36–37
International Marxist Group (IMG), 127
International Movement for an Imaginist
    Bauhaus, 24
International Socialism (IS), 127
International Union for the Conservation of
    Nature
    (IUCN), 303
International Union of Socialist Youth (IUSY),
    3, 106
International Union of Students
    (IUS), 159
Intesa, 85
Ioannidis, Dimitrios, 261–62
Irish Republican Army (IRA), 139, 144–46,
    148
Isou, Isidore, 23

Jablonski, Henryk, 182
Jagger, Mick, 64
Jancsó, Miklós, 216
Jasienica, Paweł, 182, 184
Jaspers, Karl, 7, 9
Jefferson Airplane, 63, 75
Jeunesse Communiste Révolutionnaire (JCE),
    120
Joplin, Janis, 63, 76
Jorn, Asger, 26

Kabouter movement, 65
Kádár, János, 209–13, 216–17
Kafka, Franz, 165
Kavan, Jan, 1, 8
Kennedy, John F., 84, 326–27
Kennedy, Robert, 326
Kex, 214
King Constantine, 256
King, Martin Luther, Jr., 38, 143, 213, 326–27,
    331
King Mob, 29
Kinks, 75
Kis, János, 211, 217
Kisielewski, Stefan, 182
Kiss, Csaba, 211
Klub Intelligencji Katolickiej (Clubs of the
    Catholic Intelligence), 181
Klub Krzywego Kola (Club of the Crooked
    Circle), 181
Klub Poszukiwaczy Sprzecznosci (Club of
    Searchers for Contradictions), 180
Kohl, Helmut, 318
Kolakowski, Leszek, 184, 225
Komandosi, 181–84
Kommune I, 29, 65, 99, 102, 105, 107, 110,
    193, 197
Kommunistischer Bund Westdeutschlands
    (KBW), Communist League West
    Germany, 103
Kommunistiska Förbundet Marxist-Leninisterna
    (KFML), Communist League of
    Marxists-Leninists, 242, 247
Konrád, György, 216
Koons Garcia, Deborah, 78
Korner, Alexis, 63
Krahl, Hans-Jürgen, 101, 109
Kriegel, František, 174
Krivine, Alain, 120
Kunzelmann, Dieter, 21, 29–30, 99, 197, 272
Kuron, Jacek, 180–81, 184, 186–87, 316–18
Kurras, Karl-Heinz, 97

Labour Party, Great Britain, 47–51, 53, 126–29, 133, 138, 142, 145, 147, 333
Lacan, Jacques, 284–85
Laing, Ronald D., , 129, 135
Lalonde, Brice, 297
Lambrakis, Grigoris, 256
Langhans, Rainer, 99
Leary, Timothy, 73
Led Zeppelin, 64
Lefebvre, Henri, 47
Lega studenti e operai, 92
Lenin (Vladimir Ilyich Ulyanov), 3, 25, 157
Lennon, John, 67, 73
Les Amis de la Terre (French branch of Friends of the Earth FoE), 297–98
Lettrist International, 23–24, 29–30
Liberty (American record company), 62
Lipovetsky, Gilles, 121, 124
Lippmann & Rau (concert agency in Frankfurt, Germany), 62
Litynski, Jan, 182, 184
London Psychogeographical Committee, 24
Lotta Continua, 96, 273
Lukács, György, 101, 109, 211, 213, 216, 218
Luxemburg, Rosa, 104

MacDonald, Dwight, 311
Machiavelli, Niccolò, 257
Magyar Demokrata Fórum (MDF), Hungarian Democratic Forum, 211
Mahler, Horst, 272
Mandel, Ernest, 225
Manson family, 76, 327, 331
Mao Tse Tung, 128, 212, 232, 251, 275
Marcuse, Herbert, 49, 100–101, 106, 109–10, 129, 215, 222, 225, 227, 231, 242, 285, 308, 312–13, 320, 322
Markezinis, Spyros, 261
Márquez, Gabriel Garcia, 255
Marxist-Leninist Communist party, Belgien, 157, 159
Marx, Karl, 3, 8, 25, 47–48, 69, 110, 224, 257, 312, 315, 321, 323, 337
Maspero, François, 115, 123–24
MC 5 64, 73
McCann, Eamonn, 140–41, 145, 147, 150–51
McClenaghan, Dermie, 144
McCluskey, Con, 139
McCluskey, Patricia, 139
McDonald, Joe, 64
McKenzie, Robert, 1
Meinhof, Ulrike, 79–80, 105, 272, 274–75, 278
Metro Goldwyn Mayer film company, 71

Metronome, Swedish record company, 70
Michnik, Adam, 180, 182, 184, 186–87, 317–18
Mickiewicz, Adam, 182, 185, 187
Mijanovic, Vladimir, 223, 228
Miliband, Ralph, 52, 54–56
Millet, Kate, 283
Mills, Barry, 76
Mills, Charles Wright, 3, 8, 95, 100, 129, 285, 326
Mitterrand, François, 307
Moczar, Mieczyslaw, 180, 182
Modzelewski, Karol, 180–81, 184, 316–17
Moon Unit Zappa, 78, 80
Moral Re-Armament, 58
Moretti, Mario, 273–74
Moro, Aldo, 276
Morris, William, 46, 48, 76
Morrison, Jim, 76
Mother Earth, 75
Mothers of Invention, 61, 78
Mouvement démocratique des étudiants (MDE), 235, 237
Mouvement pour la liberation des femmes (MLF), 284, 287
Movement of March 22, 112, 115, 123
Movimento giovanile progressista (MGP), 235, 237
Muste, Abraham, 35, 38, 43

Nagy, Imre, 209
Nairn, Tom, 54
NASA, 303
National Council for Civil Liberties, 140
National Council for the Abolition of Nuclear War Tests, 39
National Organization of Women (NOW), 283
National Union of Students (NUS), 127
Nationalist Party, Northern Ireland, 139, 141
Natolin Fraction, 179–80
New Left (Neue Linke, Nuova Sinistra, Nouvelle Gauche), 3, 8, 13, 20–21, 28, 41–56, 66, 72, 74–76, 79–80, 86–91, 94–95, 97–98, 100, 106–7, 113–14, 117–21, 123, 126–27, 129–36, 141, 143, 147, 151, 155–57, 159, 190–91, 193, 213, 215, 222, 224, 227, 231–32, 234, 237, 240, 242–43, 249, 259, 283–86, 297, 300, 308, 311–15, 322, 328
New Reasoner group, 46
Nietzsche, Friedrich, 73
Nieuwenhuys, Constant, 14, 25–26
Non-Alignment Movement, 220

Non-Violent Action Against Nuclear
  Weapons, 40
North Atlantic Treaty Organization (NATO),
  41, 56, 97, 102, 240, 275, 279
Northern Ireland Civil Rights Association
  (NICRA), 140–41, 146–49
Northern Ireland Labor Party (NILP), 139
Nouvelle Résistance Populaire (NRP), 270
Novomeský, Laco, 166
Novotný, Antonín, 166, 172
Nuclei Armati Proletari (NAP), 281

Ochotnicza Rezerwa Milicji Obywatelskiej
  (ORMO), Voluntary Reserve of the
  Citizens Militia, 183
Ohnesorg, Benno, 97, 103, 130
Old Left, 44, 52–53, 86, 114, 117–19, 283,
  322
O'Neill, Terence, 148, 150
Ono, Yoko, 73
OPEC, 285
Opus Dei, 254
Orbison, Roy, 71
Organización Latinoamericana de Solidaridad
  (OLAS), 123
Oriach, Frédéric, 270
Orpheo group, 214
Overney, Pierre, 270, 279
Oxford Labour Club, 46
Oxford Union, 131

Pacifist Socialist Party, Netherlands, 13
Pahlewi, Rehza, 103
Palach, Jan, 172, 177
Papadopoulos, Georgios, 253, 256, 259, 261,
  263
Papandreou, George, 256
Paris Commune, 115
Parisian Bohemians, 23
Partito Socialista Italiano (PSI), 84, 86–87
Patriotic Guards, 202
Peace Societies, 33–34
People's Democracy (PD), 140–41, 144–45,
  147–48
People's Liberation Front (FLP), 255, 269
People's Socialists Party, 170
Petrescu, Dan, 204–5, 207
Petroulas, Sotiris, 256
Pinochet, Augusto, 259, 266
Plant, Robert, 64
Plato, 257
Poland's Solidarity, 203
Polityczny Klub Dyskusyjny (Political
  Discussion Club), 181

Polska Partia Robotnicza (Polish Worker Party),
  180
Polska Zjednoczona Partia Robotnicza (PZPR),
  Communist Polish United Workers'
  Party, 179–84, 187
Pompidou, Georges, 116
Popular Front for the Liberation of Palestine
  (PFLP), 269
Praxis group, 224–28
Profesores No Numerarios (PNN), 255, 265
Progressive Organisationen der Schweiz
  (POCH), 236, 331
Proll, Thorward, 105
Proudhon, Pierre Joseph, 114
Provisional IRA, 142–43
Provisional Republican movement, 141–42,
  145–47
Provo, 5, 13–21, 29, 66, 106, 151, 248, 300
Pugwash Movement, 35, 37
Pulawski group, 179–80

Quaderni Rossi, 86

Racial Adjustment Action Society (RAAS), 127
Radio Free Europe, 215
Radio London, 61
Radio Luxembourg, 61
Radio Nord, 61
Radio Veronica, 61
Rákosi, Mátyás, 209
Randle, Michael, 38
Rankovic, Aleksandar, 220
Reasoners, the, 46–47
Reclaim the Streets, 302
Red Army, Soviet Union, 164, 179, 200
Reform Communists, 171, 211–12
Reich, Wilhelm, 285
Republican Club, 99, 147
Republican Wolfe Tone Societies, Ireland, 147
Resistenza, 271, 273, 275–76
Revolutionary Cells (RZ), 271
Revolutionary Socialist Students' Federation
  (RSSF), 56, 127, 135
Rewolucyjny Zwiazek Mlodziezy, Union of
  Revolutionary Youth, Poland, 180
Rigas, 259, 266
Rocard, Michel, 307
Rokkan, Stein, 248
Rolling Stones, 6, 63–64, 68, 75, 77, 331
Romanian Workers' Party, 201, 207
Rossi, Paolo, 88
Rostagno, Mauro, 85
Rote Armee Fraktion (RAF), Red Army
  Faction, 76, 80, 99, 102, 105, 108, 110,
  269–70, 272, 274–79

Rotman, Patrick, 121–22
Rousseau, Jean-Jacques, 319
Rowbotham, Sheila, 132, 134–36
Rubin, Jerry, 66, 331
Rustin, Bayard, 38, 44

Saint-Simon, Henri de, 114
Salzinger, Helmut, 66, 70
Samuel, Raphael, 51, 52, 55–56
Sander, Helke, 288
SANE (the Committee for a SANE Nuclear
  Policy), 36
Sartre, Jean-Paul, 27, 48, 123, 231,
  277, 313
Savage Rose, 64
Saville, John, 46, 52, 54, 56, 126
Schleyer, Hanns-Martin, 276
Second Socialist International, 33
Seweryn Blumsztajn, 182, 184
Shah of Persia, 97, 103
Sinclair, John, 73
Sindicato Español Universitario (SEU), 255, 257
Sinn Féin, 139, 141–42
Situationist International, 14, 18–19, 23, 26,
  29–31, 106, 313
Skjervheim, Hans, 248
Slonimski, Antoni, 182
Smolar, Aleksander, 181
Smrkovský, Josef, 171
Social Democratic and Labor Party (SDLP),
  141, 146–47
Social Democratic Party (SPD), West
  Germany, 13, 98–99, 108, 299
Social Democratic Party, East Germany, 189
Socialist Party (PSU), 13, 307
Socialist Unity Party (SED), 76, 189–90, 193,
  196
Socialistisk Folkeparti (SF), Socialist People's
  Party, Norway, 240–42, 246
Society for Human Rights, 170
Soehnlein, Horst, 105
Sofri, Adriano, 85
Solzhenitsyn, Alexander, 317
Soós, Baksa, 214
Sorbi, Paolo, 85
Sosialistisk Valgforbund, 241
Sosialistisk Venstreparti (SV), Socialist Left
  Party, Norway, 241, 246
Soviet Red Army, 179
Sozialistischer Deutscher Studentenbund
  (SDS), Socialist German Student League,
  53, 66, 97, 98–101, 103–7, 109–10, 228,
  288, 307
Spinelli, Altiero, 326
Sponti–Bewegung, 99

Springer, Axel, 103–4, 277
SPUR, 24, 26
Stalin, Josef, 48, 251
Stomma, Stanislaw, 183
Strasser, Gregor, 175
Strauss, Franz-Josef, 98
Student League of Yugoslavia (SSJ), 221, 225,
  228
Student Nonviolent Coordinating
  Committee, 42
Student Peace Union, 37, 41–42
Students for a Democratic Society, 3, 42, 66,
  326
Subversive Aktion, 99–100, 106, 110, 315
Survivre et Vivre (Survive and Live), 297
Sviták, Ivan, 170
Syrius, 214, 222
Szabad Demokraták Szövetsége (SZDSZ),
  Alliance of Free Democrats, 211
Szabad, György, 211
Szelényi, Iván, 216
Szlajfer, Henryk, 182

Tangerine Dream, 63
Tempel, Hans-Konrad, 38
Teufel, Fritz, 99
Thatcher, Margaret, 133, 318–19
Thompson, Edward P., 46, 48, 52–53, 55–56,
  126, 129, 132
Tito, Josip Broz, 175, 220, 223, 225–26, 228
Todd, Olivier, 297
Togliatti, Palmiro, 168
Tomorrow, 18
Ton Steine Scherben, 64
Touraine, Alain, 8, 121–23, 305, 307
Trotsky, Leo, 104, 175
Tudoran, Dorin, 204
Tupamaros, 76, 271–72, 277

Ulbricht, Walter, 173, 195–96
Ulster Unionist party, 137–39, 142
Ulster Volunteer Force (UVF), 148
Union des étudiants Communistes (UEC),
  114
Union Nationale des étudiants de France
  (UNEF), 111–12, 322
Unione goliardica italiana (UGI), 85
*Unione nazionale universitaria rappresentativa
  italiana* (UNURI) 85
United World Federalists (UWF), 35
Universal Coloured People's Association
  (UCPA), 127

Vaculik, Ludvik, 194
Vajda, Mihály, 216

van Ree, Frank, 16, 21
Vaneigem, Raoul, 26, 31
Vänsterpartiet (VP), Party of the Left, 249
Venstresocialisterne (VS), Left Socialists, 241, 251
Vester, Michael, 106
Viale, Guido, 85, 93–94, 96
Vietnam Solidarity Campaign (VSC), 126, 128, 135
Vlahovic, Veljko, 219
Voice of America, 215
von Amsberg, Claus, 17
von Rauch, Georg, 272

Walesa, Lech, 317
Walterowcy, 180
War Resisters' International (WRI), 34, 36–38, 41, 43
War Resisters League, 38, 40, 42
Who, the, 63, 70, 75
Williams, Raymond, 49, 52, 55, 129, 135, 176, 313
Willis, Ellen, 72, 80

Wilson, Harold, 126, 130, 135
Wolff, Karl-Dietrich, 1, 8
Women's International League for Peace and Freedom (WILPF), 35–36
Women's Liberation Movement, 132, 237, 281, 284, 287
Working Committee on Civil Rights, 147
World Wide Fund for Nature (WWF), 296, 303

Young, Nigel, 51
Youth International Party, 66

Zappa, Frank, 64, 78, 80
Zawieyski, Jerzy, 183
Zengakuren, 37
Živkov, Todor, 173
Životic, Miladin, 225
Znak, 183, 185
Zwiazek Literatów Polskich (Union of Polish Writers), 182
Zwiazek Mlodziezy Socjalistycznej (ZMS), Union of Socialist Youth, 180–81, 184